MAVERICKS

*An Incorrigible
History of
Alberta*

ARITHA van HERK

PENGUIN
VIKING

VIKING
Published by the Penguin Group
Penguin Books Canada Ltd, 10 Alcorn Avenue,
Toronto, Ontario, Canada M4V 3B2
Penguin Books Ltd, 80 Strand, London WC2R 0RL, England
Penguin Putnam Inc., 375 Hudson Street, New York, New York 10014, U.S.A.
Penguin Books Australia Ltd, Ringwood, Victoria, Australia
Penguin Books (NZ) Ltd, cnr Rosedale and Airborne Roads,
Albany, Auckland 1310, New Zealand

Penguin Books Ltd, Registered Offices: Harmondsworth, Middlesex, England

First published 2001

1 2 3 4 5 6 7 8 9 10

Author representation: Westwood Creative Artists
94 Harbord Street, Toronto, Ontario M5S 1G6

Printed and bound in Canada on acid free paper ∞

NATIONAL LIBRARY OF CANADA CATALOGUING IN PUBLICATION DATA

Van Herk, Aritha, 1954–
Mavericks : an incorrigible history of Alberta

Includes index.
ISBN 0-670-88739-0

1. Alberta—History. I. Title.

FC3661.V36 2001   971.23   C2001-902679-X
F1076.V36 2001

Visit Penguin Canada's website at **www.penguin.ca**

for my mother and father,

Marretje van Dam van Herk
and Willem van Herk

Contents

Acknowledgements

Grateful thanks to the helpful archivists and librarians at the Provincial Archives of Alberta, the Glenbow Archives and Library, and the University of Calgary Library. They were wonderfully patient and generous. Thanks also to the local museums and collections all across Alberta that offer a view of the past, the present, and the future.

Robert Sharp, Robert Kroetsch, Elizabeth Flagler, Carolynn Hoy, Brian Stanko, Joy Fehr, Pamela McCallum, Nicole Markotic, Peter Oliva, Rudy Wiebe, Pat Sharp, Christl Verduyn, and Miriam Grant helped in untold ways.

Special thanks to my sister, Bertha, and to my parents, who dared to immigrate to Alberta.

Thanks for their faith in this book to Cynthia Good, Alison Reid, Maryan Gibson, Shannon Proulx, Cathy MacLean, Sandra Tooze, and particularly Jennifer Barclay and Hilary Stanley.

Introduction

If I have learned anything writing this book, it is how devoted, dedicated, and amazingly perceptive historians of Alberta are. They are each a special kind of visionary, accumulating the details of the past and writing them in the present for the benefit of the future, and I read them with admiration and delight. I have no historical training, and so it was a challenge even to contemplate writing about this province. I knew in advance that I would fail to provide any historical perspective sufficiently rigorous or knowledgeable to compete with the brilliant historians who have worked and who continue to work on Alberta. I had to decide that I would be content to tell the story of this place from my own idio-syncratic and biased point of view. Any mistakes are mine. The omissions, and unfortunately there are many, deserve books of their own. The most frustrating aspect of writing this book was how much I had to leave out. History is about what we keep; its secret story is about what is lost. That story is one we all long to find.

I was born in Alberta, in the middle of one of the wettest, muddiest Mays on record. It had rained so much that my parents could not even manage to get their car up our dirt lane. The day they brought me home from the hospital was bright and warm. They parked the car at the end of the driveway and waded through the mud. I remember that first short journey. I remember the sky slamming its brilliance against my baby eyes.

My parents are Dutch immigrants who arrived in Canada just five years before I was born. In March of 1949 they boarded a boat at Le Havre and set out on the journey that enabled me to write this book. They disembarked at Pier 21 in Halifax and boarded the train, beginning that long, long journey all the way to Wainwright, Alberta. There, they were picked up by the farmer who had served as their sponsor and taken to Fabian, a small town hovering on the edge of the Battle River. From Fabian they moved to Wetaskiwin, where they were living when I was born, in an old farmhouse close to the ancient and mystical Peace Hills, bending their backs to the task of making a living in this challenging country. When I was two, they moved to a farm close to the village of Edberg in the County of Camrose, but still close to the Battle River. The land was better, and my parents wanted to buy a farm of their own, which they eventually did, struggling and saving and working, working and saving and struggling.

We worked beside them, my siblings and I. We were poor, but we enjoyed a childhood that must count as one of the most blessed in the world—rafting on the slough in summer, skating on the slough in winter, roaming free through the bush, picnicking at Dried Meat Lake or Buffalo Lake, and taking a butter-yellow school bus into town every morning. We knew the habits of gophers and coyotes, we milked cows and chased pigs, we drove the tractor and waded in spring ditches catching tadpoles, we were "Caesars of our own small world." And Alberta in the fifties and sixties was a marvellous place, full of energy and conviction, endlessly expansionist, crazily unpredictable, seeded with evangelists and dust-driven gravel roads and the wild optimism of oil strikes and growth. There was so much promise in the air that we could tip it out and drink it.

I left Edberg to go to the University of Alberta in Edmonton, and when I graduated I moved first to Calgary, then Vancouver, a wonderful city, but too different for my blood to take. So I moved back to Alberta, to Calgary, and I have lived here ever since, with shorter sojourns in Leeds and Marburg and Kiel and Wollongong and Trier and Wierden and Yellowknife and Oviedo and Vienna and London. I do have some worldly comparisons to draw upon.

They say that writing about home is the hardest task to undertake, for the writer can never see clearly what she is closest to. I can only say to this province, to the people of this province, that I have tried to tell some of its story, tried to show Alberta's energy and wit and anger and passion, so often invisible to outsiders, who see only our extremes, our difficult and recalcitrant side.

Alberta is a kingdom that resists description, that defies definition. The truth is, to understand Alberta, you really have to live here. I hope that reading the pages of *Mavericks* will be the next best thing.

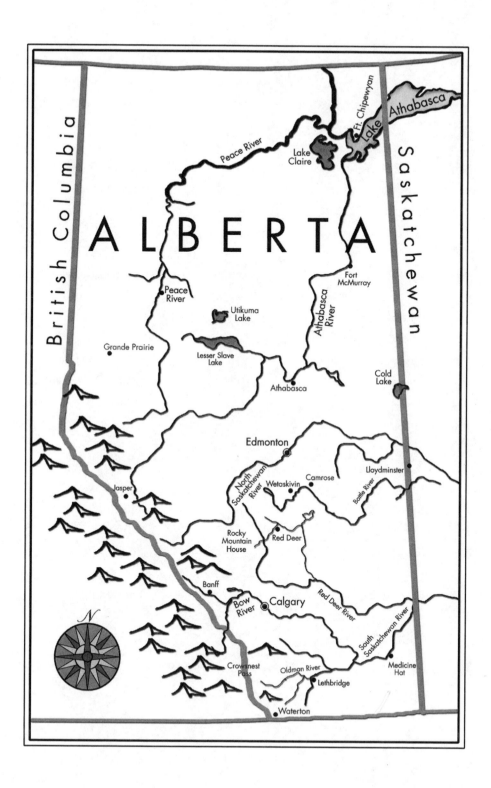

1 | Aggravating, Awful, Awkward, Awesome Alberta

Those people out there are different.
                    —Jean Chrétien

Few people actually dare to come out and say, "I'm from Alberta." The very admission is a social gaffe. Albertans are regarded as creatures from the swamp, Neanderthals, figures of fun, fools and daredevils, lunatic Bible-thumpers, gun-toting renegades, and crazy oilmen who really don't appreciate their tolerated position within this great nation. And when those same marginal heretics get annoyed and start agitating for respect from the Centre of Canada, they're branded as crybabies and whiners and illogically well-off hillbillies. It's a tough position to occupy.

I was recently having a glass of wine with the renowned Québécoise poet and novelist Nicole Brossard. Usually we talk about words, but somehow we stumbled into the territory of separation. She expressed astonishment at the disaffection of Albertans and the rising emphasis on Alberta separation. While I assured her that the attention paid to the separatists was more a function of media boredom than an actuality, I nevertheless expected her to demonstrate a modicum of understanding. Did she not, I asked, recognize the West's disaffection with federalism? "You cannot separate," she said. When, for argument's sake, I asked her why not, since Quebec has been trying to separate for years, she said, "But you cannot separate from us."

Who is us? I wanted to ask. We didn't have time to explore this interesting contradiction, but the conversation made me think. Quebec's dreams of independence are based on a history and cultural integrity distinct from the rest of Canada. Albertans, on the other hand, are merely allergic to how they have been treated by Central Canada. The implication that Quebec can separate, but that Alberta cannot, puts a finger on the pulse of Alberta's reactive behaviour. We are still and have always been, as the writer Peter Newman says, wrongly considered a child of the East, a stray adopted into Confederation but never quite a member of the family, sent out to do the chores and made to eat in the kitchen. Expected to put the good of Central Canada above our own, Albertans have developed a rebellious streak.

The habit of treating Alberta as an exploitable and resource-rich hinterland goes back three hundred years. And why should a self-centred Centre change its attitude? Canada as a country is an act of imagination so unlikely that it is hard to believe its actual success. For that reason it is wildly attractive, as Alberta, perhaps better than any other province, knows and respects. But Albertans are also very different from the rest of the nation. Our history is different, our politics are different, our ways of thinking are different. Even Ontarians who move west to Alberta discover themselves being chiselled into a different shape, with other expectations, another accent.

I am not a member of the Canadian Alliance Party or its forerunner, the Reform Party of Canada. I don't subscribe to independence movements or agree with the right-wing intellectuals who want to erect a firewall around the province. Such political manoeuvres are symptoms of Alberta's discontent, not measurements of its beliefs. Like most people in this province, I believe in the impossible dream called Canada.

But I was born in Alberta, I grew up in Alberta, and I live in Alberta. My pride is local, and like everyone else out here, I grow impatient with the Central Canada's obtuse, narcissistic, airy dismissal of the West's valid and distinctive desires. Albertans are mavericks, people who step out of bounds, refuse to do as we are told, take risks, and then laugh when we fall down and hit the ground. We know our own abilities and failures only too well, and we are perfectly aware of how often we shoot ourselves in the foot. We just bandage our toes and limp on.

Peter Newman has more succinctly and directly than any other commentator or historian put his finger on the moment of Alberta's discontent. In a recent article in Maclean's, *Newman summarizes exactly Alberta's conundrum:*

> There is in Alberta today a ferocious craving to be heard. The province's discontents keep multiplying without ever being debated, much less resolved. Central Canada's political elite has yet to accept the notion that westerners are anything more than bubbas in the boondocks, whose lives are consumed in envy of the lucky few plugged into action central in Toronto, Ottawa and Montreal. That elitism has little appeal to most Albertans, but gaining official recognition of their distinctiveness does have. What they will demand with increasing ferocity is greater control over their own destiny. At the moment, they feel abandoned by a country that continues to mobilize its best and brightest to satisfy the demands of Quebec, without ever

realizing that another large chunk of valuable geography has aspirations that are just as urgent and just as valid.

The riddle of Alberta has no answer. We are the country of deadly and spectacular storms, our wealth as itinerant as rain, our foliage wild oats and slough-side willows. And yes, we want to be heard.

• • •

To the rest of Canada Alberta has played a succession of roles, from "Rupert's Land" to "the Great Lone Land" to "the Territories" to "the Promised Land" to "the Garden of the Desert" with lyrical "unshorn fields." Whatever Alberta is called, it has through time and experience become a sophisticated outlaw, a place where pedigree is unimportant and where migrants are encouraged to reinvent themselves, attracting a mélange of characters, from religious groups to mad scientists to crazy stock promoters to mall builders. Hyperbole and racism, tenderness and neighbourly concern jostle family values and Christian schools, rampant impatience, and inventive financing. Alberta operates by a creed less interested in frontier individualism than in creative initiative. This is a province that promises low-tax living, cheap booze, video-lottery gambling everywhere, and the freedom to enjoy inappropriate opinions. Meanwhile, Albertans assiduously pay taxes, try not to drink too much, and practise an astonishing degree of charity, while serving as good-natured scapegoats for the rest of Canada's wilful ignorance.

Alberta is succinct as a blade, dangerously predictable as an anarchist, a land of hoodoos and high skies, bellicose booms

Princess Louise Caroline Alberta, after whom the province is named, not necessarily pleased with the honour

Glenbow Archives, Calgary, Canada: NA-900-2

and busts, oil derricks and bush planes, sudden chinook winds strong enough to tear away house shingles. With mountains and prairies and parkland and boreal forest, Alberta has landscape enough for innumerable movie sets, and Hollywood has been coming here for years, drawn by expressive locations, talented technicians, and a good return on the US dollar. Alberta backdrops *Cameron of the Royal Mounted, River of No Return, His Destiny, Pajamas,* Clint Eastwood's *Unforgiven,* and most recently, Steven Seagal's *Exit Wounds.* We've got the scenery, so let the American cameras roll, although Alberta often gets disguised as another place, somewhere just as beautiful. We're doubles for Americans—we dance with Americans more readily than Centrals, flirt with Americans, move south/north as easily as PEI plants potatoes. We almost became Americans, a fact that the Centre just doesn't understand. Their influence is reflected in our restlessness, annoyance, exuberant mutiny. Nearly American, we've almost shaken off the dust of Central Canadian United Empire Loyalists and their stock in trade.

Disguise suits us; we can become any place we want. Changeable as the eye of a moment, quick to turn into a snowstorm or a tornado, the weather is part of our character, and while a snowstorm can cause a hundred accidents, Albertans always expect a chinook just over the horizon, knowing that when they wake, that thick, lazy roll of warm cloud will be lowering to the west. (Chinook: a warm, dry wind that tumbles over the eastern slopes of the Rocky Mountains, pushing optimism and migraines ahead of the melting snow.) Northern Alberta gets them too, although they are more frequent in the south, Pincher Creek and Calgary blessed with thirty-five chinook days a year, a big break in winter's bite. The chinook invests in surprise and contradiction; winter winds aren't supposed to melt the snow, and migrants from the centre are always surprised at the mildness of Alberta winters.

Edmonton and Calgary. Two circling huskies, equal in size and clout, 185 miles apart and connected by the north-south ribbon of Highway 2. Books and studies and reports discuss their rivalry, blue collar versus white collar, Redmonton versus Tory-blue Calgary, Oilers versus Flames. Edmonton hosts the legislature, the civil servants, the mandarins of the latest swept-in majority government. Calgary parries with oil men and bankers and corporate head offices, 204 of them, second only to Toronto.

Albertans are enigmatic, full of contradictions. We take our skiing seriously, our sunshine for granted, and our politicians with a huge sprinkling of salt. We're wildly intolerant and paranoically tolerant, home to Holocaust denier Jim Keegstra from Eckville and contemporary eco-outlaw Wiebo Ludwig. We have a reputation for edge-of-ledge citizens, some of whom we own proudly, others we'd like to disown, but freedom of speech is as dear to us as some of the unfortunate things we say. Our extremists are a part of the character of this place, part of what makes it unique. And the Centre conveniently forgets that Ernst Zundel came from Toronto.

If Manitobans are the most charitable Canadians, Albertans are the most generous, ordinary people proud to contribute to charities, eager to prove they can take care of their own and creative about the way they help the less fortunate. In December 2000, Edmonton chefs put the final touches on a 2,500-kilogram yule log, a cake big enough to feed nearly twenty thousand people and heavy enough to make *The Guinness Book of Records*. After the weigh-in, it was sliced up with a saw and served to the needy public. The nature of Alberta charity is hyperbolic, and if Albertans seem outwardly self-serving, they believe in being responsible for one another without resorting to paternalistic handouts. In the larger altruism of medical research, University of Alberta scientists in Edmonton continue developing a cure for diabetes and at the University of Calgary an innovative research program measures and evaluates the cause and effect of strokes.

Like the rest of Canada, we worry about crime. We have our share of car thieves, pot growers, drug gangs, and those who traffic in black-bear parts. In Calgary one famous thief robs convenience stores with a crowbar for a weapon, his trademark disguise the women's panties he wears over his face. He favours black—with a black jacket and black pants to match the lacy black underwear. This is an Alberta bandit, straight out of folklore.

Homespun heroes, like the Okotoks homeowner who scared off a thief with a shovel or the old lady in Edmonton who tripped a bank robber, are common. We refuse to be a conduit, and the law cracks down on cocaine shipped through Calgary and Edmonton to Yellowknife, that newly booming centre of diamond discovery. We're interested in punishment more than human rights. Correctional centres in Alberta have recently installed a computerized phone system to track inmates' phone calls, presumably to ensure they cannot harass their victims or witnesses. Our retributive impulses go so far that the government plans to introduce legislation to allow the seizure of assets from criminal gangs, but how much of that money will go to support victims of crime is of course a question. We're smart and cynical enough to suspect that it might get waylaid by government coffers, just as video-lottery machines tax untaxed Albertans.

Schools in Calgary and Edmonton and Lethbridge regularly go into lockdown. In November 2000, police upgraded charges against two teenagers in Edmonton who attacked and beat a fourteen-year-old boy so badly that he eventually died. And a sixteen-year-old was charged with first-degree murder after a shooting at a Taber school in 1999. If sleepy Taber has school shootouts, the potential for violence is everywhere. Albertans worry about kids, so the province dumps about $10 million into funding for agencies and safe houses to get child prostitutes off the street, contentiously passing the Protection of Children Involved in Prostitution Act, which allowed minors suspected of being engaged in the sex trade to be confined for up to seventy-two hours "for assessment." That law was struck down in July 2000 by the federal Supreme Court as unconstitutional, because its failure to provide a court review for children taken into custody put it in violation of the Canadian Charter of Rights and Freedoms. Furious at Central interference, the Alberta government immediately changed the law so that every child taken off the street is informed in writing of the reason for detention and given the right to contact a lawyer or legal aid, but can still be confined for up to five days. Emily Murphy, the family judge who worried so much about vagrancy and prostitution, would have approved. But we secretly adore rule breakers, love breaking our own rules. We tolerate maverick citizens, encourage them, connive with them, admire criminal ingenuity that results in economic gain.

Central Canada dismisses us as a male culture, cowboy and roughneck, but Calgary was the first big city in Canada to appoint a female police chief, Christine Silverberg, who was wooed west from Ontario. When she retired in October 2000, the press questioned whether, as a woman, she had had any special effect. Silverberg herself calmly claimed to have brought about massive changes because of her focus on human dignity. She had become an Albertan, tough and hard to intimidate, and the objections to a woman taking the credit she was due were overruled by the respect she had earned. Meanwhile, two male city police officers were charged with bribery and obstructing justice because they accepted a good bottle of alcohol for tearing up a ticket. Drinking and driving are no more prevalent in Alberta than in civilized Central Canada, although drinking drivers in Fort

McMurray are famous for eluding the Mounties, so much so that judges in the oil sands capital send even first-time offenders to jail. These are the images attached to Alberta: fists and bottles and blue jeans, horses and hailstones and half-tons, and hard-drinking guys in hard hats. No wonder visitors from Toronto express surprise at the number of sidewalk cafés, theatres, and black-tie galas.

Alberta culture is alleged to be the funniest oxymoron in the Canadian lexicon, but despite getting minimal government support, the arts in Alberta fight hard. We take our dancing seriously, and our music covers the whole octave from hurting songs to arias. A Tina Turner concert will sell out, but so will the Edmonton Opera. The Esther Honens Piano competition, established with a $5-million legacy from Honens, a Calgary businesswoman and classical music lover who died in 1992, is held every four years, its phenomenal success an example of how Albertans support cultural causes. The Fringe Festival, the largest theatrical event in Canada, gets bigger every year, and in August it is impossible to get a hotel room in south-side Edmonton. Calgary First Nations actor and singer Tom Jackson's "Huron Carol" now travels across Canada every Christmas raising funds for local food banks. Albertans often tie culture to fundraising. The Udderly Art Cow Auction, which sold off 117 fibreglass cows decorated by local artists, a herd of art that roamed downtown Calgary during the summer and fall of 2000, raised more than a million dollars for charity. The party was flashy and competitive, with big companies belly-ing up to display their wealth and community spirit. Albertans like to throw their cash around, and every money clip has the big bills on the outside.

Visiting Centrals are surprised by the number of good coffee shops and interna-tional food spots that sprout around Alberta. Yes, Albertans eat beef, melt-in-your-mouth, homegrown beef, although you have to know where to find it. When one of the Richler boys came all the way out west to review a steak house, he picked the worst place in town. Calgarians snickered in their sleeves, but the Toronto magazine that printed the review had no idea how far behind fashion it was. Yes, too many restaurants feature a ranch or settler theme, with saddles on the ceiling and miniature oil derricks as stir sticks, but tapas and chioppinos are common, and we know where to find bento boxes, pita, kumquats, gelato, and celeriac. We're well acquainted with goat cheese, good osetra, and low-fat biscotti. We know the difference between a *digestif* and single malt scotch. Event planners are as common as caterers, and lattes come in every variety—without

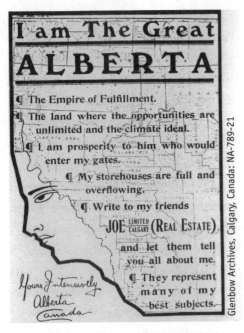

I am The Great

ALBERTA

❧ The Empire of Fulfillment.

❧ The land where the opportunities are unlimited and the climate ideal.

❧ I am prosperity to him who would enter my gates.

❧ My storehouses are full and overflowing.

❧ Write to my friends

JOE LIMITED CALGARY (REAL ESTATE)

and let them tell you all about me.

❧ They represent many of my best subjects.

Yours Intensively
Alberta
Canada

Glenbow Archives, Calgary, Canada: NA-789-21

I am the Great Alberta, an advertisement for the province, June 1910

the embellishment of a provincial sales tax. Nothing trendy gets past Albertans, although they are likely to make it just a little to the west of eccentric.

In analyses and articles, pundits and poll takers are fond of remarking on Alberta's rawness. Calgary still chafes over the late Mordecai Richler's famous contention that the city was uncrated yesterday. What happens to old buildings, to character? Do we really tear down everything more than thirty years old? Alberta historical societies wage losing battles to save abandoned train stations or brick warehouses, all subject to the quick reductions of the wrecking ball. Soon Albertans won't be able to tweak their memories of how amazing structures like grain elevators built the imagination of the West—except for the elegant blue silhouette of the Brentwood Light Rapid Transit station in northwest Calgary, a perfect copy of the shape of a grain elevator.

What Centrals cannot know is that building here one hundred years ago had to be quick and dirty. Western cities could not build with brick and granite, so log and sandstone historic buildings are less likely to withstand the passage of time. When we save a place, it's out of a combination of monetary gain and local pride, like the Anderson Apartments, once a "bachelors' hotel," a baroque red-brick, five-storey apartment house built during the pre–First World War boom. Until 1950 it was the tallest residential structure in Calgary, perched on the edge of elegant Mount Royal; now it has been renovated into trendy condominiums. The people who lived there are a roster of Calgary's famous: Archibald Dingman, one of the businessmen who first discovered oil at Turner Valley; Charles Jamieson, lawyer and newspaper columnist during the 1930s; Edward Curlette, photographer; Fred and Maude English, Calgary pioneers; and later, Jann Arden—twang-and-warble queen. Ghosts refuse to let the place be torn down.

Albertans remember and forget, and when we forget we argue about what we ought to remember. At the end of 2000 the Western Heritage Centre, Alberta's tribute to its ranching roots, in Cochrane, the town that sprang out of the old Cochrane Ranche (meaning a really big ranch), closed its doors because of insufficient funding. The minister of community development—remember, the word "culture" is forbidden—was publicly unsympathetic. No visitors, no funding. The centre promised to attract as many tourists as the Royal Tyrrell Museum, that emporium of dinosaur bones, in Drumheller, and failed. Pragmatic we are, as pragmatic as our south-of-the-border cousins. But we're not Americans, just a strange hybrid of northwestern pride and narrow-eyed suspicion.

With a larger area of national parks than any other province, Alberta takes credit for scenery. After the federal government capped growth in Banff at 1.5 percent a year, Parks Canada decided that the way to award building applications exceeding that ceiling was by lottery. Every year Banff businesses wishing to expand throw their plans in the ring and pray for luck, another Alberta tendency. Our minister of economic development accused Heritage Minister Sheila Copps of threatening ordinary citizens' access to the parks, and Copps came back with the argument about how the national parks belong to *all* Canadians, while Albertans think these magnificent playgrounds belong mostly to them. The fact that the Centrals have cut funding is a major issue, bigger than the federal focus on ecological integrity. Nothing irritates Albertans more than being questioned about our integrity.

We're also known for systemic discrimination—particularly against gay and lesbian and transgendered persons. The Alberta Marriage Act sits in the law books like a spectre of nineteenth-century homophobia. Red Deer MLA Victor Doerksen, who spearheaded the private member's bill of "one man and one woman," intended to restrict marriage licences to heterosexual couples, is utterly unapologetic. Although the Supreme Court claims that the word "spouse" can apply to same-sex couples, Alberta stubbornly differs. Still, in November 1999 an Alberta court granted same-sex couples the right to adopt children. And for all its bigotry, overt and covert, Alberta passed a bill creating an annual Memorial Day to honour the Holocaust and those who died in other genocides. Premier Ralph Klein says he

The Banff Springs Hotel, late 1800s, set in the most beautiful scenery in the world

believes that the act will "strengthen Albertans' resolve to speak out in the face of persecution and to help those people who need help."

Alberta's politicians are without question its craziest asset. Ralph Klein, the popular working/drinking-man's premier, doles out verbal gaffes with more panache than a stand-up comic: he has even called the Swan Hills waste-treatment plant a "tourist attraction." Klein's success is sometimes hard to fathom, but as the poster boy for conservatism, he rides some tough bucking broncos. Albertans indulge Klein, think of him as a good guy, a buddy, the type you might run into at the local pub. But Klein is tame compared to the exaggerations and inventions and scandals of William Aberhart and Ernest Manning, John Edward Brownlee and Alexander Cameron Rutherford. We have a habit of electing parties in huge waves, then tossing them out of office when they don't stand up to our standards.

In Alberta, as in Quebec, Ontario is the enemy. Ottawa has still not figured out that treating regions as if they are slightly malfunctioning limbs attached to the country's torso is not a good idea. The arms and legs are likely to develop frostbite. Quebec and Alberta record similar reactions to the power the federal government exerts. Questions about health care, for example, elicit similar answers. Forty-seven percent of Quebeckers approve of privately owned companies being able to deliver some health care services, with only 39 percent of Albertans recording a similar sentiment. And if a clever pollster asks if the provinces are "content that they are treated with the respect they deserve," 77 percent of Ontarians answer yes, followed by 52 percent of Albertans, while in all the other regions, less than 50 percent says yes. Alberta is simply the country's canary for discontent. We're not so different from the other regions; it's the Centre we hate.

In a changing Canada, where then does Alberta stand? Accelerating mergers and acquisitions, unparalleled takeover of Canadian businesses by American companies, the strange virtualities of information technologies, the sticky fingers of government are all perversely Albertan issues, and Albertans are ahead of other Canadians in considering them. We may seem to march with a different placard, but in truth we are an early-warning signal of disgruntlement. If Canada is going to survive, it has to understand its own nature, that the places "out there" are pieces of a diverse puzzle and not a construction of regionalisms.

Albertans are married to energy. We're connected to what lies underground, the depth charge of the forces below. Despite the Alberta Advantage—the phrase coined to promote our economic leadership—the skyrocketing prices of gas and electricity cut both ways. Oil and gas companies flourish and the economy booms, filling provincial coffers with energy dollars, but the average person pays through the nose, just like the rest of Canada. Newspapers cartoons show wolves named "heating prices" and "electricity rates" lurking around a snowbound house. Ralph Klein tried to soften the cost of energy with $150 rebate cheques to every tax-filing Albertan, but that hardly took care of one month's markup. "Winter Energy Tips" and price hikes came at the same time as the cold snap started, twenty below zero and counting. Alberta's electricity prices, once the lowest in North America, have deregulated into the highest. Klein, under pressure from business and agriculture, starts to do the backwards shuffle, explaining that usually deregulation works, but in this case, well, we'll have to look at the issue again. Gotta keep those voters happy.

Albertans' most predictable noise is our provincal cheer: tax cuts, tax cuts, more tax cuts. Politicians promise there will be no sales tax, Albertans' worst fear. When the provincial government sends out a survey asking what Albertans want to do with their surplus funds, the answer is always the same—cut taxes, cut taxes, we hate taxes.

The business of business means that Alberta's long tradition of boom and bust works through mergers and acquisitions, takeovers and sneaky raids in the night. Telus, that meek Alberta company, first merged with BC Tel, then bought Clearnet and now owns a large percentage of QuebecTel. Alberta's economic climate was jet-fuelled in 2000. WestJet quietly made millions, carrying passengers with just peanuts and prayers. Oil companies were bought and sold every day, Alberta's oil giants sharing boards and goals with American companies. A province once grounded in agriculture started to duck behind techno development. Farmers facing cultural and financial ruin know that bread and potatoes have a hard time competing on the world market, and while Alberta pretends to resist subsidies, it still wants federal hand-outs for agriculture. In the booster tradition, everybody's interested in money—getting it, keeping it, and making more. Migrants to Alberta come to get rich, even if they stay for other reasons.

We are an enigma to those who don't understand our love of contradiction. After the federal election of 2000, the whole of Central Canada wondered out loud what in hell was going on in Alberta. But while most of the province elected Alliance Party members, the party did not "sweep" Alberta, with Joe Clark (PC) in Calgary, and Anne McLellan and Dave Kilgour (Liberals) in Edmonton winning seats. Alberta might seem hypnotized by the snake-charming Alliance Party, but Joe Clark, the Alberta boy who was prime minister for a few short months in 1979, staged a triumphant win over the Alliance candidate, and although the Centre views Clark as a bit of a hick, a stumblebum, at home he is respected and admired. Like any real Albertan, Clark is no quitter. With trembling jowls, he fights on.

While the federal Liberals haven't stopped gloating over their majority, they have begun to worry about that incurable rash called Western alienation. The situation wasn't improved by Chrétien's suggesting, just before the November 2000 election, that politicians and people from Alberta are "different." Implying what? Difficult? Recalcitrant? We are! All of us. And proud of it. But more insulting were Chrétien's attempts to douse the ever-present smudge pots of Western angst and fury. "Damage control in the West" makes Albertans roll their eyes and clench their fists. Western grumbling is a staple of Canadian politics, and being perpetually fed up with Ottawa is such an Alberta trademark that we've become unhealthily attached to our hostility. We want to be alienated.

The new Alberta Independence Party, which sprang up in the early hours of 2001, reflects exactly that recalcitrance. A mere two hundred people disgruntled enough to believe in secession showed up for the first meeting. The real result, which no one wants to say aloud, is that Alberta would be immediately annexed by the United States, who have always courted us. Of course, that doesn't seem a bad thing to the separatists, although they are too small in number to be significant. And when a group of right-wing intellectuals released a manifesto outlining suggested provincial "initiatives," including withdrawing from the Canada Pension Plan, collecting our own revenue, creating a provincial police force, and pushing ahead with a divergent health care policy, Klein yawned and took the "letter to the premier" under advisement. The fear motivating the manifesto is that once again Ottawa will try to redistribute Alberta's wealth to the rest of the country, while Alberta will resist, refusing to sell its wheat and oil at cut-rate prices, harbouring its disgruntlements. We believe in exaggerated promises, we elect crackpot provincial goverments and vote for right-of-right-of-centre parties, we pretend that nothing can ever be conservative enough, and we refuse to accept centralization. Cheap gasoline prices are fine but we will never, absolutely never, endorse a sales tax, and we wish a pox on the GST.

We're contrarians, dwellers of an elaborately deceptive labyrinth. If we say no, we mean yes; if we say yes, we mean no. When we run aground, we pretend that was where we wanted to be all along. When we fall in love, we jump in the back of a pickup truck and ride out of town. We commit suicide often, we eat ice cream steadily, we grow skull-sized potatoes and sweet Taber corn, we run raspberry canes from our neighbours' yards, and we pick buffalo beans to decorate our designer tables. We build skating rinks and ski jumps, we drive too fast, and we always come home, knowing exactly where home is. We're modest beneath our bluster, closer to cunning than quiet. We dare to be surprised by the beauty of our landscape, have to pinch ourselves to believe that the mountains aren't an elaborate painted set looming to the west, have to persuade ourselves that we deserve them. We are a people who embrace cold, skiing, and snowmobiling, the air crisp against our teeth. We live in our skins, believing that every rule is made to be broken. We sleep naked. Of all the provinces, Alberta has the largest percentage of people who sleep nude, some 68.6 percent compared to BC, where 65.1 percent do the full monty. Statisticians expect this from sexy Quebec, not Alberta, and in modest Ontario only 56.9 percent claim to sleep in the raw. Perhaps the pyjama factory is in Ontario. Or Albertans just like bare skin.

We're exhibitionists who love to shop, burn plastic without hesitation. Of the top ten urban retail streets in Canada, Alberta boasts three: Whyte Avenue in Edmonton, and Stephen and Seventeenth Avenue in Calgary. Not all of us ride horses, although we all own cowboy boots. We hate teachers and scowl at new-fangled education, but have the highest percentage per capita of post-secondary degrees in Canada. We're quick to take offence, ready to lob insults we are slow to retract. We'd rather die than say sorry, but we love it when Gretzky sheds tears. We approve of shady deals, but Peter Pocklington will need a passport to get back into the province. We glance at mirrors peripherally, we dance with winter tires and hailstones and snowflakes and long, late nights, and we deliberately face into the wind every chance we get.

If there is an Alberta that's truly itself, it's Alberta in the plush blue of a November twilight, light so dense it feels like cloth, so sharp that it tastes of ginger. Alberta's light sears the sight of memory, marking every person who lives here for even a short time. This place is like no other. Insanely inventive, it is a tall tale, a mudside, a raging hailstorm, a rustling poplar tree, a shout of fierce delight, a dusty hayfield. The unofficial Alberta, the one not measured and counted and public, is a kaleidoscope of celebration under a turbulent heaven.

So what the hell is an Albertan? And why are we the way we are?

Listen. Meet Alberta, one of the most amazing characters in the story of Canada.

2 | Primordial Time

Time, depth, and distance fall away;
a cozened reader in a future age
will find a calmness in a rage
of river flouting time and space,
in meeting wildness face to face.
        —Jon Whyte, "Nivation"

I am at a special regional conference of the American Association of Canadian Studies. This is a respectable body of scholars, serious, dedicated to close and generous study of our country, its habits, its politicians, its literature. For historical ambiance, the conference is being held at the Palliser Hotel in Calgary, that CPR landmark conveying with its sheer bulk the power and muscle of the "sea to sea" railroad. The Palliser Hotel was built in 1911, but it is a venerable site in a city as young as Calgary. It bespeaks dignity, situated beside the tracks like an elderly dowager with an ivory cane.

I attend a session on Calgary writing, particularly interested in a paper on Nancy Huston who, although she is now a Paris writer, was born in Calgary and is still described as a Canadian writer. She seldom returns, although she has used the city in her writing, and I expect the presenter to offer some interesting comparisons between Calgary and Paris. But I am wrong. He declares that this is his first visit to Calgary, he knows next to nothing about Alberta, and he is horrified by what he has seen a few steps from his hotel. It is unclear exactly what he has seen on the downtown streets, but he concludes that there is no reason for him to concern himself with this place. He states that it is perfectly clear that Nancy Huston left Calgary because she would never have been able to write the books she writes in what he calls "a mono-cultural place, less than one hundred years old."

In historically tilted arguments about age and venerability, about culture and its attendant snobbery, this is an infuriating assumption. "Alberta," I cannot resist telling him, leaping to my feet perhaps more forcefully than I should, "has a culture that goes back far beyond a mere one hundred years." He is disdainful of my comment. I know that he will board the plane with relief, look toward what he thinks of as the "scenery"

15

*of the mountains to the west and dismiss forever this postmodern encampment mas-
querading as a city.*

*His is the mistake commonly made about "young" places. They seem like brash
upstarts, running around without clothes, needing lessons with knives and forks. But
age and its wisdom are merely a matter of perspective, and the body, the landscape, the
voice of this place are more complex than Rousseau and revolution. Alberta's culture
goes back deep under its crust, behind the flanks of its mountains, layered in secret stories of escape and metamorphosis, fiery upheavals and glacial grindings. The characters
of Alberta's early drama are great sea creatures and wonderful dragons, humans who
could do battle with mammoths, and sophisticated priestesses who knew rituals that
would cure broken hearts.*

• • •

In an act of post-Victorian optimism, Alberta was declared a province of Canada in
1905. But its geological formations tell us that this land began billions of years ago,
during one of the oldest eras of earth's history, the Archean. This place is not new,
not innocent of change or history, not mono-cultural or mono-historical.

The oldest known rocks on this planet Earth lie just north of Alberta, close to
Great Bear Lake in the North West Territories. More than four billion years old,
these rocks are neighbours and relatives to Alberta's slightly younger three-billion-
year-old rocks, which lie in the northeast corner of the province, near the Slave
River. The ground beneath our feet bears witness to ancient transformations;
imagine this land quarrelling with its own composition, moving and grinding
into the argumentative place it has become.

Back in time, as the earth's proto-crust coasted above subterranean earthquakes
and volcanoes, younger segments of rock welded to those earliest Archean blocks,
making Alberta's basement a mixture of geological plates, all stuck together as part
of an early supercontinent. That combined land mass rose above sea level as a
rocky, barren world that shed its bulk along great river systems emptying into a
basin to the west. Eventually this basin subsided, deepening into what is now the
Pacific Ocean. During the Proterozoic era, 1.7 billion years ago, Alberta was the
edge, the seashore of what would ultimately shape itself into the North American
continent. Sand and water together left behind, along that ancient coastline, sedi-

mentary deposits shed from upland areas.

When the coast subsided, the sea moved eastward again, creeping over the flanks of that early continent. Near Jasper, marine life began to settle, building their homes one paper-thin layer at a time, as algal mounds. The seas washed in and out of western Alberta for millions of years, leaving behind sandstone, shale, and limestone. There were no plants or animals on land; all life was sheltered in the womb of the ocean.

When the oxygen content of the atmosphere increased, so did the abundance and complexity of the creatures in the oceans. Soft-bodied animals like worms and jellyfish developed. (Their taxonomy is embedded in the Burgess Shale, that fossil graveyard lying just across the British Columbia/Alberta border, Rosetta stone for the entire Cambrian period, from 590 to 505 million years ago.) These were early ancestors of the first Albertans. During the same period, the trilobites and brachiopods evolved, their hardened carapaces deriving from the minerals in seawater. The trilobites were the first true Albertans, mobile and prolific. They didn't know they were Albertans, and being small and singularly happy organisms, they did not even care they were trilobites, but there they were, primitive living things preparing a complex future.

As the millennia sped by, an enemy quietly entered the paleo-Albertan sea world: the cephalopods. These squid-like creatures had a voracious appetite for the plump and peaceful Albertans, especially those lacking protective shells, who fell prey to their tentacled grasp and deadly beaks. The armour of the trilobites and brachiopods saved them, and soon they were joined by an increasing number and variety of hard-shelled neighbours. As these citizens spread through the warm, shallow Alberta seascape, their hardened calcite shells slowly accumulated on the sea floor, and layer after layer, century after century, developed into deep piles of limestone. Alberta was growing a skin, accumulating a graveyard of trilobites, corals, and brachiopods.

Seas washed in and out of Alberta, which lay along the western flank of a large continent called Laurasia. Waters washing into the shallow basin carried sands, silts, and limestone, establishing a broad, low platform of land with a solid continental crust for a foundation. Meanwhile, the northeastern part of this early continent had shoulder-checked Europe, driving Greenland's east coast deep into the flank of the northern British Isles. This collision of continents slowly pushed up the Laurasian land mass, lifting it high above sea level so that the seawater drained south and westward, once again leaving Alberta high and dry. Tropical storms swept over this new land, huge rivers raged and aqueous plant life began to transfer its allegiance from salt to fresh water, slowly creeping onto the land. As the great orogeny—mountain formation—in the east subsided, the land again relaxed beneath a warm, shallow sea, populated by algae, sponges, shellfish, and primitive corals. There were no Rocky Mountains yet, just happy beachfront, the persistent rumble of rolling ocean breakers on Alberta's broad western shores.

Along this edge, new Albertans appeared. More and more of the sea creatures had grown carapaces. And fish, the first vertebrates, began to develop, flexing their way between the ocean-bottom plants. Corals and sponges built pinnacle reefs that grew upward toward the sunlight filtering into the water. The stromatoporoids—bulbous sponge-like creatures—were the most energetic of these reef builders, forming the porous structures that would hold oil and gas. The Leduc-Rimbey reef, famous for Leduc No. 1, modern Alberta's 1947 oil strike, became an environment perfect for hosting Alberta's future energy wealth. Euryptorids, a primitive form of oil field scout, began to move between the ocean and land, probably snacking on land plants. This area was then a shallow sea colonized by organisms and populated by prehistoric fish. Over millions of years, the shoreline changed, and the land alternately drowned and dried. But by the end of the Devonian period, 360 to 410 million years ago, an incredible network of fossil reefs, reservoirs for oil and gas, had grown. In that tropical water, an organic sludge rich in hydrogen and carbon created an amazing soup that, buried by layers of sediment, was blended by heat and pressure into the liquid that we know as oil, which conveniently pooled in those handy reservoirs made by the coral reefs.

Throughout, the continental plates kept colliding and after millions of years, converged into the supercontinent, Pangeia, a global land mass suggesting the shapes of current continents. Alberta's swampy seaside provided a perfect environment for the formation of tropical forests, curious insects, and the forerunners of amphibians, rhipidistians, who hauled themselves out of the water onto land and evolved into air-breathing creatures with four legs. These tetrapods stayed close to the water's edge, but time ultimately gave rise to cotylosaurs, lizard-like creatures who laid their eggs on land and who bridged amphibians and reptiles. No longer confined to an aquatic environment, they migrated and adapted to diverse landscapes and became the great-great-grandmothers of all other reptiles, dinosaurs, birds, and mammals. This was a heady Club Med world, with hundreds of land- and seascapes, and thousands of species of different life forms.

But that incredible zoo did not last; between the Paleozoic and the Mesozoic eras, about 250 million years ago, something in the world's environment changed, resulting in a mass extinction that left, in less than one million years, few sur- vivors. Although there are many hypotheses, no one knows the cause of this global die-off, and 95 percent of early Albertans did not make the cut. They died, but left behind their fossils. In the Mesozoic era, the period that followed the great extinction, new life forms evolved from the few survivors. In the Jurassic part of the Mesozoic, the sea crept up the rivers and along the delta of the moving shore- line. This tropical mud was perfect for the costuming of dinosaurs, which evolved from those early reptiles. Albertonia and Bobasatrania, strange-shaped fishy crea- tures with lots of teeth and absurd appendages, slid through the coastal waters. Exotic reptiles moved between land and sea, dodging and darting and hunting for prey. Tiny coiled ammonoids, radiating from a central spiral, found nutrients in silt. Deep cool waters, shallow, warm waters, and salty tidal flats alternately layered the western edges of Alberta, every slice another story.

The time of Pangeia moved between rain and drought, brine and lush growth, warm swamps and forests. Thecodonts, the forerunners of crocodiles, appeared, and by the end of the Triassic period, from 250 to 210 million years ago, were chas- ing little balls of fur, ancestors of mammals. Pangeia was peaceful, a heavenly breather in the cycle of upheavals, until it succumbed to the inevitable pressures that ground the continents together. When it did, the oceans boiled up again and covered the land, leaving only a few islands lolling above.

Alberta's astonishing scenery was inventing itself. Plants began to take over, curious tentacles spreading across the landscape and serving up a smorgasbord of tastes to vegetarian dinosaurs who enjoyed the flavour of flowers and berries, and were themselves tasty dishes for their carnivorous cousins, each part of a complex food chain. Early mammals, tiny rodents, scurried for their tiny lives. They stayed small, size no advantage to them, leaving the territory open for the most famous of all Albertans, dinosaurs, those "terrible lizards" that evolved from thecodonts. During the late Triassic, Jurassic, and Cretaceous, the dinosaurs were, for some 130 million years, the undisputed Caesars of Alberta's changing landscape.

Dinosaurs ruled Alberta for longer than humans have even existed. Theirs was a paradise of water lilies and cattails, vines and katsura trees, dawn redwoods and breadfruit trees and evergreen torreyes, warm, shallow seas sheltering whale-size lizards and *protosphyraena*. On oxbows and levees and reed fields and sandbars, turtles and aquatic salamanders and web-spinning spiders and *chasmosaurus* took one another's measure. *Centrosaurus* aimed their horned brows at their enemies; clawed dinosaurs could disembowel their prey with one strike. The bipedal *Albertosaurus*, twenty-five feet long and weighing several tons, could outrun every enemy, its tail, one-half its entire length, serving as a counterbalance while its ridiculously small forelimbs, with their two-fingered hands, flailed uselessly. Warm-blooded and cold-blooded creatures mingled. A few sprouted wings and took to the skies, and *hadrosaurus* eggs, big as grapefruits, nested in layers. *Edmontosaurus*, naive and impressionable, roamed the edges of the delta in herds, gulping plants, and swaying on large, three-toed feet. And rarest of all, *Tyrannosaurus rex*, at six tons the largest carnivore ever recorded, shook the earth when it stomped over to a dead carcass it intended to scavenge. Though their brains might have been small, they were happy, gregarious animals whose names live in Alberta's imagination.

The last great sea drowning the province, the Bearpaw Sea, began to retreat seventy-two million years ago, and slowly marine life scuttled away. The lush swampy world changed, became less hospitable. And one evening, the winds from the southeast began to push an ominous cushion of air. An asteroid about ten kilometres in diameter hit the Yucatan Peninsula, an explosion more than a thousand times stronger than one produced by all the world's nuclear explosions together. That collision created the Chixulub crater, and the dust and debris and heat that rained back into the atmosphere profoundly changed almost every ecosystem in North America. Any creature surviving the fireball and the resultant tidal wave would have had a hard time, for the haze that blocked the sun brought about severe planetary cooling.

Scientific arguments about the asteroidal effect abound. Was there only one asteroid, or several? Did it cause the dinosaurs' extinction or merely cause an environment that contributed to the finale? Some argue that volcanic eruptions, leading to high levels of carbon dioxide and increased global temperatures, did them in. Some argue that an exploding supernova destroyed the favourable climate. Some say that they were already dying. A few creatures, like birds and crocodiles, survived, and plants evolved to accommodate a different climate. Scientists do agree that between 60 and 80 percent of all species suffered extinction at the end of the Cretaceous period, sixty-five million years ago. It took ten million years for plant and animal life to recover, and the ghosts of that long-ago paradise still haunt us with their questions. Present-day Albertans read their bones, their eggs, their coprolites, and mourn them.

One of the most important events occurring during the Cretaceous period is that Alberta's neighbour to the west arrived, not with a whimper but a bang. A whole series of subterranean shrugs and ripples pushed volcanic islands toward North America, resulting in a jigsaw geology, different chunks of land jamming together on the west side of the continent. These slivers of land skiing up the western coast, colliding and grinding against its flank, caused Alberta's land mass to rise, and over twenty million years of terrible pressure the mountain ranges of the West rose. The land uplifting to form those ancestral Rocky Mountains tilted Alberta, and all the inland water flowed toward the northeast, creating a shallow sea that followed the direction of the Slave/Athabasca river systems. The great rivers emptying into these estuaries carried the sediment that ultimately gave rise to the Athabasca oil sands. During the swampy, damp Jurassic period, vegetation decayed and layered, decayed and layered. When the western edge of Alberta was tipped up like a plate, the land sagged into a basin to cradle a silt-rich arm of the sea, a superb environment for the accumulation and decomposition of peat, which over millions of years hardened into the bituminous shine of coal. More than 150 million years ago, these pressures and upheavals produced the coal beds of the Crowsnest Pass, which would become legenday for its miners and bootleggers and unions. All the while the dinosaurs prowled and proliferated. The western uplift continued, caused by five great crashes, each one lasting some ten million years and followed by a few million years of quiet before the next collision. Slowly, British Columbia was glued to Alberta, the land mass pushing itself higher and higher. Every crash made the central basin of Alberta collect more mud and debris, marine sediment layering more deeply and thickly. The land mass of British Columbia and Alaska increased pressure and elevated western and northern Alberta even more. That made the ocean in the northeast of the province recede, and by the end of the Cretaceous period a new continental sea had deluged southeastern Alberta.

We imagine the Rockies as ancient, but they are really very young. Alberta's landscape tiara was formed by slow-motion continental collision, which occurred at the rate of two inches a year, virtually unmeasurable but inexorable. The top layers of the Pacific plate were pushed and folded and distorted, piled up in several stages over the past two hundred million years. Each range between Alberta and BC represents a different upheaval. From Calgary westward, the first range is the Alberta foothills, then the Front Ranges, where Banff is situated, then farther west the Main Ranges, where the town of Jasper lies. The western edge borders the Rocky Mountain trench, that magnificent divide symbolically separating Alberta from British Columbia.

When the construction of the mountains was complete, the Rockies were not yet the way they are today. They would be irrevocably altered by ice, the advance and retreat of glaciers. The first of these was the Great Glaciation, which took place 240,000 years ago. The Rockies were so blanketed in ice that only the tops of the highest mountains showed. Ice scoured the surfaces, ground rocks into flour, and altered the contours of the mountains. After 100,000 years, this first mega-glacier began to melt and retreat, resulting in huge rivers rushing along the eastern front of the Rockies. The channel they opened became the route by which early man and animals travelled from Asia to Central and South America, along the western shoulder of Alberta. That first ice age was followed by four others, not quite so extreme. One ice sheet moved westward from the Canadian Shield, and met, in a roar and scrape of glacial fury, the ice fingering its way out from the valleys of the Rockies. The most recent ice ages to creep from their mountain aeries were minor: the Crowfoot Advance about 11,000 years ago, and the Cavell, or Little, Ice Age about 750 years ago. In 1898, the Athabasca glacier of the famous Columbia Icefields just reached the valley where the Icefields Parkway now runs.

But the effects of those ice sheets are visible. The water of the mountain lakes is a startling blue-green, coloured by rock flour. Crevasses that trigger the imagination of painters and writers are caused by the stretching and shrinking of the ice. Thomas Wharton's novel *Icefields* explores the fascination humans feel for these seductive fields of frozen water. Cirques scooped out of solid rock formed small lakes. The drumlins and kettles of central Alberta are hills and hollows left by melting ice and littered piles of till or moraine. The river valleys that invited settlement at Edmonton, Calgary, Lethbridge, and Medicine Hat are glacial signatures. Here in

Alberta we now live on the great outwash plain of the retreated glaciers from that last ice age. Even the hot springs in Banff come from moving mountains. Between the folded and pressured layers of the Rockies, water melting from snow or rain seeps into cracks thousands of yards deep and is slowly heated by the surrounding rocks. The deeper the water trickles, the hotter it gets, dissolving and carrying along rock flour and minerals. Trapped within rock faults and under pressure, the water works its way back to the surface, magically transformed into the healing mineral springs.

Ice age life had to be adaptable and recovery from the ice age was slow. In the Cenozoic era, which we are in today, grasses evolved. With grasses came the mammals that eat grass, and with those mammals came the mammals that eat mammals. The corridor that ran along Alberta's western edge was home to mammoths and dogs, horses and llamas, sabre-toothed tigers and short-faced bears. The animals who lived at the end of the last glacial period first encountered humans, then slowly disappeared, perhaps because the humans hunted them, perhaps because relatively speedy environmental changes forced them into extinction. But, like the dinosaurs, their spirits have not left. We still hear the screams of sabre-toothed cats, the thundering hooves of ancient bison with horns six feet wide, the gnawing teeth of the giant beaver.

One theory about early Albertans, based on archaeological tool types, suggests that they migrated from Asia over the Bering Strait and Alaska land bridge in the last great ice advance. Humans followed the ice-free corridor southward between two receding ice sheets, along the rain-shadowed eastern flank of the Rockies. Were they following game? Curious? Struck by the carelessly spectacular bounty and beauty around them? Scientific arguments about when humans arrived are unresolved. A newer theory argues that humans came via the Pacific Ocean and then overland. Did people know this landscape some 24,000 to 45,000 years ago, or did they show up a mere 13,000 years ago, the more conservative estimate based on carbon-dated readings of the Clovis Spearpoint, a hunting projectile point used during the earliest post-glacial period? Because early Albertans didn't leave many permanent structures or visible marks, reading their history remains an exercise in mystery and speculation, aided by oral stories that have been passed down from generation to generation.

One of the biggest controversies about early humans surrounds the Woodpecker Island Taber Child remains. In 1961 John Nunan, a member of

Canadian geologist Dr. Archie Stalker's Geological Survey field party, found some bones in a hole halfway up the bank of the Oldman River, just north of Taber. Stalker describes the bones as occurring in "interglacial or inter-till deposits." A geologist, he could read the strata the bones were sandwiched between, even though his party did not immediately identify the bones as human. They were buried by nineteen yards of soil, which Stalker carefully measured, the strata alternating glacial with non-glacial sub-units. The field party dug the bones out, still within their matrix, and sent them to Ottawa—which, as any Albertan can tell you, is always a mistake. When the fragments were identified as human, archaeologists circled them again and again. If the matrix where the bones were found was an indication of their age, these were the oldest human remains in the Americas. Based on geological surroundings, Stalker estimated them at 25,000 years old, but surrounding wood fragments were later carbon-dated at between 32,000 and 49,000 years old. Every scientific body with an interest in human antiquity had a different opinion, and the bone fragments of that disinterred skeleton were subjected to batteries of tests that dated them from 25,000 years old to less than 4,000 years old. Ultimately the National Museum of Man in Ottawa decreed, based on the findings of accelerator mass spectrometry, that the Taber Child was only 3,500 years old. But Stalker adamantly disagreed, arguing that those bones were laid down before the advance of the last glacier, and that their minimum age is 14,000 years. The Cordilleran ice sheet, which flowed from the mountains, met the Keewatin ice sheet, which came from the east, somewhere around Nose Creek in the Calgary area, and was deflected southward. When the glacier began to retreat, a lobe of ground opened up in southern Alberta, while northern Alberta was still covered with ice. That open area was tempting to animals, which would eat the grasses growing in the water at the base of the glacier; and of course people would follow the animals.

Stalker's version of the bones is a poignant one. A baby between four and six months old died. The body lay on its left side somewhere at the point of an ancient braided river in a spot only occasionally covered with water. But the bed of the river, through silt deposition, grew, and that small body was buried by sand or silt. The sand in which the bones rested was eroded and more sand deposited both by the river and by the next encroaching glacier, which pushed till over the site. The weight of the glacier crushed the skeleton's skull and added to the blankets of soil that covered it, which is how the bones could lie undisturbed until recent changes in the valley's erosion exposed them. Stalker was fierce in his defence of the bones' age, and arguments over the protein and radiocarbon dating of the bones still erupt, further complicated because the dates attributed to the skeleton differ from the dates of the material that filled the cavity of the skeleton. There are other questions, too. The Museum of Man apparently replaced two of the bones with reproductions so the real ones could be sent to the Canadian Conservation Institute for protein analysis. Embarrassingly, the real bones were lost and have never been found. Stalker's estimate of the skeleton's age would situate Canada's first humans in the West. What does that say about patterns of civilization? If people were traipsing through Alberta that long ago, all our preconceived notions of human habitation would have to be adjusted. Unspoken but even more important is the actual political significance of the dates on aboriginal land claims.

Glaciers are beautiful but destructive forces. They grind everything in their paths to powder, and leave behind piles of debris pushed from elsewhere. We might, were we not such a glaciated country, have much more evidence to locate the comings and goings of ancient people. Once the glaciers retreated, some 14,000 years ago, Alberta's First Peoples hunted and lived in a land as bounteous as it was demanding. Their creation myths, their inventive means of survival, and their tribal wars gave them a history as complex as any that has been written. Powerful in their intricate cultures, these people's children continue to speak with resonant voices. And we, clumsy detectives, continue to find faint traces that human beings were here long before Europeans even imagined sailing off the edge of the world.

Alberta novelist Rudy Wiebe describes in his afterword to Robert Kroetsch's 1993 *Alberta* how the Trans-Canada Highway crosses the earliest site of human habitation known in Canada. Found when backhoes began to widen Alberta Highway 68, forty miles west of Calgary, the artefacts that were revealed belonged to people from the Fluted Point Tradition, who camped there beginning between 10,000 and 11,000 years ago. This marvellous campground, called the Sibbald Creek site—after the first white man to graze cattle there—continued in use until the twentieth century. There, sheltered in the lee of the mountains, surrounded by trees for firewood and plentiful game, early nomads enjoyed the bounty of Alberta's foothills. They possessed the strength and intelligence to

Pictographs at Writing-on-Stone

withstand cold, travel long distances, and hunt huge and threatening animals with mere stone hammers and pointed projectiles. But they knew a good camp spot when they found it, and this south-facing slope, with at least six micro-environments and many, many plant species, from lodgepole pine to buffalo berry, snowberry, anemone, and kinnikinnick, was not merely beautiful but replete with everything needed.

To endlessly mobile humans, stories, songs, and dances were more portable than any material possession. The few marks that they did leave are evocative and eloquent. Across the southern plains, great stone circles, initially presumed to have been teepee rings, read the starry skies. They resemble, from the air, the wheels of awkward bicycles. Central rock cairns extend spokes toward concentric rings and other cairns, their location aligned to capture exactly the line of the sun rising at the summer solstice, the first ray of summer's light. Always built on a height of land, with sweeping views, the spokes of these medicine wheels, so named because of their sacred history, point toward distant rock mounds like a network of signs, their positioning revealing sophisticated astronomical readings. Close to them are always teepee rings, but also stone effigies, outlines of humans dancing and gesticulating, as if to participate in heavenly conversations.

Calgary archaeologists, in dating the artefacts in the centre of a stone circle located close to the ghost village of Majorville, found evidence that the circle was made 4,000 to 5,000 years ago. Those first stones had been positioned in the earth by human hands when the Egyptian pyramids were still being built. This astonishing fact puts the lie to every dismissal of this country as "young" and "unsophisticated." Even more suggestive are the sacred petroglyphs of the Milk River, *Kin-nax-is-sa-ta*, in southern Alberta, an eerie river whose glacial meltwater pours white as milk between sandstone beds. On the open prairie above, the wind scoured the landscape, but in the coulees and valleys of the riverside, trees and plants flourished. This was liminal space, a terrain that contained different worlds, a crossover for the spirits, or as P. S. Barry says in his *Mystical Themes in Milk River Rock Art*, "the wasteland and the paradise combined." On these rock walls, pilgrim Albertans drew their journeys, told stories of their daily and spiritual lives. The area is now preserved as a provincial park, called rather prosaically Writing-on-Stone. The earliest evidence of human visitors is about 10,000 years old, but most of the petroglyphs appear to originate with the practice of communal buffalo hunts. With the incredible cross-tribal co-operation and organization required to herd buffalo over a jump came concomitant rituals to ensure the hunt's success. *Kin-nax-is-sa-ta* was a secluded, otherworldly place, where shamans could prepare themselves. Although experts cannot assign a time to individual pictures, engravings of horses clearly date from after the First Peoples' acquisition of horses around 1730. Chimeric creatures, symbolic shapes and animal figures on the walls bespeak a holy place, where animals and birds run and fly, where ghostly figures ride and hunt, where warriers with shields and spears take part in great battles, where skeletons rattle their bones and babies are born, and where humans with raised arms and floating hearts address their own transformation. Iconographic studies claim that these drawings are not simple cartoons but spiritual and mystical symbols and guides.

The womb of the world, the Milk River valley became a place of religious pilgrimage, where, even into the twentieth century, the devout brought offerings and prayers to the pictures on the walls. Alberta historian Hugh Dempsey, in *A History of Writing-on-Stone*, describes a Blood family's pilgrimage to the pictures, to present "gifts for the ghosts."

Glenbow Archives, Calgary, Canada: ND-8-246

Buffalo—should have been the name of the province

Next morning the children were taught the ceremony which would be performed when the gifts were presented to the spirits. The wagon was loaded and the party made its way to the pictograph site. The mother then sorted the gifts into several bundles while "our father also got busy with his medicine bag to get out his ochre to begin his other ritual to paint our faces." It was almost midday before the offerings were finally left at the holy place. There they went through the ritual of "approaching the site to leave the gifts without any talking. Only our dogs were making any noise."

The power of this place, its long history, continues to exert an ineffable force. Both oracular site and sacred text, the walls dance and gesture with figures who invite us, blinded by our contemporary ignorance, into the history of an Alberta that may seem relentlessly modern but that harbours in the whisperings of time a long, long poem of landscape and language, creature and creation.

This is, truly, where the world began.

3 | Fur

Canada is useful only to provide me with furs.
        —Madame de Pompadour

In late January, bent under the weight of my fur coat, head down against a tearing snow-storm wind that sucks away heat and breath, I find myself becoming David Thompson in 1799, my sextant heavy on my belt as I plod forward, following the North Saskatchewan River toward the Athabasca, dreaming of Rocky Mountain House. The snow stings my forehead, the wind crusts small drifts against my eyebrows, and I dream of the eloquent tributaries of maps, their lines scouring paths of discovery.

Thompson knew that when he reached the trading post, he would have to tabulate bales of beaver, count stacks of blankets, and align the handles of cast-iron pots, but here, against the wind, we are both permitted the solitude of thought. Alone in this invisible white, I imagine the teeth of the Rockies biting at a brittle sky that tomorrow will be pierc-ingly bright. But for now I am buffeted by a blizzard on the eastern side of the Rockies, leaning into a cold that intends to carve crystals into my bones, to make of me a skeleton, a bleached frame reduced to the ash of snowflakes. And yet, here is when I feel alive, com-pletely aware, intoxicated by the slow burn of cold.

I share with David Thompson the knowledge of how to face an Alberta wind. Pay attention to where you are. Notice landmarks. Check the stars, if they are visible. Wear fur. It is only slightly less fashionable, in this hyper-judgemental world, to be walking in a blizzard than to be wearing fur. Very few people do either.

Why, when Canadians turn their attention to the fur trade, that three-hundred-year-old economic gamble that shaped and exploited the West, is Thompson the figure who leaps to mind? Does he, with his incredible map and his own resistance to the trade, sweeten the greed, make the exploitation of the West's people and resources somehow palatable, even romantic? Does the figure of Thompson persuade a still-ruthless Centre that some good came out of the North West Company and the Hudson's Bay Company's fierce competition, their willingness to trade in death and debauchery, as well as in axes and blankets?

Thompson was a Westerner who paid attention, who listened and learned from the aboriginal people he met and the landscape he transferred to a two-dimensional imagi-

nary manifestation called a map. He worked, body and soul, for two trading companies, and understood their opportunities and their limitations. And he understood fur. Fur keeps you warm, keeps you close to the ground, close to its animal source. Fur, so wonderfully rich and plentiful, was the first resource that the Centre stole from the West.

• • •

In the mid-1600s, when Oliver Cromwell was making life difficult for royalists, when Pieter de Hooch was painting the Dutch home as an exemplary place with impeccable tile floors and polished windows, when Sweden and Denmark, France and Spain were at war, a spirit of uneasiness prevailed, not only in the Old World, with its constant inventions and discoveries, but in the New World, the newest part of the New World.

The Dutch and English divided up eastern North America, while the Spanish built missions in Florida and explored Alabama. The French were well established on the St. Lawrence River, and from the city of Quebec, the adventurous Pierre-Esprit Radisson and his brother-in-law, Médard Chouart, Sieur des Groseilliers, set out on a journey. These coureurs de bois were an intrepid pair, and their adventures are recounted in Radisson's wonderfully hyperbolic *Voyages*, which now resides in the Bodleian Library in Oxford, England. Radisson and Groseilliers were, in the spring of 1659, the first Europeans to go as far west as Lake Superior and the upper Midwest of North America. So interested were they in exploration that on their return, when the governor of New France, one very foolish Marquis d'Argenson, refused to give them permission to move beyond Lake Superior, they changed their allegiance from the French to the English. Marquis d'Argenson thereby altered forever the fortunes of the French in North America and indirectly affected how and why the West came to be dominated by English- rather than French-speaking people. If Quebec wants to blame anyone, they ought to begin with d'Argenson.

It is unclear whether Radisson and Groseilliers ever made it to Hudson Bay, but their enthusiasm and their reports of the area that would become Minnesota were noticed by Colonel George Cartwright, visiting the New World to try to collect taxes for Charles II from the somewhat resistant colonies of New England. Cartwright persuaded the brothers-in-law to return with him to England, hoping to use them to enlist royal support for ventures in search of the thick and lustrous beaver skins that the fashion slaves of the day found so desirable.

By then, the English were thoroughly sick of Cromwellian repression and the Restoration had kicked in. The theatres had re-opened, the Anglican Book of Common Prayer had been revised, libraries had just been founded in Berlin and Copenhagen, and the French were exporting domestic furniture to the rest of Europe. Charles II of England, in granting a charter to the Royal Society in 1662, emphasized the new interest in scientific discovery; Isaac Newton and Edmund Halley were hard at work. In 1665, when Radisson and Groseilliers sailed up the Thames, London was in the throes of the Great Plague, which killed 68,596 people, about one-sixth of its population, a disaster that would shortly be superseded by the Great Fire of London. After hanging around for a year, presumably entertaining the Old World with their exploits in the New, the two actually met Charles II, on October 25, 1666. They must have spun a good yarn, because they were granted royal protection and a weekly pension. More important, they had sown the seeds of the Hudson's Bay Company, which set out to trade in a new way, not via the French route on the St. Lawrence, but through Hudson Bay, named for the mariner Henry Hudson, who had met his end when cast adrift there in 1611.

Radisson and Groseilliers also spoke with Prince Rupert, a member of the Stuart family who was particularly interested in the mineral potential of the land beyond Hudson Bay. He financed an exploratory journey, stocking two ships with trading items and commissioning Radisson and Groseilliers to sail to Hudson Bay, build forts, trade, prospect, and return. On the way, Radisson's ship nearly foundered and was forced to turn back, but the other sailed on and anchored at Rupert River, then prepared for winter on Hudson Bay. It was, as usual, a bleak season, but in the spring, several thousand James Bay First Nations people came to trade prime beaver pelts for hatchets, scrapers, muskets, and needles, an exchange that set in motion the initial relationship between western aboriginal peoples and whites. That first trip didn't make much money, but it proved that Radisson and Groseilliers had told the truth; it was possible to sail to Hudson Bay, winter there, and return with a ship's bellyful of fur. The economic exploitation of the West's resources had begun.

And such is the force of commerce that Charles II, on May 2, 1670, "granted, ratified, and confirmed" to Prince Rupert and his Company of Adventurers of

England a charter—in effect, a total monopoly and perpetual succession over all the sea and lands of Hudson Bay and its entire drainage system. Under the governorship of Prince Rupert, the Company of Adventurers were deemed "true lords and proprietors" of something like 40 percent of what we now know as Canada, some 1.5 million square miles. What a kingly gesture, to bestow on a faithful cousin the proprietorship of a tract of land beyond all European imagining! Of course, the true lords and proprietors of this vast territory were conveniently designated as suppliers of the goods that would be taken from the area. They were not even given the dignity of recognition as a conquered or occupied people. So began the configuration of the West as a land that could be ransacked for the trading floors of Europe. Ironically the mercantile success of the Hudson's Bay Company gave Prince Rupert so much cachet that he presided over the laying of the cornerstone for the Royal Exchange.

By the terms of that charter, the area that now includes Alberta was virtually owned by the HBC until it was resold to Canada in 1869—when the Deed of Surrender, the act for the Temporary Government of Rupert's Land, provided for the region to be transferred back to the British Crown, which agreed to give it to Canada. In short, the West was passed from one colonial power to the next, the Hudson's Bay Company compensated with $1.5 million and one-twentieth of the region's arable land. They retained, as well, title to 120 trading posts. Canada had scant idea what it had been handed; their plans for this territory were to annex it and then "open it up" to agricultural settlement. But Rupert's Land was first designated a cornucopia of fur to be hauled back to London and sold to enrich its shareholders. Of course, no European had yet laid eyes on the area that would become Alberta. It was still quietly minding its business, greening and blooming through spring and summer, then slowly retreating into winter. It would be a few years before traders got that far west.

Although it was all their entrepreneurial fault, it is doubtful that Radisson and Groseilliers ever laid eyes on Alberta. Certainly Radisson explored the Nelson and Hayes rivers, now in Manitoba, but his narrative contains very little in the way of geographical markers, and historians are still arguing about where, exactly, he travelled. In the end, examples of poetic justice, they too were disillusioned with the trade. After much argument, with the two jumping between the French and the English, Groseilliers retired to his gooseberries at Trois-Rivières and died peacefully in 1696, while Radisson, with a French price on his head, died poor and uncelebrated in London in 1710.

• • •

Once European awareness of the West's wealth had been piqued, it was only a matter of time before entrepreneurs tried to find ways to access that wealth. Pressure on the original inhabitants began long before whites got anywhere near them. As each aboriginal group was pushed farther back by white settlement, they in turn pushed other tribes back, so that territorial shift was the first indication of contact. The second was the slow spread of trading items: kettles, axes, sewing needles. The Cree traders of present-day Ontario who got guns from the French and English traders used them to trade with and pressure the prairie and parkland bands.

Map-maker David Thompson's storytelling wise man, *Saukamappee,* related to Thompson his first encounter with guns, somewhere around 1730. The Peigan people, with the help of the Cree, used them to defeat the Snake Indians, who lacked guns but possessed another amazing import, horses, brought to America by the Spanish. Alberta's mightiest people were squeezed between those big dogs as swift as deer, ridden by the Snake people from the southwest, and the weapons brought by the quick-footed Cree traders from the northeast. There was nothing for the Peigan to do but engage with the white trade, albeit indirectly, and by barter or capture, borrow both guns and horses, which became their markers of power and wealth.

Alberta hosted French peddlers long before the English got up enough energy to leave the shores of Hudson Bay and travel inland. By the mid-1700s, the French were diverting the best of northwestern furs to Lower Canada via the long trade route from the Saskatchewan country to Lake Winnipeg, the Great Lakes, and the St. Lawrence. It was only when the English realized they were losing money that they began to rethink their strategy of using the Cree and Assiniboine as middlemen who bought furs in the west and north and transported them to Hudson Bay to sell to the Company posts there. The French peddlers, who took their goods straight to the source of income, clearly had the advantage.

The Indians were pragmatists. If they could trade with the French, why should they drag their furs all the way to Hudson Bay? The energetic Montrealers of the

North West Company first monopolized the Saskatchewan River area, establishing inland trading posts while the HBC slept at "the edge of a frozen sea." The HBC reduced the number of made-beaver (full beaver pelts) required for guns and blankets, and for a while the Indians enjoyed the competition, playing the French and English against one another—they preferred English tobacco and French brandy. Both English and French were often helped out by Indian women, and the role of women in facilitating trade became vital. To complicate matters, in 1745 the British Parliament offered a £20,000 reward for the discovery of the Northwest Passage, which made activity grow even more intense. It was obvious that the HBC was losing trade to the tent-to-tent French peddlers, far more convenient travelling salesmen to the First Nations people than the remote Baymen.

And then, in 1754 Anthony Henday, an HBC net-maker and former smuggler, volunteered for a mission to the interior, its object to persuade the Indians there to travel to the Bay to trade with the HBC. Henday is named by every historian as Alberta's earliest white visitor, although what were the French if not white? Since the French peddlers kept no journals, Henday is the first on record.

During his year-long journey, from June 1754 to June 1755, he encountered intolerable "Musketoes," drank nothing but stagnant water, learned the difference between deer and moose flesh, and developed "swelled" feet. Henday connected with the people he met, and even getting necessities gave him pleasure; he describes buffalo hunting as "fine sport," "the buffalo so numerous [that we are] obliged to make them sheer out of our way." He was impressed with the incredible hunting abilities of the Indians. "So expert are the natives, that they will take the arrows out of them [the buffalo] when they are foaming and raging with pain, & tearing the ground up with their feet & horns until they fall down." He met various tribes, who all told him, over and over again, that they were conveniently supplied by the French.

Henday, intelligently enough, but also by necessity, travelled with Indians. He was under the care of a Cree middleman called *Attickasish*, one of those who traded furs and carried them to the Bay. He was also accompanied by a Cree woman, who obviously shared his bed and, if one reads between the lines of Henday's journal, kept trying to explain local matters to him. After four months of uncomfortable travel by canoe, they reached Alberta, about September 11, 1754, crossing the Battle River, also called "the stream flowing in the tremendous valley," somewhere north of Wainwright. Henday recorded a few days later, "Level land, few woods, & plenty of good water . . . Indians killed 8 Waskesew." Close to present-day Edmonton they met a number of French traders who were loading their canoes. Because he was protected by his Cree companions, the French left Henday alone, but that encounter signals the French presence in Alberta long before the English bothered to investigate the region's potential. Somewhere around Irma, on September 20, Henday "came to 7 tents of Asinepoet [Assiniboine] Natives. I smoked with them and bought a horse from them for a gun, to carry my provisions." Although he did not initiate the long Alberta tradition of horse trading, which the original people had been actively engaged in since 1730, he probably made the first white man's horse trade.

His companions showed Henday the bountiful parkland of the North Saskatchewan River, then moved south to the Red Deer and Battle rivers. Around October 1, 1754, near present-day Innisfail, close to Red Deer, Henday was taken to a large gathering of Blackfoot. He recorded an impressive camp of more than two thousand people, some two hundred bleached teepees in two regular lines on either side of a broad street. These were the mighty people who controlled the approaches to the foothills of the Rockies. He was escorted to the tent of their leader, who "received us seated on a clear [white] buffalo skin, attended by twenty elderly men." They smoked silently, then ate buffalo flesh together, and Henday says, "I was presented with ten Buffalo tongues," the prairie's greatest delicacy.

Although he was met with hospitality, Henday's suggestion that these people should travel to the HBC to trade for powder, shot, guns, cloth, and beads was met with indifference, even suppressed laughter. When he suggested that some of the young men return with him, Henday recorded their sensible answer that "it was far off, & they could not live without Buffalo flesh; and that they could not leave their horses and many other obstackels, though all might be got over if they were acquainted with a Canoe, and could eat Fish, which they never do. The Chief said they never wanted food, as they followed the Buffalo & killed them with the Bows and Arrows; and he was informed the Natives that frequented the Settlements, were oftentimes starved on their journey." This scene is almost comic—a ragged white man, completely unable to survive without being cared for by his Cree guides, suggesting to this wealthy and powerful people that they undertake an arduous, lengthy journey in order to purchase a few kettles.

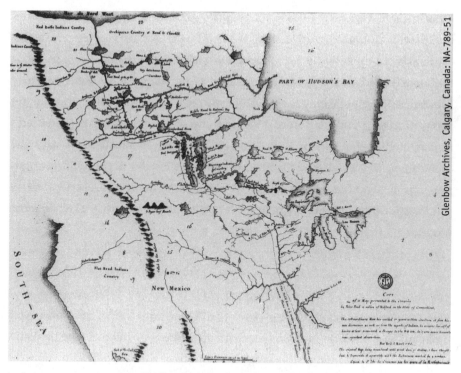

Peter Pond's map of what he thought the West was like

Over that winter Henday happily joined in the drumming, dancing, smoking, and feasting. He was willing to eat everything, even dog. And, in his favour, he was smart enough to pay attention when the Indian woman who lived with him advised him to stop pestering everyone about trapping—he was making himself ridiculous. He recorded the Indians' laughter at some of his stupider questions, and he noted a moderate winter, with women "knitting snowshoes." The native tendency to adjust to the weather and to enjoy what they had was at first puzzling to him, but slowly he, too, relaxed, although occasionally his irritation at their refusal to trap more fur than they needed recurred. "The Beaver and Otters are swarming about us in the Creeks and Swamps, [but] not one went out to-day but myself, & I killed two Otters." He still had a lot to learn.

On December 24, 1754, Henday recorded climbing a hill to say farewell to the Rocky Mountains, *"Usinee Wutche."* "On a rising ground, I had an extensive view of the Arsinie Watchie [he is a bad speller] which will be the last this trip inland."

He was the first white man to witness a vista so breathtaking that it would certainly stay with him for the rest of his life.

Henday camped with his Cree guides along the banks of the North Saskatchewan River and at the end of April 1755, when the ice went out, they paddled east, again meeting the Blackfoot who traded the Cree all their winter fur and pemmican. Henday recorded, "We are above sixty Canoes and there are scarce a Gun, Kettle, Hatchet, or Knife amongst us, having traded them with the Archithinue Natives." Henday made other journeys but did not keep further journals. Like many other employees who contributed to the HBC's success, Henday was treated badly, not promoted, and after he left the company in 1762 no more was heard of him.

• • •

Alberta's territory came into its own only with the formation of the North West Company in 1779. That entrepreneurial group pushed beyond the structured grid of the HBC, which stubbornly clung to the shore of Hudson Bay. The Montreal peddlers, white and Métis, were the first to forge their way into the great hinterland of Lake Athabasca, the Slave, Peace, and Mackenzie river basins, the country's richest storehouse of quality beaver. Although the Treaty of Paris in 1783 was supposed to end the fighting between English and French, the traders were far away, and in the spirit of competition were as quick to ignite a feud as they were to play friendly games between their adjacent posts. The Nor'Westers, famous for their bellicosity, impudence, and humour, differed sharply from the more rigid functionaries of the HBC. Their trading canoes came all the way from the St. Lawrence, a supply line more than three thousand miles long. The economic turnaround was slow; thirty months separated the purchase of trade goods and the sale of furs. Nor'Westers were French or Scottish, but not English, and their unruly spirit reflected the spirit of the West. They can be credited with saving Western Canada from being annexed by the United States, they can be blamed for leaving behind alcoholism, syphilis, and many mixed-blood children, and they predicted the strange affinity between Alberta and Quebec—a mutual hostility to the bureaucrats in between. True Canadians, these traders made Montreal home to their celebrations and retirements, while Fort William was their transshipment centre, its location on the shoulder of Lake Superior a perfect staging point from which to leave the centre and head for the Wild West.

One of their founding members, Peter Pond, never wrote much about his time in the northern part of what would become Alberta. An eccentric man who wanted only to make money, he contributed a great deal to initial knowledge and exploration of the area, without necessarily setting out to fulfil that goal. Born in Milford, Connecticut, in 1740, the son of a shoemaker, he became a shoemaker himself. In 1756 he enlisted as a private in the British colonial army; he served with the British troops that took Fort Niagara in 1759. After the conquest of Montreal in 1760, he headed for the West Indies, and when he returned worked in both shipping and trading around Detroit. At some point during this period, he killed a fur-trading opponent, and although he confessed to Detroit authorities— he said he was threatened and abused by the other man—he was never prosecuted. Pond seemed to have an affinity for murder; he was twice more involved in the murder of rival traders, and he was known for his violent temper. He wrote an account of his early experiences that survives to this day (held at Yale University), but the narrative ends abruptly in 1775, the year he travelled northwest to winter at Fort Dauphin, his first foray into Western Canada.

Was Pond's effectiveness in negotiating with the Indians enabled by violence or experienced Yankee guile? He felt no qualms about intercepting Indians who were bound to trade with the HBC, offering them goods and relieving them of their best furs. After two years' trading in Manitoba and Saskatchewan, in the spring of 1778 he formed a loose joint venture with several other peddlers (the forerunner of the North West Company) to trade in the Athabasca. The region's luxuriant beaver pelts had long been the subject of mesmerizing stories told by First Nations traders.

Pond spent the winter of 1778–79 about forty miles south of Lake Athabasca on the Athabasca River, not far from present-day Fort Chipewyan. How he got there is unclear. Was he guided by Indians? Did he follow a native trail? The Scottish-born fur trader and explorer Alexander Mackenzie, who was Pond's assistant during his last year at Fort Chipewyan, claimed that Pond's House was the only post in that region until 1785. And the Cree and Chipewyan there were pleased to see Pond, for trading with him saved them making the long trip to Fort Churchill on Hudson Bay. They had better things to do.

Pond was on his best behaviour when he was the only trader in town. As the one post there, Pond's House was favoured with energetic trade. The Indians were willing to give him favourable terms and to part with furs for less than they would at Hudson Bay. They were also happy to supply him with provisions. Pond enjoyed an easy exchange, incidentally impinging on the HBC supply line and, according to Mackenzie, collecting more than twice as many furs as his canoes would carry. Historians still argue about the total number of pelts Pond brought out that year. Some say he collected a fantastic eighty thousand skins. Ironically, the last untapped source of beaver east of the Rockies became the first meagre European settlement in what would become Alberta, manned by an American murderer, whose only creed was making money.

Whatever his motivation, in 1778 Pond trudged over the portage between Lac La Loche and the Clearwater River, just a few miles from the Alberta/Saskatchewan border, to winter on the Athabasca River, some forty miles north of Lake Athabasca. Pond bragged about the convenience of the Methye Portage or Portage La Loche, but he exaggerated its comforts. The Methye Portage is a boggy quagmire of muskeg and brush that rises some 1,200 feet and whips the body with tamarack and pine, poplar and scrub. That climb, especially carrying two hundred pounds of freight, was hellish, fourteen miles across the height of land to the Clearwater River, and so demanding that it took his men eight days to portage. Mackenzie described it as well:

> The Portage La Loche is of a level surface, in some parts abounding
> with stones, but in general it is . . . covered with the cypress, the
> pine, the spruce fir, and other trees natural to its soil. Within three
> miles of the North-West termination, there is a small round lake,
> whose diameter does not exceed a mile, and which affords a trifling
> respite to the labour of carrying. Within a mile of the termination of
> the Portage is a very steep precipice, whose ascent and descent
> appears to be equally impracticable in any way, as it consists of a
> succession of eight hills, some of which are almost perpendicular;
> nevertheless, the Canadians contrive to surmount all these difficulties,
> even with their canoes and lading.

Perhaps that portage reinforced the temptation of a cross-continental trading route. Pond was the first white man to use it and to encounter the Athabasca and Clearwater rivers in the elbow crook where now the town of Fort McMurray bursts past the seams of its oil-sand overalls. He was the first to trade there and the first European trader to use pemmican as survival food. Pemmican allowed traders to travel faster than they had before; they didn't have to carry so many provisions, and they could concentrate on trading because they didn't have to hunt or fish to feed themselves.

Pond wanted to keep the competition away from his territory, but he needed allies and in 1783 his partnership with a group of like-minded men grew into the initial North West Company. Pond held one share of the sixteen who had joined; other early members included Peter Pangman, Joseph Frobisher, Alexander Mackenzie, and Simon McTavish. Contentious as ever, Pond felt that he should have been offered more than one part for all his hard work, so he at first refused the share and considered forming a joint venture with John Ross and Peter Pangman, but he eventually accepted the North West Company offer and returned to the Athabasca in 1785.

Pond gleaned everything he could from the Indians' descriptions of the country to the west and north. He believed he had a clear sense of Great Bear and Great Slave lakes, as well as the Peace and Mackenzie rivers. More than anything, he wanted to push deeper into unmapped territory, and over the winter of 1784–85 he worked hard at preparing a map, purely invented, of where he planned to go. Claiming that his discoveries, as well as reports from the Indians, gave him cartographical authority, Pond was convinced that he had discovered a passage to the northwest sea. He revised his map four times—at least, there are four versions, intended for audiences as diverse as the Empress of Russia and the Honourable W. W. Grenville, the British cabinet minister responsible for colonial matters—but his imagination bested him and he drew the Mackenzie River as draining into the Pacific Ocean rather than the Arctic. However inaccurate, his map inspired considerable interest, even that of Sir Joseph Banks, the English naturalist who had accompanied Cook on his voyage around the world, and it is possible that Alexander Mackenzie carried it on his voyage down the river he named after himself.

But for all his desire to explore further, in the spring of 1788 Pond left

Athabasca for good, his reputation for cartography and discovery outweighed by his quick-draw violence. With the shooting death of another competitor, John Ross, Pond had been responsible for the demise of one man too many, and the Nor'Westers forced him to retire. He sold his share in the company to William McGillivray for £800 and, frustrated and dissatisfied, returned to the United States. Very little is known of his later years, which he seems to have spent drawing maps and reading travel stories. He died in 1807, like many other fur traders, a poor man.

Still, Pond had made a mark and a map. He found and initiated the most challenging portage in the entire northwest. He never wrote a word about that remote country. What we know about him is mostly second-hand, derived from the journals and writings of his contemporaries, especially his young apprentice, Alexander Mackenzie. And yet he seems a fitting harbinger for Europeans in the area that would become Alberta. An American and a murderer who drew a map that misled more than a few people, he fits right into the tradition of this province, long before anyone could have predicted the maverick place it would become.

• • •

This country was not particularly friendly to the invading whites. In 1781–82 the Canadians found that smallpox had ravaged people beyond Portage La Loche, and the Indians refused to trade with them. Despite such natural mistrust, the North West Company and its venturesome gamblers were not easily discouraged. Alexander Mackenzie describes the NWC as "no more than an association of commercial men, agreeing among themselves to carry on the fur trade, unconnected with any other business." The company included some 50 clerks, 71 interpreters, 1,120 canoemen, and 35 guides, an impossibly small number of people considering the territory they covered.

We know most about the trade via the pens of the bourgeois, literate men who could record their versions of events. But the real muscle behind the western advance was the canoemen, or voyageurs. Their lives were broken, itinerant; they lived in Montreal or Upper Canada and were away from the beginning of May until the end of September. Some of them signed three-year contracts and did not return until their terms had expired. What they saw, for all that it remains unwritten, can be imagined as the West before it was irrevocably altered by the advent of settlement and churchification, money, and law. Fuelled by pemmican, the canoeman worked eighteen hours a day, toiling against the current of swift glacial rivers. They portaged across deadfall and along treacherous cliffs carrying at least 180 pounds on their backs. Romantic descriptions depict only colourful sashes and broad moustaches, but their culture was much more complex. The wonderful paintings of Frances Hopkins, who accompanied her husband on at least one long overland voyage (he served as secretary to Sir George Simpson), capture the private pleasures and physical weariness of these amazing men. Theirs was a life of carrying, paddling, walking, smoking, and singing, carefree, dangerous, and demanding.

Their internal divisions were based on their abilities; the middlemen, who knew the rivers less well, paddled and followed orders from the bowmen and steersmen, who had memorized every subtle clue of shoreline and rapids. The guide who led each brigade was the most experienced riverman, responsible for the ultimate success of the journey. Such service was not easy. They paddled and ate and drank rum and swore, and they sweated and died—of heart attacks, strangulated hernias, drowning. They were short—under five foot five. They fought with vigour, snored under overturned canoes, and served no man, enslaved only to their paddles and the rivers they followed. Their canoes, caulked with resin, were made of birch, as light as three hundred pounds, yet able to carry four tons. The red-cedar paddles were brightly painted, and the best crews of the express boats could paddle sixty strokes a minute. Even an Olympic athlete with light-as-a-feather modern equipment might blanch at such physical extremes. These extraordinary men paddled a thousand miles in four months from Lachine, Quebec, to Fort Chipewyan on Lake Athabasca. They carried their loads—some as much as five hundred pounds—with a tumpline, a twelve-foot leather thong, three inches wide in the middle, and tapering at the ends. Each end was tied around a pack, and the man braced the loop in the middle against his forehead. They could claim *"Je suis un homme du nord,"* for they, not their bosses and the accountants back in Montreal, opened the West. But they were unlettered, and their stories died with them.

The arduous voyageur experience and the North West Company developed the talents of that stubborn Scot, Alexander Mackenzie, who at age twenty-nine in 1793 declared himself the first European to cross North America by land or, more precisely, in a battered fleet of birchbark canoes manned by Indians and voyageurs. Regarded as far more than a trader, Mackenzie called himself a "scientific geographer," a more dignified appellation for a man who navigated some of the greatest rivers in the northwest and, in the explorer/fur trader tradition, mapped them with precise detail and deliberation.

Many of the Nor'Westers had left behind a poor and struggling Scotland, finding, for all their hardship, at least some opportunity in the trade. The Scottish Highlands were not particularly comfortable, and the Scots actually found the northwest a reasonably easy place to survive in. Mackenzie was no exception. He was born in Stornoway, Scotland, in 1764, his mother died when he was ten, and his father brought him to New York, which he quickly left for Montreal. Rapidly gaining experience in the fur trade, he joined the Nor'Westers and was posted to the Athabasca, first as Peter Pond's assistant and later as his replacement.

History suggests that westward-moving Europeans marvelled first at the sweep between the prairie and the parkland, then eyed the Rockies and found them temptingly scenic. But no, the first European experience of what would become Alberta was crossing the mucky muskeg of the Methye Portage, the steep, nasty height of land that separates the waters flowing into Hudson Bay from those that flow into the Arctic Ocean. Mackenzie's first glimpse of the area was impressive; when he reached the chief precipice on the portage, he became as breathless as any tourist, and offered one of the first descriptions worthy of being used in Travel Alberta brochures:

> This precipice, which rises upwards of a thousand feet above the plain
> beneath it, commands a most extensive, romantic and ravishing
> prospect. From thence, the eye looks down on the course of the little
> river [the Clearwater River], beautifully meandering for upwards of
> thirty miles. The valley, which is at once refreshed and adorned by
> it, is about three miles in breadth, and is confined by two lofty
> ridges of equal height, displaying a most delightful intermixture of
> wood and lawn, and stretching on till the blue mist obscures the
> prospect. Some parts of the inclining heights are covered with
> stately forests, relieved by promontories of the finest verdure, where
> the elk and buffalo find pasture.

Mackenzie recognized beauty even before economic interest, although he remarked on that as well. "At about twenty-four miles from the Fork, are some bitumenous fountains, into which a pole of twenty feet long may be inserted without the least resistance. The bitumen is in a fluid state, and when mixed with gum, or the resinous substance collected from the spruce fir, serves to gum the canoes. In its heated state it emits a smell like that of sea-coal. The banks of the river, which are there very elevated, discover veins of the same bitumenous quality." The oil sands. That bitumen is still serving to gum canoes, although now canoes have become automobiles on rubber tires. After reading Mackenzie's description, men tried to find those fountains into which a twenty-foot pole could be inserted. They never have, although for years now the honey-coloured wealth of the oil sands has been shovelled into trucks and refined into sweet crude.

Present-day Fort Chipewyan is no longer located at the site of the original post—it is now on the north side of Lake Athabasca—but that small log shack was Mackenzie's headquarters for some eight years, and from there he departed on his intrepid expeditions. Mackenzie droned through his first long winter with Pond, complaining of being "deprived of every comfort that can render life agreeable." He did mention that Pond "had formed as fine a kitchen garden as I ever saw in Canada," so the Athabasca was not without fresh vegetables—in the summer at least. But the life of a trader condemned to an inland post waiting for winter to pass and aboriginal people to bring in fur was certainly challenging. The laden canoes didn't arrive at Fort Chip until late September, and then they were quickly dispatched up the Peace River to trade with the Beaver and Rocky Mountain Indians. Mackenzie had arrived with almost one hundred men, and without any provision for their winter sustenance, which meant they had to fish like hell for food. He recorded in detail the best times to fish and the best way to preserve fish. And like every Scottish overseer, he complained about his men, writing that "the voyaging Canadians are equally indolent, extravagant, and improvident, when left to themselves, and rival the savages in a neglect of the morrow." They might have been not so much indolent as tired.

Mackenzie's observations were detailed and pragmatic. He noticed salt ponds in the area, that the people who lived on venison were less healthy than those who lived on fish, and that scurvy was unknown. He described the rituals of trapping and trading: in the fall the Indians met the traders at the fort, bartered furs for provisions, then went out to hunt beaver. Mackenzie even recorded words in different aboriginal languages, Knisteneaux (Cree) and Algonquin, words for numbers, for the body, for animals, for family relations, but also expressions for emotions, like "I am angry" and "I fear." He learned cautiously, conciliatory but suspicious, making idiosyncratic notations: "We could not but observe, without some degree of surprize, the contrast between the neat and decent appearance of the men, and the nastiness of the women." It is difficult to decipher what Mackenzie actually meant and whether his comments are to be trusted.

He wrote that the Chipewyan numbers were not commensurate with the huge territory they covered, which he attributed to the ravages of smallpox, and survival was never far from his consideration. The Chipewyan women, he observed, did not stop working during pregnancy, which Mackenzie concluded contributed to the healthy delivery of their children. He also noted the mothers' custom of cutting off a piece of the umbilical cord of newborns, decorating a cover with porcupine quills and beads, and hanging it around their necks, a spiritual connection with the separated child. These people managed to survive by the snare and the spear. The fur they layered themselves in was so warm that they could lie down on the ice in the middle of a lake and sleep comfortably, although they might, in the morning, have to dig themselves out from under a crust of snow. Although they were popularly accused of abandoning their old and infirm to perish, Mackenzie witnessed a man afflicted with palsy who was tenderly carried about by his people. He recorded their overt sorrow at death, their long periods of mourning, and that they were not cannibals. His Chipewyan lexicon included the phrases "I am to be pitied" and "I love you." He must have wanted to use them, or heard others expressing those sentiments to him. In fact, although he was described as suspicious and curt, Mackenzie had two children with an Indian wife.

In early June 1789 Mackenzie embarked on his first great journey, one of two he made in the hope of discovering the elusive Northwest Passage. He left Fort Chip with four Canadian voyageurs, two attended by their wives, a German, an Indian named English Chief and his two wives, as well as two other young Indians. The aboriginal people were engaged to serve as interpreters and hunters. As well, he travelled with a trade canoe outfitted with merchandise and a Company clerk. The image of the lone explorer travelling with two paddlers is very much dispelled by this retinue. Mackenzie travelled in a flotilla, with lots of help, men to row and women to cook. The women were especially important because they kept the group in footwear as a pair of moose-skin shoes "does not last us above one Day."

The river they followed loses itself in the Peace River, then becomes the Slave River. After various embarkations to get around rapids, living on geese and ducks and fish, which the Indians killed, they got to Great Slave Lake, still frozen although it was June. Unable to canoe across, they had to tramp around its perimeter, stumbling through marshes and deadfall for days before they could locate the actual outlet of the great river that would be named after Mackenzie. Because the river first flows west, it seemed they were on the right track, but then the river turned north.

It rained and rained and rained. Every night the canoes had to be taken out of the water to be gummed. Mackenzie doggedly described the weather and the geographical aspects of the river—how wide the banks, how deep the water, the dwarf woods growing on the banks, the mosquitoes whining in clouds around them. He observed all the details of a summer solstice in the North, where the sun does not set. He saw the bones of the great white bears and he never quite reached the Arctic Ocean, because fog along the coastline shrouded it completely. Still, the incoming tide of the Beaufort Sea dampened their feet, and from a high hill Mackenzie could see vast rafts of ice clogging the shore, obviously not the benign salt of the Pacific. Mackenzie's 102-day journey to what he called the Frozen Ocean aroused little interest among the partners of the fur trade when he reported it at the annual North West Company meeting on Lake Superior. Geography mattered less than beaver pelts.

But Mackenzie had tasted travel and, even more intriguing, had heard from the natives of the North that the Inuit had, less than ten years before, traded with large canoes full of white men who came from the West. He could not shake his persistent fixation on the Northwest Passage. Persuaded that if he wanted to be a "scientific geographer" he needed to get more surveying and astronomy under his belt, he went to England to study. When he returned, he was ready to follow Pond's second river, sure that it would flow to the Elysian West.

By this time the Nor'Westers controlled three-quarters of the fur market, so Mackenzie did not have to fret about economics. He could, with relative ease, leave Fort Chip in the hands of his cousin, Roderick Mackenzie, and embark on his second trip. He left the fort on October 10, 1792, determined to proceed to the company's most distant settlement on the Peace River, and from there prepare to set out in the spring.

Waiting for winter to pass, Mackenzie recorded the weather. "On the 29th [of December], the wind being at North-East, and the weather calm and cloudy, a rumbling noise was heard in the air like distant thunder, when the sky cleared away in the South-West; from whence there blew a perfect hurricane, which lasted till eight. Soon after it commenced, the atmosphere became so warm that it dissolved all the snow on the ground." He had met the magic chinook, or snow eater. Still, impatient to go west, Mackenzie could hardly wait for the snow to disappear completely. Finally, on May 9, south of Berwyn at the Fork Fort, he set off. His canoe was huge, 25 feet long, with a 26-inch-wide hold, and a 4-foot-9-inch beam, but light enough that "two men could carry her on a good road three or four miles without resting." This one canoe carried provisions, gifts, arms, ammunition, baggage (three thousand pounds' worth), and ten people—Mackenzie, six voyageurs with French names, a Scottish company clerk, two Indians, and a large panting dog.

He landed at the present site of Dunvegan, Alberta, on Sunday, May 12, 1793, where he encountered a group of Beaver Indians—obviously they knew that white men brought trade goods, and they were practised in exchanging furs for these goods. They informed Mackenzie that he would, in ten days, get as far as the Rocky Mountains. Mackenzie and his entourage travelled hard, leaving at four every morning and paddling until seven in the evening. It was a freezing-cold May, and the Rocky Mountain Indians they met pleaded ignorance of the country beyond the first range of mountains. The Beaver Indians with Mackenzie were apprehensive and wanted to turn back. On the last day before Mackenzie crossed the as-yet-undrawn boundary of Alberta and proceeded west up the Peace, May 13, he noted seeing the dens of grizzly bears. He wanted to kill one, but intelligently desisted, writing, "the Indians entertain a great apprehension of this kind of bear, which is called the grisly bear, and they never venture to attack it but in a party of at least three or four." On May 14, he was in northern not-yet British Columbia.

Navigating gorges and rapids, climbing sheer rock faces hand over hand, he and his group made slow progress. Mackenzie, of course, could enjoy a short doze in the canoe while the others paddled. At one point, nervous about their survival, he tucked a letter detailing their progress into a rum keg and sent it down the river. Then, at the confluence of the Parsnip and the Finlay rivers, he hesitated. Which way? Advised by an Indian, he turned south into the Parsnip, luckily the right choice. Despite violent storms, fog, heat, mosquitoes, and impassable cascades, Mackenzie navigated through the mountain ranges of British Columbia and gained the Pacific on July 22, 1793, where with vermilion and melted bear grease he inscribed his famous graffito, "ALEX MACKENZIE, FROM CANADA, BY LAND, 22d JULY 1793." With Scots determination and an ability to threaten and cajole the First Nations people and the voyageurs who paddled him there, Mackenzie initiated the route over the Rockies to the Pacific.

They were all, including the large panting dog, back in Alberta on August 22 or 23. Mackenzie, having accomplished his goal, stayed at Fort Chipewyan, bored and eager to get to Montreal to brag about his accomplishments. The North West Company was superficially happy that he had outflanked the Hudson's Bay Company, who had been commissioned to find the Northwest Passage. But some of the Montreal partners were annoyed at the cost of Mackenzie's expedition. They didn't give a damn about how much country Mackenzie had covered. They wanted furs and money. Perhaps because of their indifference and his feeling unappreciated, Mackenzie first proposed the idea of merging with the Hudson's Bay Company, suggesting that jointly they could ward off the infiltrating Americans. For some years thereafter he instigated competition and its side effects, beginning a new company and then selling it, stirring the trade stew until eventually, tired of fur-trade politics, he returned to England, a colonial hero in a Britannia-rules-the-waves world. Perhaps he dreamed of the chinook.

• • •

The surveyor Peter Fidler is not as well known as his flashier map-maker colleagues, and his journals offer a less arrogant version of the fur trade at the end of the eighteenth century. Fidler worked for the Hudson's Bay Company and not the intrepid Nor'Westers. Like David Thompson, he was trained by the HBC surveyor Philip Turnor, a man whose most profound contribution to the company was his teaching the rudiments of measurement and compass to promising young apprentices. And like Thompson, Fidler was an instrument for the company.

Hudson's Bay advertisement for fur fashions, 1912

Born in Derbyshire in 1769, Fidler joined the HBC as a labourer, arriving at York Factory (on Hudson Bay) in 1788. He was either a well-educated labourer or a quick study, because he rose swiftly in the company, demonstrating a natural aptitude for geography, and was promoted to "writer," the man required to keep the post's journal. In the summer of 1789 Fidler tracked inland and spent the following winter getting trade experience in Saskatchewan, then in the spring of 1790 went down to Cumberland House to acquire under Turnor "all the information in my power respecting finding the latitude and longitude of any place he may be sent to." Once again the circuitous route to the Athabasca country, via that hellish Methye Portage, was at issue. To get to this rich source of beaver, the traders had to go from Cumberland House across to the Churchill River, then up to Île-à-la-Crosse, from there over Peter Pond Lake and up the Methye River to the portage, which took them to the Clearwater River, down that river to the confluence of the Clearwater and the Athabasca, where Fort McMurray is now, and then down the Athabasca River to Lake Athabasca, involving hundreds of miles of doubling back and forth. Everybody was eager for a shortcut and Turnor was sent out to find it. David Thompson was supposed to train as Turnor's assistant, but when Thompson broke his leg, Turnor instead took Fidler with him to the Athabasca in September 1790.

Until April of the following year, Fidler lived with Chipewyans in northern Saskatchewan, a practical apprenticeship in language and custom. He met up with Turnor again in the spring, and they took a circuitous route into Alberta, and on their way down the Christina River north of Fort McMurray, Fidler records, on June 21, 1791, "Found great quantities of bitumen a kind of liquid tar oozing out of the banks on both sides of the river in many places, which has a very sulphurous smell and quite black like real tar and in my opinion would be a good substitute for that useful mineral." The HBC had actually seen this substance in 1719, when a Cree middleman—*Wa-pa-su,* or Swan—brought a sample. It is probably a good thing that neither trading company could foresee the value of the oil sands. If they had, Alberta and possession of her natural resources would have been even more contentious.

Fidler spent the winter of 1791–92 with a group of Chipewyans who had been given provisions by the HBC; he was to ensure that they were not seduced by the Nor'Westers, and that they brought their furs to the HBC in the spring. Crossing and recrossing what would become northeastern Alberta, he kept a wonderful record of domestic life among the Indians. In it, he is funny, self-parodying in requiring scientific observations of himself, while recognizing their contradictory value. His tongue is tucked firmly in his cheek. "The Nautical Almanack & requisite Tables—composed the whole of my Library—with 1 Shirt besides the clothes I had on my back also composed the whole of my wardrobe," an apt library and wardrobe for an intrepid wandering Albertan.

Fidler seems to have been especially curious about and sympathetic to native women, describing their activities so carefully that we learn a great deal about their ingenious survival tactics. "The Women employed making Bone fatt in a Birch rind kettle by heating stones red hot & frequently immersing them into it which makes a tolerable shift for want of a Metal one." He remarked gratefully, "Got a Cap made of a Beaver Skin after the manner of the womens which is very well adapted for keeping the Snow from ones neck going thro the woods." He recorded the tradition of women's living separately when they menstruated, but without the lip-biting prissiness of other traders, and he noted that the women sometimes used menstruation as an excuse for assignations with other men.

At one point, Fidler was driven to cut off both sleeves of his leather coat to make a pair of shoes. Completely without backup shoes or clothing, he had to trade a blanket and moose skin with a dour Canadian, Daniel Mackenzie of the NWC, for some old shoes and socks, and complained about Mackenzie's predictable stinginess, concluding sarcastically, "Such was the generosity of that man." Because his lack of clothing was so desperate, he was forced to wear a blanket around him like a petticoat, and he accused the Canadian traders of "debauching" the Indians to get their best garment skins. All through the winter, Fidler struggled with his clothes; he was at one stage both coatless and trouserless in the perishing cold. Since his trousers were utterly worn out, and the petticoat blanket was insufficient, he had no choice but to try to make himself a pair of trousers. One of his men kindly gave him some skins from the bottom of his tent, and Fidler set to work, learning to sew as he went. The leather was so stiff and hard that he broke all his needles and was forced to resort to awl and sinew, which gave him a healthy respect for the sewing of the Indian women.

As well as cold, he complained of hunger, especially about the aboriginal tendency to eat irregularly—when they had food, they ate it all, then starved until they got some more. Later, Fidler realized that this feast-and-famine existence was because the Indians had always lived in places where there was food. Hoarding or saving food seemed ridiculous—their larder walked past their tents. Fidler is most European in his irritation at the Chipewyans' ironic regard for work: "The more a European does of work with them, the worse he is respected by them & gets generally the worst victuals & frequently little of it when he complys to do every thing they bid him, whereas if he stiffly refuses from the first that he is with them they will be very kind to him & will give him a larger allowance of provisions than had he listened to every request of theirs..." Ah, Mr. Fidler. These are Albertans, contrarians, shamans of inverted logic.

At the height of winter everyone was hungry and frostbitten. Fidler learned how hard it was to pull a sledge through deep snow in the boreal forest. Other traders joined them, and at one stage he complained about sharing his small tent. "They thronged it up so very much that I was obliged the whole to lay in a manner double & could not get any Sleep—before morning I often wished our new comers at the Devil & I am afraid that they will remain with us, & eat what we should require for ourselves—as none of them are any thing of even tolerable hunters."

Fidler learned sufficient Chipewyan to communicate well, which he was very proud of, and on February 7, 1792, he recorded, in a poignant moment, his intimacy with this new language: "This night dreamed in the Chepawyan Language— the first time and I appeared to have more extensive command of words when asleep than when awake..." His delight fairly leaps from the page. Nor is he afraid to confess to ignorance and fear. Hearing noises one night, he thought the bears were going to get him, but when the Indians told him that the noises he heard were moose deer, he was wise enough to laugh at his own consternation. Like most fur-trading Europeans, he was a combination of intelligence and stupidity. He burned off his beard by sitting too close to the fire, and he survived primarily because of the women, who pitched his tent and took care of him. He tells the story of coming upon a pregnant, starving woman whose husband and son had died. The Chipewyan took her with them, and at one point had to "put up short of where we intended to go on account of the deceased mans wife being delivered in the Track when hawling a very heavy Sledge. The other womin wished to erect the small Tent for that purpose but she was too quick for them. She had a boy—got two large beaver." The combination of "she had a boy" and "got two large beaver" shows how Fidler had adapted to his friends' rhythms of survival. The next day he notes, "The woman that was delivered yesterday took her heavy sledge to drag as usual—the same as if nothing had happened to her." Fidler does not hesitate to share their joy and fear. When two young men who were presumed lost returned, he saw "tears of Sorrow and affection upon every ones countenance."

When he arrived back at Fort Chip on April 10, he concluded, "Upon the whole this has been rather an agreeable winter than otherwise. The principal difficulty we laboured under was the want of a Kettle & being at some few times reduced to very short allowance in provisions which last is ever the case with any person that may accompany Indians." He froze his ears but kept his sense of humour. Turnor was well pleased with his performance, observing in his journal that Fidler "is a very fit hand for the Country as he stands hunger and the weather well and can eat anything the Indians will."

Despite his pragmatic experience in the Athabasca, Fidler was next sent to push up the Saskatchewan River. As interested in the Plains Indians as he was in the Chipewyan, Fidler did not mind being passed over for the Athabasca, and happily headed west with another HBC man, William Tomison, noting again the effect of the Europeans on territorial movement: "Formerly the Snake Indians used to inhabit about this hill but since Europeans have penetrated into these parts and supplied the surrounding nations with fire arms these Indians have gradually retreated back to the south west woods." He and Tomison built a post, Buckingham House, on the north bank of the North Saskatchewan, close to present-day Elk Point, Alberta. Directly downstream the Nor'Westers were busily erecting Fort George. Competition between the two companies was escalating, and all the activity and bustle of building was watched by curious bands of Blackfoot and Tsuu T'ina from the south and Cree from the north. Indians who associated with the HBC were not given credit by the Canadians, and Fidler watched the growing trade war between the Nor'Westers and the HBC. He noted that because the Canadians of the North West Company did not speak English and the HBC men did not speak French, the two were obliged to converse the little that they did in whatever Indian tongue they shared, an ironic Babel-cross.

Traditionally a trader went out to winter with the Indians as an act of diplomacy. Fidler did so, and his journal entries recording his 1792–93 journey with the Peigan overland from Buckingham House to the Rocky Mountains west of Fort Macleod are simple and entrancing. His wanderings took him through the heart of the Alberta, from east of current-day Edmonton south through the parkland and down to the prairie. On that trip he became the first white surveyor to locate the Battle, Red Deer, Bow, and Highwood rivers and to spend a winter in the foothills. Intrigued, he recorded far more than latitude and landforms and the daily necessities of survival. While Thompson and Mackenzie's impressive tomes were revised and rewritten long after their respective journeys, Fidler's journal is as fresh as the moment.

On November 20, 1792, right around Innisfail, Fidler saw what Henday must have seen some forty years earlier from almost the same spot. "Here I first got sight of the Rocky Mountain, which appeared awfully grand, stretching from SSW to WbS by Compass, very much similar to dark rain like clouds rising up above the Horizon in a fine summers evening." Even today, everyone who visits Alberta experiences that pure, magical moment, when the Rockies, stretching all the way south and west, blue and daunting, speak. Fidler was no exception.

Not far from present-day Beiseker, he witnessed the excitement and fury of a buffalo drive. The Peigan used a high face of rocks on the east bank of a creek as a buffalo "jump," where they drove "whole heards before them & breaking their legs, necks, &c. in the fall, which is perpendicular about 40 feet. Vast quantities of Bones was laying there, that had been drove before the rock. This kind of Places in the Plains are very useful for the Indians." Fidler's detailed description reveals his fascination, and although he does not differentiate between jumps and "pounds"—where buffalo were herded into a corral-like structure and slaughtered—he provides a first-hand account of the way the plains people shopped for food. Since buffalo were the mainstay of their existence, they never began a hunt without appropriate prayers and ceremony. When they could not use a pound or jump, they hunted the beasts on horseback, killing them with arrows, at which they demonstrated a spectacular skill.

Fidler's sojourn with the Peigan was a happy experience. After seeing the loveliest parts of Alberta and wintering by the Oldman River, he arrived back at Buckingham House on March 20, 1793, to find all well. "Thus ends our Journey to the Rocky Mountain. The Indians during our whole stay with them treated us in a very hospitable and friendly manner, tho' we were near 5 months with them." It is as close to a thankful acknowledgement as any white man has made.

After scouting the Saskatchewan River up to the Sturgeon, where he concluded that the lack of timber made it a poor place to build a post, Fidler and Tomison headed back to York Factory on Hudson Bay, Fidler carrying with him all the experience of geography and sky that his senses had absorbed. Kicking around York Factory doubtless drove him crazy, and following the custom of the country, he married a Cree woman called Mary, with whom he lived the rest of his life, years later marrying her again in a Christian ceremony.

Until returning to Alberta in 1799, Fidler worked all over the West. The war between the Nor'Westers and the HBC men was heating up; a territory that had once seemed infinite was now contested. Finally assigned to the Athabasca again, Fidler tried, between 1802 and 1806, to establish a trading post at Fort Chipewyan. This was enemy territory, for the Methye Portage delineated the edge of the HBC charter, and the Nor'Westers considered the Athabasca theirs.

The hostilities between the two companies at Fort Chipewyan mixed murder with tricks and frights, bullying and malicious traps. One Nor'Wester, Samuel Black, followed the HBC men everywhere, shouting to scare away the birds and game they were trying to hunt so that they virtually starved. HBC governor George Simpson would later describe Black as "a Don Quixote in appearance—ghastly, raw boned and lanthorn jawed, yet strong vigorous and active. Has not the talent of conciliating Indians by whom he is disliked, but who are ever in dread of him, and well they may be so, as he is ever on his guard against them and so suspicious that offensive and defensive preparation seem to be the study of his Life having Dirks, Knives and Loaded Pistols concealed about his Person and in all directions about his Establishment even under his Table cloth at meals and in his Bed." It is amazing

that he would bother with a tablecloth at all, but he was the sort whose participation in the company warfare at Fort Chip defeated Fidler. Determined to drive
him away, the Nor'Westers tormented him, covering his chimney to smoke him
out, surrounding his house in the middle of the night, beating on the walls and
setting up an unearthly howling. Shots were even fired, although no one in Fidler's
party or family was killed. When the ice went out of the river, Fidler abandoned
Fort Chip and left Alberta for good.

Although ultimately the Hudson's Bay Company took over the North West
Company, the animosity between the two groups subsided but never quite died.
The competition between them had been too fierce.

• • •

David Thompson, Canada's iconic map-maker, was poor. Years after completing
his journeys, as an old man in Montreal, he rewrote his thirty-nine volumes of
notebooks into a narrative, hoping to make some money. Thompson covered so
much ground, an estimated fifty-five thousand miles, on foot and by canoe and
horseback, that we can only marvel at his reconstruction of those footsteps, those
notched trees, those rivers. He mapped the sources of the Mississippi, the upper
region of the Missouri, the interior of British Columbia, and the whole of the
Columbia River system to the Pacific. He laid out Quebec's Eastern Townships, surveyed Muskoka, and later drew the border between Canada and the United States.
Despite what he had done for the fur-trading companies, he died in poverty in
1857. Afterward, his sons sold the words of his labour to Charles Lindsey of
Toronto, the West yet again falling into the hands of Upper Canada. Lindsey
apparently intended to edit and publish Thompson's work, but as an Ontario man
who knew nothing about the country the narrative described, he ultimately
decided not to, and for a long time the journals languished.

In the late 1800s J. B. Tyrrell, a geologist for the Geological Survey of Canada,
after whom the Royal Tyrrell Museum is named, was mapping in the Rocky
Mountains. Impressed with the amazing accuracy of the maps he was using,
Tyrrell sought the originals and discovered that they had been drafted by David
Thompson and were in the possession of the Crown Lands Department of the
Province of Ontario. Of course. Tyrrell published a paper on Thompson's maps in

1887–88, prompting Lindsey to write Tyrrell and inform him that he was in possession of Thompson's narrative. Tyrrell bought it from Lindsey. Because his journeys had been so similar to Thompson's, he could appreciate the map-maker's meticulous observations. By that time Thompson himself had been forgotten by Westerners and Canadians alike.

Tyrrell ranked David Thompson as one of the greatest geographers of the world. He scolds: "It is not creditable to Canadians, proud as we are of our country and its limitless natural possibilities, that this pioneer who did so much without remuneration to render the country known to us and others should remain neglected." Albertans could snort and say, So what else is new? but Tyrrell's approbation was sincere. There is no portrait of Thompson, no monument to him, and we must imagine a face that his daughter once said resembled John Bunyan's, a daunting thought. It is better to picture him striding through the sweet-smelling forests of the Rockies, pointing his Dolland's, a ten-inch brass sextant, toward the stars. More than anything else, Thompson was a brilliant surveyor, accurate and methodical. Like Fidler, he was trained by Philip Turnor and, like Fidler, took to surveying with enthusiasm. It drew him far more than fur-trade merchandising.

Thompson was born in England of poor parents and sent to a school for poor boys, the Grey Coat School, which received, on December 30, 1783, an application from the secretary of the Hudson's Bay Company, wanting to know if "this Charity could furnish them with 4 boys against the month of May next, for their settlements in America." The schoolmaster wrote a letter informing the HBC that there were only two boys who had been taught navigation, Samuel John McPherson and David Thompson.

Samuel John McPherson obviously didn't fancy the idea of going to the wilds of America, for he went missing and was expelled, never to be heard of again. But David Thompson, for the sum of £5, was apprenticed to the HBC and sailed from London in May 1784. He arrived at Churchill at the beginning of September and spent the winter of 1784–85 under the tutelage of the same Samuel Hearne who had travelled up the Coppermine River to the Frozen Ocean. Hearne certainly made an impression on the young Thompson, but more impressive, the boy was sent, on foot and with two Indian guides, from Churchill to York Factory, a journey of some 150 miles. Imagine that chill autumn walk for a fifteen-year-old English boy along the shores of Hudson Bay. Thompson must have arrived at some bargain with this wild, beautiful country and made up his mind to stay. At York he spent a year doing accounts, working in the store and adding to the post's provisions by hunting. He was serious and industrious, and he did not purchase brandy. He had arrived just when the HBC was starting to realize that they needed to compete with the intrepid French traders and so had decided to establish some trading posts on the Saskatchewan River.

In July 1786 Thompson was given a trunk, a handkerchief, shoes, shirts, a gun, and a tin pot and sent out to do exactly that. He and his Métis companions journeyed inland and established Manchester House, a huddle of huts just to the west of the confluence of the Battle and North Saskatchewan rivers. But fierce competition between the traders meant that the HBC had to work hard to persuade Indians to bring furs, and Thompson was chosen to go farther west to befriend the Indians and convince them of the desirability of trapping beaver and bringing their skins to the Baymen. That was the beginning of his legendary journeying.

After travelling southwest to the Bow River, making Thompson the first white man to see the site of Calgary, he encountered a large camp of Peigan Indians somewhere in the foothills. He settled down with them and spent most of the winter with an old chief named *Saukamappee,* who told him stories and showed him the life of Western Indians before they were compromised by Europeans. This is the stuff of romantic adventure, a seventeen-year-old from a charity school in London soaking up the wisdom of a generous aboriginal chief. *Saukamappee* related to Thompson the myths and history of the Plains Indians, how they acquired horses and guns, their pleasures and battles and the terrible smallpox epidemic of 1781–82, laying the foundation of Thompson's sympathy for aboriginal people. *Saukamappee* was surely the guiding spirit behind those great maps. After this winter of education, Thompson returned to the trading post on the Saskatchewan, continued visiting other posts, and then fell and broke his leg, an accident that would affect his physical abilities all his life. (It also meant that Fidler got to accompany Turnor and train as a surveyor.)

It took Thompson a long time to recover his mobility, but once he did, he travelled from post to post, trying to persuade the Indians to trade with the HBC instead of the French peddlers. He began to take astronomical observations, his precision astonishing. In 1790 he spent the winter with Philip Turnor, and under the chief surveyor's tulelage devoted himself to the requirements of surveying and astronomy. Those first four years in Saskatchewan country turned David Thompson into the observant, meticulous man that he became.

The company's interest in money was a constant irritation to Thompson. In his narrative, he claimed that he was told to stop surveying and to focus on furs, and that was the cause of his decision in 1797 to leave the HBC and join the Canadians of the NWC. The immediate reason for his defection is not clear; the HBC record says only "Left Service." During his thirteen years with the HBC Thompson had travelled some nine thousand miles, mapping virtually every step. In his last letter to the resident chief at York, he complained bitterly about lacking a nautical almanac and getting no support for his surveying. The North West Company, by contrast, seemed eager to find out more about the country and they welcomed Thompson, assuring him that he could map to his heart's content and offering him a large increase in pay. They were gaining a star employee—a surveyor, a clerk, a linguist, and an experienced trader.

Once Thompson was their man, the North West Company sent him out on a continuous surveying trip completely unhampered by matters of trade. That ten-month journey wended some four thousand miles from Grand Portage down to the Missouri, and around the south shore of Lake Superior to Sault Ste. Marie and back to Grand Portage. The Nor'Westers were happy with his work and asked him to continue as a surveyor and fur trader, sending him out in 1798 and 1799 to Lac La Biche, where he surveyed the Athabasca River and the Methye Portage, only stopping for a few days to marry Charlotte Small, daughter of a Chipewyan woman and a North West Company partner.

In March 1799 Thompson started for Fort Augustus, next to Edmonton House, and from there proceeded to Rocky Mountain House, the westernmost post on the Saskatchewan River. He spent the next years exploring the flanks of the mountains from the Saskatchewan to the Bow. All the while he was trading, building posts, repairing posts, and keeping company with the stars. In 1804 he became a partner in the North West Company and in 1805 went up to Rocky Mountain House in order to cross the mountains and lead a trading party into the interior of British Columbia. Thompson carried out every task with unusual diligence, always travelling with his wife and family, and several times having to sneak past the Peigan, who objected to trade being conducted with the Kootenay Indians of the interior; they did not want their old enemies supplied with knives and guns. Sent to survey the Columbia to its mouth, he did not reach the Pacific Ocean until July of 1811, an anticlimax, for Jacob Astor of the Pacific Fur Company, the NWC's American rival, was already there, claiming the estuary of the Columbia for the United States. Much has been made of Thompson's wandering around in the mountains while Astor hustled out to the Pacific, but Thompson never did anything in a rush. He worked deliberately, methodically, surveying the best routes for travel and conducting trade with the Indians. Even now, it is hard to imagine anyone knowing the mountains as Thompson did. Finally, in 1812, after twenty-eight years of roaming the West, he crossed those mountains one last time and followed the rivers east toward Montreal. He never went west again, although it is certain that the West lived in his imagination, fuelled his meticulous maps and the narrative he culled from his notebooks.

Thompson was an enigmatic mix of the pragmatic and the mystical. His French was terrible, but he insisted on reading the Bible aloud to his restless Canadian voyageurs after a long day's paddling. He opposed using liquor for trade, and once made sure that the kegs he was forced to carry were put on a recalcitrant packhorse who rubbed them to splinters against the rocks. He was an avid naturalist, watching a mosquito suck his blood with the aid of a magnifying glass. He treated the aboriginal peoples with respect, complaining that white men who expected Indians to behave as they themselves did were unfair. There are apocryphal stories that he had been challenged by the devil to a card game and, having won, gave up gambling forever. The Indian name for him was *Koo-Koo-Sint*, the man who looks at stars.

He mapped more of North America than any other cartographer, filling in the great spaces of the northwest. He wanted, ambitiously enough, to delineate the entire Western continent, and he almost succeeded. He is still a silent presence behind every map published by the Canadian government, some part of each deriving from Thompson's work. His life's art, his great map, is quite simply beautiful.

This Map made for the North West Company in 1813 and 1814 and delivered to The Honorable William McGillivray then Agent Embraces the Region lying between 45 and 60 degrees North Latitude and 84 and 124 degrees west Longitude comprising the Surveys and Discoveries of 20 years namely The Discovery and Survey of the

Oregon Territory to the Pacific Ocean the survey of the Athabasca
Lake Slave River and Lake from which flows Mackenzies River to the
Arctic Sea by Mr. Philip Turnor the Route of Sir Alexander Mackenzie
in 1792 down part of Frasers River together with the Survey of this
River to the Pacific Ocean by the late John Stewart of the North West
Company by David Thompson Astronomer and Surveyor

sgd David Thompson

David Thompson, astronomer and surveyor, was one of the first to understand
the complexities of Alberta's geography and people, our impossible contradictions.

• • •

After the North West Company established Fort Augustus on the banks of the
North Saskatchewan River in 1794, the competitive Hudson's Bay Company
quickly built Edmonton House, the post that would, by the mid-1800s, dominate
the trade. Edmonton was struggling to its feet while the 1804–1821 fur war
between the Nor'Westers and the Baymen raged, while Lord Selkirk was trying to
impose his utopian and HBC-approved settlement on Red River. The repercussions
of the Battle of Seven Oaks, the fight between the Nor'Westers, led by Cuthbert
Grant, and Selkirk, who wanted to forward agricultural settlement, echoed
throughout the northwest, even though that spat was far away from Alberta, in
Red River, Manitoba.

Although it was a guerrilla war waged along a four-thousand-mile front, the worst
of the fur trade war took place in the rich beaver country of the Athabasca, where the
Montrealers and the HBC men skirmished and argued and threatened and
ambushed one another. Those desperate and heady times, with many of the traders
throwing themselves enthusiastically into the feud, hindered both companies' commercial goals. Even Canada's governor-in-chief Sir John Sherbrooke's proclamation
that all parties in the fur-trade war were to cease and desist had no effect. After all,
the traders reasoned, what could he do to them way out in Indian country?

Into this pirates' mess walked a tough, miserable Scot called George Simpson,
newly minted interior head of the Hudson's Bay Company. To him the HBC allotted the task of quelling the war. Character studies of Simpson are not flattering; he

was wily, energetic, and full of bravado. He swore to defend the rights and interests of the company and set out to vanquish the wild Nor'Westers. Simpson never adopted or grew to love the West. He belonged to that separate province called politics, and no politician's manoeuvre was beneath him. He plied everyone with liquor, threatened and cajoled the Indians, and even arrested and imprisoned the Nor'Wester chief executive, Simon McGillivray, although McGillivray managed to escape back to his fort by, his country wife claimed, vanishing up the chimney. NWC and HBC forts were often within throwing distance of each other—so that they could spy on each other—and their proximity fuelled their inventive hostilities. Ultimately the two came to behave exactly alike, which is how the more regimental HBC won out over the dashing, flamboyant Nor'Westers—by adopting their swashbuckling approach. The HBC expanded the number of its posts and began to undercut the competition's prices. Because the company enjoyed the favour of the British banks, they could afford to engage in a price war that eventually destroyed the Nor'Westers, who did not have access to long-term loan guarantees and who had severely overextended themselves, thanks to the huge distances of their transportation system. Montreal to Athabasca is a lot farther than York Factory to Athabasca. On top of everything, the North West Company partners depended on their profits to support their upkeep and their Montreal pleasures, the costs of which were prodigious; they were running, from year to year, on a very slim margin.

By the fall of 1820, the competitors were deadlocked. If they merged into one solid, reliable firm, the British Colonial Office wheedled, the joint company would be granted trading rights over not only Rupert's Land, but all the way to the Pacific. With the persuasive Edward "Bear" Ellice acting as political broker, the marriage was neatly arranged. It joined both companies' assets, each valued at £200,000, but the new company would be given the Hudson's Bay Company name and governed by the HBC charter. There were one hundred shares, twenty for the HBC directors and twenty for the NWC partners, with the extras subdivided for each chief factor or governor. They feathered their nests well, and as promised, the new company was granted complete control over all of British North America except for the colonies already established in the east and the centre of the continent—Upper and Lower Canada were quite safe from HBC control. On July 2, 1821, the Hudson's Bay Company was anointed as a transcontinental trading empire, controlling an area from Hudson Bay to the edge of the Pacific and into Oregon country, all for the token payment of five shillings a year. If Rupert's Land had seemed an unimaginable concession, this new charter was beyond belief, a hubristic coalition given dominion over an enormous land mass that harboured the richest resources in the world. The 173 posts that were amalgamated under the HBC controlled one-twelfth of the Earth's land surface. The West's position as colonial property, to be traded and exploited, was once again reiterated.

The redoubtable George Simpson was appointed chief of the new Northern Department. The first meeting of the factors and traders of the amalgamated companies in the summer of 1821 was tense, but Simpson plied them with alcohol, his favourite trick, and pushed them together as cannily as any American president eager for a peace prize. Slowly, what might have been a brawl became a party, and by dawn they were swearing allegiance to the very men they had the year before threatened to kill. It was not for nothing that Simpson was dubbed the "Little Emperor." A driven, self-aggrandizing despot, he willingly enslaved himself to nineteenth-century mercantile capitalism. His resemblance to Napoleon was deliberate, a characteristic he cultivated, and by 1826 he controlled both Northern and Southern departments. Of course, he was not the actual ruler of the HBC, but a servant acting for the London Committee, who pulled his strings as he pulled the strings of those beneath him. Simpson at least had experience of the West, while the London directors merely fingered the money that poured in from that distant Eldorado. The Hudson's Bay Company actually had the power to act as the territorial agent of the British Empire and everything it stood for, with Simpson its effective judicial, legal, and commercial authority.

Simpson travelled, restless and ruthless, across the continent, making twelve transatlantic trips and three journeys to the Oregon and Columbia River area; he roved back and forth across the prairie, the parkland, sweeping from Edmonton to Winnipeg, and once even going overland by snowshoe from Lake Athabasca to Great Slave Lake, back to Lake Athabasca, then to the Peace River and across Lesser Slave Lake to Edmonton. Cruelly assiduous, he tried to carve a few hours from every journey, his poor crews forced to paddle faster and faster.

Simpson wrestled and throttled his empire, and through a combination of lightning inspection tours and terrible cutbacks that he christened "Economies," he succeeded in keeping everyone off balance and himself high in the saddle. He measured and restricted everything at each post from mustard consumption to the cost of tin plates. He promoted a scorched-earth trapping program that left not even baby beaver alive. He controlled the Oregon and the New Caledonia areas as long as possible, despite the inevitable loss of everything south of the forty-ninth parallel to the Americans. Most of all, he dominated the Indians, keeping them "in a proper state of subordination." No more gift-giving, no more toasts with company rum. Prices for beaver went down, and prices for trade goods went up. The Indians had to supply the company with profits, profits, profits. They viewed Simpson with quizzical suspicion. Although he was convinced that tricks like attaching a music box to his dog's neck impressed them, they were wary. Swooping down on a sleepy post, Simpson's fleet would be announced by a bugler, a bagpiper, and the voices of his paddling Candians, a performance that puzzled the Indians, who were skeptical of shrieking pipes and men in plaid skirts.

Simpson made a number of material changes that increased profit margins quickly. He replaced the *canot du nord* with York boats, which could carry three times as much. Nor did the crew of a York boat need to be as skilled; those tub-like vessels demanded strength rather than finesse. He himself found them too slow for his impetuous pace, and travelled by a specially made oversized express canoe, some thirty-three feet long and paddled by a dozen—usually Quebec Iroquois—boatmen. He had a personal servant and secretary, and sometimes travelled with his longest-kept country wife, Margaret, whom he described in a letter to a friend with the dismissive line, "The commodity has been a great consolation to me." He felt, of course, that every beautiful woman in the country should be made available to him, and had a string of mistresses, whom he called "bits of brown" and treated much as he treated company pots and pans, with finely honed contempt. Historian Grant MacEwan claims that he "fathered seventy sons," but nobody kept count, and Simpson himself was not eager to recognize his illegitimate children. His rapaciousness made it clear that he was not of this country, but an imported dictator who felt it his right to prey on its wealth and people. Because he had contempt for what had always been *"à la façon du pays"* ("the custom of the country"), he did not feel compelled to abide by its rules, and the effect of his 1830 marriage to his British-born cousin, pale and insipid Frances Simpson, broke down the unwritten but respected custom of marriage between white men and aboriginal women.

Simpson treated everyone except those who met his standard of brute workaholism cruelly, and recorded in a little red "character book" his evaluation of every man's weaknesses and abilities. A tyrant made more dangerous by the distance between Europe and the interior of Canada, he enjoyed virtual carte blanche over the territory he ruled. The Colonial Office felt no compunction about his power, just as long as he administered some version of law and order. Convinced that only the HBC prevented the British North American West from succumbing to the Americans, they supported the HBC's mercenary

Glenbow Archives, Calgary, Canada: NA-1747-1

John Rowand, the roaring factor of Edmonton House

interests. The patent unfairness of Simpson's administration, especially for Indians and Métis—he never promoted them—was of no interest to London. In 1838, with Queen Victoria's tacit approval, the Hudson's Bay Company monopoly was renewed for another twenty-one years. Although by this time fashion was starting to turn away from fur, they had reached the height of their mercantile power. Simpson was knighted in 1841, making him even more arrogant. His heightened station suggested to him the grand gesture of undertaking the first journey around the world, which he did, accompanied by his ego and a ghostwriter to record his exploits. Some say he is the model for Jules Verne's *Around the World in Eighty Days*.

If there were any justice, one would hope Simpson died miserably. Perhaps he did, but not until 1860, having enjoyed all the benefits of wealth and privilege. The official certificate claims that he was overtaken by "haemorrhagic apoplexy, attended with epileptiform convulsions," but others speculate that he died of syphilis or just plain nastiness.

• • •

Of all the posts pouring money into the London coffers, Fort Edmonton, the largest settlement west of Red River, glowed like a star in a far-flung constellation. Perched on the high bank above the North Saskatchewan, and an impressive two hundred by three hundred feet, Fort Edmonton was picturesque but practical, a key supply point, a destination and a distribution centre for the interior trade. Edmonton had many names and moved many times; it was called Fort Des Prairies when the NWC dominated the Athabasca region, and its most noted controller, John Rowand, first worked for the Nor'Westers. Under the HBC he was promoted to chief factor at Edmonton in 1823, and from there he pushed and shoved the Saskatchewan district around for thirty years. If Simpson was a birchbark Napoleon, Rowand was a rumbling grizzly bear, who roared for respect and who earned it with his fists more than any innate authority. Once the inconvenience of the Methye Portage was substituted by the North Saskatchewan route and the Carlton Trail, which meandered cross-country from Fort Garry to Fort Edmonton, Edmonton House became a pivotal fort. Under Rowand's stewardship, it blossomed.

Rowand did all he could to make the post more than a temporary home. He loved racing (Edmontonians still do—they gamble on horse racing more than any city in North America) and he bred horses, testing their speed and endurance on his two-mile racetrack. Most of all, he was Falstaffian lord and master of the "Big House," a three-storey residence and office that boasted the West's first glass windows, shipped from England in barrels of molasses to keep them from breaking en route. There was an armoury, a large serving kitchen, and even a ballroom, mostly used to dazzle visitors and high-ranking Indians. We know, from the artist Paul Kane's description of Christmas at Edmonton, that the Big House could seat 150 for dinner, and the celebratory dances that followed such feasts were famous. Rowand's Métis wife, Louise Umphreville, was as large and stubborn as he and Rowand did not put her aside or inflict on her a white replacement. Living his whole life on the Saskatchewan, he might not have had either the inclination or the chance to find a European wife, or perhaps, as the stories go, Louise kept Rowand in line.

At the end of Fred Stenson's wonderful novel, *The Trade*, the narrator imagines the betrothal of Louise and Rowand. Rowand, in galloping a horse across the prairies, had fallen and fractured his leg. The popular story is that when his horse returned without him, Louise went out and found him, set his leg, and while nursing him back to health professed undying love. But Stenson's version claims that Louise came upon the injured man, and simply sat in her cart and stared at him while he raved and cried in agony on the ground. Finally she got down and sat beside him, still unspeaking, her silence telling him clearly that he was in her power, that if she chose to whip her horse back toward the fort, he would be nothing but supper for the wolves. Or, if he chose to trade with her fairly, she could bind his leg and save his life. Rowand and Louise made a deal—they would marry according to the custom of the country, but he would behave better than the custom of the country. When that was settled, she dragged his injured body onto her cart and trundled him back to the safety of the fort. Rowand, to his credit, kept his bargain, constantly reminded by the limp that he retained until he died.

Rowand governed and guzzled with a broad, foreshortened girth. Not tall, he weighed some three hundred pounds and carried with his weight an apoplectic temper, which he used to advantage. He believed, he claimed, only in God and the Company, and if he had to choose between the two, God would take a back seat. But he did manage, by fierce bossiness, to prevent a good deal of competitive bloodshed among different Indian tribes, and among his often recalcitrant men. Big Mountain, as he was called, had both admirers and detractors. His unorthodox governance, and his determined love of horses and the prairie defined him as an Albertan who had imbibed the spirit of the place to the extent that it overrode his pedigree—he was the son of a Montreal doctor. When he died of a sudden stroke or heart attack in 1854, trying to stop a fist fight between two Métis crewmen at Fort Pitt where his son was chief trader, he was mourned with genuine sorrow.

He had asked to be buried in Montreal, so in the spring of 1855, his body was dug up, and an Indian woman set to work to boil the flesh from the bones. Even after a year in the ground, there was enough fat rendered from the remains to make a useful batch of soap. His bones were sealed in a keg of rum and a canoe commissioned to carry the keg to Red River, where it was to be shipped back to Montreal. But when a heavy storm came up over Lake Winnipeg, the frightened crew, believing Rowand's bones to be cursed, threw the barrel over the side. It bounced around in the water, eventually washed up again, and was transported to York Factory on Hudson Bay. Ships from York Factory sailed only to London, so the keg was sent to Britain, where the Hudson's Bay executive who benefited so much from Rowand's bluster and rage gave the barrel a funeral full of pomp and circumstance. Still, the barrel was not buried, and it migrated to Liverpool, where it rolled around a warehouse for a few years before an astute warehouseman figured out what it was and shipped it back across the Atlantic to Montreal. At last, exactly four years after his temper killed him, John Rowand, a mountain reduced to a rum keg, finally reached the place were he had requested burial. One final irony remained. When the barrel was unsealed and opened, the rum that was supposed to preserve his bones had been transformed to water. One can only hope that the poor Indian woman who drew the short straw of boiling Rowand down to his skeleton had the company of good rum to help her through her task.

• • •

The Hudson's Bay Company enjoyed its monopoly, but as time ticked by, Upper Canada began to make noises about the vast prairie sea between Lake Superior and the Pacific coast. The Canadian provinces felt that the West rightly belonged to them, and they resented the HBC's resistance to settlement.

Added to that, busybody missionaries had begun to infiltrate the previously unministered-to prairies. So many souls to be saved! The missionaries' adamant notions of sin, combined with a new awareness of class and race largely brought about by the introduction of white wives, changed the freedom and ease that had made life in Rupert's Land so amazingly outside moral considerations, an amorality that had been for the benefit of all.

The missionaries' emphasis on chastity and fidelity imported social smallnesses that the West had never concerned itself with. And not just missionaries but the occasional determined settler, military man, and entrepreneurial cowboy was starting to appear. The West was no longer the sole preserve of its true and original inhabitants and the fur traders who had come to buy their furs.

In 1857 the Hudson's Bay Company and its privileged charter were finally cross-examined by a select committee of the House of Commons in London. It was revealed that the equivalent markup on goods sold to the Indians was something like 300 percent, an obscene profit that made even British parliamentarians raise their eyebrows. The information that liquor was still an active item in the trade was not impressive either. And a number of unsympathetic witnesses charged that the HBC was interested only in monetary success. Of course, the real issue had become the suitability of the Territories for settlement and cultivation. Even more damning was the contrast between the company's dividend profits, some £20 million, and the extent to which it had lied about spreading God, law, and civilization among the Indians. It was obvious that it had not been following "civilization's" mandate but its own mandate, profit.

Because no one had the money to purchase what they claimed as assets, the HBC's charter was renewed for a dozen years, but now that Canada's interest was out in the open, those assets, which had just been privatized, could be sold for a value even greater than the wealth the company had previously taken out of the country in furs. The trade was beginning to soften; now the HBC's biggest muscle was the huge tract of land, four million square miles, that they titularly "owned" and hoped to sell to the highest bidder. Politicians eyed the situation from every angle and finally reached the conclusion that they would have to pay for those Hudson's Bay Company commitments. Sir John A. Macdonald, that sly old fox, said it best: "Canada looks forward with interest to the day when the valley of the Saskatchewan will become the back country of Canada." The HBC had been given the right to take the land's resources, but had never actually been given title to the land itself. And yet here Ottawa was, having to grapple with buying the best of settlement land from the company. Such a sleight of hand can only be admired.

In the end, a conglomerate planning a trans-Canada railway came up with the money, £1.5 million in exchange for its right to build a railroad—which the government of Canada would finance—and colonize the interior on its way to connecting up with the coast. In November 1869 the Hudson's Bay Company signed the Deed of Surrender as requiem to its centuries-long monopoly. The HBC retained more than forty-five thousand acres of land around their trading posts; they were granted the right to claim some seven million more acres of arable land; and they were guaranteed the right to continue the trade, without hindrance or competition. It was a win/win situation. No longer the only spatial authority in the West, the HBC was now the largest private landowner, even better. Once immigrants and settlers began to arrive and fur trading gave way to farming, the company turned its hand to new monopolies, new ways of making money, like supplying settlers with the goods they needed. In the non-arable North, of course, they still dominated the fur trade, and would do so for another hundred years.

In 1875, the company gave up the entirety of its territorial claims to Canada. What would become Alberta was sold again, and the fur trade, although it was not over, entered the world of history. Beaver was out of fashion; the great buffalo herds were dwindling; the native peoples were starving. Silk top hats and the closed railway carriage scuttled the fur trade. What had once prompted the continent's greatest mercantile adventure—beaver—is nothing more than a flat-tailed reminder on our five-cent coin.

4 | First Peoples

The rawhide loops
are gone, the
hand is gone, the
buffalo's skull
is gone;

the stone is
shaped like the skull
of a child.

—Robert Kroetsch, "Stone Hammer Poem"

I grew up on the banks of the Battle, or Fighting, River, a muddy outwash stream that meanders through Alberta's parkland without much ceremony or water. The river itself, which rises above Battle Lake in the forests far below the flanks of the foothills, is unimpressive, reedy and stony and lazily ox-bowed, but it drifts through a cupped cleft as wide and high-banked and magnificent as if it were a rushing torrent, a major waterway long plied by imperial boats. The valley is simply beautiful, lush and treed and mysterious, as tempting to a prairie poet as daffodils to William Wordsworth. Its high shoulders speak of the Battle's long-ago history, that when glacial melt carved those incredible banks, a huge wall of water swept through, and only in the recent past has the power of the stream subsided to a trickle, a dreamy twisting path loitering toward those soft shoulders to join with the North Saskatchewan at Battleford in Saskatchewan.

But while it seems inconspicuous now, the Fighting River was a momentous landmark for the First Peoples. They knew its watershed as an idyllic refuge, with plentiful game, copses of trees, and grassy meadows. It is still an earthly paradise. Summer buzzes with insects and light; and winter shelters deer and mice under the deep, snow-laden limbs of the spruce trees. Fall blazes the poplar trees yellow, and in the late, lazy heat, seeds scatter and hawks test their vision from high above. The tenderest of green strikes the light of spring, when beaver and muskrat splash the slow water.

Long ago it was called the Chacutenah River, a rough geographical division between

*the sea of prairie grass to the south and the wooded brush to the north. But then it became
another boundary. After the Blackfoot acquired horses, the Battle River separated sworn
enemies, the Blackfoot and the Cree, who used the line of its wavering water—"the stream
flowing in the tremendous valley"—as a territorial boundary. Crossing the Battle meant
going to war, and war echoed through the coulees and dips as often as the cries of children
and the barking of dogs, the snort of horses, the rumble of buffalo hooves.*

*When I dream of paradise, it looks like the Battle River valley. When I cross a Rubicon,
I cross the Battle River. When I drown, I drown in the Battle River. It twists through memory, and of all the magnificent rivers in Alberta it is perhaps the one closest to the hearts
of the First Peoples, who revelled in its lush gifts, its miraculous bounty.*

• • •

Who were these people that Central Canadians, wanting a sea-to-sea nation, were
trying to imagine and rule and govern and manage and pacify and push around?
Indians in the East had two hundred years to adjust to whites and the changes
they brought, but Indians in the West had only two decades. Without ever having
seen them, the Centre imagined Alberta's First Peoples as not quite people, wild
and intractable, "savages" in need of civilization. Whites who had gained some
first-hand knowledge, like scientist Dr. James Hector of the Palliser expedition in
1857–60, argued that the Indians should not be treated as if they were inconven-
ient animals, or "the natural evils of a new country, which are in time to be
removed in the process of settlement." That was the Centre's position on the original inhabitants of the West. They had lived here longer than forever, and they
were a troubling presence—something needed to be done with them.

Despite descriptions and summaries, various oral and written accounts of adventurous white travellers, the First Nations people who lived in this as-yet-undefined
province were as various and complex as the landscape itself, and are as various and
complex today. The many different tribes were of different origins, spoke different
languages, and depending on their geographical location lived different lives.

These roving humans were roughly divided between those who lived in the
northern forests and those who lived on the southern plains, while a few lived
along the foothills of the Rockies. Each landscape provided a particular livelihood.
The woodlands people travelled over wide distances, surviving on moose, deer,

and fish; they were as much at home in canoes as they were on foot, and they used the rivers and lakes of the north as natural highways. The people of the south had to rely on their feet, at least until they acquired horses in the early 1700s; they followed the buffalo, that walking emporium. Both groups used dogs as beasts of burden. Both lived according to complex interpersonal and intertribal relationship systems.

This was a time of fearsome magic and unpredictable plenty, where people fitted themselves into the environment instead of trying to make the environment fit them. Their technologies were the fruits of pragmatism and what nature provided: stone, bone, wood, and leather. There is no question that First Nations groups, depending on weapons and strength and food sources, pushed one another back and forth, killed one another and fought for displaced territory. Warfare was as inevitable as occasional hunger, as fierce as the weather. Indeed, war could be interesting, contributing excitement and honour to life. Battles led to new movement and were the subject of great stories. But battles could also mean defeat, rout, death. Survival was always elusive. The people clustered, as was economically practical, in small bands or family groups, each a unit with its own social and religious framework. All lived intimately with the natural world; the rivers were havens of wood and water, while plants and game offered a varied diet. The valleys tucked inward for shelter, and the hilltops offered spectacular lookouts for both sunsets and enemies. And although life was difficult—one of constant movement, of hunting meat, then drying it and pounding it for pemmican—the world was also beautiful, woven with the flicker of leaves and light, the rush of wind through grass, the shy purple of spring crocuses.

When the seasons shifted emphasis, the people did too. With winter came long months of hunkering down in the shelter of the hills, hoping that the animals they hunted would not stray far. Spring offered respite from cold, the new grass promising young buffalo, melting ice, a softening earth. Summer was the dry time, when the grass first greened and then browned, when fires raged on the horizon. And fall, when the berries and the bears fattened, when the geese flew in huge arrows overhead, meant that winter's cold arms were waiting just around the wheel of the sun. Over every season hung the dome of Alberta's sky, a cerulean blue so crystalline that it seemed drinkable. Sky and earth together formed a sacred, magnificent cradle.

Alberta's original peoples were restless by necessity, yet pragmatically adaptable. Long before whites themselves came west, their tools—hatchets, knives, copper pots, and steel sewing needles—began to exert pressure by accelerating the jostling for territory. From far away, Europeans sent two incredible gifts, different in their outcome and their effect. The first was the fleet, four-footed horse, which Albertans acquired from the tribes to the south, who had in turn acquired them from farther south. Horses had actually roamed the plains earlier, but like the mammoth, become extinct, only reintroduced to North America when the Spanish brought them to Mexico. Tough and playful, intelligent and useful, these "big dogs" transformed life on the prairie, enabling people to move faster and more efficiently than before. The second and more doubtful gift was the firearm, which made survival easier, but war more common.

The Cree, who acquired these "shouting sticks" from the French and English traders, brought them in from the north and east, at first using them to push the Blackfoot south and west, and then trading them to the same Blackfoot enemies. Northern Cree, Athapaskan, and Assiniboine people exchanged goods with whites long before the Blackfoot. Those woodlands people, who were most at home in a canoe, became natural go-betweens, the traders' traders. But for all the wealth and knowledge that the fur trade gave the Cree, when the southern tribes became monarchs of both guns and horses, they enjoyed a prosperity that made them spectacularly independent, almost scornfully indifferent to the white man's goods. The plains people, not paddlers but riders, had no interest in making pilgrimages east to Hudson Bay. For a while, mounted and armed, they were the undisputed lords of the prairies, true occupants of its succulent reaches.

The relationship of the horse to Albertans, past and present, cannot be overestimated. *Saukamappee* related to David Thompson a description of First Peoples encountering horses: "Our enemies the Snake Indians and their allies had Misstutim [big dogs] on which they rode, swift as the Deer, on which they dashed at the Peigan, and with their stone Pukamoggan knocked them on the head, and they had thus lost several of their best men. This news we did not well comprehend and it alarmed us, for we had no idea of Horses and could not make out what they were."

Saukamappee describes the victory battle, won with guns, over the Snakes, and after the war ceremonies, he says, "We were anxious to see a horse, of which we had heard so much. At last, as the leaves were falling we heard that one was killed by an arrow shot into his belly, but the Snake Indian that rode him got away; numbers of us went to see him, and we all admired him, he put us in mind of a Stag that had lost his horns; and we did not know what name to give him. But as he was a slave to Man, like the dog, which carried our things; he was named the Big Dog." Of course, this is Thompson's translation of *Saukamappee*'s story, but the mixture of admiration and pleasure that the horse elicited is obvious. Later, the Blackfoot renamed the horse *Ponokamita,* or "elk dog."

Before the First Peoples of Alberta, who had no immunity against alien germs, ever laid eyes on whites, white diseases had effectively erased half their population. Smallpox was a far more terrible gift than guns or kettles, and *Saukamappee* also related to David Thompson their encounter with that dreadful scourge:

> We caught it from the Snake Indians. Our Scouts were out for our security, when some returned and informed us of a considerable camp which was too large to attack and something very suspicious about it; from a high knowl they had a good view of the camp, but saw none of the men hunting, or going about; there were a few Horses, but no one came to them, and a herd of Bisons feeding close to the camp with other herds near....
>
> Next morning at the dawn of day, we attacked the Tents, and with our sharp flat daggers and knives, cut through the tents and entered for the fight; but our war whoop instantly stopt, our eyes were appalled with terror; there was no one to fight with but the dead and the dying, each a mass of corruption.... It was agreed to take some of the best of the tents, and any other plunder that was clean and good, which we did, and also took away the few Horses they had, and returned to our camp.
>
> The second day after this dreadful disease broke out in our camp, and spread from one tent to another as if the Bad Spirit carried it. We had no belief that one Man could give it to another, any more than a wounded Man could give his wound to another. We did not suffer so much as those that were near the river, into which they rushed and died. We had only a little brook, and about one third of us died, but in some of the other camps there were tents in which every one died.

When at length it left us, and we moved about to find our people, it
was no longer with the song and the dance; but with tears, shrieks,
and howlings of despair for those who would never return to us.

Guns and horses transformed the Blackfoot into magnificent riders and buffalo runners. The horse extended trade, and ownership became a display of wealth and status. Herds of horses symbolized prosperity, and the Blackfoot, especially, began to enjoy a renaissance wealth. Hunting and travelling were much easier, and the resultant free time could be spent on other activities, decorative and artistic. Horse stealing became a measure of honour—horses bestowed glamour, horse stealing was an excuse for skirmishing.

The rules of plains civilization were flexible yet pragmatic, governed by a version of public democracy. Leaders were made chiefs for eloquence or for bravery, but even the role of chief was advisory rather than disciplinary. Every person followed his or her own conscience within a larger social structure. Their measure of satisfaction was shaped by the contingencies of their world; white notions of right and wrong were puzzling to a people who could take neither their territory nor their survival for granted.

They fought and took scalps, but not thoughtlessly or without cause. Their code of honour understood shame. They formed uneasy or necessary alliances, then ruptured them again. Cree raiding parties into Blackfoot territory sometimes succeeded and sometimes failed, and over every battle hovered spirit protectors. One famous story tells of Cree chiefs Big Bear and Sweetgrass leading a small horse-raiding party into Blackfoot country south of the Red Deer River. Accidentally stumbling on a huge Blackfoot camp, they were attacked so suddenly that they barely had time to barricade themselves in a small copse of trees. For three days, completely outnumbered, they held off the Blackfoot warriors and even though they were pinned down ultimately killed nineteen Blackfoot chiefs, asserting a magical power that astonished and frightened their enemies, who finally lowered their weapons and walked away. Only twenty Cree, mostly green braves, had held off hundreds of Blackfoot. They later counted no fewer than thirty-two bullet holes in Sweetgrass's clothing, although he had not one physical scratch.

This intricate social world, a form of civilization that Europeans could not possibly understand or translate, changed with every new encounter. It had to. The byzantine motivations of white men, their laws and rules and prayers and bargains with God, were puzzling to Alberta's early people. Accustomed to adaptation and adoption (children and families were commonly adopted by relatives and friends), they shifted shape with every test that nature presented. And their cultural history, recited in songs and stories, dances and ceremonies, is beyond the reach of a feeble post-oral comprehension that expects real cultural and religious practices to be written down.

The horse and the fur trade together contributed to the flourishing of a prairie golden age (1750–1880). But the effect of trade and contact was that the repository of Western wealth, the great buffalo herds, began to diminish drastically. The North American continental herd is estimated to have once numbered more than fifty million, the land always thick with grazing beasts, the people's mainstay. Repeating rifles and unscrupulous hunters, intent on sending hides east to make belts for factory machines, reduced the number so quickly that the people of the plains had barely the blink of an eye to deal with a terrible social, cultural, and economic loss. Between 1871 and 1875, American buffalo hunters killed ten million migrating buffalo, and brutal traders eagerly supported the slaughter, saying, "Kill every buffalo you see; every buffalo dead is an Indian gone." By the mid-1870s none could be found north of the Red Deer River. By 1879 they had almost disappeared and an American game count in 1886 found only six buffalo. In two decades, the source of all abundance was gone and the people were defeated—first by starvation and then by encroaching white settlement.

Indians were puzzled by white notions of ownership and property, by political or legal authority. Obedience was an unheard-of constriction. Their loyalties were dependent on moment and context, a fluidity necessary for nomads. Now their natural faith was being threatened by missionaries. In the confusion, warfare between the tribes increased. And worst of all, the whisky traders, sure that they would not be challenged now that the HBC had been sold to Central Canada, sidled up over the border. Although rum and whisky had always been a staple item of trade, the people had never been poured such copious amounts of drink, and drink of such vile character, continuously and in their own camps. These traders were without scruples, intent only on debauchery. One of them, Alexander Stavely Hill, even went so far as to claim, "If we had only been allowed to carry on the business in our own way for another two years, there would have been no trouble now as to feeding the Indians, for there would have been none left to feed: whiskey, pistols, strychnine, and other like processes would have effectively cleared away these wretched natives." Keeping the First Peoples starving, demoralized, and divided was the effective strategy that "pacified" them even more than Mounties and settlers and preachers. They were reduced to skeletons, forced to survive on dogs, gophers, porcupine, even their precious horses. Facing famine and privation, they had no choice but to capitulate to the promises held out by the white man's treaties.

• • •

When whites first sniffed the delicious air of the West, some ten tribes and four broad language groups lived in what would become Alberta. Northern Alberta, the boreal forest of tamarack and spruce between and around the Peace and Slave rivers, was home to people of the Athapaskan linguistic group. They included the Beaver people, *Tsattine*, or those who lived along the river of beavers, the Peace. Before whites arrived, there were several bands of Beaver people, but disease reduced their number and the Cree pursued them westward. Alexander Mackenzie records that Peace Point, on the Peace River, is named for the Cree and Beaver finally making peace after a long conflict, settling on Peace Point as the boundary between their territories. From traders, the Beaver obtained guns early, enabling them to stop the Cree, and in turn push their enemies west. The Beaver were famous as trappers and hunters, but knowing the unpredictability of survival, they welcomed spiritual help in finding food. Their coyote trickster carried songs on his back, and used dancing and singing to catch fat ducks for food.

To the east of the Beaver were the Chipewyan, famously fierce warriors; at Bloody Falls Samuel Hearne witnessed their merciless massacre of an enemy Inuit group. Tough and resilient, they hunted the area from Hudson Bay to Great Slave Lake, especially the lower Peace and Athabasca rivers, migrating with the caribou. Currently they live as far south as Cold Lake. Early traders with whites, they at first refused to touch alcohol, wanting nothing to do with its mind-altering effects. Their herbal-medicine practitioners were helpless to prevent a smallpox epidemic from killing nine-tenths of their tribe in 1781. As trappers, they were indispensable to the fur trade, and well aware of the value of their land; when they signed Treaty

Eight (1899), they sagaciously asked for better terms than were first offered. One of their enduring legends is of a guiding star in love with a little girl.

The peaceful Slavey or *Acha'otinne* people first lived just west of Lake Athabasca, then were forced north and west by the invading Cree. Because they disliked the dismissive name Slavey, given them by the Cree, they now call themselves *Dene Chaa* or *Dene Thaa*. Wandering in small family groups, they preferred woodland and water areas and lived primarily on fish, which they caught in weirs or with nets. Excellent moose hunters, they loved beautifully decorated clothing and relied on animals as guardian spirits to help them hunt other animals. Although considered quiet and unwarlike, they were feared for possessing supernatural powers, and one of their legends recounts how a beaver bored through a wall of rock and opened a passageway so that the Mackenzie River could spill from Great Slave Lake to the Arctic Ocean. They were an intensely emotional tribe, and Alexander Mackenzie recounts the force of their mourning, how when one of their family died, they fired their guns to warn their friends away, women cut off a joint or two of their fingers, and families threw away every belonging in order to forget the deceased. The most remote of Alberta's peoples, sociable and easygoing, they suffered most from the terrible effects of influenza and tuberculosis.

The Sarcee, or Tsuu T'ina, who were related to the Beaver Indians, had always lived between the Athabasca and the upper North Saskatchewan, but by the 1700s had begun to move south toward the plains, where they made alliance with the powerful Blackfoot and transformed themselves into prairie Indians. Their separation from their Athapaskan cousins is recounted in a tale about a tribe crossing the ice of a large lake, shaped like a buffalo, in midwinter. Some of them had already crossed when a small boy noticed a buffalo horn sticking out of the ice. "I want that bone," he said to his grandmother, who began to hack at the horn, trying to break it. She tried to pull the horn free from the ice until suddenly there came a great crack and the ice split open. All the people on the ice fell in, and the ones on either shore were separated forever, those on the north staying close to the Beaver people and those on the south travelling to the land of the Blackfoot. The trader Alexander Henry described the Sarcee as being "the bravest tribe in all the plains, who dare face ten times their own numbers." During the 1800s the Sarcee and Blackfoot lived and travelled together, and Treaty Seven allocated them a common reserve close to Blackfoot Crossing. The two nations argued so much that the

Sarcee Indian camp near Calgary, late 1890s

Sarcee, under the leadership of Bull Head, left to follow the few remaining buffalo. They roamed south of the border, but almost starved, and in 1880 they were compelled to return to Blackfoot Crossing. There was so little food on the reserve that the Sarcee encamped at Fort Calgary, and in desperation tried to burn down a trading post. The Mounties finally persuaded them to go south to Fort Macleod, but the winter trip was hellish, and they lacked provisions. Bull Head's dislike of the Blackfoot Crossing reserve intensified and he kept complaining. When promises made to his people were repeatedly broken, Bull Head finally sent an eloquent petition to Ottawa explaining his many grievances. The government, always nervous of a squeaky wheel, and this one a warrior, finally gave the Sarcee the reserve they wanted, 108 square miles from prairie to foothills on Fish Creek, now virtually a part of the city of Calgary. The Sarcee suffered severely from tuberculosis, so much that a physician was appointed as Indian agent. He turned the entire reserve into a sanitorium, and finally the group began to conquer the illness that had so reduced their numbers. Now surrounded by the burgeoning city, they have sold some 1,500 acres of land, but generally resisted white encroachment and economic pressure well.

Around the same time as the Sarcee came to southern Alberta, the Gros Ventres moved south to the United States. Always in an uneasy position, the Gros Ventres more than once plundered and attacked trading posts, and they were feared for their tempers and their long-held grudges. Pressured from every side, this nation slowly moved southward until they settled in Montana.

The eastern and northern parkland was home to the Woodland Cree, who roamed from the North Saskatchewan River to Hudson Bay. As the first people to trade with whites, they became both backbone and intermediary of the fur trade, the middlemen who carried the furs east and carried trade goods west, slowly moving up the North Saskatchewan toward the Rockies and pushing the Beaver people back to the upper Peace River until they controlled most of the woodlands of Alberta.

After they became partners with the white traders, the Cree revised their cyclical habits to incorporate trading practices. Their resourceful and comely women formed alliances with the fur traders, and out of those marriages came the Métis people. But their long association with whites gave them no advantage; they, too, suffered from smallpox and tuberculosis, were nagged by missionaries to convert, and lost their children to residential schools. Naturally the Woodland Cree were suspicious of government promises, both the Treaty Eight offerings for status Indians and the concomitant Scrip Commission, which offered the Métis "scrip" entitling them to 160 acres of land. To a people who loved hunting and trapping and fishing, farming seemed a ridiculous invention, and they followed their seasonal patterns as long as they could.

Their cousins, the Plains Cree, lived north and south of the leafy wooded basin of the North Saskatchewan River. Part of large nation, the Frog Lake People, the Beaver Hills People, and the Rocky Mountain People were three specific Cree groups who ranged through Alberta. Fierce warriors, they were the sworn enemies of the Blackfoot, often raiding their camps for horses. Adaptable to any landscape, and dependent on the buffalo, they moved toward the foothills in winter and out onto the plains in summer. It was the Plains Cree who joined with Louis Riel in 1885, the Cree who fought white incursion most vigorously, even though the

Cree Indians in Central Alberta, around 1890

Blackfoot were the ones with the warlike reputation. Most of the North West Rebellion took place in Saskatchewan, but at Frog Lake, thirty miles northwest of Fort Pitt, warriors killed eight people, and at Hobbema some looting occurred, prompted not by hostility but starvation. But the defeat of Riel and the subsequent surrender of their chief, Big Bear, was a sad conclusion to this final resistance, and from a life of roaming the entire prairie, the Cree people settled down to a combination of hunting, fishing, and farming on their reserves. Their leaders' names, Ermineskin, Samson, Sweetgrass, and Poundmaker, are echoed in the names of contemporary reserves.

From the North Saskatchewan River south roamed the legendary Blackfoot peoples, traditional enemies of the Cree. Linguistically Algonkian, the Blackfoot Confederacy included the Blood, Peigan, and the Blackfoot who gave their name to the nation. These *Soyi-tapi*, or prairie people, rode the area south of Battle River and during their most powerful period controlled a territory from the eastern slopes of the Rockies to the Dakotas and the Missouri. Famous as warriors, the

Blackfoot teepee near, Cluny, Alberta; note the ominous presence of a grain elevator

Blackfoot stole horses to become, within one generation, astonishing riders. They were totally uninterested in trade until the death of the buffalo, the mainstay of their lives and to them the holiest of animals. They had always revered the beasts, used every part of the animal, and left the hides of white or albino buffalo as gifts to the Sun.

The Blackfoot Confederacy was the most romanticized of all First Nations groups, especially to those in the Centre who imagined them as howling dervishes eager to scalp unwary settlers. The "Blackfoot war," which resulted in the United States cavalry killing 173 Peigan in the Baker massacre of 1870, drove most of the people in the confederacy north of the border to the British-controlled area of their ancestral lands. Still, they could not shake the Americans, who doggedly followed them with barrels of whisky. The American trade was deadly; in one year, for example, drunken arguments caused the deaths of seventy Blood people. The Mounties were white, but they were a relief from whisky traders, and the Blackfoot established a complex, almost philosophical relationship with these representatives of Canadian law. They at first tried to remain aloof, only to realize that the increasing numbers of whites meant that their land was being invaded, and despite many qualms, in 1877 signed Treaty Seven at Blackfoot Crossing, under Crowfoot's leadership taking a reserve on a brow of the Bow River. But their land was always tempting to others, and in 1912 the Blackfoot sold half of their reserve; in 1918 they sold a further fifty-five thousand acres. This sale gave them temporary wealth, but it was quickly devoured by rising costs of living. It seemed as if every time the Blackfoot people reached a moment of equilibrium, the white man's system tilted the playing field again.

The Blood, or *Kainai*, Indians were part of the Blackfoot nation, but jealous of their status and situation, and when the treaty talks were planned for Blackfoot Crossing, they almost boycotted the gathering. Finally, two days late, they arrived, and their chief, Red Crow, gave Crowfoot authorization to speak for all. On the strength of Colonel Macleod's consistent honesty—and the fact that the Mounties had always kept their promises—both chiefs signed the treaty. The Blood reserve first allocated was a barren stretch of land between Blackfoot Crossing and Medicine Hat, a flat space where the wind blew twice as hard as anywhere in Alberta. The Blood people decided that they preferred their winter camping ground close to the Belly River, and in 1883 they accepted a 362,600-acre reserve between the Belly and St. Mary rivers, still the largest reserve in Canada. But it was hard for them to give up their pride, and frequent skirmishes over stolen horses resulted in a few Cree being killed. Also, Blood warriors loved crossing the border to Montana to steal horses—if they could get back into Alberta undetected, they could not be punished, an irresistible challenge. Their wonderfully anarchic arrogance convinced others that they felt superior to every person, believed they were the "cream of creation." Increasing numbers of European settlers made the Blood land very tempting to government agents, and again and again the tribe was asked to surrender land for sale or development. But the Blood people resisted, and to this day have sold not a single acre.

The Peigan people, or *Aputoksi-pikuni*, with formidable family connections in Montana, are in Canada the smallest group within the Blackfoot nation. Rich in horses and very industrious, the Peigan sought early to adapt to a world without buffalo, finding that cattle ranching was the most effective way to use their land. Unlike the Blood Indians, the Peigan were not successful in keeping their property out of white hands, and in 1909 they sold 28,496 acres of their reserve. One Peigan man called Strong Buffalo, who had raised a large herd of cattle, decided to travel in 1895 with the local Anglican priest to England to visit the much-discussed Queen Victoria. His story is a refreshing reversal of Victorian travellers recounting their visits to the West. Although he never did get an audience with the fat old queen, he spun amazing tales of his voyage across the water, the houses he saw, and the bizarre antics of Englishmen, who were truly strange and uncivilized.

The Stoney, or Assiniboine, people, who long ago were separated from the Sioux, roamed north of the Blackfoot, from the Eagle Hills to the Beaver Hills and west all the way to the foothills of the Rockies. Both warmly hospitable and extraordinary horse thieves, they were fascinated by white religion. The presence of Methodists George and John McDougall, who had established Morleyville on the Bow River, divided the Stoney groups, although at the signing of Treaty Seven, the Stoney were under the sway of McDougall's missionary influence and several Stoney bands shared a reserve close to the Morleyville mission. Because they were located close to the foothills, they could still hunt deer and elk, and despite white intervention they continued to argue for their right to hunt for food, a precursor of current legal arguments about First Nations people being allowed to hunt and fish outside game regulations. More than any other group in Alberta, the Stoney people fought hard to retain their language and culture. Stoney Chief Walking Buffalo, who always wore a buffalo head and horns in the Banff Indian Days parade, and who erected a yellow teepee on the campground, told until his death the story of the powerful buffalo who came to him in his dreams. Although concerted efforts were made to stamp out what the missionaries and many whites considered "barbaric" ceremonies, Chief Walking Buffalo also argued for the importance of the Sun Dance.

Finally, almost on the edge of Alberta, along the foothills south of present-day Banff, lived the isolated Kootenay. From having earlier roamed the prairies, they were pushed west by the Peigan to become mountain dwellers. Occasionally the Kootenay ventured out onto the plain to hunt but they were more mountain people than prairie people.

These many nations, who knew a magical past and dream a living future, call Alberta home. They are still a paradoxical people, friends and enemies, accommodating, but not easy for whites to understand. They are, like coyote, shapeshifters and tricksters who know that the whitewashed stories of discovery and civilization are inventions. These people have lived in Alberta forever, and no matter how many bargains are made with them, no matter how many lies come sneaking over the horizon, they know who and where they are.

• • •

The furs that Alberta's First Peoples exchanged for European goods were so bountiful that they did not hesitate to trade them for the tobacco and kettles and knives and guns the whites brought. They were especially quick to apprehend the advantages of firearms; hunting became more efficient with firearms and steel traps, but guns made intertribal wars both more tempting and more lethal. Trading posts became the locus of social life for gathered bands, and leadership became a contested issue, since white traders would deal only with one trade chief, who negotiated all terms of sale. Community structures were profoundly altered by the cumulative effect of these new habits and new possessions. And while the Hudson's Bay and North West companies had always recognized that their employees worked only with the sanction and co-operation of the original peoples, later traders and inhabitants did not appreciate that mutual dependency.

Whites competed in an utterly ruthless way, unfathomable to people who had always been rich in prospects if not possessions. With game and fur-bearing animals disappearing, treaties seemed a means to ensure at least a modicum of assistance from the men who made strange black marks on paper. These acts of surrender were constructed as elaborate rituals, but pacification came about as a combination of necessity and subjection. The people had no choice but to give up their ancestral rights in return for a few acres, a pittance in treaty money, and the vague promise of assistance in farming, health, and education.

Central Canada negotiated the treaties as an extension of their overall plan to first confine the Indians to reserves, and then slowly "assimilate" what they assumed was a vanishing group with a vanishing way of life. They read the treaties as agreements by which the original peoples ceded entitlement of all land to the Central government. The First Peoples, on the other hand, understood them as peace treaties that merely allowed the newcomers "use" of their land. The coercion behind the signing of the treaties, the terrible starvation that the people suffered, is seldom considered as a weighted factor in the legal wrangling that continues even now. And the oral but unrecorded treaty negotiations, with their gaps between intention and understanding, are completely unexplored. These talks sometimes went on for days; so what was said that was never written down?

In true colonial fashion, Canada's attitudes toward Alberta's First Peoples evolved from methods and policies that had been applied by the British long before Confederation. The principle that the Indians needed "protection" formed the very core of a paternalistic and ultimately destructive relationship. At first the British had openly purchased lands that they wanted to use or to settle, seeking the First Peoples as political and military allies, but this pragmatic exchange was irrevocably altered by the arrogance of evangelism. The effect of nineteenth-century missionary movements, those new crusades out to Christianize the world, advocated "protecting and civilizing" the Indians to give them access to the cloudy reaches of white man's heaven. The missionaries who settled among the Indians, determined to "teach" them, were government tools, and under the willing blessing of this system, various churches happily served as instruments of assimilation almost until the end of the twentieth century.

The Indian Act of 1876 laid the foundation for the way First Peoples would be treated for more than one hundred years, and set out to indoctrinate them in the principles of private property. While this act was primarily directed at First Nations people east of Lake Superior, its attitudes drifted westward. Because Western peoples were reluctant to relinquish their traditional beliefs, Ottawa decided to prohibit expression of these beliefs, making the Thirst Dance and the Sun Dance illegal, and even prohibiting Plains Indians from appearing in ceremonial garb. Most aggressively, knowing that children had very little interest in attending schools on the reserves, the governor-in-council, in 1894, was empowered to take whatever steps necessary to force children to attend residential and industrial schools, which meant wrenching children from their families. Because the missionaries were so eager to promote their particular salvations, they became the regulators and directors of residential schools, the poisonous effects of which still fester. Only after the incredible contribution of First Nations enlisted men in the Second World War was interest in the political rights of Canada's aboriginal peoples awakened, and in 1951 a new Indian Act, albeit remarkably similar to the old one, was passed. Recently government and the settler usurpers have begun to look at Alberta's original peoples with a different set of eyes and in a different context. But we are not yet sufficiently ashamed.

Treaty Six, signed in 1876 at Fort Pitt and Fort Carlton by the Cree, Assiniboine, and Ojibwa peoples, surrendered the centre of Alberta, from the source of the Red Deer River to Jasper House and along the Athabasca to Lac La Biche, and then along the Beaver River in the north and, finally, following east from the Rocky Mountains along the Red Deer River to the south. By this treaty, paid for with approximately $47,000, Ottawa purchased 121,000 square miles of the richest soil in Canada.

In 1877 the new lieutenant-governor of the North West Territories, David Laird, and Colonel Macleod of the NWMP were entrusted to make further treaty with the Blackfoot. Laird was royally welcomed to Fort Macleod by a Mountie horse parade, and then troops and a baggage train of goods (gifts and bribes) set out for Blackfoot Crossing, where negotiations with the Blackfoot Confederacy were to proceed. The people were offered the usual terms—a $12 signing bonus, plus $5 a year; the chiefs also got a suit of clothes, a medal, and a flag, the very things, of course, they needed most. The reserve allocation, a square mile for every five persons, was the same as the other treaties, but the Blackfoot were offered cattle instead of farming implements. In what seems now an obvious lie, Laird promised the Blackfoot that they could continue to hunt all over the prairie and that should they wish to sell any of their land or coal or timber, they would receive fair prices. War chief Medicine Calf, sometimes called Button Chief, who had actually signed American treaties and seen them broken, gave the most interesting speech, saying, "We want to be paid for all the timber that the Police and whites have used since they first came to our country. If it continues to be used as it is, there will soon be no firewood left for the Indians." Laird responded facetiously that "you Indians ought to pay us rather, for sending these traders in fire-water [alcohol] away and giving you security and peace, rather than we pay you for the timber used." This was obviously a slightly different negotiation from Treaty Six, but the result was similar. Not knowing that Crowfoot was only the chief of his tribe and not chief of the entire confederacy, the police and Laird put him in the uncomfortable position of speaking for everyone, although he repeatedly requested that his brother chiefs speak first. But because he had a long history with whites and seemed to understand them, all the people looked to Crowfoot for leadership and finally, after days of discussion, Crowfoot was forced to summarize. He said, "I will sign the treaty."

The Alberta historian Hugh Dempsey, in his biography *Crowfoot: Chief of the Blackfeet*, describes Crowfoot's doubts well. He had gone to consult with a very old and wise medicine man named Pemmican, who told him, "I want to hold you back . . . because your life henceforth will be different from what it has been. Buffalo makes your body strong. What you will eat from this money will have your people buried all over these hills. You will be tied down, you will not wander the plains; the whites will take your land and fill it. You won't have your own free will; the whites will lead you by a halter. That is why I say don't sign. But my life is old, so sign if you want to. Go ahead and make the treaty." There were the tempting presents behind the Mounties, while facing those piles of food and blankets were the hungry people. Most of the chiefs were prepared to accept the treaty, and so Crowfoot spoke, and Treaty Seven, symbolically signed in 1877 by the Blackfoot, Blood, Peigan, Sarcee, and Stoney tribes, surrendered the entire south of Alberta. Or . . . was that treaty really signed? Hugh Dempsey says that Crowfoot, when asked to touch the pen to signify his agreement, only made a gesture, purposely refusing to touch the instrument that would inscribe the people's subjection. Which might make for an interesting battle in a court of law today.

After a Mountie salute of thirteen guns, the commission secretary recorded the subsequent celebrations. "On Sunday afternoon the Indians fought a sham battle on horseback. They only wore the breech-cloths. They fired off their rifles in all directions, and sent the bullets whistling past the spectators in such close proximity as to create most unpleasant feelings. I was heartily glad when they defiled past singly on the way back to their lodges, and the last of their unearthly yells had died away in the distance." The combined fear and contempt evident in this man's written observation show the duplicity behind the treaties. Later, Father Constantine Scollen, one of the missionaries in attendance, said that given their long-standing nomadic relationship to the land, the First Peoples could not possibly have absorbed the implications of the treaty, with its focus on ownership. Others now argue that they signed a deal and knew the consequences, that land-rights questions should not be reconsidered. In northern Alberta, where settlement did not so quickly overrun hunting grounds, the people could continue living with the land for a few decades, but not long. Treaty Eight was signed by the Chipewyan,

Cree, Beaver, and Slavey in 1899. Reserves today comprise only one percent of Alberta's total area, while Métis settlements occupy slightly less than one percent.

• • •

After signing Treaty Seven, the Plains Indians struggled through the terrible winter of 1878–79. In the summer, only a few scattered beasts could be found. Without buffalo, the door of the future closed tighter and tighter, and although they begged the Indian agents for help the people slowly starved on a diet of gophers and mice. Even worse, American hide hunters had set prairie fires that trapped the few remaining buffalo herds south of the border.

Finally, gaunt and desperate, the Blackfoot had no choice but to follow the buffalo to Montana. The Americans were unwelcoming, believing that the Blackfoot had been encouraged to go south in order to save the Canadian government the cost of feeding them. Private government letters support their suspicions—the Canadian officials looked as if butter wouldn't melt in their mouths, but they were not above sending trouble across the border. And the moment that the people found buffalo in Montana and were able to gather some meat and a few hides, the whisky traders reappeared, their vicious potions reinstating the cycle of debauchery and death. This led to renewed hostility, and several times Crowfoot had to intervene in potential warfare between the Blackfoot and the Plains Cree, who had followed the buffalo south as well.

In 1879 there in Montana, a fiery-eyed Louis Riel paid Crowfoot a visit, arguing that the Mounted Police and the Canadian government could not be trusted and that if the First Peoples joined forces with the Métis, together they could capture the entire Northwest and oust the whites entirely. Crowfoot was wise enough to be doubtful; he did not see war as a ready solution to any of his people's difficulties. But Riel's version of white betrayal was persuasive, for they already had plenty of evidence that whites broke their promises. Despite failing to enlist the Blackfoot as allies, Riel had already set in motion the crusade that would lead to the 1885 Rebellion, based on his belief that "the N.W.T. is the natural property of the Indian and Half-breed, [and] ought to be set apart for their exclusive use, ruled and governed by them alone." Crowfoot doubted that Riel could win any war with whites, but the suspicion lurked that Riel was right about white betrayal.

Meanwhile, the buffalo grew still scarcer, and to share the limited hunting, Crowfoot made peace with the Sioux chief, Sitting Bull. Lambs and lions had no choice now but to lie together. With hunger a daily visitor, Crowfoot sent a message asking if the Blackfoot people would be fed if they returned to Canada, but Commissioner Dewdney replied that they ought to stay with the buffalo—in short, keep trouble south of the border. The Canadian government's terrible abnegation of responsibility has never been redressed, and in the subsequent winter, misery and destitution dogged the heels of the people. They turned to horse and cattle theft, and the Americans raged about being overrun with hordes of "alien Indians." There was nothing for the great confederacy to do but scatter into small groups, ranging far and wide in search of what now appeared to be an utterly vanished buffalo. The dam had to break, and when Crowfoot's warriors, the Black Soldiers, triumphantly stole seventy good Crow horses, some with ranchers' brands, Crowfoot understood only too well that the US cavalry now had an excuse to attack his people, and that as long as they stayed in the States they were vulnerable. Although he personally oversaw the return of the horses, Crowfoot knew there was finally no choice but to return to Canada. Even though they were disgruntled and restless, and although they threatened revolt, the Black Soldiers followed their chief. But they made the trip unpleasant and dangerous, trading scarce food and hides for whisky, and then grumbling when hunger struck again. The trek was miserable. The children had measles, the skeletal horses could barely walk, the few remaining dogs fought, and there was almost no pemmican left. Their slow trip home was marked by the graves of their dead. Crowfoot, his face carved with sorrow, walked at the end of the long caravan, having given his horses to the needy to ride.

But Canada had become as hard-hearted as the United States. When the people finally trickled into Fort Walsh in the Cypress Hills at the end of June, the Mounties gave them a few meagre rations and told them to move along. Slowly the Blackfoot tottered west, six weeks later coming in sight of Fort Macleod, where the Indian agent reported, "Crow Foot arrived here . . . with 1,064 followers, all in a most destitute condition. A large proportion of his followers consisted of old men, women, and children. They were nearly all on foot." Although no one knows the true extent of their losses on the walk home, at least one thousand Blackfoot people died between 1879 and 1881. The once-bountiful world had become a vale of tears and defeat.

After resting, they crawled on to Blackfoot Crossing, the beautiful spot that had always been theirs and that was now their designated reserve. There was so little game that they had no choice but to beg for white hand-outs. The food they were given was substandard, the flour crawling with maggots, and the beef a meat the people found too sweet, of the wrong texture. Worst of all, the employees of the federal Department of Indian Affairs treated the people with contempt.

It seemed hopeless. When Commissioner Dewdney and the Marquess of Lorne, Governor General of Canada (who later named Alberta after his wife), on an official tour of the Northwest, came to visit a few weeks later, Crowfoot made Lorne a present of one of his last horses and gave a heartbreaking speech asking for assistance for his vanquished people. Lorne made a grand speech in return and—out of bad manners or compassion?—refused to take the horse. Then, symbolic of the double messages that the Centrals were so handy at doling out, he in turn gave Crowfoot a gun and advised him to turn to agriculture.

Doubt and misery battled for supremacy, and the people grew hungrier. Crowfoot tried to impress the seriousness of the situation first on the farm instructor, then on the senior government man, but they both refused to listen and told the Indian agent in Fort Macleod that Crowfoot was becoming intractable. Irritated warriors threatened to shoot the government men. Finally, in frustration, they fired a few rounds into the log ration house, which sent the farm instructor hightailing off to Fort Macleod with a story exaggerated enough for a detachment of ten Mounties, under the command of Francis Dickens, son of the nineteenth-century English novelist, to appear at the reserve. Although the presence of the police imposed temporary peace and quiet, Crowfoot no longer trusted the Mounties. The tension came to a head, literally over a steer's head. Offal and heads of beef were a favourite food of the people, but the government men held these parts back and sold them instead of including them as rations. Obviously the whites were making a few extra dollars on the side. One day a man named Bull Elk and his wife wanted to buy a steer's head, but the rations man thought there was too much meat on it and refused to sell it for the usual dollar. That first head was retrieved, and Bull Elk got another, but when he was about to leave with the second head, another white employee ordered him off the premises, claiming he had not paid. A tussle ensued, Bull Elk saying that he had paid for the head and the government man accusing him of stealing, both snatching it back and forth.

Finally, furious, Bull Elk went home, got his rifle, and fired a few shots toward the ration house. As might be expected, all hell broke loose. Inspector Dickens marched out to arrest Bull Elk, but suddenly armed warriors surrounded everyone and the police were powerless. Dickens called for Crowfoot, but meanwhile the people pulled Bull Elk free and knocked Dickens to the ground. Now, a Mountie on the ground is a dangerous thing, and pretty soon everybody was firing guns into the air. Crowfoot, when he arrived, had no sympathy for Dickens; the white men treated the people like curs, and Bull Elk should never have been arrested, he said. Finally, to calm the situation, he persuaded Dickens that Bull Elk should be left in his custody until a proper magistrate could come and try the matter.

But Dickens, instead of abiding by his agreement, sent an hysterical message to Fort Macleod. A group of twenty Mounties set out immediately and arrested Bull Elk the moment that they arrived at Blackfoot Crossing. The trust that Crowfoot had always felt for the Mounties was irrevocably shattered. He expected the white government workers to be liars and cheats, but never the Mounties. To make matters worse, they got busy turning a government building into a barricade, with sacks of flour, the food that the people needed so much, piled up as protection. Crowfoot walked straight up the barricade and demanded that Bull Elk be returned to his custody, but the Mounties refused. Looking at the fortified building, Crowfoot inquired if they intended to fight, and the police replied that if the people did, they would too. The gauntlet was on the ground.

Despite Crowfoot's anger, the Mounties took Bull Elk to Fort Macleod, but it was hard to prove that he had done anything wrong, and he could only be charged with firing a weapon. Colonel Macleod, who heard the case, gave Bull Elk a light sentence, but even he could not know to what extent the Mounties' relationship with the people was changed. Because they had failed to listen and they had broken their word, Crowfoot would never trust the police again. Dewdney did have enough experience to realize that the situation on the reserve was explosive. He replaced the nervous farm instructor with an ex-Mountie who had always had good rapport with the people, and he made Inspector Cecil Denny responsible for clearing up matters on the reserve, which Denny did, getting rid of the corrupt government men and ensuring that matters of rationing and farming were standardized.

For a few months everything went smoothly, but Ottawa kept intervening. The burgeoning federal Indian Department was rife with political favours and trade-offs. Central Canadian men who needed to be rewarded with a political sinecure were often appointed to administrative positions on reserves in the West. Inexperienced and without a sense of aboriginal culture or a language to communicate with, these were generally young men whose rudeness created endless difficulties. However much the Mounties tried to stabilize matters, mistrust had eroded the earlier confidence that the people had placed in them, and the aboriginal people now treated everyone with suspicion.

Meanwhile, settlers and homesteads began to seed Alberta, telegraph crews strung a line through Cree lands to Fort Edmonton, and Ottawa announced a new leasing agreement. The wide-open spaces where the buffalo had roamed were perfect for grazing cattle, and ranchers could lease that land for a penny an acre a year. Soon, railway surveyors began to stake lines for the great steel stitching that would sew the country together. Swarms of rough, exploitive men camped close to the reserves. Drinking, gambling, and prostitution accompanied construction and, of course, affected the First Peoples. Although Crowfoot resisted the CPR's building its track along the reserve, even he could not prevent the railway's progress. The reserve towns of Cluny and Gleichen both had a train station where tourists would disembark to stare at the Indians who watched the train's arrival.

Until his death in April 1890, Crowfoot talked with his many confederates and friends about ways to make the people's life better. He was sometimes reviled and insulted, and he suffered the sadness of seeing his people slowly reduced in number and circumstances. In a final irony, after a long, bed-ridden winter, he was the subject of an argument about whether he was a Christian. Father Albert Lacombe insisted that he had converted but if he was baptized, it was only a few days before his death. The people did not want him buried in the ground, according to the white custom, and so his coffin was placed partly above ground and covered with a log shelter outside the palisade of the Catholic cemetery. His grave rests at the most spectacular point overlooking Blackfoot Crossing.

• • •

As surveyed land was taken up by white settlers, the children of the prairie suffered even greater misery, and their unrest grew. Riel's dream of a nation for Métis and aboriginal people struck a stronger and stronger chord, and eventually the Métis of

Saskatchewan sent for Riel to return to Canada and lead their cause. The West, angry at Ottawa's mixture of neglect and repression, was ripe for rebellion. In an effort to control potential unrest and in response to threats of armed resistance, the Mounties made numerous arbitrary arrests, seizing and imprisoning any Métis or Indian who seemed suspicious.

In the summer of 1884, discontent flowered. Why should the people not wish to drive the whites out of their country? Perhaps if the whites were gone, the buffalo would return. Tribes gathered for their annual summer celebrations, and stories of happier days, recounted through long twilights, fuelled the people's sense of betrayal. Indian agents who overheard rebellious talk ran the scared-rabbit-run to the Mounties with stories of the people getting ready to fight. The Mounties tried to arrest troublemakers, only to cause more trouble. Sham battles, with bullets whizzing through the air, relieved some tension, but inevitably led to more charges and more arrests, and the terrible circle of doubt and mistrust continued.

In a rare act of wisdom, Governor Dewdney decided that sending some of the plains chiefs on a tour of information and appeasement would be a good strategy. He invited Red Crow of the Blood, Crowfoot and Three Bulls of the Blackfoot, and Eagle Tail of the Peigan to travel on the hated smoke-belching railway to the cities of Winnipeg and Regina. He wanted to persuade the leaders not to join the rebellion. The chiefs toured the cities and, as Hugh Dempsey says, "saw the true strength of the invader. Winnipeg alone had a population of more than fifteen thousand, with enough men and weapons to defeat the entire Blackfoot nation." Clearly, a battle with an enemy so numerous would be futile. Perhaps even more persuasive, the chiefs visited Stony Mountain Penitentiary, where some of their people were imprisoned.

Central Canada had no coherent plan for the Western tribes. With the Canadian economy in decline in 1883, John A. Macdonald had decreed across-the-board cuts to every department, with disastrous results. The Bear's Hill chiefs, Bobtail, Ermineskin, and Samson, wrote to Macdonald directly, their letter reproduced in the new *Edmonton Bulletin*. "We were once a proud and independent people and now we are mendicants at the door of every white man in the country; and were it not for the charity of the white settlers who are not bound by treaty to help us, we should all die on government fare. Our widows and old people are getting the barest pittance." The money-saving measure of cutting rations to the plains people and the Centre's dismissal of concerns expressed by those in daily contact with the people were ignorant and short-sighted. Ottawa's next stupid move was to change the food that was distributed. Some accountant in Ottawa, who saw that the northern Cree took their rations in bacon, realized that bacon was less expensive, and decided that for the nations of Treaty Seven, bacon should be substituted for beef twice a week. The Blackfoot, who mourned the taste of buffalo, found bacon even less palatable than beef. Anger over the inedible food and the near-starvation-level rations they were expected to survive on grew. The death rate accelerated.

Cree chief Little Pine argued that the Blackfoot should support the Cree in any fight; and Cree chief Big Bear invited the Blackfoot people to join him and the Métis in resisting the whites. In Saskatchewan, Crowfoot's adopted son Poundmaker, increasingly restive and pressured by his warriors, prepared to fight beside the Métis. Meanwhile, the winter of 1884–85 was even hungrier, and it was clear that spring would bring every discontent into the open. Riel's general, Gabriel Dumont, had indicated to the clerk of the North West Council the Métis position on the Indians: "They are our relatives and when they are starving they come to us for relief and we have to feed them. The government is not doing right by them." But the North West Council, a mixture of elected and appointed white men, seemed to have no pull at all with deaf-in-both-ears Ottawa. Petitions sent east were ignored or met by threats and misunderstanding. Even Indian agents and Mounties tried to persuade Ottawa that rations and policies needed to change. But nothing changed, and if it were up to the Centre nothing would change, until, in March 1885 at Batoche, Louis Riel declared a provisional government, replacing the authority of the North West Territories. The West was ready for one spark to flare into an uncontainable wildfire.

Wildfire was indeed the result. From Fort Carlton, Mountie Superintendent L. N. F. Crozier telegraphed Colonel A. G. Irvine, NWMP commissioner: "Half-breed rebellion liable to break out at any moment. Troops must be largely reinforced. If half-breeds rise the Indians will join them." The Centre was spoiling for a good fight, and Major-General Fred Middleton, British-born and -trained commander of the Canadian Armed Forces, such as they were, raised a militia, which was immediately dispatched to assist the Mounties in quashing the rebels. At last the CPR had real business instead of the odd assortment of settlers they had transported west so far. The only fear to which the central Canadian boys who rode the troop train west would confess was that the Mounties would finish the fight before they got there.

Meanwhile, at Duck Lake on March 26, the Saskatchewan Métis under Gabriel Dumont had clashed with the Mounties and the Prince Albert volunteers. That confrontation left twelve Mounties dead and eleven injured, while the Métis suffered only five deaths and several wounded. So effectively did the Métis fight that the Mounties had the idea that there were hundreds of them, although there were only twenty-five on horseback.

The conflagration had begun. News of this first Métis victory swept across the prairies, making young Indian men eager to join the fight, although the old chiefs were still wary. Around every new settlement, Edmonton, Fort Macleod, Calgary, settlers and whites barred their doors and clutched anxiety close. They knew firsthand the extreme condition of the starving people and feared their taking up arms. The telegraph helpfully relayed nervous news to the East, and in Toronto wild excitement mustered volunteers along with the Royal Grenadiers and the Queen's Own Rifles. Within four days, the Centre, which had ignored Western messages and petitions for weeks, which left questions unanswered for months and years at a time, mobilized six hundred men and saw them off with cheers and brass bands. It might have been 1885, but the imperial position of the East was suddenly asserted in what would become a repetitive pattern.

The hungry Indians were more interested in food than killing. They looted Battleford and at other posts demanded provisions. From Buffalo Lake to Lac La Biche, they seized food and ammunition from Indian agents and HBC stores. If they were not given what they wanted, they took what they needed, and the whites who owned the trading posts scurried away, telling exaggerated tales of hostilities—in only a few places was actual violence committed. At Frog Lake, just inside the present-day border of Alberta, the Hudson's Bay store and the police barracks were ransacked by a group led by Imasees, the son of the Cree chief Big Bear. The whites were taken prisoner, and when they refused to obey the orders of a warrior called Wandering Spirit, nine men, including two priests, were killed. Only one white man, William Cameron, was spared. Chief Big Bear, who tried to control his furious warriors and prevent the killing, managed to keep two women, Theresa Gowanlock and Theresa Delaney, whose husbands had been killed, from harm.

At Fort Pitt, where the incompetent Francis Dickens had been moved, the Indians shot and barbecued some cattle, which settled their hunger a little, and then spent a day parleying with the HBC man, W. J. McLean. The McLean family, who spoke Cree, were astonishingly calm, perhaps because they had always had a positive relationship with the Indians. They negotiated the safety of the forty-four whites who were at Fort Pitt, and because they served as hostages, Mountie Dickens was allowed to flee with his Mountie troop. Dickens and his detachment spent the next seven days floating a leaky scow down the North Saskatchewan in an effort to reach Battleford, a cowardly performance indeed. And although the braves looted Fort Pitt, the whites in their captivity were treated well, and the McLean sisters' stories of the time spent with Big Bear's Cree became celebrated captivity narratives.

Meanwhile, Major-General Fred Middleton and half the Toronto troops disembarked from the CPR train at Qu'Appelle and marched north, while Lieutenant-Colonel William D. Otter and the rest of the troops went a little farther, got off at Swift Current and marched north from there. The Ontario boys were in good spirits, although they suffered from sunburn, blisters, and swollen feet, and had some trouble pushing themselves and their guns and ammunition through unexpected spring blizzards. Their leaders, wanting to engage in a military-style campaign, had little sense of the guerrilla tactics of the Métis and Indians, and relied on utterly inappropriate military strategies. Fred Middleton himself was a high-handed liability. A British officer, he mistrusted his troops, who were mostly Canadian, and treated them with condescension. He advanced so cautiously that everyone was impatient, from his own men to the Métis carters, spies who were happily sending daily reports to their general on the Métis side, Gabriel Dumont.

The First Peoples of not-yet-Alberta watched. Cree and Blackfoot, who were old enemies, might now unite in fighting their new enemy, the whites. Many of Crowfoot's young warriors were eager to join the fray, but he wanted to wait and see what the Blood and Peigan thought. Peigan war chief Running Wolf voted to join the rebellion, but Chief Eagle Tail dissuaded him. Blood chief Red Crow, who had been on the fact-finding journey to Winnipeg, mistrusted the Cree and refused to join the fight. Still, the tribes were eager for the energy of battle instead of their demoralizing day-to-day drudgery and hunger. Father Lacombe, the missionary trusted by all, made a point of discussing the rebellion with Crowfoot. "Among the

Indians of the North-West there was a kind of general feeling, with the old and the young, that the time was at hand to finish with the white policy," he wrote later, and although he understood the people's discontent, he tried to persuade them to stay on their reserves and wait. He was confident enough in what he observed to write to Macdonald in Ottawa: "I have seen Crowfoot and all the Blackfeet. All quiet. Promised me to be loyal no matter how the things may turn elsewhere." To pacify the restive people, Mountie inspector Cecil Denny increased rations, reasoning that rebellion was less likely to be prompted by full bellies.

Crowfoot waited. Cree messengers and scouts visited, recounting each battle and victory, each tantalizing looting, tempting and daring the Blackfoot to join them. On the opposing side, Dewdney, Denny, and Father Lacombe visited too, asking the Blackfoot for their continued co-operation and reassuring them that the Eastern soldiers would not harm those loyal to their treaty. Crowfoot listened to both sides, finally agreeing to send a telegram to wily old Macdonald in Ottawa, saying, "We will be loyal to the Queen, whatever happens." Despite hunger and privation, the doubly wily chief had decided to take the route that would most protect his people. Macdonald, that most forgetful of men, even replied: "We ... shall never forget the good conduct of yourself, your minor chiefs and warriors."

Meanwhile, at Fish Creek, in current Saskatchewan, Middleton made a strategic mistake. He split his troops, making them vulnerable to attack. Métis general Dumont hid some 150 men in the Fish Creek ravine, and snipers fired on the inexperienced soldiers as they appeared over the shoulder of the hill above. When the artillery finally managed to focus on the well-camouflaged rebels, some of them fled, but although they were surrounded by troops, a mere forty-five Métis held off hundreds of heavily armed soldiers, a battle eagerly reported across the West. That symbolic defeat put Middleton in his place for a couple of weeks, long enough for the Métis to consolidate their forces. If they had then been able to persuade Poundmaker and Big Bear's warriors to join them, they might have chalked up a few more victories, but the lengthy discussions among the different Indian bands, their indecision and procrastination, in the end left the Métis fighting pretty much on their own and ultimately contributed to their defeat at the battle of Batoche on May 12, 1885. By then, the Métis had no ammunition except stones and nails, and Middleton defeated their courage only with his superior guns.

Crowfoot's adopted son, Poundmaker, was painted as particularly hostile and dangerous. At the beginning of April, because the Indian agents had fled the reserve, Poundmaker had no choice but to bring his entire band of Cree to Battleford to collect their much-needed food rations. Their visit unfortunately coincided with the unrelated killings of two other whites, and the entire community, terrified without cause, sought uncomfortable shelter in the NWMP barracks. Poundmaker demanded his rations, then returned to his reserve, but some unrelated Indians looted the HBC store and a few private houses. Despite evidence that much of the looting was carried out by whites after the Indians had left, the whites inside the palisade sent out moaning telegrams about Poundmaker being on the warpath, demanding that Ottawa do something. As fast as he possibly could on hearing this news, Colonel William Otter marched his troops north from Swift Current, where they had disembarked from the train, to relieve the besieged fort. Once they reached Battleford, where the edgy but unhurt settlers were jubilantly freed from their cramped quarters, Otter could not contain his soldiers, and without provocation or reason, except the excuse of "punishing" the band for frightening the white settlers, Otter proceeded to the Poundmaker reserve to "surprise" the Cree there.

With 325 men, forty-eight wagons, two seven-pound guns, and a Gatling machine gun, Otter marched right up to the Cree encampment at Cutknife Hill and, like a true soldier of the Queen, started firing, while Cree men, women, and children fled in every direction. Amazingly, no Cree was hurt, and in a few moments the soldiers were astonished to realize that the warriors, under the superb leadership of war chief Fine Day, were returning fire. A genially retained hostage of Poundmaker's, a reserve instructor called Robert Jefferson, described the battle's beginning: "I lost no time in getting to Poundmaker's tent. He was just per-forming his toilet, and appeared in no way perturbed by the unexpected attack. He told me that an old man . . . had detected the rumble of the wagons [and] had roused the sleeping camp. . . . Poundmaker donned the fur cap that he always wore and proceeded to invest himself in what looked like a patchwork quilt. In my ignorance, I ventured to ask him what it was. With great dignity he informed me that it was his war cloak; that it rendered its wearer invisible to an enemy. Then he got up and stalked out of the tent without another word." Legend has it that Poundmaker, armed with only a whip, led his people in the daring fight. Exposed to the Cree warriors sheltered in the trees, and by noon virtually surrounded, the soldiers were easy targets. By nightfall, Otter knew he had to retreat or succumb, and with great difficulty he pulled back, carrying on his supply wagons his eight dead and thirteen wounded men. Although the warriors were prepared to pursue the soldiers, Poundmaker's influence prevented Otter's force from being utterly routed. As Jefferson says, "There was no pursuit. A number of Indians had mounted and were about to start after the retreating soldiers, but Poundmaker would not permit it. He said that to defend themselves and their wives and children was good, but that he did not approve of taking the offensive. They had beaten their enemy off; let that content them. So there was no pursuit." If only the Central army had been so punctilious. The victory at Cutknife Hill gave the warriors confidence that they could defeat the whites; but before they could join the Métis at Batoche, that final battle was lost and over, and the 1885 Rebellion drew to a close, with Métis and Indian alike scattering to save themselves from capture. Pursued more by hunger than defeat, Poundmaker surrendered to Middleton at Battleford on May 26; weeks later, on July 2, Big Bear and his son Horse Child surrendered to the police at Fort Carlton.

Although much of the 1885 Rebellion took place in what would become Saskatchewan rather than Alberta, the connections between the First Peoples were deep and indissoluble, and the whole West was consumed by what transpired. The settlers feared the Blackfoot, and despite Crowfoot's reassurances no one trusted that he would not join with the Cree. According to Sam Steele, it was the state of alarm of the citizens of Calgary that prompted Major-General Strange, whose ranch adjoined the Blackfoot reserve there, to take charge of the defence of the District of Alberta by organizing a scout troop and Home Guard. Based on wildly exaggerated reports of hostilities, the settlers, ranchers, and townsfolk became incredibly nervous. When Steele arrived at Calgary on April 11, he found "the inhabitants in a very excited state. Many ladies were at the train with their families, on their way east." Steele and Strange reassured everyone in Calgary that all would be well, although the small community still slept with guns under their pillows. Before marshalling his volunteers to march off to Edmonton, Strange sent the Reverend John McDougall ahead to inform the northern settlements that troops were on their way to effect their relief.

Under Strange, a mixed bag of cowboys, Mounties, and scouts marched north, crossing rivers swollen with spring runoff, reassuring settlers along the way that all was well and that a significant force defended their interests. At the Battle River they met Father Lacombe and fellow priest Father Scollen, who were dogging the footsteps of Cree chiefs Bobtail and Ermineskin in order to constrain them to keep the peace. The Cree had looted the HBC stores for food; Strange, whose show of military force was obviously designed to discourage Alberta's native people from joining the rebellion, pompously warned them that "on the conduct of themselves and their bands their future treatment would depend." Steele hyperbolically describes Bobtail and Ermineskin as "a most forbidding pair, and their bands the most depraved in the north west," his words undoubtedly seasoned by fear. Of course, these armed men were having enormous fun with their heroic protection of the country. Most of the anxious settlers in central Alberta had taken refuge at Fort Edmonton, and when Strange and his troops arrived they calmed them down considerably.

From Edmonton, then, Strange's guard moved east along the old Edmonton-Pitt-Carlton trail. They met no opposition at all, although they were eager to, and so trigger-happy that every movement had them firing into the wind. Steele describes how, "one night the 65th, according to orders, had tied up their scows for the night and were resting, when one of their sentries gave the alarm of Indians! No more was necessary for the corps. They were under arms in a moment and, led by their gallant commander, charged up the heights with loud cheers and swept the prairie with a shower of bullets. Five of my scouts who were out had to lie down in a deep hollow, where there was cover for themselves and their horses, until it was discovered that the sentry's Indians were young poplars waving in the wind!" This ridiculous scene of soldiers firing at the waving branches of young poplar trees marks the height of war in the West.

Reports of the killings at Frog Lake and the siege at Fort Pitt were greatly exaggerated, but suited what everyone wanted to believe, that the Indians were "on the warpath." The cumulative effect of fear and anticipation was to create more fear and anticipation. Although meticulous count was kept of the whites who died halting bullets that spring, there is no precise count of how many Indians and Métis were killed. The romance of this prairie war was undeniable, and even Steele succumbs to its seduction in his description of the "enemy" they faced: ". . . a fine-looking band of Indians appeared on the summit of a large round butte, about 1,500 yards distant. They were galloping in a circle to warn their camp, their excellent horsemanship and wild appearance making a remarkable picture as they were silhouetted against the blue sky. Directly they were sighted General Strange gave them a shot from the 9-pounder; the first fell short, the next swept the butte, the shrapnel tearing up the grass and gravel a second after the wild horsemen disappeared from the summit." This rhetoric helped to make palatable what Strange and Steele and Middleton were doing, which was chasing through rain and mud and soggy muskeg after Big Bear's remarkably elusive Cree. Ultimately they found the main body of the band and negotiated with them to release their white captives, an ignominious and rather humble end to what the military troops wanted to believe was a glorious campaign. For without Strange or Middleton's knowledge, Big Bear, alone with his youngest son, Horse Child, had quietly surrendered to three Mounties at Fort Carlton who were not even looking for him.

The North West Rebellion is still a scar on the hearts of Westerners. The effect of Riel's trial and execution was to incite ongoing suspicion of Ottawa politics for a century to come. The inherent justice of the Métis cause and the Centre's cavalier treatment of the West's legitimate concerns all contributed to this intensely bitter historical moment. Although history is reluctant to acknowledge the possibility, it was a good thing that Louis Riel didn't seek an alliance with the Americans, or the West would have a different complexion today. American sympathy was commonplace, especially in Alberta, where many settlers came from the United States. Had Riel pursued an alliance south, Canada might have stopped at Manitoba. And Riel's trial sparked rising tension between French and English Canadians for years to come. Quebec, seeing in Riel a passionate representative of French cultural rights, cried for his acquittal, while Orange Ontario bayed for Riel to dangle, and Macdonald famously declared that Riel would hang "though every dog in Quebec bark in his favour." When Riel was found guilty of high treason and hanged on November 16, 1885, his noose choked the Conservative Party in Quebec and enabled Wilfrid Laurier's Liberal electoral triumph in 1896.

Even more questionable was the way General Middleton, once he could claim to have won the war, arbitrarily arrested any Indian he thought had been rebellious. New and even more constrictive rules were applied. Indians caught stealing horses were sentenced to six years in jail; arrested Indians, who thought they were prisoners of war, were tried for treason. Wandering Spirit, Big Bear's disobedient warrior, and five other Cree and two Assiniboine warriors, were sentenced to death and hanged, while their families were brought to Battleford and barbarically forced to watch. Big Bear was convicted of treason-felony and sentenced to three years in Stony Mountain Penitentiary. Poundmaker too was sentenced to three years there. Crowfoot had written to Governor Dewdney begging clemency for his son, but to no avail, although because there was concern that he would die in prison Poundmaker was released after serving six months of his sentence. The moment he was able to travel, he went to Blackfoot Crossing to visit Crowfoot, and father and adopted son had a moving reunion. But their meeting was shadowed by the sadness of many defeats. At one of the ceremonies celebrating the Sun Dance, Poundmaker, who had been warned by a shaman not to eat any saskatoon berries, sipped at a bowl of sacred saskatoon berry soup, coughed, choked, and died. A white doctor claimed that he had suffered a burst blood vessel, but the Blackfoot people believed that he had encountered a greater spirit.

Peace did not improve the daily life of the people. Disease claimed children and adults alike, and now they had to get a pass from the Indian agent before they could travel off the reserve. Although the Mounties did not enforce these laws too strictly, they were still in place. Even more distressing, the missionaries redoubled their efforts to prohibit the First Peoples from practising their religious festivities. The people continued to celebrate clandestinely, but the ecstatic power of those ceremonies was forever eroded. Sir John A. himself came west to shake hands with the Indians who had been "loyal," and he and Crowfoot actually met just after Poundmaker's death. What they said is probably erased by official reports, but they must have looked each other up and down appraisingly and wondered at the implied power behind the frail frames of mortal men.

When a monument to Mohawk chief Joseph Brant was to be unveiled in Brantford, Ontario, in 1886, the feds decided that the occasion would be a perfect opportunity to bring east some of the chiefs who had not joined the rebellion, both to show them that Canada could never be challenged and defeated, and to show Centrals that these same chiefs were loyally subjected. Although Father Lacombe opposed Crowfoot's invitation, he nevertheless accompanied Crowfoot, Three Bulls, and an interpreter called Jean l'Heureux on a tour of the East that rivalled that of a contemporary rock star. Everyone was curious to see the Blackfoot chief who spoke for the Indians of the Wild West, and who, despite temptation, had not taken up arms against the whites. Reporters besieged him with questions, and people stared and pointed.

The chiefs' trip was an odd mixture of tourism and indoctrination. In Montreal they visited the Bank of Montreal, a Catholic convent, and shot the Lachine rapids. They met CPR magnates Sir George Stephen and William Van Horne, who presented them with a perpetual pass on the railway that they hated so much. They visited the citadel of Quebec City—in particular the many cannon guarding the walls—as well as the Quebec legislature, where Crowfoot sat in the speaker's chair. In Ottawa they were joined by Red Crow, One Spot, and North Axe, all being feted for their loyal obedience. There they met with the prime minister, and Crowfoot again reminded Macdonald of his promises: "We hope the Great Chief will think of our people. Since the white man came the buffalo have gone away, and now we need to be helped by the white chiefs." Lacombe made sure that the chiefs attended High Mass, conducted by none other than himself, at Ottawa's basilica. Every ceremonial symbol of white power—church, state, and monetary—was deployed to impress these indigenous Western eyes. The irony of their own cultural erasure by these same institutions was doubtless not lost on any of the chiefs. By the time they returned to their reserves, they were tired and overwhelmed, especially Crowfoot, who, although he was only fifty-six, was ill, overburdened, and sad. The whites, it was clear, outnumbered his people. They would never leave, would never be defeated. For the rest of their lives, those wise old men tried to help their people adjust to this different and now inevitable life. Both Red Crow and Crowfoot worked hard to persuade hot-blooded young warriors to give up horse thieving and adopt the far less interesting pursuits of farming and ranching.

But more promises were broken. The winter of 1886–87 brought even worse starvation, and in 1888 the people were reduced to eating their horses and dogs. Treaty or no treaty, they were subject to a genocide of irrational thoughtlessness, pushed and pulled by the whims of Central policies that seemed structured for defeat. Indians were never very interested in agriculture; cattle and horses were closer to their experience than planting and harvesting. When newly minted Indian Commissioner Hayter Reed determined in 1889 that Indian farmers, because they were "primitives," should farm by hand, using primitive methods, lunacy reigned. After having been told for years that they should adopt white agricultural practices, undertaking farming as a commercial enterprise, suddenly machinery and commerce were prohibited, and the First Peoples were instructed to behave as if they were farmers living before the age of tools and mechanization. Even successful Indians quit farming in disgust. Historian Sarah Carter, in *Lost Harvests*, contends that this Ottawa edict was not only a mad sociological experiment, but a deliberate policy meant to undermine ownership of their land. If they could farm only a quarter of their land, then eventually the surplus arable acres would revert to white control. Fortunately, in 1897 Reed was fired by the new Liberal minister of the interior, Clifford Sifton, and that was that.

Still, this was an example of the way the people were used as guinea pigs. Worst of all, their children were forcibly removed to residential schools, where an even more horrible destruction was benignly perpetrated. The schools exposed children to communicable diseases, and at some schools an unfathomable number of children died. At Old Sun, for example, 40 percent of the students died of tuberculosis, but because the deaths occurred after the students left (the school was careful to send them home once they got sick) the school itself was never held responsible. Almost every child who went to residential school contracted some form of tuberculosis, and families regularly lost children, so their mistrust of white institutions, and the white religions operating them, was no surprise.

When the First Peoples tried to live among whites, they were further degraded; systemic discrimination made it difficult for them to survive white treachery and expectation, and the contrast between "town" Indians and those who stayed away from their conquerers was remarkable. No matter where, survival was difficult. The people, poignantly, had to sell their resources to those who had displaced them. Some tribes operated sawmills; they sold land to the railway; they ran coal mines; they sold Christmas trees, berries, and firewood, their former wealth commodified for white settlers. And over all ruled the Indian agents, go-betweens, censors, bankers, moral and social arbiters, while the dictatorial and far-distant Indian Affairs Department simply had no conception of the habits and traditions of the people they controlled. They could not grasp the inherent difficulty of this adjustment or the peoples' ingrained resistance to being confined to one spot.

Added to these complexities, throughout the first half of the twentieth century, the people had to fight to hang on to their allocated reserves. If they weren't perceived as "using" the land, agents and settlers would try to persuade them to sell pieces of it. The Métis, too, were subject to erasure and "pacification," and although they were given scrip to settle their claim to the country, those lands were often cheated from them by unscrupulous land agents who subsequently resold the land to settlers. Contemporary events suggest that Alberta's dominant culture has still not figured out the language or the texture of First Nations values.

What has changed is that oil and gas findings have given some reserves tremendous wealth, leading to legal wrangles with the province and the federal government over land rights. Forest resources, too, have conferred economic wealth. Now Alberta's aboriginal people invest in real estate and rental properties, house construction, cattle and feedlot enterprises, grain-handling systems, film production, and even banking companies. There still exist tremendous inequities among reserves, and some are much more reliant on assistance than others. This economic impact, however, has given Alberta's First Peoples a new political awareness, so that no longer are white decrees necessarily accepted or believed. Several First Nations people have served as Alberta cabinet ministers and MLAs, an inside relation to government that has put their fingers on the pulse of power. Ralph Steinhauer was Alberta's first aboriginal lieutenant-governor. Overall, Alberta's First Peoples demonstrate increasing action and visibility, along with an energetic resistance that has grown out of their long oppression. And as one of the fastest-growing segments of Alberta's population, they have the numbers to change the face of this difficult province.

At the same time, some legal struggles have resulted in victorious recognition of First Nations' ownership. The Peigan band in southern Alberta was recently offered a federal/provincial deal to persuade the band to drop its lawsuit against both governments over the Oldman River Dam. The deal offered the band some $64 million, ten thousand acres of land, and an annual payout for use of Peigan land, at the same time claiming that Lethbridge Northern Irrigation District's water diversion system is essential to farming around the Oldman River, because food processing and intensive livestock farming rely on the irrigation system. Earlier, the construction of the Oldman River Dam had led to several protests—the Lonefighters Society unsuccessfully built their own diversion to try to turn the Oldman River away from the irrigation district. In 1990 the ever-attentive RCMP raided the reserve, charging people there with every possible crime and misdemeanour in order to disable the protests. The December 2000 settlement offer suggests that both levels of government recognize that they have not adequately recompensed the band for use of their lands, an ironic reversal of usual process.

Alcohol and drug-related deaths are extremely high for Alberta's aboriginals, who say that a strangling sense of hopelessness contributes to a despair that whites simply cannot understand. Suicide is a contemporary epidemic, often tied to alcohol, so much so that reserves are questioning whether or not they should try to ban alcohol. For example, the Siksika nation, some 2,500 residents, in southern Alberta, recorded seven people committing suicide (twenty times the national average, which is 13 per 100,000) and some 247 people attempting suicide in the last nine months of 2000. These horrific statistics are difficult to fathom, especially because most of the victims are young, as if the energy and drive of contemporary Alberta offer them nothing at all. Suicide rates have always been higher on Alberta reserves than for the general population, and despite "improved living conditions" are on the rise. The Alberta Advantage is advantageous for only a few.

Demolished by diseases like smallpox and tuberculosis, struggling with byzantine and ridiculous rules, fighting to stay alive, Alberta's First Peoples have enacted an astonishing feat by refusing to fade away and vanish. For all the deliberate or accidental attempts to erase their presence, the original inhabitants of Alberta mark this province as powerfully as any politician or historian. They colour the background of many Albertans, from Senator James Gladstone to Lieutentant-Governor Ralph Steinhauer to the Honourable Peter Lougheed to architect Douglas Cardinal. Ultimately, however much recent arrivals may claim this province, it has always been theirs.

5 | From Space to Territory

I would be quite willing, personally, to leave that whole country a wilderness for the next half century, but I fear if Englishmen do not go there, Yankees will.
—John A. Macdonald

My father's central Alberta farm wasn't large, only half a section, land divided by sloughs and windbreak rows into fields where we grew wheat, barley, oats—those civilized crops. There was a hayfield too, where clover burst tight and green, but for me as a child the most important part of the farm was the bush, a small chunk of land that had never been cleared. It was really a rough pasture for the cows to graze, but it managed to hold separate from the cleared land surrounding its dense tangle of growth, and to stay mysterious, even wild.

The bush was our Great Lone Land. We could discover there rare lady's slippers and huge puffballs, the pussy willows and the buffalo beans of spring. Coyotes lived there, mice and porcupines and skunks. We could build treehouses and forts, raft the green surface of the slough and hide from adults determined to give us chores. I thought the bush was still primeval forest, untouched.

It wasn't actually forest. It contained the common mix of central parkland growth, poplars and chokecherry and saskatoon bushes, willows, the tangle of wild roses. But in the middle of the bush was a huge pine tree that seemed like a beacon or landmark, that grew sturdy and untouchable, aloof. I believed that pine tree was the tallest tree in the world. I knew it had secrets, power, a connection with the landscape before any human had found it. In secret, I worshipped the pine tree, brought it small offerings, touched its bark, talked with it. It was a perfect tree, shapely and eloquent. The other growth of the bush was mongrel, unruly, without nobility.

I made the mistake of pointing out that tree, which was visible, its top rising in contrast to the rest of the bush, to a kid visiting from the city.

"Look," I said, "that's the tallest tree in the world."

He looked at me as if I were crazy.

"It is," I insisted.

"But," he said, "the poplar trees on either side are taller."

My eyes measured and compared, and the difference of the pine diminished.

He was right. And I hated him. For I had given this tree meaning and magic, made it a shrine in my universe, my wilderness, my territory.

• • •

Upper and Lower Canada began to develop opinions, even learned how to put on airs, and their merger in 1840 into one province, "Canada," gave them the confidence to believe that they were finally somewhere, a real place. A cookbook addressed to the "taste, habits, and degrees of luxury of the Canadian public" was published; systematic colonization was under way; cholera made its terrible immigration voyage; York was incorporated as Toronto; Upper Canada went through spates of rebellion and invasion; and Canada issued its first threepence postage stamp, sporting that infamous hewer of wood, the beaver. William Wordsworth and Herman Melville, Franz Liszt and Robert Schumann, Florence Nightingale and chloroform were changing the world. And in 1854 Prince Albert appeared in public wearing a hat made not of beaver but silk.

Once the West had stopped being Rupert's Land and become something known as "the Territories," it was subject to the influx and infiltration that happens to territories everywhere. England and the United States both started eyeing what had earlier seemed like an endless, uninhabitable tract of land riddled with beaver dams, and instead began to calculate its value as a potential space for settlers, gold mines, and other pipe dreams. The Americans who trekked over the Oregon Trail managed to oust the all-powerful Hudson's Bay Company. And Central Canada, now feeling that it was a nation-in-waiting, began to take a proprietorial interest in the West when before it had been a territory to avoid, much as Europeans on the Trans-Canada claim that they can sleep from Winnipeg to Calgary.

Until 1850 the West, to most whites, was shrouded in mystery, a wilderness beyond both Canadian and European imaginations, populated by nomadic natives and secretive Métis. The trading centres were little more than one or two log cabins, and the only white residents were fur traders, explorers, missionaries, and the occasional adventurer. But such a place also had romantic appeal, and from the mid-1800s onward travellers began to eye it as a challenge, a source of high adventure, a destination. Almost everyone visiting the "Great Lone Land" relied on the hospitality of Edmonton House, the fort in the heart of the wilderness, stockaded and rustic, but a source of food and shelter, a jumping-off place. Chief factor John Rowand's hospitality was as famous as his fierce ledger-keeping and his terrible temper, and under his rule Edmonton House became a considerable establishment. Traders and HBC employees passed through, going east and west, natives came to trade, boats arrived with goods bound for the Athabasca and departed loaded with furs for York Factory. Edmonton was more than a trading post, it was a food depot, a boat-building centre, a gathering point, the high spot on every adventurer's list of bed-and-breakfasts.

By this time, American settlement threatened to move into and engulf the British prairies—that is, if the British did not actually begin to demonstrate interest. But official gestures were lazy and expensive. The Hudson's Bay Company, which had monopolized the West since 1821, was now facing free and illicit traders who simply ignored the company's privilege. Governor Simpson could rage and froth as much as he wanted, blame "the Americans and their half-breed allies," but the West was beginning to exercise what would become a tradition of subversion. In England the Hudson's Bay Company was having to defend its monopoly, its cavalier treatment of Indian and Métis people, its antagonism to settlement. Meanwhile, in Upper Canada (or Canada West, as the Centrals began to call themselves after 1841—why is it that the word "West" has so much romance, so much beautiful resonance?) newspaperman George Brown declaimed about the necessity of Canada's extending its borders to the Pacific—to him, all that territory was like honey in a beehive.

Suddenly Canada West decided that the Territories should be theirs, not a loose region ripe for American picking, not a rich hinterland belonging to that old imperialist counting house, the Hudson's Bay Company. Fur, although it was a victim of fashion's caprice and no longer such a hot commodity, began to fly. Settlers in Red River, the Manitoba colony struggling on despite failing crops and difficult times, made it obvious that either the British or the Canadian government would have to take a stand on the issue of settlement. The Hudson's Bay Company was no longer undisputed lord of the West, and settlement and its terrible complexities became a driving issue. But the West was a conundrum, a storied area full of weather and wind. Would it actually allow itself to be settled, or would it resist, starve anyone who tried to touch it with a plough? Every traveller and expert who set foot in the Great Lone Land had an opinion he was more than willing to share.

One of the most famous visitors was artist Paul Kane, who "determined to devote whatever talents and proficiency I possessed to the painting of a series of pictures illustrative of the North American Indians and scenery." That he conflates Indians and scenery is evidence of the common attitude toward what were considered the two most intriguing aspects of the West. Scenery and Indians were repeatedly lumped together, objects of every outsider's bright-eyed curiosity. Rupert's Land called like a siren, and although Kane was strongly advised against trying to enter that "forbidding" territory, he persisted and, having successfully gained an interview with Sir George Simpson, persuaded him that a hitchhiking artist was not a complete burden to the fur brigades. Simpson agreed that Kane could go along to Winnipeg, and if all went well he might then, with the aid and succour of the company, proceed farther west.

So on May 9, 1846, Kane set out from Upper Canada with Simpson. Left behind at the Sault, Kane was able to commandeer canoe and company assistance all the way to Red River and beyond. Impressed by Kane's determination, Simpson ("I have to request the favor of your showing that gentleman [Kane] your kind attention and the hospitalities of such of the Company's posts as he may visit; and you will be pleased to afford Mr. Kane passages from post to post in the Company's craft—free of charge") gave Kane entrée, and he used it effectively.

Kane's thirst for experience served him well. South of the Pembina, "very anxious to witness buffalo hunting," he met a Métis hunting party. When they found a large herd, Kane joined the chase and, although he was thrown from his horse, instantly remounted, determined to make a kill. He shot a huge bull, and then dismounted to make a sketch of the animal, who stood pawing the ground. When the wounded bull charged, Kane leapt to his horse, and only when the bull stumbled back to the herd was Kane able to recover both his gun and his sketchbook, along with a nice story. Like many travellers, Kane was intrepid and foolish, but since he was young and strong, he survived, and witnessing a buffalo hunt in one of the last years of the great herds provided with him an indelible memory.

But Kane was not satisfied with merely having reached the plains below Fort Garry. Full of romantic images of "wild tribes," he wanted to travel the westerly stretch of the prairies. Kicking around Norway House, waiting for the

Saskatchewan brigade to return from Fort York, he dismissed the Cree who lived there as "rather diminutive in comparison with those who inhabit the plains." How did he know? He hadn't yet reached the plains, but he had already decided what version of "noble savage" he wanted to encounter. Kane demonstrated a lively interest in the physical attributes of the men he met. He particularly admired a Métis voyageur named Paulet Paul, saying that he was "certainly one of the finest formed men I ever saw, and when naked, no painter could desire a finer model." Kane's interest may have been professional, but then again, the West offered a freedom from social strictures that permitted Kane's aesthetic sensibilities full flight.

With square, noisy John Rowand, Kane set out from Norway House in the York boat fleet, progressing up the Grand Rapids and westward, with Kane drawing various portraits, enjoying the "danger from the Blackfeet," and commenting on both wildlife and the open scenery. At Fort Carlton, Kane met Wesleyan missionary Robert Rundle, and the three men, Rowand, Kane, and Rundle, together decided to take a shortcut and travel on horseback cross-country to Fort Edmonton. On that journey, Kane witnessed a different kind of buffalo hunt, where the buffalo were driven into a stone pound and then killed. Kane complained that the Indians wasted the buffalo by killing too many this way; but it is clear that his romantic spirit preferred the excitement of the hunt on horseback. Enjoying various hunting and horse adventures, the men stopped briefly at Fort Pitt, and three days later reached the palisade of Fort Edmonton.

Eager to cross the Rockies, Kane did not linger at Fort Edmonton but joined a cavalcade west. As they proceeded up the Athabasca River, the weather grew steadily colder, and Kane commented sourly on the scenery: "This is the most monotonous river that ever I have met with in my travels. Nothing but point after point appearing, all thickly covered with pine, any extensive view being entirely out of the question." Kane was less interested in the landscape than in the "views" it was supposed to provide him with. Only when he saw the vista of the Rockies did he begin to cheer up. They reached Jasper House, "three miserable log huts," and then on snowshoes they crossed the Athabasca Pass and rolled themselves downhill to Boat Encampment in present-day BC.

Kane spent the remainder of the winter and the following summer on the West Coast, only undertaking another mountain crossing east very late in the fall of

1847. The Pacific slope of the Athabasca Pass was daunting, and the cold overwhelmed Kane's appreciation of the surrounding beauty; "last night was the coldest I ever camped out," he complained on November 3. The lateness of the season kept them at Jasper House until the Athabasca River froze hard enough to support travel. Only on November 14 could they set out, their supplies pulled by sled dogs. But although the lakes were frozen, the rivers were not, and their journey was perilous, with the dogs barely surviving. Kane suffered terribly from *mal de racquet*, a sharp pain in the instep of the foot, caused by an amateur's wearing snowshoes. The small party made it to Fort Assiniboine, where they were able to rest and recover, gorging themselves on whitefish and sleeping for a few days before proceeding to Fort Edmonton.

Kane arrived at Fort Edmonton on December 5, 1846, and settled in for an Alberta winter, replete with both work and comfort. Provisions were plentiful, buffalo ranged close to the fort, and to Kane's delight seven of "the most important and warlike tribes on the continent are in constant communication with the fort." Kane had reached his own version of heaven, and over the winter he sported and sketched, hunted and relaxed. He killed a buffalo so large that its head weighed 202 pounds—which he had stuffed and mounted and took back East with him. And he celebrated Christmas in the northwest manner, his famous description of that holiday perhaps the first writing that gives Edmonton the honour of a place, with a style and tradition. Their appetites sharpened by the minus-forty-degree temperature outside, Kane, Mr. Thebo (the Roman Catholic missionary from Manitou Lake, about thirty miles away), HBC chief Harriet and his clerks, and missionary Rundle feasted on boiled buffalo hump, boiled buffalo calf, dried moose nose, whitefish browned in buffalo marrow, buffalo tongue, beaver tails, roast wild goose, potatoes, and turnips. After dinner all the "inmates of the fort" were invited in, and although few of the locals spoke English, that did not prevent Kane from joining the celebratory dancing: "another lady with whom I sported the light fantastic toe, whose poetic name was Cun-ne-wa-bum, or 'One that looks at the Stars,' was a half-breed Cree girl; and I was so much struck by her beauty that I prevailed upon her to promise to sit for her likeness, which she afterwards did with great patience, holding her fan, which was made of the tip end of swan's wing with an ornamental handle of porcupine's quills." The subsequent portrait shows a beautiful woman indeed, her appearance possibly coloured by Kane's perspective, but nevertheless as seductive a face as any to be found in the world.

That winter, Kane made one dogsled expedition downriver to Fort Pitt, where he stayed for a month, and another upriver to Rocky Mountain House. On May 25, with the eastward-bound Saskatchewan brigade, he began his journey back to Upper Canada, where he complained that the "greatest hardship I had to endure, was the difficulty I found in trying to sleep in a civilised bed." He had truly been seduced by the West.

Where are Kane's paintings now? Mostly in Orange, Texas, in Toronto, and in Ottawa, where tourists and Centrals gaze at the world they depict and imagine that it is still the same now, romantic and forbidding. Only occasionally in the shadowy depths of the canvases do we catch a glimpse of spontaneous motion. Even more seldom, as in the lurid glare of *A Prairie on Fire*, is a tinge of Kane's own awed incomprehension of this untameable world captured.

• • •

Visitors to the West proliferated. Interest in the Territories was piqued and debates about their suitability for settlement and farming continued. Sir John Richardson, who crossed a part of Rupert's Land on a search for the lost Franklin expedition as early as 1852, took an authoritative position: "From Fort Edmonton down to Carlton, . . . a range of five hundred miles, the country and climate invite the husbandman and the plough." Indeed? Did Richardson stop to break some ground, or did he proceed from an imagination that he must have relied on to fuel his own futile search for another Englishman determined to enter this landscape the English way?

The missionaries had by then begun to infiltrate the territory with their conversions and proselytizations—Wesleyan Robert Rundle and his cat, James Evans and his Methodism, Father Bourassa and Father Taché with their desire to convert northern Alberta to a Catholic heaven. Civilization was stretching its well-meaning fingers west, and no matter how the Hudson's Bay Company resisted religious men and speculative settlers, their iron hold over Rupert's Land was loosening.

The dispute over Oregon had made everybody nervous. When the Hudson's Bay Company succeeded in losing everything south of the forty-ninth parallel, the

British began to worry about the West falling under the spell of the Americans. Along with finally reconsidering the Hudson's Bay Charter, they commissioned the Palliser expedition, the first concrete demonstration of official interest in the land between Red River and the Rockies. Palliser's Report was the first of many external reports interested in dictating the future of the West, and it helped to initiate the West's skepticism and mistrust of external "experts" who visited in order to tell the West what is good for the West, experts who are still making these pilgrimages.

Captain John Palliser himself was a man of many parts. Although he has been described variously as a geographer and civil servant, he was really an Irish country gentleman, relative of many earls, conservative to a fault, a man of Anglican leanings, tall, with good connections, who owned not just land but "estates." He conducted his education at Trinity College in Dublin itinerantly, with results so desultory that he was "cautioned." He had a good voice, could play the piano and pray with equal energy, was well travelled, and could manage German, French, and Italian. No Cree. Not one First Nations language. That was the province of the Métis and fur traders.

Palliser's life was consumed with travel and sport—especially hunting. He and his friends had particular opinions about colonization, botany, and mountaineering, as if they were all equally *sportif*, marvellously available to gentlemen in search of thrills. Palliser had first sought North American adventure in 1847, on an expedition to hunt bear and buffalo. He had so much fun and was so taken with the American West that he was determined to return.

Palliser proposed to the Royal Geographical Society an expedition to "survey" a part of North America, "from the headwaters of the Assiniboine River to the foot of the Rocky Mountains, and from the northern branch of the Saskatchewan to the 49th parallel of latitude." Palliser drew a dotted line west across the most recent map of British North America and said, "That's where I want to go," and sure enough, the government invested his joyride with all the weight of a "scientific enterprise."

Why was Palliser put in charge? He had little science, was fairly lax in discipline, enjoyed flattery, and was easily influenced by the Hudson's Bay Company and Sir George Simpson. Perhaps the HBC encouraged his appointment because they knew he would not describe the company's practices too negatively. Palliser hated rows, loved jokes, was not ruthless but rather easygoing, all traits that probably contributed to the survival of the expedition. But why would the British government endow a man of such careless aptitude with such power? Because he was not invested in the controversy over the future of British North America? Or because he was just the right kind of man—aristocratic, with a passing interest in science and the "wilderness"—who happened to be in the right place at the right time?

The real question the expedition was asked to answer was the question of settlement. Were the Western plains suitable for farming? And if the British didn't get there soon, would the Americans sneak in and take over the "British" West? Was the Hudson's Bay Company a good steward of this huge tract of land? What about the mythical tribes of nomads

Glenbow Archives, Calgary, Canada: NA-3148-1

Peter Erasmus, the Métis man who guided more lost white men than anyone else

whose land it really was? What about the new nation of Métis people who were rising in social and political strength? What about the lack of communication between the prairies and the Pacific coast? What was out there?

While Palliser planned his expedition, the Select Committee on the Hudson's Bay Company met, arguing over the great northwest, full of opinions and advice. The committee's contentious findings—that the Hudson's Bay charter be renewed, but with caution—probably encouraged support for Palliser's venture. Finally, the funds for the expedition were approved on the basis that this country was "almost unknown," terra incognita. Were the current maps correct? Where exactly was that forty-ninth parallel that was supposed to keep the Americans south?

These colonial committees laboured under their own ignorance. David Thompson's work was forgotten; shockingly, the British had never heard of him, had never seen his magnificent map. Most offensive of all, Governor Simpson, when asked about Thompson's cartographical work, described it as "worthless," probably because Thompson had left the Hudson's Bay Company for the Nor'Westers. Peter Fidler's work, too, was unknown. The bewigged members of the Royal Geographical Society and the Colonial Office had no idea that Thompson and Joseph Howse, fifty years earlier, had crossed the Rocky Mountains, nor any idea of what the Rocky Mountains were. The British once again demonstrated the predictable nature of colonial bigotry: only one of their own, a British expedition, could possibly give them accurate information.

So Palliser was chosen, and the expedition mounted, ostensibly by the Colonial Office; but to complicate matters the scientists with Palliser also took orders from their various mentors within the Royal Geographical Society. In the beginning everyone argued about who would pony up the funds; however, imperial challenge won, and the undersecretary of state pushed through treasury support. Of course, there were plenty of political motives as well, but they were best left unspoken. In the end, the expedition cost £13,000, which made the Colonial Office see first purple and then red.

Meanwhile, various knowledgeable men and scientists were consulted, various characters examined, their physical and moral attributes checked against the expectations of the day, and finally the expedition members were chosen, five men who could be considered a metaphor for nineteenth-century rectitude. The Swiss botanist Eugene Bourgeau, who pined for mountains, was kind and enthusiastic, and enjoyed his botanical tasks. On the expedition, he collected twenty-two packets of dried plants and 110 different seeds. He spoke no English, and so got along well with the Métis, who appreciated his enthusiasm and his reverence for plants. He also became fast friends with Father Lacombe, who by that time had made the West his permanent home. In contrast, the magnetical observer, Thomas Blakiston, was an English zealot who made everyone's life miserable. He was grumpy throughout, and by the end happy to leave.

James Hector, a naturalist-geologist from Edinburgh, did most of the expedition's scientific work. The tough little Scot, actually trained as a doctor, was far more interested in geology than medicine, and overall showed himself to be wise and tolerant. John Sullivan, who served as astronomer and secretary, was an Irish mathematician, and assistant master of a nautical school at Greenwich. Easygoing and somewhat inexperienced, he garnered most of Blakiston's scorn and the two became bitter enemies. Not quite a ship of fools. More like a party of innocent savants, armed with the scientific knowledge of the day but hampered by the difference between what they expected to find and what they did find.

These gentlemen were to recruit their assistants, boot polishers and carriers, guides and hunters, locally, which meant that they needed the co-operation of the HBC, a nice way of putting the expedition in the company's debt. At last, gathered and commissioned, they were just about to sail when Palliser contracted typhoid fever and they were delayed. Finally, on May 21, 1857, they left—except for Blakiston, who was to follow on an HBC ship.

They had been charged with examining the route between the head of the Great Lakes and the Red River settlement, with examining the southern prairies, and with discovering a suitable pass through the Rocky Mountains—repeating already accomplished work. They were also required to record features and agricultural details, flora and fauna, geology and climate, and most of all, to keep careful daily records, which they did not manage to do. It is difficult, from a contemporary perspective, not to laugh at the craziness of this endeavour—the Colonial Office sending out a party to record a country that they had trouble seeing except with their particular bias. They learned an enormous amount, that much is true, but while the tendency is to read the Palliser Report as a description and explanation, it might be better read as a report on the education of five Europeans who encountered a world beyond their imagining. That their report was referred to as gospel by other newcomers—the Mounties, the railway—is even more laughable. And in the end, it was something of a hodgepodge, field reports and journals mixed with descriptions and maps. There are errors that occasionally put forts or camps in the middle of the prairies instead of west of the Rockies, that confuse the Porcupine Hills with the Cypress Hills, that mismeasure the heights of mountains. Recorded distances do not always match with where the expedition went, and even today scholars argue about which coulee is where, and which boulders they actually saw.

They in fact did little "discovery and exploration," but travelled on well-established trails, generally the easiest contour of land that the people native to the country had been using for years. Those same trails, which have subsequently been adopted by railways and highways, still whisper under our feet. They had the wherewithal to hire guides who knew the country intimately, first James McKay, a Métis trader and later Manitoba MLA, who led them across Manitoba and Saskatchewan to Fort Carlton, where they spent their first winter, later Peter Erasmus, who was engaged by and travelled with Dr. Hector from 1858 until August 1859. What Hector "discovered" is largely attributable to this astonishing Métis interpreter, guide, hunter, freighter, builder, horseman, traveller, and native to the West.

At Fort Carlton that first winter, they hunkered down and sent letters off to London complaining that they needed more men and more money. To press his case and ask for money for a third season (they had initially planned only two), Palliser went back to New York and New Orleans—but that journey seems to have been undertaken for his own pleasure and to provide the service of carrying mail for various important personages. He probably looked around the few huts of Fort Carlton and thought, "I'm not staying here all winter. I had better find an excuse to return East." Palliser's report accusing the Red River Colony of laziness and lack of diligence infuriated the residents of Red River. But his letters must have been persuasive, because the Colonial Office promised him more money. In the sociable Centre, Palliser wined and dined with Simpson in Montreal and other officials in Toronto. He also conferred with Dr. John Rae, later of Arctic renown. Rae was considered an expert on the prairies even though he had hardly spent any time there. Finally Palliser rejoined his party at Fort Carlton, who, locked together all winter, quarrelled mightily. Blakiston felt that no one was working hard enough, Hector hated Blakiston's sarcasm, Sullivan was not sufficiently assiduous, and Bourgeau took refuge in his own language and his botanical samples. Relations with the Hudson's Bay Company people, on whom they relied, were no better. Bored and hungry, they suffered from a severe bout of cabin fever. Hector had been the most assiduous, actually getting to Fort Edmonton and Rocky Mountain House, and thus becoming the first member of the expedition to travel into Alberta. He had been sent ahead to hire Métis men for the coming season of work, and he had the happy experience of spending the New Year at Fort Edmonton, a carefree, celebratory time. Hector also seemed the most adaptable, claiming that he was never so cold in the northwest as he had been at home in Edinburgh, a truism that most

Captain John Palliser and Sir James Hector. Did they know what they were looking at?

people from the prairie, who know the difference beween dry cold and damp, could endorse. Following the North Saskatchewan River back to meet his colleagues, Hector mapped its progress, but of course it had been mapped—quite accurately—before.

That second journey west was rough going for Palliser. The ice had not yet left the rivers, and Palliser's horses were in poor shape. He finally got back to Fort Carlton, where he had to organize the work for the coming season and play peacemaker between the irritated men. In mid-June 1858, the crew set off west, and finally reached Alberta, crossing the Battle River, passing Buffalo Lake, crossing the Red Deer River, and stopping to hunt buffalo close to the present-day site of Irricana.

From there they divided, Palliser and Sullivan going south to Big Chief Mountain, actually south of the border, Bourgeau and Hector going up the Bow River. While Bourgeau stopped to record botanical observations, Hector wandered around in the mountains, following different divides, until he crossed over Bow Pass, then went west along the Howse River and down the North Saskatchewan to Edmonton. His most interesting story was about his getting soundly kicked by his horse, so soundly kicked that his guides—these were visitors, always guided—were sure he was dead. Legend has it that they were about to shovel dirt over his body in a shallow grave when he winked at them. That narrow escape gave its name to the Kicking Horse River and the subsequent pass that the railway would use, although Hector was skeptical about the possibility of building a railway linking the Pacific and the Atlantic.

Blakiston, meanwhile, was supposed to explore the mountain passes to the south, but he was in a foul temper and chose not to follow directions but rather to explore the passes known to the Kootenay Indians. He crossed the Oldman and the Crowsnest rivers, then went over the mountains via the North Kootenay Pass, down the Kootenay River and into the United States. He came back over the South Kootenay Pass and into Waterton Lake before returning to Edmonton, grumbling all the way.

Palliser himself crossed the Rockies using the Kananaskis Pass, also called Stunning Pass, stunningly beautiful to this day. Originally Palliser had planned to meet Captain Hawkins of the International Boundary Commission, but the Kootenay Indians refused to guide him south, so he was forced to return to the foothills and wend his way north, via the present-day site of Calgary, along the old Middle Blackfoot trail. None of his travels was very original.

Back in Edmonton, the impatient Blakiston declared that he was leaving the expedition, thus disqualifying himself from service with the Colonial Office. He spent the winter waiting at Red River, and then returned to England. Meanwhile, the remaining members of the expedition waited out the winter of 1858–59 in Fort Edmonton. Other English adventurers, hunters, and thrill-seekers had worked their way to the fort, and two of them, Arthur Brisco and William Mitchell, joined Palliser's party. Palliser and his buddies spent the winter hunting and "getting ready" for the following summer, which really meant hiring Indians and Métis to work for them and tell them where to go. Hector spent the winter testing various routes along the foothills of the mountains. He was the most enthusiastic member of the expedition, the most engaged with the country he was visiting. Sullivan and Bourgeau looked after their horses and whiled away the time. They were all entertained by the grand ball that Palliser and Mrs. Christie, the wife of the factor, threw at Christmas. Bourgeau enjoyed working as both carpenter and cook, but in the spring he returned to England.

When the expedition set out in May 1859, they were eighteen strong, a collection of Métis and Americans, even a Dutchman and a Canadian. Palliser followed the Blackfoot Trail south, rounded Buffalo Lake and headed to the Hand Hills. The Blackfoot, again at war with the Cree, were not happy to see the Stoney Indians who travelled with the expedition, and their war-like gestures made the whole group nervous. Palliser hadn't brought enough presents, and even his Indian guides were reluctant to go on. Finally Palliser simply insisted, and they followed the Red Deer River east, Palliser under the mistaken assumption that the landscape was similar to an area he had examined more than a hundred miles away. They went all the way to the Cypress Hills, then split up, Palliser and Sullivan travelling west. Intent on finding a route to the coast, they muddled around in southern BC. Meanwhile, Hector actually found a route through the Rockies, Howse Pass, which the Indians knew well and which David Thompson had used. Then they all met up again, dawdled around Victoria, went down to California, and finally returned to England, mission accomplished.

Much has been made of Palliser's expedition, how they visited most of Alberta, covered the arms of the North Saskatchewan River and crossed the mountains at six different passes. True, they passed through a lot of territory, but their work in no way matched Thompson's and Fidler's; and for all their adventurousness, they relied on guides who knew far more than they did. The documented result of their travels was a generalized account that has coloured readings of the West to this day, not a favour but a curse. Yes, the expedition confirmed certain geographical features, corrected and amended inaccurate mappings; their latitudes were relatively accurate, but their longitudes, because of inaccurate chronometers, were wildly out. Hector's challenge of the earlier reported heights of the Rocky Mountains was probably the most enduring legacy—his mapping of the Rockies south of Athabasca Pass was commendable, even trustworthy, and his geological sections especially contributed to real knowledge. But overall, Palliser's report was useful only insofar as it documented what had formerly been orally communicated in people's memories and thoughts.

Producing the report took some time, during which Palliser, having overspent his budget in the tradition of every good government employee, had to beg for more support. It is interesting to note the contrast between Palliser's delight in throwing huge balls at every outpost—he threw not only the Christmas ball at Edmonton but one for the whole city of Victoria!—and his inability to balance his budget. For years after his return to England, the HBC sent acrimonious letters about how much he owed them. With few friends left in the Colonial Office, Palliser had to argue for the value of his work. His bills were outrageous—for everything from the balls he loved to the cost of instruments, to the cost of his horses. The HBC was annoyed at his claiming to have made discoveries that their employees had long ago made, and there were repeated questions about whether the government had got its money's worth. Palliser was seen as an adventurer, a man with a lust for travel who had protracted the expedition just to have fun. Poor Palliser, first to freeze and burn and suffer, and then to come home, not a conquering hero, but an embezzler of public funds for a wilderness lark. He did win some gold medals, and when his massive Report was ultimately published, scientists consulted it avidly. Fittingly, Palliser died in debt, leaving not much in Ireland, but his name all over Western Canada.

Ultimately Palliser is best known for his famous triangle, the stretch of land from the forty-ninth parallel to the fifty-second, and from longitude 100 degrees to 114 degrees west:

> ...let us imagine a line drawn from 60 miles south of Fort Carlton,
> which is on the verge of the great prairies, to [southern Saskatchewan],
> and thence produced to the site of old Bow Fort. This line marks the
> boundary of two natural divisions of the country, viz., the ancient for-
> est lands and the true prairie district. To the north of this line gener-
> ally there is timber, a good soil for agricultural purposes up to 54

degrees north latitude, and superior pasturage; to the south there is no timber, the soil is sandy, with little or no admixture of earthy matter, and the pasture is inferior. Exceptions of course may be found, as for example in the neighbourhood of swamps and gullies, where the soil and pasture are better.

It is true that the area has suffered drought and devastation, but Palliser ascribed to the prairie characteristics of infertility and aridity that it still fights. Why not call it lush and open, with soft breezes and the chirping of gophers? John Palliser would have needed a different imagination.

Palliser believed that Canada could not govern the West and that the HBC could not maintain its monopoly. He suggested that the West be retained by England as a separate colony, which, if his recommendation had been followed, would have made for a very different Canada, and possibly the West as an independent country. The British did not bite. The West was too much territory, and neither the British nor the Canadians were anxious to subsidize the transportation system that would be needed to "civilize" that space. Most particularly, the British did not want to shoulder the burden of the government and defence of Rupert's Land. And so, to prevent the United States from taking over, a negative motivation, it was left to the nascent government of Canada to annex the West.

• • •

Not to be outdone, the Centrals, under the sponsorship of the Canadian government, sent out their own expedition to report on conditions in the West and to construct a map. George Gladman was in command, but most of the work was carried out by geologists Henry Youle Hind and Simon Dawson, who was also a professional surveyor. Their mandate was to determine whether agriculture was feasible and a transportation link from Canada possible. In the end their report more or less concurred with Palliser's delineation of fertile and arid belts.

Henry Youle Hind's *Narrative of the Canadian Red River Exploring Expedition of 1857 and of the Assinniboine and Saskatchewan Exploring Expedition of 1858* records some interesting First Nations perspectives on the HBC and the coming of the white man to the West. The expedition was mostly concerned with topographical and geological features, particularly the forces that had shaped the beautiful river valleys. Hind described the area south of the North Saskatchewan River as "the Great American Desert," but also argued that the "fertile belt" could be "settled and cultivated from a few miles west of the Lake of the Woods to the passes of the Rocky Mountains and any line of communication whether by waggon road or railroad, passing through it, will eventually enjoy the great advantage of being fed by an agricultural population from one extremity to another."

A confident if not arrogant professor of chemistry at Trinity College in Toronto, Hind perceived the West in a way that reflects a newly minted Central Canadian nationalism, eager to see the West annexed to the burgeoning aspirations of Canada. His description of the prairie betrays that occupying impulse. "The vast ocean of level prairie which lies to the west of Red River must be seen in its extraordinary aspects, before it can be rightly valued and understood in reference to its future occupation by an energetic and civilised race." Obviously he thought the race that already occupied the prairie was neither energetic nor civilized.

In 1859–60 the Earl of Southesk, a weedy Scottish aristocrat, travelled west for adventure as a variation on the European grand tour. Self-described as a "prisoner of civilisation," he looked to the West to provide him with a combination of health spa and good hunting. His elaborately eloquent paean to his trip was titled *Saskatchewan and the Rocky Mountains*. Advised to veer south from Jasper House and then into the front ranges of the Rockies to encounter terrain that had not been seen by white eyes (which was probably untrue), the well-guided Southesk (he travelled with no fewer than ten men) comforted himself with the splendid aspects of nature. On first seeing the Rocky Mountains, he described them as "a glorious sight, stretching along the horizon as far as eye could reach. Below us rolled the river among dark pines, hills then for many miles, then the foothills of the loftier range, and then uprose the mountains themselves, rugged and peaked and scored with gashes; not magnified hills but rocks in very archetype, steeped in a soft mellow gray against the blue sky, with masses of snow glittering in the sunlight." Probably hearing coyotes, he reported, "The little wolves kept up a chorus all night long, beginning each fresh strain with mewing whines, like a family of peevish kittens, then bursting into tremulous, melancholy howls. The effect was very pleasing; it harmonised so well with the savage loneliness of the scene, that I should have been sorry to miss this wild wolfish music." Southesk marked his name on various fir trees and recorded every event with a romantic's eye. On saying goodbye to this wonderful scenery, he refused to use the word "forever," asking, "Who can tell what powers of travel the spirit may have after death?" Southesk was an early example of the starry-eyed tourists who still flock to the Rockies, eager for respite and succour, determined to see a bear and buy a postcard and claim that they have climbed a mountain.

Albertans could be forgiven for wishing that tourists like this might be eaten by bears. From the 1850s onwards, the West's "pristine wilderness," suffered an influx of such romantic ninnies, ostensibly serving some scientific purpose or another. Viscount Milton and Dr. Walter Cheadle were exactly this type of wealthy Victorian tourist. Milton was a pale and pugnacious young aristocrat who, with Cheadle, his personal physician and tutor, claimed to be in search of the most direct route through British territory to the gold regions of the Cariboo, although the real purpose of their journey was pleasure. The account of their 1862–63 expedition, *The North-West Passage by Land*, was published in 1865.

They asserted that one of their principal objectives was to draw attention to the importance of establishing a highway from the Atlantic to the Pacific, not only to connect the different English colonies in North America but to afford more direct communication with China and Japan. Their trip was further justified by their interest in colonization, and they described the West as "65,000 square miles of a country of unsurpassed fertility, and abounding in mineral wealth, [which] lies isolated from the world, neglected, almost unknown, although destined, at no distant period perhaps, to become one of the most valuable possessions of the British Crown." They were correct about the area's value, and they noted too the Hudson's Bay Company's lack of interest in settlement. "It is the interest and policy of the Company to discourage emigration, and keep the country as one vast preserve for fur-bearing animals."

While these two had much to say about the monopoly of the HBC, Milton and Cheadle's own unexamined privilege was evident in their enjoyment of the exciting prospects of a buffalo hunt and in their description of the rustic balls held in their honour (although they were expected to supply the rum). Nor did they hesitate to pass judgement on whether northwest women were good-looking. Their incidental comments show exactly their presumptions. They remarked that Indian children seldom cried, and that wives and children looked up to their husbands and fathers with respect, which Milton and Cheadle approved of. After a tedious buffalo hunt, with many setbacks, they declared with gusto that "truly the pleasures of eating are utterly unknown in civilised life." They must have been, for the first time in their lives, hungry.

Despite having excellent guides, they proceeded by trial and error, frostbite and mishap. They suffered from snowshoe lameness and "bachelor disorder," whatever that was. At one point, there was nothing for it but the homesick Milton simply had to make a plum pudding—after sifting out fruit and flour and sugar, which were mixed at the bottom of a box with loose shot, caps, fragments of tobacco, and other dust and grime. When they were bored, they tried to train their dog, Rover. They actually noticed the real threat of looming starvation for the native inhabitants. "The days when it was possible to live in plenty by the gun and net alone, have already gone by on the North Saskatchewan." Only a few buffalo remained, and they were hard to hunt.

Their incidental descriptions are the most interesting part of their narrative. At one point along the trail, they passed a team of dogs standing frozen, stark and stiff in their harness. They discovered that a skunk skin served as an effective weather-glass—when it warmed up it stank—and they learned that the Indians used the scent gland as a cure for headache. Cheadle, as a doctor, was frequently consulted on medical ailments and did his best to cure everything, implying all the while the superiority of English medicines.

Arriving at Fort Edmonton on May 14, 1862, they described the fort not as the rough, sprawling stockade that it was, but "prettily situated on a high cliff overhanging the river on the northern side." Their time there appeared to be as delightful a diversion as the rest of their journey. Richard Hardisty, the chief trader, gave them every kindness and hospitality. They visited Father Lacombe, compared stories with miners from White Mud Creek, who were panning for gold dust, and heard tales of other gold-seeking Americans who were beginning to come through. They traipsed out to St. Albert looking for bears, but "the bears had evidently left the neighbourhood." Still, and probably because they did no work, they found day-to-day life at the fort monotonous, and required constant amusement. "We wandered from one window to another, or walked around the building, watching for the arrival of Indians, or the sight of some object of speculation or interest."

Setting out from Fort Edmonton in that spring of 1862, Milton and Cheadle had supplies consisting of two sacks of flour of a hundred pounds each; four bags of pemmican of ninety pounds each; tea, salt, and tobacco, the latter the only luxuries they could afford. "We were ignorant of how long the journey would take," they declared. The fact was that they were merely ignorant. The journey, from St. Albert to Lac Ste. Anne, through dense bush to the Pembina River, followed a trail just one horse wide, encumbered with roots and fallen trees. Their horses sank up to their hocks and floundered through bogs. They crossed the Macleod and Athabasca rivers, and from a bare knoll got their first thrilling glimpse of the Rocky Mountains. After three weeks they reached Jasper House, which they described as sitting in a perfect garden of wildflowers. They stumbled on, from one post to the next, and by July 9 discovered that they had crossed the height of land and gained the watershed of the Pacific.

Milton and Cheadle, for all the popularity of their account, were rich, lazy Englishmen whose trip was a comedy of errors. They named mountains after each other, set forests on fire, had to kill one of their horses for food, and would have perished had it not been for their native guides. The true mark of their origins is best summarized by Cheadle's putting his boots outside the door of the tent one night, expecting them, the next morning, to be clean and polished.

Milton and Cheadle were but the forerunners of the remittance men (Englishmen whose families regularly remitted funds to them for their support) and carpetbaggers who would flood west, determined to make their fortunes. The prospectors were already on their way. News of gold in the rivers of British Columbia brought all kinds of people through Edmonton, some of them genuine workers, some of them speculators. In 1862, when the Cariboo Gold Rush made Barkerville the largest city north of San Francisco and west of Chicago, the whole of the northwest felt the reverberations.

Miners and adventurers from the East gathered at Fort Garry, near Winnipeg, and dreaming of gold, decided to travel via the oxen-powered squeaky-wheeled wooden Red River carts across the prairies to the Cariboo. These 175 men split into roughly two groups, both leaving Fort Garry in June 1862. Because they chose to follow the old fur-trade route, these gold seekers, most of them from Ontario, were called the Overlanders. And they weren't all men. Catherine Schubert, who accompanied her husband, brought along their three small children. At Edmonton they rested and assembled provisions for the long trek to Lac Ste. Anne, Jasper, and then through the mountains to Kamloops. Some exchanged their carts for horses. Edmonton began to take on the air of a supply station, a point of departure, a role it would continue to enjoy for the next century.

Henry Youle Hind's younger brother, the accomplished artist William, joined one of these groups; his paintings of the journey and of the interior of BC are quite informative. And the Schuberts, despite their three-thousand-mile journey, despite the whirlpools and rapids of the Fraser smashing their raft to splinters and a long trek through unbroken forest with nothing more than a few bites of pemmican and flour, survived. A day after their arrival in Kamloops, Mrs. Schubert calmly gave birth to their fourth child, a daughter. The West attracted tough women.

In Edmonton early Alberta mining promoter Tom Clover's exaggerations about gold in the North Saskatchewan persuaded a number of men to desert the Overlanders and stay. They dredged and shovelled for years, but found only enough gold dust to keep them in flour and whisky. For all the rumours and the trace showings, that was the extent of gold in Alberta. Little did any of the prospectors know that within one hundred years the rush would be for black gold, liquid gold, oil sands gold.

• • •

Back in the Centre of the country, the West, or what came to be called "the Saskatchewan," was discussed and dissected, and as early as 1848, George Brown's Toronto newspaper, the *Globe*, under the banner of "Canada for Canadians," groused about the Hudson's Bay Company monopoly and claimed that the territory should belong to Upper Canada. Already the Toronto Board of Trade was licking its lips, imagining what westward expansion would do for Canada's economics. Canada, meaning Toronto, planned to become Brown's "great tollgate for the commerce of the world," just as long as it could somehow get control of the resources waiting to be discovered between Red River and British Columbia. These Centrals had little idea that variations of Cree were the West's most practised tongue, and that more French than English was spoken; they had even vaguer knowledge of the volatile temper of the West, or they might have been less eager to annex it.

The people of the Territories, distant and removed from politics though they might have been, were shocked to be informed, in 1863, of the sale of the Hudson's Bay Company to the International Finance Company. Rupert's Land had been sold right out from under itself. Not-yet-Alberta, all 255,000 square miles, had been handed over to her next owner without any consultation or input from those people who called her home.

Knowing of the reverberations of that exchange, and every day more aware of the insatiable American greed for land, John A. Macdonald was slowly working toward a different confederation, his own path for annexation of all those delicious miles. Ottawa was the compromised-on capital of the province of Canada, and Daddy John thought it might be good if it were the capital of a really BIG territory. The Yankees were even more interested than John A., and they had an army that had just tested itself in the Civil War. But Macdonald was determined to win any battle against the nasty Americans, those republican rascals, and his constitutional coup, the British North America Act, Section 146, neatly spelled out the future of the West in relation to central Canada. "It shall be lawful for the Queen, by and with the advice of Her Majesty's Most Honourable Privy Council, on Addresses from the Houses of Parliament of Canada . . . to admit those Colonies or Provinces, or any of them, into the Union, and on Address from the Houses of Parliament of Canada to admit Rupert's Land and the North-western Territory, or either of them, into the Union, on such Terms and Conditions in each Case as are in the Addresses expressed and as the Queen thinks fit to approve, subject to the Provisions of this Act. . . ." By getting the BNA Act approved, Macdonald enabled the domino progression of acquisition; having once been a colony, Canada now wanted to acquire a colony. His mutton-chopped and heavy-browed Fathers of Confederation were happy to concur.

Macdonald's federal blueprint was modelled on the old system of ownership and exploitation, designed to make the interests of the parts subordinate to the interests of the whole—not a bad philosophy, at least for the Centre. And it wasn't long before Canada moved to annex the West, its 1867–68 request, prettily framed in an address to Queen Victoria, ostensibly representing the good of the Canadian people. "It would promote the prosperity of the Canadian people and induce to the advantage of the whole Empire, if the Dominion of Canada, constituted under the provisions of the 'British North America Act, 1867,' were extended westward to the shores of the Pacific Ocean." The letter threw in several nostrums about the welfare of the population already inhabiting those remote territories and expressed earnest assertions that the fertile lands and the mineral wealth were wanting "stable government for the maintenance of law and order." It was a weaselling, sycophantic address, appealing to every imperial instinct of Britannia and her commonwealth appetites to unite "Rupert's Land and the North-western Territory with this Dominion, and to grant to the Parliament of Canada authority to legislate for their future welfare and good Government; and we most humbly beg to express to Your Majesty that we are willing to assume the duties and obligations of government and legislation as regards these territories." In the West, we say, it would make a pig laugh. But it worked. What was Queen Victoria going to do with a scrabble of trees and water, prairie and mountains and Red Indians? Better let the colonies deal with the colonies.

John A. Macdonald actually believed that local governments were temporary and that they would ultimately be absorbed by an overarching, larger governing body. If he were alive now, witnessing the pitched battles between local, provincial, and national levels of power, he would probably have to pour himself a stiff scotch just to steady his disbelief. He had already decided that the West would enjoy being annexed as a subordinate and obedient territory, and no one could have prepared him for the resistance of that fiery insurrectionist Métis Louis Riel, who represented far more accurately the doubtful feelings of the West about being made to obey some Orange Ontario rules.

Canada quickly passed "An Act for the Temporary Government of Rupert's Land and the Northwestern Territory When United with Canada" in 1869. They were ready to control the uncontrollable, eager to fence the unfenceable. But to assume governance of the territories, Canada had to settle with the Hudson's Bay Company, who still held their charter and had a good idea of what the territories were worth. There were offers and counter-offers, threats and negotiations and plenty of sulking, until finally, by the 1869 Deed of Surrender, Rupert's Land was transferred to Canada. Handsomely compensated, the HBC was secretly pleased to rid itself of a territory full of dead buffalo, smallpox, and American whisky traders.

The messiness of this period of history is difficult to decipher; it is a web of trades and intrigues and double-dealing, and much happened behind the official communiqués we read now. That the West was a "problem" was unspoken but evident. That it was both feared and desired as an adjunct to Canada was obvious.

That it was seen as recalcitrant but valuable was a subtext. And that Canada was damned if it was going to let the Americans annex that much British North American land was a truism. In absolute truth, the West was roped into Confederation because of the powerful anti-American sentiment of Upper Canada/Canada West/Central Canada, the same Centre that now so assiduously courts all things American, while the West, for all its affinities with below-the-belt-border, holds the Yankees at bay.

The people who had lived in Red River for generations could not quite swallow being sold to a government that had never been very interested in their survival or their future. When a survey party arrived, prepared to carve their traditional long river lots into mile-square sections, the residents reacted like anyone whose home is invaded. In 1869 Riel and his people rode into Fort Garry, lowered the HBC flag and declared a provisional government (still loyal to the Queen), which would speak for the people of Assiniboia. Affronted by Riel's pre-emptive strike, Macdonald dispatched William McDougall as governor-designate to perform one of those heroic flag-raising ceremonies that claimed the territory for Queen and country. But Riel dispatched a courier with a politely threatening note that sent McDougall scampering back to safety. Rupert's Land was not behaving as expected. Nervously Macdonald asked the Queen to hold off on the transfer of the Territories and commissioned Donald Smith to go and figure out what was happening. Even Brown's Toronto *Globe* shook a finger at Macdonald, blaming the trouble at Red River on the Dominion government's failure to recognize "the opinions and feelings of the inhabitants."

Sending Smith to negotiate was a political acknowledgement of Louis Riel's strong position, although the provisional government's subsequent buffalo-hunt court martial and execution of the traitorous Thomas Scott, a Protestant trouble-maker living at Red River, made both polite conversation and persuasion difficult. The American Congress eyed a bill to annex the rebellious territory, Sir John had a severe gallbladder attack, and Ontario citizens vented their indignation at public meetings, demanding that the traitors who had killed Scott be hanged. But the Centre was forced to take seriously this pesky settlement run by pesky half-breeds, and the resultant Manitoba Act, which poured oil on troubled prairie, created the province of Manitoba. The territories were demonstrating a distinction and stubbornness that the Centre had not expected and that they now began to understand would need to be controlled. Manitoba was allowed to join Confederation as a province but not quite a province, a province semi-equal to the "real" provinces, since Ottawa, for the good of the Dominion, retained absolute power over public lands and natural resources. The double-dealing with the Territories had begun.

Even more infuriating was the arrival in Manitoba of Colonel Garnet Wolseley's expeditionary force, sent west to "keep the peace," but really to symbolize the presence and the interests of Central Canada. Arriving at Upper Fort Garry, they advanced in battle formation, hoping to fire a few bullets, but were disappointed to find the fort empty—the Métis had simply dispersed over the prairie. Wolseley's occupation force and the subsequent flood of Ontario settlers into Manitoba did not bode well for the country farther west, now called the North West Territories. The Court at Windsor, which had no clue about prairie or parkland or boreal forests or aboriginal peoples or buffalo, admitted Rupert's Land and what they called the North-Western Territory into the Union on June 23, 1870, whereas, whereas, and whereas. For all they knew they could have been talking about the moon. An act for the temporary government of this huge area was passed by Ottawa in 1871, and under those terms the Centre casually, without much information or even curiosity, administered the West until 1875. Aside from the squeaky voices in Manitoba, the other inhabitants of the Territories were never much consulted.

The incorporation of Rupert's Land and the Territories into the new Canadian Confederation was an autocratic gesture that would cast a long shadow. The Centre's disdain for the opinion of the people affected, whether Métis or Indian or white, was not even a consideration. When the great Chief Sweetgrass spoke, his words were not heeded: "We heard our lands were sold, and we did not like it. . . . We do not want to sell our lands; it is our property and no one has a right to sell them." But the West had been sold—or in governmental language, annexed. Now it was no longer the natural resource of an absentee commercial firm, but a colony dependent on a Canada that wanted this land as an extension of power and occupation through settlement. Even historians admit that Confederation was a device to increase the economic base of Central Canada.

• • •

William Butler loved his dog, Cerf-vola, more than anything

Glenbow Archives, Calgary, Canada: NA-249-27

In true administrator fashion, Lieutenant-Governor Adams G. Archibald of Manitoba, who was supposed to be responsible for the entire West, decided that an official report might be a good idea. But who would be willing to undertake such a journey? Only a romantic Englishman—or an Irish Catholic with an English patina. In 1870 Captain William F. Butler was sent west to check on Indian unrest and disease, rumours of which had begun to reach the oblivious Centre. Butler, an Irish officer in the British army who had sailed for Canada purely to attach himself to the Winnipeg Expedition of 1870, possessed more military intelligence than local awareness. But after Butler's demonstrating his "intellectual superiority" to Wolseley during that first Riel encounter, influential financier and railroad builder Donald Smith (he's the one pounding in the last spike in the famous picture) suggested that Butler be commissioned to travel as far west as the Rockies and to report on the "Great Lone Land" to Canadians. By this time, the pattern of visiting experts was beginning to seem repetitive.

Butler was eager to have a good look at this wilderness. Certainly a strong physical specimen, he travelled in the winter and seemed equally at home on foot, horseback, or dogsled. His narrative *The Great Lone Land*, a romantic travel epistle published two years after his journey, revealed much about his approach to this indescribable world. From his opening declaration that he sailed for North America in search of the excitement of war to his nostalgic regret at the close of his narrative, where he "needs but little cause to recall again...the image of the immense meadows where, far away at the portals of the setting sun, lies the Great Lone Land," Butler demonstrated a romantic engagement with what he saw as transcendent and exotic nature. So delighted was he with his first official journey that he undertook another three years later in 1873, travelling from Fort Garry into the Peace River country, and then on across the Rockies and down the Fraser River to the Pacific. That journey resulted in another travel book, *The Wild North Land*, where Butler rhapsodized, "He who rides for months through the vast solitudes sees during the hours of his daily travel an unbroken panorama of distance. The seasons come and go; grass grows and flowers die; the fire leaps with tiger bounds along the earth; the snow lies still and quiet over hill and lake; the rivers rise and fall, but the rigid features of the wilderness rest unchanged. Lonely, silent, and impassive; heedless of man, season, or time, the weight of the Infinite seems to brood over it." The weight of the Infinite, indeed.

Like so many other interlopers, Butler travelled with guides and assistance, and he had the cachet of acting on behalf of the government, with all the power such a commission entailed. In fact, he had been appointed a justice of the peace and was to confer the same title on two other men in the Saskatchewan, Ontario's attempt to exert some legal authority. Butler was specifically asked to examine matters of law and order from an independent point of view, particularly regarding the "necessity of troops being sent" to the Saskatchewan country, as that wild land was named. He was to ascertain the extent to which smallpox raged—he was supposed to carry medicine for the treatment of the disease, but he insisted that its weight would impede his progress; he left eight boxes behind, taking only two, which were broken before his arrival at Edmonton. Further instructions charged him to obtain information about the different Indians between Red River and the Rockies, but he was to make no promises whatsoever to those Indians. Lastly, he was expected to report on the fur trade, particularly the presence of free traders and American traders. He left Fort Garry on October 24, 1870, expecting to reach Edmonton in a month. That he departed at ten o'clock at night says more about Butler's romantic inclinations than the urgency of his charge. "The night was cold and moonless, but a brilliant aurora flashed and trembled in many-coloured shafts across the starry sky."

When Butler reached Edmonton, he conferred appropriate judicial functions on the "officer in charge," at the same time noting that judicial functions meant nothing at all in the West. He described in exaggerated detail the "most desperate set of criminals" that he encountered there; his lurid interest in their "crimes" makes it obvious that Butler was torn between admiration and stern disapproval. From Edmonton, he set out on the most demanding part of his journey, south toward the country of the Blackfoot, that mythologized tribe. "Who and what are these wild dusky men who have held their own against all comers, sweeping like a whirlwind over the arid deserts of the central continent?" Butler asked hopefully. Later he wrote, "I believe the Blackfeet and their confederates are not nearly so bad as they have been painted." He crossed the Battle River and then headed west, through Three Medicine Hills toward the Rockies, a vista that he declared the most spectacular sight he had ever seen. Without irony, he said of the Indians that "no man can starve better than the Indian—no man can feast better either." His portrayal of the First Nations people he met was exactly what might be expected of a Victorian gentleman encountering "savages."

His report concluded that "law and order" were unknown in the West, and that serious crimes had been committed by "persons of mixed and native blood, without any vindication of the law being possible." Proper punishment was the only way to measure proper civilization. Butler argued that as a mercantile body, the HBC could not be expected to serve as a governing power, and he rightly predicted increasing tension between First Peoples and whites because of the rapid disappearance of the buffalo and the decline of the fur trade. The settlers' habit of poisoning wolves (which then poisoned other animals), the incidence of smallpox, the use of alcohol in trade, all, Butler argued, contributed to Indian discontent. He praised the work of the missionaries but commented on the confusion created by their competitive approach to conversion.

Like any civil servant, Butler made recommendations that all related to strategies of control. He recommended that the West be governed first by the appointment of a "Civil Magistrate or Commissioner" (much like Ireland or India); then the organization of a federal police force, specially recruited and engaged for two or three years' service; and third, the establishment of two government stations, one around Edmonton and the other below Fort Carlton. Last, he advised that "all precautions should be taken to prevent the outbreak of an Indian war." The Indians, he stated, had dealt too much with white men who cheated them; but if the government were to enter into peaceful treaties with the Indians, those same Indians would likely abide by them. It might in the end be Butler who should be blamed for the "treaty pacification" of the western tribes. His ambivalence toward the original inhabitants of the prairies is shown by his horror at how they had been exterminated by the Americans and yet his subtle contempt for their complex social systems. And one of his most ironic comments describes the Indians as the only perfect socialists or communists in the world because they hold everything in common, share everything, and thus never change their stations in life. How could he possibly understand such a philosophy?

The West sprawled on the threshold of enormous changes, the biggest change the place would experience since the mountains had cracked the earth's crust. This time the alterations would be human, subtler but more devastating than changes to landscape and climate. These shifts in culture and survival destroyed people, revised the face of a previously untampered-with space, and introduced unpredictable social and political variants. The character of the West was about to be pushed and shoved in an entirely new direction.

• • •

Sandford Fleming, chief engineer of the proposed transcontinental railway and the man determined to synchronize the watches of the world, conducted his longitudinal and latitudinal measurement of the country in 1872. With the urgency of the need to construct the promised railway uniting BC with the rest of the country hanging over the Centre, Fleming wanted to see "the main features of the country with his own eyes." He determined that the Yellowhead, or Tête Jaune, Pass should be the one used by the nascent Canadian Pacific Railway, although the CPR would ignore that good advice and take the southerly, more difficult pass named after American surveyor Albert Bowman Rogers. Fleming's trip repeated the follies and observations of earlier travellers, although with a slightly more scientific bent.

By this time, travellers through the Territories were commonplace. Fleming's expedition was detailed by his secretary, George Grant, who complained about having to take notes in the bottom of a canoe or leaning against a tree. Grant kept an assiduous daily record, but the real intent of that expedition is recorded in his conclusion that "we have a great and fertile North-west, a thousand miles long and from one to four hundred miles broad, capable of containing a population of millions. It is a fair land; rich in furs and fish, in treasures of the forest, the field, and the mine; seamed by navigable rivers, interlaced by numerous creeks, and beautified with a thousand lakes; broken by swelling uplands, wooded hill-sides, and bold ridges; and protected on its exposed sides by a great desert or by giant mountains. The air is pure, dry and bracing all year round; giving promise of health and strength of body and length of days. Here we have a home for our own surplus population and for the stream of emigration that runs from northern and central Europe to America." Behind Grant's flowery language is the old impulse for ownership and annexation, settlement.

Because it was expedient that the laws respecting the Territories be amended and consolidated, the North West Territories Act of 1875 laid out the rules. This act determined all manner of administrative processes, but contained two striking details. One was that an area not exceeding one thousand miles could become an electoral district within the Territories by proving that it had a population of one thousand inhabitants (not counting "aliens or unenfranchised Indians"). The second was an entire section devoted to the prohibition of intoxicants, either the manufacture, sale, exchange, importation or barter of any intoxicating liquor.

The West was about to be civilized.

6 | Moustache Mounties

In the evening the Major...and a squad of men paid us an official visit. They acted with courtesy toward every one, but all appeared "dry," which after a 4 months' march on arid plains is perhaps not to be wondered at. They asked for whiskey, but when we regretted our ability to give them a drop, they evidently took it as a joke, for several details, under command of proper officers were soon engaged in trying to find the "critter."

—Whisky trader Charles Schafft

I am driving the highway between the Forks and Rocky Mountain House, a spectacular road that turns east from the Banff/Jasper Highway through the Howse Pass. It is the height of summer, a dark blue August evening, between afternoon and sunset, and there is not another car in sight. I drive a small sports car, with awesome cornering ability, and so I put my foot down and fly. I'm with a German friend visiting Alberta to do research on Canadian literature. We meet no one, not another car, for kilometre after kilometre, and the light and the air and the cooling of a hot August day between the mountains and the river are like a dream of space and time. And yes, I am speeding.

And a mere twenty kilometres from Rocky Mountain House, a white car comes over a hill straight at us, and I know, even before he spins around behind me and turns on his lights, that he's a Mountie. There's no point in doing anything except slow down and pull over. I stop, dig out my licence, my registration, my insurance, roll down my window, and wait.

"But you weren't really speeding," says my friend, who is used to German Autobahns.

"Oh yes, I was," I say. "The speed limit here is one hundred."

She looks puzzled at this irrational law—that a wide, seldom travelled road would have a speed limit so low. But I can't explain the traffic laws of Alberta to her right at that moment. There's a Mountie at my window.

He is flawlessly polite. "Good evening, ladies. How are you this evening?"

Were he a waiter, I would explain that we do not appreciate being called ladies, but he is a Mountie, and so I say nothing, except the usual "Fine."

He is very tall, so tall that he has to bend down to talk into the window. He is neither young nor old, but rather of that undefinable middle age that could be late thirties or forties or even early fifties. He sports a walrus moustache, the pride of prairie Mounties who are apparently not allowed to grow beards, but may decorate their upper lips with brooms of no insignificant bristle.

"And where are you off to this evening?"

"We're on our way to Rocky Mountain House."

"Do you know how fast you were going?"

"Yes," I say, as decisively as I can. "138 kilometres an hour."

"Why"— he looks amazed—"that's exactly what I clocked you at."

I say nothing, relieved that he hasn't clocked me at 160.

"Where are you going in such a hurry?"

"Rocky Mountain House," I repeat as neutrally as possible.

"Where do you live?"

"Calgary."

"And your friend?"

"She's visiting from Germany."

"Oh, and she thought you should be driving as if you were on an Autobahn."

"No," I say. "I am entirely responsible for my driving."

He looks amazed again. "Do you know the speed limit?"

"Yes, it's one hundred kilometres an hour." There is no reason to fight with him. He'll win anyway.

He takes my papers and looks at them. "So you are the registered owner of this vehicle."

Now that's a Mountie word. Vehicle. "Yes," I say.

He takes the documentation back to his vehicle, does the usual check on the records. I know that everything is legal except my speed.

When he comes back, he still expects me to make excuses. "Now," he says, "a highway traffic violation of that speed calls for a $210 fine, and I'm sure you can do without that."

"Yes, sir," I say quietly.

"But because you were honest and you didn't make excuses, I have dropped the amount, so you'll only have to pay a $50 fine." He seems very pleased with his justice, and although I wish he wouldn't give me a ticket at all, I listen patiently while he outlines the terms and conditions, and cautions me to slow down.

I even say "Thank you," before putting the car in gear again.

As we drive away, my friend looks at me and starts to laugh.

"What?" I ask.

"He was so polite," she says. "His moustache was so big, and he was so polite."

• • •

Although no one could have predicted the extent to which the Mounties would capture the attention of popular culture for more than a century to come, when William Butler first suggested the formation of a police force for the West, the Centre took up the romance of that idea with alacrity. What would be more fun than to form a band of merry military men in the East and send them out West to impose law and order on an unruly and difficult place? Sir John A. Macdonald knew how important that stretch of land between Red River and the Rockies was, and until he got the railway built across that tempting expanse it needed to be kept under control. So on May 20, 1873, the North West Mounted Police Act, establishing a new police force for the North West Territories, was passed. One of Canada's most marketable symbols, with their red coats and pillbox hats and flourishing moustaches, was invented solely because the West needed to be pacified, monitored, and given one hell of a curfew.

The force was supposed to be called the North West Mounted Rifles, but at the last moment, John A. decided that "rifles" was too explosive a word and changed the name to police. They were modelled on the Royal Irish Constabulary, whose job was similar—to quell rebellion, in spirit or deed. Given a hybridized mandate, they were to ride horses, do the work of an army by enforcing Canadian sovereignty along that long undefended border, as well as serve as a civil police force dealing with local crimes and misdemeanours. They were to be "of sound constitution, active and able bodied, able to ride, of good character, able to read and write either the English or French language, and between the ages of 18 and 40 years." Their red coats signalled their distinction from the much-hated American army, whose "blue coats" had come to imply to the natives vicious punishment; the government hoped that the cheerful scarlet would allay the natural suspicions of the Indians and signal protection and consistency. Later, an American would observe, "The boys after their four months' march looked hearty in physique, but

F Troop on parade at Calgary, 1876

wear a most abominable uniform—a short red coat, leather britches tucked into boots, all supplemented by a white cover that looks no more like a head covering than a coal scuttle." Abominable they might have looked, but they couldn't be mistaken for Americans.

Tales of the whisky trade, both exaggerated and real, titillated the sobersides in Toronto, while Macdonald, who knew the power of whisky, knew also how it could make the most tractable men ungovernable. The American whisky traders, who were virtually toasting the Canadian government with contempt, had to be stopped, sent back across the border; and the Indians the trade corrupted needed to be both protected and pacified. To add fire to alcohol, the Cypress Hills Massacre in April had scared everyone. The stories that filtered back east were both unfactual and exaggerated: it was reported that American whisky traders had killed a large number of Assiniboine Indians in the lush hills crouched between southeastern Alberta and southwestern Saskatchewan. Getting a force out west as soon as possible seemed urgent. So before they could even break in their boots, the Mounties were on their way.

The Cypress Hills, a wooded haven on the otherwise open prairie, still sheltered a few buffalo. But the massacre was far more complicated than mere whisky trading, and studying it might have taught the Mounties some valuable lessons. A group of American and Canadian "wolfers," not whisky traders, had caused the trouble, although drinking had contributed to the conflict. Wolfers were a form of hunter gone rancid. These men would kill a buffalo, then saturate the meat with poison and leave. Hungry wolves would congregate, eat the poisoned buffalo and die horribly, carcasses in rictus around the carcass. The hunters would return and skin the wolves for their pelts. The buffalo were already terribly depleted by mass slaughter—hide hunters with high-powered guns killed and killed and killed, then took only their hides, which were used to make belts for the industrial machinery of the Centre, leaving behind the meat. The result was grotesque waste, the prairie a stinking mass of rotting carcasses and bleached bones.

Unsurprisingly the Indians did not appreciate this depletion of the animal that had provided them with sustenance for years; nor were they happy about the wolfers whose poison killed not only wolves but their working dogs. So when a group of Blackfoot encountered a band of wolfers on their way across the border to Fort Benton, it seemed mere justice for the Blackfoot, adept horse thieves, to steal the wolfers' horses. To give the impression that the horses had been stolen not by them but by the Cree or Assiniboine, they chased the animals toward the Cypress Hills, then rode away west. The furious wolfers, determined to recover their horses, tracked them to the Cypress Hills and ended up at two sleazy whisky posts, Abe Farwell's and Moses Solomon's. The horses were gone, but whisky flowed, and along with a group of Assiniboine Indians who had just completed a trade, the wolfers had quite a few drinks. When another horse belonging to the fort wandered off, the wolfers believed that this group of Indians had stolen it too and, deciding to take justice into their own hands, slaughtered between twenty and one hundred (the numbers vary wildly) Assiniboine children, women, and men before heading back to Fort Benton without their horses, but with a powerfully satisfied sense of retribution. This was the spark that sent the Mounties on their way, before they even knew where they were going.

What and who were this force? The 150 men of Divisions A, B, and C were quickly recruited. "WANTED IMMEDIATELY BY GOVERNMENT," an ad read, "20 Active, Healthy Young Men, for service in the Mounted Police Force in the North West Territory. They must be of good character, single, between the ages of 20 and 35 years, capable of riding. They will have to serve for a term of 3 (three) years. Their pay will be 75 cents per diem, and everything (uniform, rations, board, &c, &c.) found, and on completion of service will receive a free grant of 160 acres of land, with right of choice. For further particulars, apply without delay to Captain C. Young, Halifax Hotel." Each officer was to recruit twenty men and report with his quotas immediately.

These men were to demonstrate all the attributes of upright conduct and discipline, and they were expected to carry the dignity of cultivated Central Canada with their pennants. The officers—actually patronage appointments recruited from what social elite was available in Toronto—generally possessed military experience, and it was to their benefit if they had some legal background; they were all sworn justices of the peace, and the commissioner had the power of a magistrate. The rank and file were still supposed to be "of good character," but many were drawn more by the spark of adventure and the promise of free land than civic righteousness. Every bored farmhand and quite a few men who needed to get out of Toronto quickly were ready to sign up.

In the fall of 1873 the first recruits were on their way to Manitoba. In order to beat the coming winter, the men were quickly put on-board boats to cross the Great Lakes. Landing near present-day Thunder Bay, they staggered more than marched the Dawson route to Lower Fort Garry, a hellish journey, cold and miserable. Once they arrived, they were sworn in and their training began, and that winter gave them all a taste of Western weather and Western temper. But they were in the hands of the best. Inspector James Walsh was adjutant, veterinary surgeon (for the animals, one presumes), and riding master. Superintendent A. H. Griesbach was in charge of discipline and foot drill, and Sam Steele was in charge of breaking in the horses and instructing the NCOs and men in riding. Later Steele's reminiscences claimed, "With very few exceptions the horses were bronchos which had never been handled, and none but the most powerful and skilful dared attempt to deal with them. Even when we had them 'gentled' so as to let recruits mount, the men were repeatedly thrown with great violence to the frozen ground; but no one lost his nerve." When a man was bucked off, Steele would bawl, "Who gave you permission to dismount?" Without him, they might have ended up as a feeble force, but Steele succeeded in giving them backbone and saddle smarts, along with some commendable bruises.

Meanwhile, in the Centre, the Pacific Scandal had finally felled Sir John, although his last act before resigning was to appoint George Arthur French as the first commissioner of the new police force. French was a humourless disciplinarian eager for advancement, and when he got himself out to Fort Garry in November to review the troops there he was displeased to discover the number of recruits who had to be discharged for gambling and drinking, along with the number who were physically unfit. Apparently, good character was a matter of interpretation, and the initial recruiting had inadvertently enlisted some tough nuts who had neither character nor physique. Steele complained that "our lawgivers must have been under the impression that we were plaster saints, not Canadians of blood and brain, with a number of the peculiarities and weaknesses of poor human nature. The only punishment that could be awarded was by fine." Obviously punishment was necessary, and fines were laughable. But for the busy men the long winter wound by pleasurably, complete with balls, parties, and rifle matches in the Winnipeg area.

French returned to Ottawa determined to gather the other 150 men promised by the North West Mounted Police Act, forming Troops D, E, and F. Those men, many of whom had lied about their experience with horses, were trained in Toronto before boarding the train for the first leg of their journey across the United States to Fargo in the spring of 1874. Ironically, a group of finely polished men with finely polished horses, who were to become Canada's premier lawmen, took the train across the United States because the northern, or Dawson, route was too difficult for them.

After a few days of fighting tangled harness and rebellious horses at Fargo, French finally got the whole mess moving—only to find that on the relatively short journey up to Fort Dufferin, Manitoba, where they were to meet up with the earlier recruits, his high-bred horses, "admitted in Toronto to be the best ever shipped from that city," balked and bloated and grew thin. Horses, like men, have a hard time changing from civilized forage to tough prairie grass, and two of them died. When the six divisions finally met on June 18, French was already nervous, and Colonel Macleod, who was in charge of the first three divisions, had already gained the confidence of his men, a contrast that would persist. The men liked French a hell of a lot less than they liked Macleod; they blamed French for everything that went wrong, and most things went wrong.

The first three divisions were full of admiration for the perfectly formed horses—until the following night when a wild thunderstorm, a common occurrence in the West, unrolled itself over man and beast. Steele remembered that "a thunderbolt fell in the midst of the horses. Terrified, they broke their fastenings and made for the side of the corral. The six men on guard were trampled underfoot as they tried to stop them. The maddened beasts overturned the huge wagons, dashed through a row of tents, scattered everything, and made for the gate of the large field in which they were encamped. In their mad efforts to pass they climbed over one another to the height of many feet.... Crazed with fright, the horses crossed the river and continued their flight on the opposite bank, and the majority were between 30 and 50 miles in Dakota before they were compelled by sheer exhaustion to halt." The local horses that the first troops had trained did not bolt, and the better riders from the merged troops (several men were injured in the stampede) had to ride south on their prairie broncos to round up a bunch of Toronto horses scared out of their wits by Western thunder and lightning. Although they managed to catch all except one, those horses would continue to be troublesome. All summer, they reared at every sound, and every small rainstorm meant that they had to be calmed and babysat.

French was convinced everyone needed a good talking-to, men and horses both. Before pulling out, he gave his best trials-and-tribulations harangue, promising the men hunger and thirst, even death, and inviting the faint of heart and the beggarly of spirit to leave while they still had a chance. He was persuasive, perhaps more accurate than he knew, and by morning, thirty men had vanished, hightailing it south across the border. The next day, July 8, at five in the afternoon, the remaining troops set out, dressed in their scarlet tunics, white gloves, and polished boots, destined to be coated with prairie dust. What a picture! Each division was mounted on a different-coloured horse, and the whole cavalcade, about two and a half miles long, included a mixture of 275 mounted armed men accompanied by 114 Red River carts with twenty Métis drivers, wagons, field kitchens, forges, mowing machines, ploughs, two nine-pounder muzzle-loading field guns, 339 horses, 142 draft oxen, and 93 beef cattle, French's notion of walking provisions.

It would have been wise to follow the fur-trade road between Red River and Edmonton, a tested and much-travelled course that provided water and wood. But no, Ottawa knew better. Colonel French and his redcoats were supposed to follow the Boundary Commission road for two hundred miles, then veer north into the Missouri Coteau hills, and then continue west, straight for Fort Whoop-Up, where they would presumably march right into the bar and announce to the whisky traders, "We're closing you down." The route was not only difficult, it was downright foolhardy, a venture into unknown country. Worst of all, Colonel French, perhaps expecting a handy water trough every ten miles, hadn't bothered with either water barrels or canteens. It wasn't long before both men and horses, forced to drink stagnant slough water, developed dreadful dysentery. A few men got typhoid.

The column sometimes stretched ten miles long. They travelled too slowly for French, the ox carts moving exactly at the pace of an ox, the cattle meandering. After a few weeks, the well-bred horses, weakened and thin, could hardly even be ridden. So French ordered that every other hour the men must walk. This caused ire, and at least one man, stating that he had joined a mounted force and not a foot parade, refused. Of course, walking wore out their leather riding boots, and soon these fine specimens of men were trudging across the prairie almost barefoot, their feet wrapped in provision sacks. Dying of thirst, suffering from uncontrollable diarrhea and from mosquito bites, they dragged their saddle-sore horses, which were skin and bones.

On July 24 they reached Roche Percée, just before the confluence of the Souris River and Rivière Courte, where, because there was wood and water and pasture, Colonel French allowed the first rest. From there, he decided, they would divide, with Division A diverting to Fort Edmonton via Fort Ellice and Fort Carlton, some 875 miles. Colonel French bestowed on Division A all the sick men, played-out horses, and slow carts. Because the main force was heading into uncharted territory, aided only by Palliser's rather inaccurate map, French obviously wanted to speed up his progress and divest himself of men and animals who might be a liability in a possible dust-up with the whisky traders, the "hot work" that he anticipated meeting at Fort Whoop-Up.

But under Inspector Jarvis and Sam Steele, both knowledgeable men, Division A nursed and roped and persuaded and pushed weak horses, sick men, and recalcitrant oxen along to Fort Ellice, where they left behind a few men, half of the cows and calves, and several sick horses. It took them eight weeks to reach Fort Carlton, encountering along the way quicksand and prairie fires and, on meeting up with a Métis hunting party, discovering pemmican as the perfect food for travellers and soldiers. Intelligently, Jarvis purchased a few sacks of pemmican for provisions. Food and water were their greatest desires; one horse trainer said, every night after eating his rations, plus a brace of boiled prairie chickens, "I wish I were in Toronto, at Gus Thomas's English Chop House, where I could get a porterhouse steak and a bottle of Guinness!" He wasn't likely to meet that bottle of Guinness for some time.

They rode and swore and hunted their way between Fort Carlton and Fort Edmonton. Every night a Métis driver played a violin while the other carters danced jigs on a door that they carried along just for that purpose. The trail was a quagmire of muck and the horses were so weak that if they fell, they could not rise. Again and again, the men had to lift them to their feet, an exhausting ritual. Those Toronto horses were almost carried along propped up by two men, one at the head and another at the shoulders, to keep them on their legs. The worst part of the journey was the short distance between the post at Victoria and Fort Edmonton. Sam Steele described it as "the hardest trek that I have yet undertaken. The trail was worse than any we had encountered. It was knee-deep in black mud, sloughs crossed it every few hundred yards, and the waggons had to be unloaded and dragged through them by hand.... The poor animals, crazed with thirst and feverish because of their privations, would rush to the ponds to drink, often falling and having to be dragged out with ropes from where they fell." When they finally reached Fort Edmonton, to be kindly greeted by Chief Factor Richard Hardisty, all collapsed into what seemed like the lap of luxury. Such an ordeal, of course, readily becomes the stuff of legend, an ironic transformation for a group of lost, stumbling, ignorant greenhorns.

Meanwhile, the main force continued by the southern route, joined by six Métis guides from Red River who were supposed to know the country, but who were nervous about moving into the territory of the Sioux and Blackfoot. The climb up the Coteau hills was daunting, compounded by the difficulties of saddle horses trying to pull the two-ton field guns up the steep slope. French was quick to arrest insubordinate officers who criticized his tactics, but they were right—saddle horses don't make good draft animals. The men were nervous; they found the silence oppressive, grasshoppers ate their canvas tents, and they were hungry. Then, having gained the Missouri Coteau, at Old Wives Cripple Creek, the Mounties unexpectedly ran into some Sioux. Matters at that moment could have gone either way, and it is to the credit of the Sioux that they looked at this limping, skinny cavalcade and gave it the benefit of the doubt. They held a formal meeting with the usual speeches and dancing and pipes and, amazingly, parted on good terms, setting a positive tone for subsequent encounters with the Indians.

But they still met adversity. On August 3 a tornado straight out of Alberta levelled their camp. By August 18 they had reached the Cypress Hills, the watershed dividing the Mississippi river system from Hudson Bay's, and the site where the massacre that had inspired their formation took place. Now they were almost in Alberta, Blackfoot country, the land of myth and plenty. The hungry men met the feast of the prairies, the buffalo, and on September 2, after an exciting hunt, gorged themselves on the delicious meat. Only a few small herds remained; the bounty of the prairie was running out but reports claimed the men ate ten pounds of meat a day.

Those same delicious buffalo had left not a blade of grass or pool of fresh water for the horses. Their guides had misled them, and although they thought they were getting close to Fort Whoop-Up (located at the confluence of the Belly and the Bow rivers), they were nowhere near it. They were, with some poetic justice, caught in Palliser's Triangle, wandering blind and thirsty over a grassless plain. A cold rain fell, so cold that it chilled the horses through. Five of them died, and French gave orders that the men should surrender one of their two allotted sleeping blankets to cover the horses. And it hadn't even snowed yet.

To add insult to injury, when they finally stumbled on the confluence of the Belly and the Bow rivers, there was nothing there, just a few roofless log cabins. Even French's information was wrong—Fort Whoop-Up was still quite a few miles west. And did he imagine that the whisky traders would hang around, offer to pour the thirsty Mounties a drink? French sent Cecil Denny on a reconnaissance trip up the Bow River and Denny ran into a group of unfriendly, although not hostile, Assiniboines. When their efforts to communicate in sign language failed, Denny and his men spent the rest of that little foray desperately trying to avoid another meeting. They scurried back to the main party and "gave a dreadful account of the country; neither wood nor grass, country very rough and bad hills ahead."

There was nothing for it but to forget about Fort Whoop-Up and head south toward the Sweetgrass Hills and what looked like shelter. Those last few days were hellish. When they finally reached the western edge of the Sweetgrass Hills, the troops were demoralized and exhausted. They had seen, from the top of the Milk River Ridge, the sharp brilliance of the Rockies. Now, at last, they had water and grass, but for many of their fine eastern horses, it was too late. So many horses died there that the camp was called Dead Horse Coulee.

French's ignorance was showing, but he made decisive decisions. He would be responsible for the welfare of the force, which meant that he would return east with Divisions D and E to plan for their ongoing situation in the West. He would send Colonel James Macleod, with Divisions B, C, and F, onward to Fort Whoop-Up. But before that, they needed food and provisions and a telegraph—so the same Mounties who were supposed to halt the American whisky trade went to its very source, the Montana whisky shop of Fort Benton, to get what they needed. French was learning. He bought some moccasins, books, stockings, and gloves for the men, and some corn and oats for the horses. He bought fifteen sturdy Western horses, not very fine but capable of survival, and left immediately to resume his journey east.

Macleod had to stay at Fort Benton a while longer, organizing supplies and gritting his Protestant teeth at the debauchery around him. But in the wisest move any Mountie ever made, by the time he left, accompanied by an I. G. Baker bull train loaded with supplies, he had hired the legendary Jerry Potts as a guide and scout. Potts, half Blood, half Scottish, had lost many of his family, including his mother and half brother, to various whisky killings, and although he liked a dram himself he worked with the Mounties toward eradication of the whisky trade for the next twenty-two years. He was the most famous of the scouts who helped the NWMP, a warrior and strategist, a man who knew the land well. In 1870 he had fought with the Blackfoot against the Cree in a battle on the Belly River, his escape from that legendary fight so narrow that he suffered powder burns on his left ear. Sam Steele recalled him vividly, as

> a short, bow-legged man, with piercing black eyes and a long straight nose. He was silent and laconic, and people said he was a fighter, and he looked it. He won the confidence of all ranks the first day out, and

when morning came he rode out boldly in front of the advance guard. It was noon when the party reached Milk River, and found him there sitting near a fat buffalo cow which he had killed and dressed for the use of the force. To those new to such life he appeared to know everything, and their good opinion of him was confirmed when on the second day he turned sharp to the left toward the Milk River ridge, selected a camp ground, and then led the force a short distance to some fine springs containing the best water that they had tasted for many a long day.

One story goes that as they were travelling, a young recruit rode up beside Potts and asked him, "What's over that hill?" Potts didn't even look at him. "Another hill," he said. Laconic he might have been, but without him the Mounties might have drifted over the prairie until they met their deaths.

With Potts leading them right up the Old North Trail, the police finally made good progress, and on October 9, 1874, Macleod positioned his men outside the rough palisade of Fort Whoop-Up. A prairie silence hung over the fort, and although Macleod had lined up the guns and ordered everyone into skirmishing order, nothing happened—they had expected a volley of gunfire. A woman went from one building to another but took no notice of them. Potts and Macleod rode to the main gate, entered, went to the nearest building and knocked, one of the most polite introductions to a police search ever. The door was opened by a man with a wooden leg, American Civil war veteran Dave Akers, who apparently said, "Walk in, General, walk in, General, and make yourself at home." (Macleod wasn't a general, but it was good politics to elevate him a little.) But where was the whisky and where were the traders? The police searched high and low and found neither. Some stories say that the two main traders, Healy and Hamilton, had left just a few hours earlier. Others claim that the whisky had been hidden or dug into the bed of the Belly River.

After the search, the usual attempt at monetary pacification followed. The Mounties offered $10,000 to buy the fort, but the traders refused. They had a misguided idea that the fort was worth more, and that the whisky trade could continue once the police got tired of this endless landscape. And so Potts guided the Mounties farther west, to an island in the Oldman River, where Fort Macleod, the first police post in Alberta, was established. The men seemed almost euphoric at being permitted to stay put. Denny says, "The location chosen looked beautiful to us after the long and weary march. And beautiful indeed it was, with the lofty barrier of snowdraped peaks to the west, the timbered range of the Porcupines to the north, and the Old Man valley as far as the eye might reach lined with sheltering woods." They went to work and built a comfortable post, the outer fort of twelve-foot cottonwood logs placed upright in trenches dug deep in the ground, the floors of the barracks packed mud, and the roof poles covered with earth, but with real window sashes and real doors. At Christmas they celebrated with buffalo and roast turkey and potatoes and dried fruits and, Denny claims, "real plum pudding."

Meanwhile, with Potts's help, Colonel Macleod went out and met with the Indians, flashing his red coat and explaining what the Mounties were doing in Blackfoot territory. Macleod had a quiet, trustworthy manner, and he established good rapport with the Indians. Most important, the people learned that the Mounties followed through on their promises. Right after their arrival, a Blackfoot named Three Bulls told the police that he had traded a pony for two gallons of whisky. The next day Crozier and Potts picked up the traders, fined them, confiscated both buffalo robes and whisky, and jailed them. Another trader, probably Hamilton, showed up and paid their bail, but the police had already demonstrated their tenacity, that they were there to stay in order to pursue their impossible mandate of policing the wide-open wide open. And by first slowing and then stamping out the liquor trade, they began to preside as law and order, judge and jury, using the very bars that they closed as the bars of justice.

It was a miserable winter, and twenty men deserted, but the following year the Mounties set up two new posts, one at the current site of Calgary, and another south and east of Fort Macleod—Fort Walsh—not far from the Cypress Hills massacre site. Inspector Jarvis was comfortably ensconced at Fort Edmonton with the fur traders, but in the spring, he moved downriver and built Fort Saskatchewan, and now the Mounties had more than a toehold. The Great March could be called a success, despite its almost disastrous outcome. French, who had never been popular, annoyed everyone, so in 1876, he was replaced by Macleod, one of the more sensible of Ottawa's decrees. Macleod had actually left the force to become stipendary magistrate for the North West Territories, so he had to be persuaded to come back.

But the police hadn't gotten smart overnight, and Calgary's founding was something of a muddle. Inspector Ephraim Brisebois had been sent to establish a fort at the confluence of the Bow and the Elbow rivers but, following tradition, got lost. For days he and his troop wandered around far north of where they were supposed to be. But Calgary was set up quickly, with the I. G. Baker Company, those purveyors of whisky, who had now become suppliers, contracted to build the barracks. Brisebois was another commander who wasn't very popular with his men, and although he wanted to name the fort on the Bow after himself, Macleod directly countermanded him and decreed that the post should be named for Macleod's ancestral home in Scotland. Calgary it was and Calgary it is to this day, Brisebois forgotten. Macleod, on the other hand, is memorialized in Macleod Trail, the main artery of neoned muffler shops and fast-food outlets leading into Calgary from the south, over the earlier tracks of the Old North Trail.

Their posts were rudimentary but persistent enough to establish a profile for these fledgling lawmen. They quickly earned the enmity of the Americans, who complained about the Mounties' seizing goods only "on suspicion" of whisky trading. The pursuit of the perpetrators of the Cypress Hills Massacre meant that the Mounties spent a fair amount of time in Fort Benton, Montana, and the connection between Fort Benton and Alberta, especially as a supply line, was continued for some years. Through its bonded bull-train freight route, which provided quicker and cheaper goods to Fort Macleod and Fort Calgary and Fort Edmonton than could possibly come from Winnipeg, Fort Benton merchants actually opened up Alberta, another American connection. If they couldn't make money on whisky, the Americans were quick to provision other needs and desires. One, named John Glenn, loaded a wagon with goods and sold them to the famished Mounties waiting on the Benton Trail for outrageous prices, $20 for a sack for flour and $3 for a gallon of syrup. The company that probably made the greatest profit out of the formation of the Mounties was the I. G. Baker trading firm, who delivered beef, bacon, flour, tea, coffee, sugar, dried apples, beans, rice, pressed vegetables and pressed hops, baking powder, salt, pepper, potatoes, oatmeal, candles, bran, coal oil, oats and hay, and probably even an occasional bottle of whisky, all for the comfort of these men and their horses.

But the most important task facing the Mounties was meeting and pacifying the First Nations people. Closely related was the unspoken but obvious mandate of occupying the West for Central Canada until there were enough settlers to ensure uncontested Canadian ownership. It was a delicate task; the police had to serve as intermediaries between the western aboriginal peoples and a Central government without a clue about what mattered to the original occupants, a rush of settlers eager for open land, unscrupulous carpetbaggers out to make a quick dollar, and political moments that begged for violence and insurrection. That the Mounties somehow succeeded in maintaining an uneasy peace, despite the fugitive Sioux who came to Canada to escape American retribution for the defeat of General Custer, the Rebellion of 1885, and the pernicious effects of starvation and disease is nothing short of miraculous. Various interpreters have lauded the Mounties for preventing potential violence; it is more likely that a combination of individually ethical policemen combined with Indian leaders who recognized the futility of resistance stumbled toward a version of mutual tolerance. There were plenty of perfidious Mounties who proceeded from ignorance rather than kindness. The much-scorned Francis Dickens, who commanded Fort Pitt during the Cree siege in 1885, was clearly a disastrous leader, discharged in 1886 on the excuse of "deafness," although his real crime was probably letting the Cree capture the fort without sufficient resistance.

Walsh might have done much to prevent the terrible starvation of the American Sioux, but his relationship with Sitting Bull was considered by his superiors too intimate, and he was transferred from Wood Mountain, close to where the Sioux took refuge, to Qu'Appelle. It was hard-case Crozier who persuaded Sitting Bull, by starving him out, to go back to the United States. And Central Canada, intent on "settling" the West, shamelessly exploited the good relations between police and the Western tribes during treaty negotiations. Treaties Six and Seven came about largely because of the trust the Mounties had earned.

By pacifying the Indians, the Mounties made sure that the railway could inch its way across the prairie, thus helping to fulfil Ottawa's national ambitions. They fought against Riel when the 1885 Rebellion raged across the prairies and, during that Rebellion, their steady presence dissuaded the nations in the south of Alberta from arming themselves. Crusty horseman Sam Steele oversaw the final leg of the construction of the railway through the Rockies, even getting up from a bout of Rocky Mountain fever to climb on his horse and stare down a group of strikers. As settlers and farmers began to take over the West, detachments and sub-posts

NWMP, ready to ride, not always sure where they were

proliferated, doubling as post offices and record offices and medical clinics. Mounties led settlers to their land, and police patrols regularly visited isolated settlers.

After the suppression of the Riel Rebellion, the Central government, eager to cut costs, claimed that the Mounties were no longer needed, but objections were loud and strenuous. In 1896 Laurier raised hackles when he claimed that the force had been formed only to control the Indians and should now be disbanded. He was shouted down, and the police pitched in to the new challenge of settlement, fighting prairie fires and smallpox and looking for lost horses and lost children. Often they themselves got lost or killed. One brief, poignant line scrawled on a note found with a Mountie lying dead as a doornail after a blizzard, read, "Lost, horse dead. Am pushing on, have done my best." Even before the Centrals understood that the West needed to be indoctrinated into their national dream, the

Glenbow Archives, Calgary, Canada: NA-949-49

Mountie dog teams at Fort Chipewyan; Mounties had to learn flexibility

Mounties were enforcing that ideal. They upheld federal laws all through the prairies, and after 1905, when law enforcement became a provincial responsibility, the federal government rented the force to the new provinces of Alberta and Saskatchewan.

At least they added variety to the social life of the province. They organized their own fancy balls and started bands, which played for all occasions. They even composed pieces, like the Mounted Police Waltzes. It is unsurprising that they came to embody one of the most enduring popular myths in Canada, stock figures of both movies and television. Paul Gross's role in *Due South* echoes back to 1910, when the Edison Moving Picture Company featured silent Mounties in *Riders of the Plains*. Actors from Nelson Eddy to Lee Marvin, from Tom Mix to Robert Preston have portrayed characters from the celebrated force. From *Rose Marie* on, the singing has never stopped.

Their motto, *Maintiens le droit* (Maintain the right), persists. They've undergone various name changes, from their initial title as the Force to the North West Mounted Police in 1879, then accorded royal status, as Royal North West Mounted Police, in recognition of their service in the Boer War. In 1904 their uniforms were upgraded too, the white helmet traded for a wide-brimmed scout-style Stetson, and the white gloves disappeared. They became the Royal Canadian Mounted Police in 1920, when they absorbed the Dominion Police, and thence had charge of various irritating duties like guarding the Houses of Parliament and the residence of the prime minister, not always effectively. They are famous for their paperwork, requiring reports on every action and every operation, and now Albertans encounter them mostly on the highways and in the national parks of the province. In 2000 the Mounties claimed that posing for pictures in Banff took up so much time that photo-snapping tourists would be charged a fee. It must be onerous to bear such a reputation and to be forced to pose next to national monuments. They would probably rather be driving dog teams across a snowy expanse or, in the tradition of their founders, galloping horses into the prairie wind.

The Mounties articulate a terrible irony. This police force, sent west to occupy the Territories for Central Canada, has become symbolic of the very place they were sent to subdue and control. When, in the 1980s, the government of Canada proposed replacing the initials RCMP with the word POLICE, the West went ballistic, objecting to Ottawa's tampering with "Western tradition." Petitions were signed, letters written, and various protests mounted. In one hundred years, the same force that represented one of the Centre's most obvious imperialistic gestures in the West had become its own pride and joy. Such was the success of the Mounties that they now represent the very place that didn't quite surrender to them but let them stay.

7 | Before Barbed Wire

Oh give me a home
Where the buffalo roam...
                —Brewster M. Higley

I do not sit well on the back of a horse. Horses are complicated animals that require clair-
voyance, intricate connection, and they seem to know I am easily unseated. I suspect that
if you want to be a cowboy who can ride any horse, rope any ornery calf, and withstand
both winter blizzards and summer heat, you need to make a deal with the Devil.

Tom Three Persons, the legendary cowboy who was the only Canadian to win big in
the first Calgary Stampede, did just that. One hot day in 1907, leading his horses across
the Blood reserve just above the Belly River, Tom Three Persons met a white man, dressed
all in black and riding a black horse. The man approached Three Persons and speaking in
perfect Blackfoot, introduced himself as Siksinum, *or "the Black One." His English name,*
he said, was Billy. He seemed to know more about Tom Three Persons than Tom himself
did, and he told Tom's future, saying that he would become the richest Indian on the
reserve, and that if he would work with the white man dressed in black, he could get any-
thing he wanted. Tom Three Persons agreed, and then his apparition rode away.

Tom Three Persons had already met varieties of the Devil at St. Joseph's Indian
Industrial School. This vision, of a black man on a horse, was far more logical than
Catholic devils, and was obviously Tom Three Persons' spirit helper. Throughout his life
as a cowboy, Tom Three Persons called on Billy, who, if he was that black angel, helped
more than he hindered.

A cowboy who worked through spring and fall roundups, Three Persons honed his
skills as a rider and took to riding bucking broncs at local rodeos and sports days, almost
always winning. Black Billy was clearly on his side. But the life of a cowboy was waylaid
by temptation, and Three Persons struggled between his character as a charming, engag-
ing bronc rider and his alter ego as gambler, philanderer, drinker, and horse thief, husband
to a number of abused and patient wives.

When Guy Weadick organized the first Calgary Stampede in 1912, he did so in
honour of ranching as a fading glory and the cowboy as a dying breed. Although there

were objections, Weadick was determined that as a part of the great tradition of the West, Indians would be participants in the Stampede. The Indian agents were nervous about the people leaving the reserves, but with the help of Sir James Lougheed and R. B. Bennett, Weadick persuaded Indian Affairs to allow the First Peoples of southern Alberta to attend and celebrate this unique occasion. Cowboys eager to win a part of the $20,000 purse flooded in from Mexico, the United States, and other parts of Canada. And everywhere were Indians, their brilliant costumes flashing between the duller shades of whites, camped out and taking part in the parade and the events. It was the first time many of the white settlers had met the people they had displaced; and it was a meeting cordial on both sides, the spirit of carnival for a few days erasing their differences.

Brought up specially from the States for his terrifying skill at throwing riders, Cyclone was the most famous bucking bronc in the West, with Tornado a close second. All week Cyclone, or "Black Terror," performed as expected, tossing every rider. When Tom Three Persons drew him for the finals, he worried about staying on the unbeatable horse, but the night before the event, while Tom sat outside his tent, his spirit helper, Billy the Black One, approached him, took off his neckerchief and gave it to Tom, who knew that the vision had come to help. True to form, the next day Cyclone "had to be thrown down and saddled on the ground for if he was saddled standing he would throw himself backwards." When Tom Three Persons got on the back of that black devil horse, Cyclone reared and plunged, "took prodigious leaps and twisted and corkscrewed his body in a fury of contortions that threatened to tear him in two." But Tom Three Persons rode him to defeat, while the crowd in the grandstands, which included the Duke and Duchess of Connaught, went wild.

That was a deal with the Devil.

• • •

By the turn of the century there was no shortage of colourful characters pushing their way west. Traders and carpenters and various other handymen found ready work; and they attracted the usual trail of store clerks and prostitutes and whisky vendors and sidekicks. The International Boundary Commission's men, a mixed bag of drovers and soldiers and cooks and supply personnel, as well as senior surveyors and scientists, had staked out the forty-ninth parallel with remarkable efficiency, despite mosquitoes and prairie fires and snowstorms, hot weather and cold. They started from Red River in May 1873 and moved gradually west, scoring the division between the Canadian prairies and the scary States with a series of markers or monuments, usually piles of earth. At a summit west of Waterton Lakes 760 miles later, they had drawn a line, the first of the artificial geopolitical fences surrounding what would become Alberta. With 388 earth mounds marking the boundary every one to three miles, no accidental drifter or whisky trader could claim that the border wasn't clear, although nobody checked passports yet. These Royal Engineers and their enormous entourage—at one point numbering more than five hundred men—undertook a trek as strenuous and exciting as that of the Mounties, but without red coats and military manners; their feat was taken largely for granted.

If a man wanted ongoing work in the 1870s, surveying was a good profession. The Centre, now that it owned the immense land wealth of the North West Territories, needed to get the place settled, but all those miles and miles had to be measured off into suitable squares, so that locations could be identified. Surveyors were as much in demand as fresh bread; there were Dominion surveyors and Boundary Commission surveyors and CPR surveyors. They studied routes and drew lines and subdivided townships—they would eventually parcel into four-sided sections 454,000 square miles of Alberta. The undulating and limitless landscape was being mathematically divided, readied for roads and taxes and railroad sidings.

By 1872, with the CPR burning a hole in Central pockets, engineer-in-chief Sandford Fleming sent out twenty-five survey parties, of which six were supposed to try to figure out the best of the seven possible routes through the Rockies. Just behind him, the first Dominion land surveyor, W. S. Gore, in 1873 measured out the Hudson's Bay Company reserve lands that had been part of the deal when the HBC sold the West to Canada, some three thousand acres around HBC forts in Edmonton, Victoria, Fort Assiniboine, and Rocky Mountain House. In 1877 surveyor W. F. King ran the fourteenth base line through what would become Edmonton; Jasper Avenue would have to move to conform to its measure. And J. S. Dennis Jr. (surveyors needed two initials and a short name), who surveyed parts of the fourth meridian, which would become Alberta's eastern boundary, in 1878 split the Barr colony settlement into two villages, later making Lloydminster the only city in Canada with a foot in two provinces. By then

Rancher John Ware and his family

Glenbow Archives, Calgary, Canada: NA-263-1

settlers were beginning to build in Alberta.

The wide-open spaces, which had been so congenial a territory for roaming buffalo, were perfect for cattle. And dogged surveyors with their straight lines could not match the new heroes called cowboys. In northern Alberta, the mysterious voyageurs dominated myth, but in the south their counterparts were surely those enigmatic men on horseback. As L. V. Kelly writes in his highly coloured history *The Range Men*, "These are the men who first braved the frontier in an effort to establish legitimate business, the men who really carved the way. They lived on the outskirts of the farthest police patrol, they herded their stock and guarded it against the untamed Indians and the wild beasts of the mountains and hills, they lived in mud-roofed shacks, eating rough foods, without any of the luxuries that are to-day considered necessities." A different variety of nomad, the range men echoed the Indians who preceded them—and many Indians worked as cowboys. In a mirror effect, the two pushed the romance of the West toward its popular, if entirely limited "cowboys and Indians" image, and although allegedly tamer than its American counterpart, the Canadian Wild West.

Conventional wisdom holds that ranching in southern Alberta spread north from the United States, but the truth is, the Methodist McDougalls first drove eleven cows and a bull down from Fort Edmonton when they established their mission at Morley, to the west of not-yet Calgary in 1873. The Mounties, too, had brought some stock along on their trek west, although it was up to Fort Benton's I. G. Baker to provide them with fresh meat. Sam Livingstone, the first settler on the Elbow River, kept pigs. A few enterprising men squatting around the posts milked dairy cows and sold butter to the Mounties, but there wasn't much market for beef, at least not yet. But settlers were starting to straggle in, and slowly the potential for business picked up. In 1876–77 hundreds of beasts bawled and dusted a trail north from Montana to establish the beginning of Alberta's golden age of ranching.

By strict definition, the first Alberta rancher was H. A. (Fred) Kanouse, son of a Fort Benton judge, a one-time whisky trader to the Indians and buffalo hunter for the Mounties. Both activities covered the rent but were risky, so he needed a new profession. In the fall of 1877, the same year as the signing of Treaty Seven, Kanouse shooed a bull and twenty-one cows off into the open prairie near Fort Macleod. No one expected to see the cattle again, but the next spring he rounded up the entire herd plus twenty-one calves, a total recovery doubled. With that lucky roundup for an example, George Emerson and Tom Lynch started driving horses and cattle up into Alberta from Montana. They sold their first lot to small operators and recently discharged NWMPs, all of them eager to try cattle ranching for themselves, and in August 1879, Alberta's first real roundup took place in the Macleod district. Sixteen men, including four former Mounties, on assorted horses, gathered together some five hundred head of cattle, discouragingly fewer than had been sent out to range the fall before. Cold weather, hungry Indians, and white rustlers had decreased the number considerably. The would-be ranchers laid the blame on the Indians and wanted to shoot anyone caught killing their cattle, but the Mounties made it known that any murderer, revenging rustled cattle or not, would hang. The disgusted group drove their reduced herd south to Montana. Maybe ranching in Alberta wasn't such a good idea.

But one bright-eyed Mountie, home in Lennoxville, Quebec, on leave from Fort Macleod, spun incredible yarns of space and wealth and limitless possibilities. Being a member of that esteemed force, Captain William Winder surely wouldn't have lied, but his enthusiasm was sufficient to raise a surprising amount of capital toward an imaginary picture he drew of an immense cattle empire. He would buy a huge herd of Montana beasts, drive them north and then, once they had grazed and fattened and multiplied, would market the resultant steers back in Montana.

Tough, long-horned cattle could digest prairie grass better than eastern horses ever could—and they got fat in the process. Both financiers and wild-eyed dreamers could see millions of acres of open grazing land, wrinkled with protective coulees, crossed by clear, swift rivers, everything that cattle needed. No fences, no farmers, and now that the buffalo were gone and the Indians confined to reserves, no competition at all. Even the weather would co-operate, with glorious chinooks a regular occurrence, melting the snow so that cattle could graze year-round. Through the smoke spiralling from their cigars, the eyes of Eastern capitalists and English gentlemen gleamed. Profit from cattle, with no overhead, required very little manpower. That dream of huge landholdings, with all the romantic associations of owning a ranch, would contribute to the development of the Alberta cowtown triangle of Fort Calgary, Fort Macleod, and Pincher Creek.

But there was one drawback. Winder had the vision but not the land. Old Tomorrow Macdonald wanted settlers in the West, but he hadn't thought about leasing huge blocks of Crown land for grazing, and he wasn't sure it was a good idea. So although Winder had financial backing, he was stymied. Until his marvellously exaggerated tales came to the ears of one Matthew H. Cochrane, a Montreal senator who had made his fortune in leather and shoes, but who had an interest in livestock breeding. Winder's story caught Cochrane's imagination—he calculated that he could run forty times as many cattle as he was currently able to in the Eastern Townships. With a vision of thousands of acres on a ranch out West, Cochrane pulled the strings of his political connections—one of his friends was the minister of agriculture, John Pope. In no time, by Ottawa standards, an 1881 order-in-council decreed that up to 100,000 acres of land could be leased for twenty-one years at the rate of $10 for a thousand acres. A penny an acre a year. And an owner could also buy 5 percent of his total lease, the "home farm and corral," at $2 an acre. Quite a bargain.

Cochrane could hardly contain himself. He immediately leased more than 100,000 acres and persuaded the Mounties to release Colonel James Walker to serve as his resident ranch manager. Maybe Cochrane thought that a Mountie would prevent rustling or could magically control wandering cattle, but Walker was a bad choice, who made mistake after mistake. Cochrane had purchased almost seven thousand head of cattle in Montana, and the drive north, to the lease just west of the current city of Calgary, was strenuous, with thirty cowboys and three hundred horses moving the cattle at a quick march of fifteen to eighteen miles a day. The poor cows barely had time to rest and snatch a mouthful of grass before they were travelling again; calves could not keep up and the cattle had no time to graze. By the time they got to the Bow River, where they were counted, then herded across to the lease land, the beasts were skinny and exhausted, and when an early blizzard hit them, more than a thousand died. It was a good thing Cochrane had his shoe factories to fall back on. But that was just the beginning. Only too often Central directives didn't quite connect with the West and its culture. Cochrane ordered Walker to ensure that all the cattle were branded, so Mountie Walker rounded up every stray steer in sight—including a neighbour's pet cow—and branded it, enraging many smaller local ranchers, whose animals he handily appropriated. In turn, they quietly rustled Cochrane's maverick cattle from coulees and hills. Not much love was lost between the big outfits and the smaller settlers. The ranchers hated farmers and treated them as "squatters," and the farmers hated the ranchers who had so much influence with Ottawa.

Walker lost even more cowboy respect when he drove a second herd up from Montana in 1882. When they were hit with a bad blizzard south of Calgary, the cattle naturally tried to take refuge in a sheltered valley, which the trail boss argued was the best course of action, but Walker insisted that the exhausted animals be driven on to Big Hill, the name of the Cochrane Ranche (the e for extra elegance) holdings. That terrible trek, combined with a tough chinook-less winter, resulted in many deaths, cattle carcasses piled deep in creek cuts and coulees. Cochrane lost more than half of his livestock, and decided to relocate to a lease much farther south, on the Oldman and Waterton Rivers, where he built a stone mansion surrounded by green lawns and tended flower beds.

A Cochrane subsidiary, the British American Ranch Company, took over the lease outside Calgary and replaced the cattle with sheep. Realizing that he was no ranch manager, Walker resigned and went into the business of sawing logs, later becoming the mayor of Calgary. The original dreamer of these dreams, Captain Winder, had got a lease of his own and started a ranch with 1,200 head of cattle and seventy-five Percheron horses. But for all his contagious vision, he died in 1885 and his holdings were dissolved.

Cowboys hate sheep as much as they hate settlers; they think sheep graze too close to the ground, ruining the grass for cattle. And Westerners have a powerful distaste for absentee landlords. Cochrane was a big shot in the Centre, with connections in Ottawa, and under various company names he eventually controlled more than 300,000 acres in Alberta. But he came west only a few times, relying on other men to run his empire. Because he hired good men and then ignored their advice, his ranches were spectacular failures. Cattle and sheep died regularly and democratically, in blizzards and prairie fires or caught in swollen rivers. Eventually, in 1905, the Cochrane lands were sold to the energetic and more pragmatic Mormons who had just come up from Utah to begin building Cardston.

By 1882 three other huge ranches joined this compelling enterprise. The Oxley Ranch syndicate was formed when an Ontario livestock breeder, John Craig, managed to raise some $200,000 for a ranch; but then he travelled to England where he fell in with a perfectly accented and well-connected Englishman, Alexander Stavely Hill. Hill persuaded Craig to drop his colonial investors in favour of English gentlemen, who presumably could invest more respectable money, in order to give the enterprise a higher tone. Hill couldn't come up with much cash, but the titled Lord Lathom could, and Craig was set. He acquired leases first in front-range country, and then along Willow Creek, but the Oxley Ranch was dogged by constant feuds over insufficient funds; cattle were often seized to cover bad debts. In 1885 Craig quit and took out his own lease, eventually publishing a book, *Ranching with Lords and Commons*, about what it was like to try to run a ranch with titled and untitled cricket-playing English directors who had no clue of ranching's day-to-day operations.

The Walrond Ranch, begun in 1883 by Dominion Veterinary Director-General Duncan McEachran, with leases along the Oldman River into the Porcupine Hills, relied on a group of similarly pedigreed British investors. Because McEachran hired an experienced American foreman, its first few years seemed prosperous, but then it, too, stumbled through unhealthy times, losing stock to fires, blizzards, and disease, especially the mange. Oddly enough, the Walrond never counted its cattle, so the ranch estimated a far larger inventory of stock than were actually alive and on the hoof. In 1895 the English shareholders "determined to quit the business," since the returns were not what had been expected. McEachran and some other shareholders bought out the British boys, but the Walrond kept on losing money, and finally it was taken over, first by William Roper Hull, then by meat-packing king Pat Burns, who actually made it work.

The most profitable of the ranches was certainly the Northwest Cattle Company, later called the Bar U, run by Fred Stimson, Captain Winder's sturdy, brass-mouthed brother-in-law. Stimson had implacable standards for both men

Cowboy on bronc

and horses, and when one of his horses was killed by a trail he remarked that a horse that couldn't outrun the CPR didn't deserve to live. The Bar U was backed by the Allan brothers, steamship magnates from Montreal, known for making the bribes that resulted in Macdonald's Pacific Scandal. Stimson had the experience to choose good cows and better cowboys, and when he trailed in three thousand head from Idaho he lost almost none. Meeting the same blizzard that destroyed the Cochrane drive, Stimson wisely let the cattle wander to an area around Fort Macleod where there was sufficient grazing to withstand the eight-day snowfall. Experienced working cowboys like Herb Miller, Tom Lynch (the king of trails), George Emerson (who'd brought the first cattle to Alberta), George Lane, and Bill Moodie were hired for the Bar U. A great horsebreaker named Henry Longabaugh, the outlaw otherwise known as the Sundance Kid, worked at the Bar U in 1890, before travelling south to join the Wild Bunch and consolidate his legend.

Best known of all was John Ware, a black cowboy who stayed in Canada because it didn't encourage quite as many vigilante groups as the United States had, although he would encounter plenty of racism and bigotry in Alberta. Because he seemed inexperienced, he was first hired by Lynch in Helena, Montana, as a cook's helper and night rider, drudgery that real cowboys despised. After a few weeks of boring night herding, Ware quietly asked for "a better saddle and a little worse horse." When the cowboys, eager for fun, presented Ware with an outlaw horse who had kicked everyone else off, Ware chuckled and asked, "What'll I do if he bucks?" But he swung aboard, and when the horse exploded into a fury of twisting and kicking Ware earned the respect of the incredulous crew by riding the bronc to a standstill, smiling all the while. At the end of the ride, with the cowboys and trail boss still astonished, Ware asked if he could keep the horse. He was instantly promoted. He was a large man, with an appetite to match, and the chuckwagon cook always served him his food on a platter; the Indians called him "bad black white man."

Although it lasted longer than the others, the Bar U, which was purchased in 1902 by George Lane, was dogged by debt and difficulty just as much as the other big outfits, and when Lane died in 1926 the place was mortgaged to the hilt. Ranching was turning out to be a romantic but elusive dream, and outfits were taken over by smaller, more economical businesses, often run by men with a ranching sideline like shipping or meat packing. But those early years were heady, optimistic times. In 1883 only about 25,000 cattle roamed the prairie, but by 1886, 75,000 cattle and some 11,000 horses rolled and trotted over the folds of the hills. And those leases were enormous. In 1888, 111 ranches leased land, each holding between 11,000 and 200,000 acres—an unheard-of spread. Most have now disappeared, although their reputations linger. Only a few Alberta families still ranch the same lands. The Copithornes west of Calgary built up their holdings slowly and carefully, actually beginning as squatters on the Cochrane lease. The McIntyres on the Milk River Ridge grew hay and green feed to feed their herds. A. E. Cross, who started the A7 Ranche at Mosquito Creek west of Nanton, supported the ranch with wealth generated by the Calgary Brewing and Malting Company and the fifty hotels he owned across the West, as well as his shares in Calgary Petroleum Products. With Pat Burns, Archie McLean, and George Lane, Cross founded the Calgary Stampede. All these ranchers had substantial family money backing them, but were cautious and smart, the only way to go if you wanted to keep a ranch in Alberta.

Those were halcyon days, and having a ranch in the West attracted various adventurers, characters as diverse as Major-General Thomas Bland Strange, leader of Alberta's home defence in the 1885 Rebellion, setting up the Military Colonization Ranche along the Bow River just for the entertainment of his fellow officers from Britain and India. There was the High River Hunt Club, solely interested in raising horses for British regiments; the Quorn Ranch, too, was backed by English investors, members of the Quorn Hunt Club in Leicestershire. The Quorn imported stallions and hound dogs and set out to raise purebred horses, but they mostly served as a dude ranch for lords and earls with wing collars and supercilious smiles, who came west to test their hounds on coyotes, their guns on air, and their riding ability over the rough, which meant that surprise gopher holes often left them gasping and winded on the ground. The Sons of England Benevolent Society Coyote Hunt had strict rules, but the coyotes, handy replacements for English foxes, probably didn't consider the society very benevolent. The English imported polo clubs and balls to such an extent that the flavour still lingers. And in the early 1920s His Royal Highness, Edward, Prince of Wales, purchased the E. P. Ranch west of High River, his occasional visits marking the social calendar of the ranching elite.

Another mythical aspect of Alberta's history got its start with Central capitalists and English gentlemen, some of whom never laid eyes on the ranches they invested in. "I have a ranch in the Territories" must have competed with "I had a farm in Africa" more than once. And following nineteenth-century fashion, young Englishmen whose families were embarrassed by their behaviour—drink or pregnant servant girls or debt—were sent off to the colonies. These so-called remittance men were often tricked or duped by locals, who treated them with a mixture of suspicion and skepticism. Stories of remittance men wiring home with outrageous excuses for more money are legion. One man claimed that he had a gopher ranch, and his father, unsure of what gophers were, wired a packet of money. Remittance men sometimes actually started ranches, with some degree of success, although often those ranches were mere shacks squatting on other leases. And if the wealthy daddy or uncle decided to visit Canada, the remittance man faced being unveiled. Some jobs bluntly advertised "No English need apply," aimed directly at a type perceived as spoiled, rich, and worst of all, green. Part of the colourful wallpaper of the turn-of-the-century West, most of the remittance men left at the start of the

Cowboy and horse, true love

First World War, enlisting for the next beguiling adventure and leaving behind only a few broken hearts and their own elevated dreams.

Adaptability was the trait most required, and Americans possessed large measures of that. Pushed back by expanding settlement, many American cowboys and ranchmen drifted north into Canada. The Powder River Cattle Company, the Circle Ranch and Cattle Company, and the Pioneer Cattle Company, all with American pedigrees, spread through the southeastern part of Alberta. In 1886 Americans drove more than thirty thousand head of cattle over the border, and although that winter devastated the herds, many, prepared for the unexpected vagaries of ranching, stayed. By 1900 the previously British balance in Alberta was tipped in an American direction: just over seven thousand citizens of British origin were outnumbered by almost eleven thousand Americans. And the myth of American individuality and frontier spirit was generally admired, despite its long association with lawlessness and liquor.

Cowboys, responsible for the finer points of running livestock on the open range, did everything from the back of a horse—man and horse together had to work as a flawless unit. Cowboys slept on the ground with their heads on feed sacks, were up before sunrise for pancakes from tin plates and coffee from tin cups, rode from dawn to dusk and never complained, although they were probably masters of the sotto voce grumble. They were no gentlemen, but tough, itinerant workers, who had nothing but their skill with cattle and horses to parlay into wages, wages that were never very extravagant. Pragmatic stockmen, they were employed by ranching overlords to carry out the gritty jobs necessary for raising cattle to be sold for beef. The work was dusty, tedious, and dangerous, not the exciting gallop that celluloid portrays. Each cowboy was expected to watch close to a thousand head of cattle, which might be spread over some twenty thousand acres. Just riding to check on a wandering herd took hours, though his ability to help them with calving, or even to save them from wolves, was limited.

Roundups combined excitement and monotony. The biggest occurred in the spring, when the cattle were counted after the winter, the new calves branded, and the male calves castrated. In the fall a smaller roundup collected cattle for shipping and sale. In preparation for the spring roundup the ranches joined forces, hiring extra hands, mending tack, preparing their string of horses—cowboys needed five to ten horses each, because horses that were ridden every day wore out. The cooks had to get the chuckwagons ready to feed the hungry men. For every dozen cowboys, some one hundred horses had to be readied, first rounded up themselves, since during the winter cowboys needed only a few horses and the rest were allowed to roam free. Finding, penning, and then re-gentling a horse used to running wild on the prairie was even more demanding than herding the less intelligent cattle, and the excitement of riding recalcitrant broncs became a favourite spectacle in rodeo. The horses had to be reminded of obedience, one at a time, and a good horse breaker was worth his weight in pancakes and coffee.

The biggest roundup in history took place in 1885, the same year as the North West Rebellion, and the contrast between the booming cattle empires and the fading force of the Métis and Indians marked it even more. About 100 cowboys, backed by 500 horses and fed by 15 chuckwagons, crossed and recrossed ten thousand miles of landscape to herd together some sixty thousand cattle.

A roundup day began long before dawn, with coffee and biscuits from the back of the chuckwagon. First the horse wranglers roped the horses selected to work that day, and after the real breakfast the entire camp moved toward the next stopping place. The range cowboys would then spread out and scour the countryside for cattle. Working in two large half-circles radiating out from the campsite, they would cover ten to fifteen miles, herding calves and cows from every coulee and creek cut. By late afternoon the cowboys would be back with the animals they'd collected, which would be held, milling and bawling, in a large open area. Riders from each ranch would go into the herd to separate those belonging to their respective ranches. The new calves would stick close to their branded mothers, and slowly, with the tremendous skill of cutting horses working against flighty cattle, the animals would be identified and herded to separate areas belonging to the different ranches, where they would be branded. This scene, of dust and smoke, horses threading between tossing horns, calves skittishly running, the branding fires hot and sparking, was a melee of speed and excitement. Cowboys quickly roped the calves, lashed the rope to their saddlehorns and dragged them to the fire, where the branding men used a hot iron to sear a permanent mark on their rumps and a cowboy wielding a penknife castrated the males. The smells of blood and burnt hair and spitting tobacco and sweat hung in the air. The noise and dust alone were overwhelming, and the terrified bawling of the calves, the quick, brutal work, all made for a scene that would now evoke either fascination or revulsion.

Of course, all these animals ranging together led to the spread of contagious diseases, mange—an eczematous inflammation—the most common. Dipping became an important part of the roundup, with animals dunked in hot water or creosote to kill the mites that caused the illness. After this treatment, branded calves and their mothers were herded away, back to the open range.

At night, circling a restless head, a cowboy's only company was the soft ballad he sang to lull the animals. Not much consolation for $50 a month, although foremen made closer to $100. Food and sleep were their finest pleasures, especially food, fresh-baked bread, fresh-roasted and ground coffee, canned tomatoes, pickles, bacon, pies. A good cook, essential to ranching life, had to make meals from the back of a chuckwagon or over a campfire as well he did in a more stable kitchen, and a roundup was often remembered by the cook's wagon. Cooks were volatile and bad-tempered, and being a cook's helper was an unlucky job. The tradition of

The cook and his chuckwagon; note the fresh-baked pies

Glenbow Archives, Calgary, Canada: NA-207-108

chuckwagons racing one another to get to a campsite first is re-enacted in the milling figure-eight and the adrenalin-pounding thunderous half-mile of hell that now crowns the Calgary Stampede's evening performances every July.

Cowboys didn't work on foot, and they didn't farm. That was part of their restless charm. Their clothing too, now considered costume, was specifically useful to their work. Their boots and chaps protected their legs from being whipped by grass and small bushes, and in winter kept their legs warm. Bandanas pulled up over the nose sifted the dust and could strain rank water; they also protected the backs of cowboys' necks from sunburn. Stetsons cut down on glare; since the sun wasn't as intense, the southern Alberta cowboy hat was slightly smaller than the American version. Boot heels were slightly elevated, to prevent feet from slipping through the stirrups. Laconic heroes, cowboys could be dirty and foul-mouthed, reeking of tobacco and sweat, with bad teeth and dirty ears, but a few managed shaves and polysyllabic sentences. Most comfortable with whisky and wolves, they were known for their determined bachelorhood, although they had a reputation for chivalry and good manners, and were willing to struggle into a jacket to sit at table with a woman. Still, women who married cowboys confessed that they were most seduced by the men's ability to ride. The cowboy code of neighbourliness, loyalty, independence, and uncomplaining persistence became a part of the West's code, unspoken but writ larger than the looming mountains. And like cowboys themselves, it lingers. Pickup trucks have replaced horses, but the work is the same.

Alberta cowboys were no saints. They carried guns, even if they claimed only to shoot rattlesnakes; they fought with one another; they rustled the odd maverick calf; and they drank long and lustily. After riding the range for months, cowboys went to town for booze and women, and after drinking and gambling and arguing and shooting up the saloons, occasionally took potshots at one another. A few were killed or charged with manslaughter. Crime was hard to control because the Mounties couldn't keep track of that much wide-open land, randomly dotted with settlers and ranchers. Patrolling from the back of a horse, they had to guess at illicit activity, and evidence of a crime long after the scene had grown cold was hard to furnish. Even if a thief or a murderer was charged, he inevitably got off with a light sentence from a tolerant judge. Whisky was sold in licensed premises, and houses of tender repute provided cowboys with that other rare pleasure, sex. Prostitution flourished and many a cowboy dumped his roundup savings in the lap of a lace-trimmed baguette. Brothels were tolerated, and prostitutes preferred the open-handedness of starved-for-affection cowboys to the more cautious and tight-fisted miners. For a long time the business of lonely men shaped the social stratification of Alberta. Pretty horses and fast women were more to a cowboy's taste than the reverse.

A frontier that had thought nothing of shooting every buffalo in sight now wanted severe penalties for anyone shooting or stealing cattle. The open range made cattle theft a tempting proposition, and unbranded mavericks were fair game. White men might have thought that they were different from the original peoples, but they stole one another's horses with as much relish as the Blackfoot ever did. Cross-border rustling of both horses and cattle was popular, but rustlers taking critters south of the border, if caught, were likely to meet with frontier justice of the rope variety, so many preferred Mountie justice, which was gentler.

The easiest way to steal calves was the "running iron" method. The thief would ride across the range, carrying a convenient branding iron rounded at the end so that it could be shaped into virtually any brand the rustler wanted. Their targets were unmarked cows or calves, and the versatile iron could even alter existing brands. If the lone figure unexpectedly encountered a suspicious owner, he slid the shorter-than-usual branding iron into the side of his cowboy boot. Brands were first ordinated in 1878; and as far back as 1876 the NWMP kept a brand book to help them identify ownership.

But rustling was also entrepreneurial sport, reflecting the historical character of a landscape that had been stolen from its original owners. Settlers and squatters alike formed rustling groups, where local thieves channelled animals to professional rustlers in exchange for grain or cash. Some thefts were elaborately conceived shipment and smuggling operations, and the Mounties learned to calculate numbers carefully. The expectation was approximately one calf for every two or three cows; any herd that had neatly doubled its numbers in a winter was suspect. And then there was grass theft. Montana ranchers would ship their cattle by train to the border and let them go. If the beasts drifted across the line, as if by accident, all the better—inexpensive Canadian grass in the stomachs of American cows, with the cattle returned from law-abiding Canada after roundup. And resolutely stiff-necked about their independence, ranchers often refused to help the police, as if the mere application of justice interfered with the philosophy of the open range. Maybe everyone was guilty of occasional rustling.

All that rustling and horse thieving led to the formation of the Western Stock Growers' Association in 1896, which authorized rewards for the "apprehension and conviction of any person or persons stealing or otherwise rustling STOCK IN THIS COMMUNITY from any member in good standing." The association lobbied Ottawa and the territorial government in Regina, and it helped to enforce branding, and roundup laws, wolf bounties, and disease control. Under the closed-lease system, eleven stock districts represented some one thousand stockmen. Voting membership was open to any cattle raiser for a fee of three cents a head of stock—which could get expensive for the larger outfits. The WSGA also got into the fight over the formation of the provinces of Saskatchewan and Alberta in 1904–5;

believing that the southern grassland had little in common with the parkland or the boreal forest in the northern half of Alberta, they wanted the boundary between the two provinces to run east/west, just south of Red Deer.

By that time, the massive open leases across the southwest began to be interrupted by the sod houses of homesteaders, the growing tension between ranchers and these settlers emphasized by barbed wire fences. Cattlemen depended on secure access to cheap grazing—guaranteed to them by their Ottawa contacts—and they exported their cattle to Chicago and Britain, where Alberta beef was gaining its reputation. Ranchers hated settlers, calling them nesters or sodbusters; they knew that if too many farmers arrived, the character of the country would change irrevocably. Sodbusters, the ranchers claimed, started fires, stole cattle, destroyed open grazing land by ploughing it under, and closed off needed water holes. Cowboys had nothing but contempt for pitchforks and wagons and hayracks; they would often make campfires of fence posts after cutting through the offending barbed wire. At first homesteaders squatting on leased land were just a nuisance, but by the mid-1890s, they were an active force. Not as much overt warfare took place between settlers and ranchers as in the States, but in the Porcupine Hills in 1890, a group of cowboys pulled down the house of a settler named Dunbar on the Walrond Ranch holdings. He and his sons had occupied the land since 1882, so they felt that their claim was just, and the settlers in that area subsequently petitioned Ottawa to change the old ranching leases in favour of homesteading.

But the business end of beef was something else, and Alberta's most famous cattle king, Pat Burns, made a fortune riding, not horses, but the cattle market. A stout, twinkle-eyed legend who brought his Irish good humour from Kirkfield, Ontario, he traded his way west from Winnipeg to Saskatchewan and then Alberta by providing just what the railway construction gangs required—meat. Arriving in Calgary around 1890 and seeing the area surrounded by grazing herds, he opened a slaughterhouse and set about marketing meat, buying cattle, and providing beef to the Indian reserves, construction gangs, and mining and lumbering camps. Burns contracted the beef for the Yukon Gold Rush in 1898, sending live cattle by boat north from Vancouver, driving them over the passes, then slaughtering the cattle beside the Lewes River and floating the carcasses down to Dawson. As a provisioner, Burns did better than the ranchers who had to nurse the four-legged beasts to market size. Entrepreneurial and ambitious, Burns brought in other goods for sale, such as potatoes and Ontario apples, luxuries the raw town of Calgary craved. By 1896 the Meat King's Calgary abattoir was killing seven hundred cattle, six hundred pigs, and fifteen hundred sheep a month. Burns often said that he would have preferred to be in the growing rather than the killing end of the business, and when, in 1907, the growers who sold to him complained about his monopoly, the government felt it had to investigate his holdings. That might have been the only time Burns lost his temper, and in testimony he asserted that he was a fair buyer, setting his prices by the stock markets in the East, and that without him the country would not eat.

His advertisements certainly suggested that P. Burns and Co. could provide dressed meats, cured meats and lard, poultry, fish, butter and eggs, oysters, sauerkraut, mincemeat, sausage makers, sausage casings, and chicken feed. Consignments of butter, eggs, and poultry were solicited, highest prices paid. Many a farmer's wife purchased a few luxuries with the butter she sold Burns. The investigating commission exonerated him completely, and he kept on making money. Even the fire that consumed his plant in 1913 did not set him back, for meanwhile, he had become a rancher himself, buying William Roper Hull's Fish Creek spread. By 1912 and the inaugural Calgary Stampede, of which Burns was one of the Big Four backers, he owned the Bow Valley, the C K, the Circle, the Ricardo, the Mackie, the Imperial, and the N F ranches, in total some quarter of a million acres of grazing land. In 1928 Burns sold most of his packing empire for $15 million and settled in to enjoying his money. As he was one of Alberta's first millionaires, no one dares to say much bad about Burns. Eventually named to the Senate, the butcher with the heart of gold is best remembered for his human rather than his financial side.

In the end, even more than settlers, Alberta's maverick climate wiped out the big ranches. The winter of 1886–87 killed thousands of animals, with cattle wading up to their bellies through snow. When they found weak and starving calves, the cowboys could do nothing but pull their guns and shoot, and in the spring, the prairie was littered with carcasses. Some ranches lost entire herds. In March of 1892 another bitter storm swept a killer path; even worse, in April of that year, a heavy rain, followed by days of freezing winds, killed thousands of cattle. During the winter of 1892–93, the weather grew vicious, temperatures falling to sixty below and snowstorms raging every three days. Against such forces, cattle had no chance. Early in the ranching years, herds flourished. But as time passed, the risks grew: mange, blackleg, wolves, rustling, prairie fires, bad winters, and drought— any one of these enough to cause economic disaster.

In 1896 the lease system, that amazing bargain of a penny an acre a year, ended, but lease holders could purchase one-tenth of their lease for $1.25 an acre. Many of them did so and continued to invest in the dream of unfenced land. After 1900 the number of settlers along the route between Edmonton and Calgary increased rapidly, bringing two of the ranchers' biggest enemies, barbed wire and taxes; ranchers were assessed $16 a square mile, whether they owned the land or just grazed it. In 1902 Alberta had some 2.3 million acres of leased land, and Minister of the Interior Clifford Sifton continued to approve individual leases of up to 150 square miles on land considered unsuitable for agriculture. But when Sifton resigned and Frank Oliver took over, Oliver, friend of farmers, reversed everything. As far as he was concerned, the climate was irrelevant, and all the land in southern Alberta was more than suitable for agriculture. Grazing leases were revoked with two years' notice. The ranchers and sodbusters were once again pitted against each other because of what the Centre thought should happen.

But southern Alberta's greatest cruelty was yet to strike. Spring blizzards killed thousands of beasts in 1904. But the bitter winter of 1906–7, when huge numbers of range stock died, dealt the final blow to rangeland optimists. The curse began when numerous fires in the fall of 1906 damaged a huge swath of grazing land south of Calgary, so cattle were already hungry when winter arrived. Then in late October it rained for two weeks, until November 15, when the temperature suddenly plummeted and three feet of snow with a frozen crust covered the grass. No chinooks broke that winter, and the cattle were desperate. Small ranchers who needed to protect their stock against scrub longhorns (rough Texas cattle that ran wild), had strung wire illegally, and hundreds of cattle drifted against the fences and died. Some desperate beasts pushed fences down and staggered onward until they found shelter or food, anything—the wood of fence posts, sapling trees, feed stacks. In Macleod one January day, scores of Bar U range cattle, hair and hide in patches, frozen and skinned, tottered through town, a ghost herd too weak even to bawl. In February so many cattle milled on the open tracks that the train could hardly get through. They literally climbed snowdrift-covered houses and barns trying to get to stacked hay. In that "Winter of the Blue Snow," one blizzard followed another, the snow getting deeper and deeper. Cattle drifted some two hundred miles, and at least half that had been rounded up in the fall of 1906 died. No matter what the cowboys tried to do, the cattle were crazed by hunger and exposure. It was May before the snow went, leaving tens of thousands of carcasses, the coulees piled deep with them; the few cattle that had managed to stay alive were just skin and bones, often too weak to stand, so they had to be shot. That was the spring they called "the Big Stink," with the stench of dead animals fouling the air. The knell of the ranching dream had sounded, and within a few years most of the big ranches had folded or sold out.

Eventually even the most diehard open-range rancher learned to put up extra hay in case the chinooks didn't blow in. Mild winters occurred often, but at least one-third were harsh. And grazing land had to be husbanded. One cow and calf needed ten acres; it took ninety acres of grass to bring a steer to market weight, and between 1895 and 1905, that steer was worth only $50. Politically assigned rangeland made overgrazing a serious problem, and the need for water reserves led to a system of "public" grazing.

Instead of cattle, wheat became king, and the plough sliced open the land. Settlement divided the newly agrarian prairie from the eastern slopes of the Rockies, which continued as rangeland. If cows could not withstand the unpredictable weather, thought some ranchers, maybe horses could, and gradually southern Alberta changed from free-ranging cows to horses. Horses did well, and even now, foothills horse ranches are almost more successful than cattle ranches. By 1920 the horse population of Alberta exceeded the human population, 800,000 horses to 600,000 people.

But the romance of ranching dies hard. The last big roundup, which took place in the fall of 1907, didn't quench the smoulder of cowboy lore. Cowboys are beloved icons, charming and bow-legged and dangerous and sexy, even though a cowboy today is an agricultural worker, ordinary, unexceptional, as likely to swing a booted foot out of the door of a pickup truck parked in a supermarket lot as off a horse. When Alberta designated 1998 the Year of the Cowboy, nobody paid more homage than usual. But on weekends Cowboys Dance Hall hosts hundreds of urban cowboys pretending to be laconic heroes, and even now the Ranchmen's Club, that elite fraternity of old range riders, flourishes. Calgary proudly calls itself a cowtown, and every year during Stampede, horses rule the streets, and bank managers and accountants don their blue jeans and their bandanas and become what every southern Albertan has always wanted to be, a range rider, a cowboy, a maverick.

As for cattle, that melt-in-your-mouth Alberta beef, not every restaurant in the West serves the real thing; you have to know where to find it and what to ask for. Now most of the meat comes from Feedlot Alley, the grassy corridor between Brooks and Lethbridge, home to the largest concentration of feedlot-grown live-stock in Canada. The smell makes people hold their noses. Everyone agrees that more studies need to be carried out on the impact on health, on pollution, on the downright stink of all those cattle eating and shitting and growing. But Alberta beef is famous, an economic mainstay. The alley may well have to address environmental concerns, but Alberta isn't about to ban beef, no matter what k. d. lang suggests.

The great ranching era lasted only briefly, but that time still sounds ghostly hoofbeats in small-town rodeos, in the dust of summer roundups, in the slow loll of grazing cattle scattered over sage-grass hills within sight of the serrated Rockies. Alberta is still, between that old world and this, a wide-open rangeland.

8 | Settlers

I had walked proudly behind my father, in the clean new furrows in my bare feet, as
he broke the new sod on our farm, and as the coulter cut the sod, and the share
turned it over, I knew he was doing something more than just ploughing a field.
—Nellie McClung, *Clearing in the West*

When you stand at the bottom of one of the huge open shafts inside a prairie grain eleva-
tor and shout, you can hear your voice echo for a million years. Dust hangs inside the
deep well like a dancer's veil and bats swoop toward the cupola-capped roofs. Beautiful
dinosaurs, those elevators rose fat with hope beside every small cluster of houses pretend-
ing to be a village, a village that included a general store, a post office, the grain agent's
house, and an elevator. They crowded against the railway, first one, then slowly prolifer-
ating into herds, white and red, green and blue, their broad board outlines signalling pros-
perity, the muscled shoulders of production and its fruits, castles of the new world, prairie
Gibraltars.

The parts of an elevator are as elaborate as hope itself. Built on concrete foundations,
elevators reach seventy to eighty feet high. Farmers in trucks and wagons pulled through
the huge double doors to dump their loads in a river of gold into the grated pit. From the
crowning gable, the elevating pulleys, rubberized belts with buckets, moved the grain to
the top, where spouts nozzled it down into the appropriate bins.

The elevator man ruling this prosperous kingdom enacted mysteries with chutes and
levers, with a mammoth weigh scale and a grading guide, a bloom of chaff clinging to his
overalls. He was always cheerful, his coffee pot brewing thick in the office beside the
ramp, his clock perfectly on time, his job reliable and well paid. He waited for the trundle
of arriving wheels, harvests gathering in the piles of rich, hard grain, this breadbasket
waiting to become flour.

I have a date with the death of an elevator, an elevator ancient enough to be pulled
down. The bulldozers attack it from one side, splintering its weakened joints, bringing it
to its knees with a wrenching groan, no longer the cathedral of the West, but a boarded
and beamed nuisance. I watch that gentle beast tumble to its knees, falling and falling
into its crumpled work, crashing toward dust.

In 1906, Alberta had forty-three grain elevators. By 1912, they had multiplied to 279, and in 1933–34 almost two thousand raised their heads into the clear Depression sky. In 2000 there were 252 again. They have lost the respect they enjoyed, their community bustle replaced by super-elevators, ugly concrete-and-metal silos, practical and leakproof, but without the elevators' granny-like capped roofs, their signs. Alberta Grain Growers. United Grain Growers. Pioneer. Agricore.

The function and parts of a grain elevator: to swallow grain and hold it until shipping. Storage for bumper crops, shelter for the secrets of growth, the sweat of labour, the waiting transformation into bread and pasta. They lumbered toward time. And they named towns, the name painted so large and loud that you knew where you were and how prosperous the town was.

• • •

Once Canada got its hands on the West, it needed to fill that West with people. Settlers effectively sealed the fate of the last fur brigade to York Factory in 1871; the fur trade and civilization could not coexist. The Hudson's Bay Company turned its hand to becoming the largest slum landlord in the West, selling the very land it had never owned to settlers. There were people here already, but they weren't buying land—it was theirs. By the 1872 Dominion Lands Act, a new system of land subdivision, ranges, townships, and sections, was established; the government offered any settler a quarter section (160 acres) of land for a $10 filing fee. The settler had three years to make the homestead his own, to live on the place at least six months of the year, to put up buildings, and to break and cultivate at least fifteen acres a year. If he failed, the $10 and the land were forfeited. It sounds like a good bargain, but as often as not disillusioned settlers turned their backs on the log and sod shanties where they had huddled through a howling winter, on the back-breaking toil they had put into the land, and left their homesteads behind. Others, though, were eager to hold out for permanent title, which was granted after the three years of "proving up."

The homesteader began with a tent, then a log shanty with a sod roof, which was fine in winter but leaked like a sieve once spring arrived. Flowers and plants grew picturesquely on the roofs, but the same roofs often caved in and showered families and their possessions with mud. Some women cried bitterly about living in a sod house and dreamed of the solid security of a frame house which no one could afford until the homestead was theirs. More fortunate settlers built a shack out of shingles and logs and finished lumber, or built tarpaper and dugout houses with straw roofs. Some could dig only shelters resembling root cellars into the sides of hills. They made furniture from poplar trees and slept on mattresses stuffed with straw. Often the first mortgage on the land was used to borrow money to dig a well, good enough for human consumption and deep enough to supply sufficient quantities of water for livestock. Settlers subsisted on a monotonous and often inadequate diet and, without a well, often contracted typhoid from drinking out of sloughs. Erecting buildings and fences necessary to keep the horses and cattle at home was next. Cutting firewood and fence posts, usually with sleigh and horses, was winter work. And if a storm struck, there was nothing to do but take shelter under the sleigh box and wait it out.

Even-numbered sections of land were allocated as homesteads, while odd-numbered sections were designated as public land, to be sold, the proceeds going to the feds. Two sections in every township were reserved for school land, and as a reward for nothing more than being the railway the CPR was given twenty-five million acres along its line. To ensure its survival, the railway needed to get people out West; it needed people to use the trains and buy stoves and shovels and harness from the Centre and send grain back to the Centre, the West paying for the cost of transportation both ways. Railways Minister Charles Tupper claimed in 1878 that the new railway would pay for itself—by selling the farmlands of the Western plains. He had the idea that there were 180 million acres on the prairies, just waiting for the touch of a plough, and that the railway could be built without raising taxes. He wasn't the first politician to be wrong.

"Canada's Colony" wasn't that simple a character, either. Scattered across Alberta were an unruly bunch of Indians, French Métis, English half-breeds, and settlers. But new immigrants in Ontario pushed to go west, and so, although there was all that trouble with the North West Rebellion, Ottawa bent to its task of surveying everything into square miles and governing a land they had hardly seen. When the last spike was pounded home on November 7, 1885, just nine days before Riel met his noose, the sound of that hammer on steel was supposed to call to settlers everywhere.

Ottawa advertised with the tempting slogan, "Free Homes for All," but at first, nobody came, certainly not the hordes Ottawa had imagined. There was a distinctly

FREE HOMES FOR ALL.

Government Lands in the Canadian Northwest,

HOW TO OBTAIN THEM.

HOMESTEADS PRE-EMPTIONS AND WOOD LOTS.

GOVERNMENT LANDS.

HOMESTEADS, PRE-EMPTIONS AND WOOD LOTS.

A "homestead" not exceeding one-quarter section, or 160 acres, is a free grant from the Government. Any person, male or female, who is the sole head of a family, or any male who has attained the age of eighteen years, is entitled to a homestead. The condition under which the grant is made is that the homesteader shall reside on and cultivate the land for three years. The person receiving a homestead entry is entitled at the same time—*but not at a later date*—to a pre-emption entry for an adjoining unoccupied 160 acre tract. The settler will not be called upon to pay for the pre-emption until the expiration of the three years that entitles him to receive a deed from the Government for his homestead. The price charged for pre-emptions within the Railway belt is $2.50 (10s.) per acre.

A settler is allowed a period of six months after date of entry for entering upon and taking possession of the land, but he must not be absent from his homestead for more than six months at any one time without special leave from the Minister of the Interior. *Only the even numbered sections of a township are open for homestead and pre-emption entries.*

Should the settler find that he cannot comply with the conditions of the three years' residence, he is allowed to purchase his homestead by paying $2.50 per acre therefor, provided that he has resided on the land for twelve months from date of entry, and has brought under cultivation at least thirty acres thereof.

Any person who has obtained a deed for his homestead after three years' residence may obtain another homestead and pre-emption entry.

Settlers that have not sufficient wood growing on their homesteads can purchase from the Government wood lots not exceeding twenty acres in size at $5.00 per acre. In addition to this, settlers are allowed, free of charge, a permit to cut timber on vacant Government lands—a sufficient quantity of wood, house logs and fence timber to meet all their requirements during the first year of homesteading. They are forbidden to dispose of wood from their homesteads, pre-emptions, wood lots, or what they may obtain under free permit, to saw-mill proprietors, or to any person other than an actual settler, for his own use. A breach of this condition, or non-fulfilment of homestead conditions, renders the entries of homestead, pre-emption and wood lot subject to cancellation. Should such cancellation be made, all improvements become forfeited to the Government, and the settler is not allowed to make a second homestead entry.

The attention of intending emigrants is drawn to the fact that the privilege of obtaining a pre-emption will be discontinued after January 1st, 1885. For those who wish to obtain large farms at a cheap rate, the coming spring will therefore be the most desirable time to emigrate. The title of the lands previously referred to remains vested in the Crown until after the Patent is issued; unpatented lands cannot be seized for debt. In case a settler dies, the law allows his executors to fulfil the homestead conditions, thus securing the estate to his heirs.

The fees charged are as follows: Homestead, $10; pre-emption, $10; permit fee, 50 cents.

LIBERALITY OF CANADIAN LAND REGULATIONS

CONTRASTED WITH THOSE OF THE UNITED STATES.

The fee for taking up a homestead or pre-emption entry is only $10, whereas it is $26, and in some cases $34, in the States.

The privilege of receiving a pre-emption entry at the same time as that for a homestead is granted is denied to the settler in the United States.

The settler must reside *five years* on his homestead in the United States, as against *three years* under the liberal regulations of Canada.

The taking of a homestead in Canada does not prevent a settler from purchasing other Government lands.

The following liberal allowance of timber is given to the settler on prairie lands free of charge: 1,800 feet of house timber, 400 roof rails, 30 cords of wood, and 2,000 fence rails—equal in value to about $60. No such grant can be obtained under the land regulations of the United States.

Particular attention is drawn to the fact that settlers, on completing their homestead conditions, are allowed the right to obtain a second homestead and pre-emption. This concession on the part of the Government has only lately been allowed, and this fact alone places the Canadian regulations, in the matter of liberal treatment of the settlers, far ahead of those of the United States.

Advertisement for free homes in the West, printed by Canadian Pacific Railway

Glenbow Archives, Calgary, Canada: NA-1472-7

Anglo-Saxon bias to Ottawa's early immigration policy, but British immigrants who came were often inept and arrogant, slow to adjust to the demands of such a demanding place. Finally it became clear that if Canada wanted to people the West, it had better start sweeping the floors of the rapidly disintegrating empires of Europe, start wooing Poles, Hungarians, Czechs, Croations.

Despite the suspicions of the Canadian government's dominant Anglos, Germans and Icelanders and Scandinavians, as well as Eastern Europeans—Ukrainians, Romanians, Poles, and Slovenians—contemptuously lumped together as Galicians, began to pour into the prairies. The English-speaking majority sought to "assimilate" the newcomers, to sandpaper away their origins and make them "clean, educated, and loyal to the Dominion and to Greater Britain." The feds essentially ignored demands for restrictions on immigration because they believed that immigration was the one way to promote economic growth. As of 1882, 25,000 new people had arrived on the prairies and were struggling to make the unfamiliar landscape home; by 1883 there were 100,000 new arrivals, and counting. They might have been forgiven for thinking themselves exiles in Egypt, tested by plagues of drought, early frost, floods, fires, and grasshoppers. But those were merely external challenges. Many a settler lost hope to loneliness, cabin fever, or "prairie madness."

But Alberta alone had 75,000 square miles of arable land. Recipients of all the monies generated by land sales, Central Canada and its National Policy turned up the rhetoric, and together the railways, government, and land companies launched the advertising campaign to end all advertising campaigns. "The Granary of the World," "160 acres of Free Land," "Two Hundred Million Acres of Land in Western Canada," "You Need Canada Needs You," "The Last Best West," and "Free Homes for Millions," the banners read. The 1892 development of Marquis wheat, which ripened seven days faster than Red Fife, technically helped to push settlement two hundred miles farther north, although the wheat wasn't available for commercial use until some years after. And the last years of the nineteenth century were blessed with above-average rainfall, so Palliser's prediction of drought and destruction in the southern triangle was discounted. By 1900 the propaganda stakes were high, and Clifford Sifton spearheaded an aggressive immigration program that relied on semi-truths and beautiful lies.

The Immigration Department had the tough task of persuading even starry-eyed potential settlers that Canada's West was not just one big snowfield, and so their pamphlets showed wheat twice as high as it grew anywhere else, groves of waving trees, and claimed that every kind of farming—"Ranching, Dairying, Grain Raising, Fruit Raising, and Mixed Farming"—was possible. Pamphlets, posters, and advertisements spread though Europe and the United States, hawking the blue skies and the mild winters of an imaginary utopia. Immigration agents got a bonus for every man, woman, and child they signed up. Why settlement followed the patterns that it did, and whether railway land-grant systems and the free-homestead system were beneficial or whether they effectively misallocated the West's scarce resources are still arguable. What if the West had been marketed as a lumber barons' haven or a watershed resource and not as a wheatland paradise to the hungry dreams of the world?

Particular groups appreciated the challenges of this remote landscape. In the United States the Mormons, or members of the Church of Jesus Christ of Latter-day Saints, faced strong persecution via the anti-polygamy Edmunds Act of 1882 and the subsequent Edmunds-Tucker Act, which appropriated the assets of the Mormon church. On April 26, 1887, the first forty Mormon settlers reached the area later named Cardston after Charles Ora Card, who had directed them there from Utah. An energetic group, they put ploughs into the ground on May 2, held their first church service on June 5, and started their first Sunday school on June

12. One woman, confronted by six inches of snow that had fallen overnight on June 3, asked, "Brother Card, is this the kind of place you've brought us to?" "Yes," he answered. "Isn't it beautiful?"

Whatever objections the United States had to the Mormons, Canadians knew them as hard-working people with a high birth rate, which was what the West needed. And they brought with them a knowledge of irrigation that would help to transform the dry grasslands of southern Alberta between Lethbridge and Cardston. Alberta had cheap land and water, which was what the Mormons were after; and they were enthusiastically welcomed by the Lethbridge area entrepreneur Sir Alexander Tilloch Galt, who was trying to find buyers for his company's land grants. The Mormons ultimately purchased not only some of Galt's land but that symbol of British snobbery, the Cochrane Ranche. In 1901 they began the town of Raymond, future sugar beet capital, and by 1906 almost four thousand Mormons, scattered between Taylorville in the south to Magrath, Raymond, and Sterling, and as far north as Taber, had settled in southern Alberta.

Although the Mormon reluctance to bow to mainstream Anglo-Protestant mores made Central Canada nervous, their loyalty to a country that offered them freedom to live and to practise their religion was strong, and the only point of contention was their belief in polygamy. At first Canadian Protestant churches campaigned against them. In his *Bulletin*, Frank Oliver, who later became interior minister, called them "the scum of creation, the cancer of civilization," an "utter abomination which no effort should be spared to rid the nation of." So although they were "intelligent, industrious and frugal," and according to Sam Steele "a very industrious people [who] have made a better show toward success than any settlement in the district," they carried a stigma and in 1890 the federal government strengthened the bigamy law specifically in response to them. Mormon elders counselled members not to marry "contrary to the laws of the land," but that did not stop their neighbours from eyeing them with suspicion, and did not completely eradicate their multiple marriages. Other settlers in the area were more nervous about their growing numbers and power in terms of land acquisition and ownership. It was twenty years before the anti-Mormon crusades of the Presbyterian and Methodist churches settled down and left them alone. Alberta's intolerance was linked to the principles of the social gospel movement, which focused on Western Canada as a Christian utopia. Within that model of "saved" society, Mormonism was considered an evil on a par with liquor and prostitution, even though Mormons do not drink or smoke, and they practise moderation in all things. Still, Albertans were much more hostile to foreign settlers, newcomers who did not speak English, considered "racially inferior."

Despite that attitude, the next core of Alberta migrants was German, a small group fleeing Austrian persecution. Following them in 1891 came a series of French groups, both from Quebec and from France and Belgium. Alberta had been French long before the English took over; and Lamoureux, started in 1872, was one of the first pioneer settlements. The new migrants settled close to Father Morin's mission at St. Albert (Morin had replaced Father Lacombe) and then slowly spread to begin the communities of Vegreville, Beaumont, Morinville, Villeneuve, Legal, and Picardville, still intensely francophone. But the French influence on Alberta was waning, and fewer and fewer French came in groups, although individual settlers did. One such settler, Marcel Durieux, whose journal, *Ordinary Heroes*, is a beautifully written rendition of pioneering between 1906 and 1914, immigrated to Canada with a father who believed that Alberta would pro-vide his sons with opportunities not possible in tradition-bound France. The fam-ily was not poor, but able to purchase stock and supplies easily, and they journeyed to a homestead on the banks of the Red Deer River. It was a spot with a view any artist would envy, but that did not mitigate the first terrible winter when Marcel and his two brothers suffered through the death of their mother and then their father. They farmed effectively despite hardship, helped to build a Catholic church in Stettler, and, with the outbreak of the First World War, all three Durieux broth-ers returned to France to fight. French settlers, unlike Québécois settlers, seemed to treat Alberta as less of an outpost and more of a home because they managed to bypass the Centre.

But Centrals, too, determined to improve their lives, were eager to move from the backwoods of Ontario and the maple groves of Quebec to the West. The colo-nizing agents of the Canadian Pacific Railway did their best to encourage emigra-tion fever; at Parry Sound in 1891, the agent craftily gave two leading citizens a train pass to Edmonton so they could check out Alberta's potential. The reeve of the township, along with a clergyman, took the passes and travelled west—in August—and, of course, returned with tales that rivalled tourist brochures for Eden. Their exaggerations made Alberta seem as distant from the stony ground of Parry

How to get to a homestead

Sound as heaven is from hell, and their glowing reports made the long-suffering colonists so restless that pretty soon everybody in Parry Sound, following through on CPR incentives like reduced train fare, made plans to go west. Most designated their possessions as security under a CPR "chattel mortgage" to pay for transportation of livestock and household effects. How many high chairs and wood-fired stoves, how many sideboards and pianos, did the CPR take possession of? And in auctioning them off, how little did they understand that they were selling people's dreams?

The proposed colony of Parry Sound left Sundridge, Ontario, in April 1892, some two hundred cars loaded with livestock and settlers' effects, 298 men, women, and children crowded into the passenger cars. The night before they left, they camped in a large hall on the main street of Sundridge, and the tales they told one another grew taller and taller. Exaggerating how little they were setting out with, how little they had to go on, their desire was for land, "virgin" land. They expected that once they had staked their claims, the land would immediately rise in value (these were early forerunners of property-flipping entrepreneurs). None of them knew anything about the West except what they had been told.

The train trip from Ontario took something like ten days. Livestock had to be let out and then reloaded at prescribed times (these were railway rules), and the two-thousand-mile journey was an ordeal, with settlers sleeping sprawled across hard seats or on the floor, the stove in the car the only place for heating water or cooking small amounts of food. Most survived on bread and cheese. Arriving at South Edmonton, everyone was pleased to leave the cramped quarters of the colonist cars and rushed to claim their dream homesteads, standing in line at the Land Titles Office. The Parry Sounders paid their $10, and then, after waiting for the spring-flooded North Saskatchewan to subside, set out for the area around Beaver Hills, at Fort Saskatchewan, about thirty miles east of Edmonton. But even after they reached their destination, they met with disorder; the absence of survey stakes meant that they spent a good two weeks trying to figure out which sections were CPR, which were HBC, and which were school sections. Some of the home-steaders threw up their hands and caught the next train back east.

For those who opted to stay, life was hard. Crops were poor in 1893, and clear-ing the land took far longer than anticipated. June and July were the best times to break the soil; otherwise the grasses were already seeded, and flies had already laid their eggs so that the following season would hatch a harvest of insects, ready to devour the sown crops. Most of the Parry Sound colonists in the first years ended up surviving by digging for gold along the banks and sandbars of the North Saskatchewan River. Enterprisingly, they made a grizzly (a gold sluice) and with the help of a blanket caught the gold dust, collected it, and took it in to the Imperial Bank of Canada in Edmonton. They hunted and lived on rabbits, wild geese, ducks, and prairie chickens.

In the spring of 1894 a second group from Sundridge, Ontario, arrived. The first settlers were at South Edmonton to meet them, overjoyed that others were joining their misery, but also, in old-fashioned custom, ready to help, with advice, if noth-ing else. Imagine this new batch of settlers disembarking to see that the friends who had departed so full of dreams two years before still wore the same clothes, much patched. Shaven faces were rare, and even water seemed scarce, for the entire welcoming committee was dirt-encrusted. Across the horizon, prairie fires

Bachelors enjoying domestic chores

glowed orange, and the houses that the Parry Sounders had constructed were mean hovels of sapling logs and sod, neither comfortable nor inviting. Potatoes and vegetables were scarce. Fruit was a luxury. The basics of survival were flour, lard, milk, potatoes, and salt pork, hardship made palatable.

The land's fertility seemed the one bankable given, for the crops in following years were bumpers, wheat, oats, and barley promising bounty just as long as the seed got into the ground. But this assumption, too, ultimately proved false. Grasshoppers descended to feast on the fields spread out below them. Pesky gophers dug pesky holes between the rows and watched every human endeavour with cheeky curiosity. Crops were hailed out, frozen out, or burned out. When it did rain, the rude trails to Edmonton turned into mires of mud and water. Red River carts, the two-wheeled wooden carts built for carrying goods, were both more durable and solid than buggies, but because the wheels were never greased, one of the most familiar sounds in early Alberta was not the chime of church bells but the screech of the axle turning within the wheel. And travel was an adventure; streams and rivers had to be forded, and muskeg avoided, which meant following the ridges of hills and coulees. Winter made travelling easier, as long as there was enough snow for a sleigh's runners, although fighting through brush was still difficult. The sheer work of going to town to buy supplies and sell produce took hours, hours that a settler badly needed for more productive work. Hogs were a practical animal to raise, willing as pigs are to eat slops and still grow fat. A cow was essential for milk, and chickens for eggs. Luxuries like canned goods, sewn clothing, and shoes were all imported from the East, the train charging the manufacturers a good price to bring them to the needy settlers, and charging the needy settlers another good price for their appearance. Railways were lifelines, tempting chimeras, illusions of hope. Some people were so convinced of the security that railways offered that they bought land as close as possible to a line, as if snuggling up to the steel track would ease the winter loneliness.

The Dominion held all the cards in the settlement of the West, slowly confining the First Nations people, then gaining the crops and trade goods from the land slaves who thought they were headed to heaven. Thrift and hard work became the main virtues, success attendant on their presence. And still the settlers came, and still the settlers clamoured for railways, roads, and schools.

In 1892–93 Scandinavians from Minnesota and the Dakotas started to arrive, taking up the land in the huge bend of the Battle River between Wetaskiwin and Camrose. Others spread along the Burnt Lake Trail from Red Deer to Cygnet Lake. In 1889 a small group of Icelandic immigrants, which included a pacifist and political radical who would become the poet laureate of Iceland, Stephan Stephansson, started the settlement of Markerville, west of Innisfail. Even while he wrote six books of poetry and hundreds of articles, Stephansson cleared his land and farmed, raised eight children, and served as chairman of the Hola School Board. That Icelandic group, with the help of the federal government, incorporated the Tindastoll Butter and Cheese Manufacturing Association, which ran a high-quality creamery, one of the first in central Alberta.

A few Ukrainians had settled on land around Beaverhill Creek and in 1895 a Ukrainian agriculture professor named Dr. Josef Oleskiw met with federal officials, toured Canada, and proposed that Canada be receptive to the controlled immigration of Ukrainian peasants. Despite Anglo-Saxon hesitancy about the suitability of "Galicians," Canada agreed, and a wave of Ukrainian settlers, eager to escape the Old World hierarchy, which bequeathed them poverty, primitive serfdom, and enforced military service, hit the West with a vengeance. By the start of the First World War, Alberta, its tolerance tested, was home to seventeen thousand Ukrainian settlers. Although Sifton declared, "I think a stalwart peasant in a sheep-skin coat, born on the soil, whose forefathers have been farmers for ten generations, with a stout wife and a half-dozen children, is good quality," there were others who called them "the scum of Europe." Settling near friends and neighbours, they formed cohesive communities whose centre was the national hall, or *narodnyi dim*, where settlers went to buy supplies, collect their mail, read Ukrainian newspapers, and visit. Anglo homesteaders tended to ostracize them, but the Ukrainians built and prospered. Their onion-domed churches, Russian Orthodox, Ukrainian Catholic, and Ukrainian Greek Orthodox, still display beautiful filigree crosses, and in Vegreville the massive coloured *pysanka*, or Easter egg, proclaims a continuing tradition. Now, 10 percent of Albertans are people of Ukrainian background, a significant slice.

But by the 1890s Alberta began to scratch a nasty case of anti-foreign itch. These attitudes reflected the racial biases and hierarchies of the time, but still were no less repulsive. The *Calgary Herald* insisted that the only question immigrants should be asked was, "Are they healthy, industrious and moral living?" These were boom years, and new arrivals were necessary to keep wealth growing. The government tried to entice as many British, northern European, and American settlers as possible, luring this immigrant elite with incentives. At the same time, the immigration touts actively discouraged blacks and Asians from applying to enter this golden province. Many Chinese men who had helped to build the railway stayed on in the West, and by 1911 there were almost 1,800 Chinese in Alberta, only twenty of them women. A marginalized group, Chinese men did many of the domestic tasks that were usually relegated to women—service, cooking, and laundry. Because of the overtly racist 1904 Head Tax ($500 on every new Chinese immigrant), very few could afford to bring their wives and families over, and most lived incredibly lonely, isolated lives, treated with scorn and ridicule, and ghettoized in the West's growing urban centres. Hostility to Asians extended to the smaller group of Japanese immigrants, who were fewer in number and concentrated in southern Alberta in the mines and sugar beet fields.

Curiously, during the great ranching era, at least one-quarter of the cattle drovers were black, and some of them stayed, notably the cowboy John Ware, who started his own ranch near Brooks. But for all that individuals like Ware were liked and respected, Albertans displayed as much xenophobia as anywhere else in Canada; and when Oklahoma's Creek-Negroes wanted to immigrate to Alberta in 1910 and 1911, headlines bawled, "Negroes Not Wanted in Province of Alberta." Every economic, cultural, and colour bias kicked in, and the federal government ultimately employed informal exclusion, keeping out as many blacks as possible by foot-dragging, discouragement, and incredible red tape. Of course, British and white American immigrants, no matter how useless, immoral, or arrogant, were welcomed.

But the great immigrant influx was on. In the fifteen years before 1914, 440,000 homestead entries were filed; in 1913, the year of heaviest immigration, Alberta welcomed 400,870 newcomers. From 1901 to 1911 Alberta's population grew from 73,022 to 374,295, an astonishing 500-percent increase. But worrisomely, to the Centre at least, Alberta was developing a distinctly American accent; by 1910, 22 percent of new immigrants to the province were American. How could the feds ensure that Alberta would not simply transfer its affections to the south-of-the-border gang? The answer was to bring in plenty of the British faithful and, later, to welcome various utopians who, even if they endorsed some strange creeds and customs, were white. Now this was a delicate balance. Religious minorities brought with them their peculiar practices, but they also developed a deep commitment to a place that tolerated their beliefs. Four different sects of Mennonites came to Alberta, eager to practise their Anabaptist pacifism. During the First World War, another Anabaptist sect, the Hutterites, who had originally emigrated from Russia to South Dakota, fled American persecution and established ten colonies in southern Alberta. They were pacifists who lived communally and held all property in common, and their insularity worried established settlers. But they garnered more land and their colonies spread, and they excite negative reactions even now. A few Doukhobors settled in Alberta after 1916, but never aroused the controversy of their Sons of Freedom relatives in central British Columbia.

Still, assimilationist Alberta preferred the glorious dreams of settler leaders like Isaac Barr, an organizer who imagined that he could establish a truly British colony in the West. Although Barr was an Ontario-born Anglican clergyman, the colony he imagined was not religion-based, and in 1903 he persuaded almost two thousand middle-class Britons, the largest group ever to leave the British Isles in one company, to abandon their lives and head for the trackless prairie in an area right on the line that would divide Alberta and Saskatchewan. Another Anglican clergyman from Ontario, the Reverend George Lloyd, joined forces with Barr and helped to formulate plans for bringing the settlers over. Even before the emigrants left England, matters began to go awry. Barr had ordered three ships, but most of the settlers were crammed into one that was supposed to hold only 550 people. They endured an uncomfortable passage and took up grumbling in a big way. When they reached Canada, there were other mix-ups related to money and baggage. Barr, who fashioned himself after Cecil Rhodes, left most of the details to Lloyd, who waxed more and more negative on the abilities of the colony's presumptive leader. And the journey west did not improve matters. It took thirty railroad cars just to handle the group's possessions, and the train trip was endless. When they reached the end of the line at Saskatoon and disembarked, they spent weeks waiting, and many of the colonists fell ill from drinking polluted water. Instead of supplies and equipment being ready, the settlers found insufficient transport and poor food. Eaton's gleefully distributed its catalogue, showing prices far lower than the settlers had paid Barr for their supplies, although they failed to take into account the two months that supplies from the Centre would take to reach the West. The angry settlers held a mass meeting, complaining about Barr's having swindled them and arguing about whether they should simply stay and settle around Saskatoon. Some did, but others chose to continue, lurching over a rough wagon trail to the tract of land that had been set aside for them, 160 miles to the west. These settlers brought along far too many dishes and far too much unnecessary finery, and almost no experience in pioneer farming. Their wagons were overloaded, the swollen rivers were difficult to cross, and when they reached their land they didn't want the sections they had originally selected from a two-dimensional map. Mutinously, the colonists demanded that Reverend Lloyd become leader and forced Barr to sign everything over. They might have been middle-class bank clerks and millworkers, but they were relatively industrious, and by the fall Lloydminster boasted a store, a church, a post office, a telegraph office, a drugstore, a saddlery, a blacksmith, and seventy-five houses. At Christmas the town

Immigration Hall in Edmonton, with woman serving food to new immigrants, 1911

celebrated the season with a hundred-voice choir. Lloydminster would never again grow so fast, and today it is a town straddling the border between Alberta and Saskatchewan, forever connected and forever divided. Arguments still persist about whether Barr was merely inefficient or downright crooked. Lloyd, respected and admired, became bishop of Saskatchewan while Barr died in poverty, in an Australian colonization scheme.

The early settlers of Alberta embodied a classic story of raw determination and terrible hope and stoic suffering. Ontario and American migrants had it easy; they came by train or covered wagon, a long but manageable trip. Europeans made a more difficult journey, packed like canned fish in sloshing, filthy holds. The ships encountered Atlantic fog and storms, even icebergs, and the optimistic immigrants must have wondered what hell they were proceeding toward. When they reached the Maritimes, either Halifax or Saint John, they were tested again, this time by immigration authorities who examined them for everything from lice to moral turpitude. The Interior Department could reject immigrants on the grounds of bad character, their likelihood of becoming a public charge, or if they suspected them of being criminals, prostitutes, or drunkards. They eliminated anyone feeble-minded, dumb, blind, or epileptic, and anyone over fifteen who could not read. After that interrogation, the settlers were free to board the train and begin a cross-Canada journey almost as miserable as the ocean voyage. When the train reached Calgary, where most disembarked, they were bedded down in the immigration hall across the tracks from the Palliser Hotel. There, for one week, the government donated a roof and cooking utensils and a communal kitchen and dining facilities; the settlers were expected to provide their own food and bedding. But immigration halls also hosted bedbugs, disease, and theft; love affairs and fights flourished between the straw mattresses lining the floor in the huge upper loft. Still, it was dry and warm, better than the leaky tents that settlers would sleep in on their way to their land once they had filed for a homestead, making only blind guesses as to which place had good soil or water.

Eventually, battling unpredictable weather and poverty and mishap and fire and flood, these hardscrabble sodbusters began to produce. Grain especially, beautiful hard wheat. Their hay and their garden vegetables were mostly for their own use, but the grain, meant to be shipped east and sold, gave them what little disposable income they had. It is no surprise that undependable grain markets became a burning question to Albertan farmers. American farmers seemed to get more money for their products and pay less for machinery. The gap between farming's hand-to-hand work and the paying results made for serious discontent. The West buckled under Central tariffs; meat, timber, and coal were all subject to tariffs—and to double the insult, they had to buy tariff-laden equipment from Central Canada in order to be able to work their land. Many a farmer tried to smuggle a harvester across the forty-ninth parallel into Alberta. Added to that were years when the elevators were blocked with wheat, and there were not enough railway cars to carry it east; farmers who could not get their wheat to market were furious. Both the farmers and coal companies of Alberta were truly at the mercy of the railway, especially in 1902, when the CPR didn't have enough boxcars to carry away Alberta's products—coal and lumber and grain.

And so those settlers, who both loved and hated the railway, turned militant, began to call for reciprocity, to voice opposition to the CPR's arrogant monopoly and excessive freight rates. Nothing has alienated the West more than the Centre's "national" transportation policies. Illustrating this anger is the often-told story of the Alberta farmer whose crops are first dried out, then hailed out; his house burns down, his horse dies, his wife runs away. Standing alone in the midst of devastation, he raises his fist and shakes it at the sky, yelling, "Goddamn the CPR!" The sentiment was justified. In 1883 the CPR set a rate schedule for transporting grain that was three times the rate charged in the East. In 1897, in order to control its monopoly, the CPR lobbied long and hard for the right to build the Crowsnest Pass railway and, in exchange, reduced its Western freight rates, although still not to the level of those enjoyed by Central Canada. As well, the CPR announced that it would not permit farmers to load individual grain cars; they had to be loaded through a grain merchant who had been permitted to use rail cars, yet another middleman for the beleaguered farmer. The 1899 Royal Grain Commission concluded that the grain trade ought to be federally supervised—once again, Central intervention in local and provincial matters. The stark unfairness of transportation costs (the West paid both ways) made for furious farmers, whose mistrust was played out in their growing suspicion of Central banks, Central manufacturers, the grain companies, the elevator owners, and of course, the CPR. The "fair discrimination" that the Centre kept trying to convince the West was for its own good might have been the only way to counterbalance the initial cost of building the CPR, but it incited resentment. Why should unprocessed products and processed or milled products be levied a different freight rate? And increases to transportation costs over the years, since they maintain the initial discriminatory rates, have not placated the West. Farmers still shake their fists at the sky and damn the CPR.

It is not only unfairness that provokes social change, but hardship. The organization known as the United Farmers of Alberta was born in direct response to centralist meddling, but also because the settlers learned that co-operation rather than competition seemed the only way to beat the devil. Farmers began to undertake co-operative projects and stand together. Private grain merchants were opposed to co-operative principles, but they had a tough fight against the UFA and the Alberta Farmers' Co-operative Company, which were active in forming grain growers' distribution co-ops to control markets and marketing. And although the horrific winter of 1906–7 killed thousands of cattle and livestock, the farmers were beginning to take the results of their hardship and their toil into their own hands.

The United Farmers of Alberta, which under the motto "Equity" was to hold such powerful sway over the province, blew into the West like a chinook, collective action determined to promote the legal and political position of farmers. After its founding meeting in Edmonton in January 1909, one hundred UFA delegates, dressed in a combination of buffalo coats and greatcoats, symbolically marched through the snow in minus-twenty-two-degree weather to demand that Premier Alexander Rutherford enact legislation in support of hail insurance and the building of elevators. Their populism followed through on many ideals of the day: respect, education, better markets, and equity. From its first big convention in Red Deer in 1910, the UFA began to work toward political power for agriculture. Its main platform stressed initiative (a vote by petition could force a voter referendum), referendum (a vote of the electorate that would bind legislation), and recall (an unwanted member could be forced to resign and face another election). Financing and credit were an important focus, articulating farmers' suspicion of Central banking institutions, a suspicion that would reach its zenith in the rise of the populist Social Credit Party, and continues even now in the Albertan habit of starting our own banks. One of the UFA's first actions was to lobby Arthur Sifton's government (he was Clifford's brother and Alberta's second premier) to establish the Alberta Farmers' Co-operative Elevator Company, which built forty-six elevators in 1913, and by 1917 was handling livestock, as well as grain, coal, flour, and binder twine.

A transplanted American, Henry Wise Wood, served as one of the UFA's most important leaders. Deeply religious, Wood believed in farmer power, farmer action, and farmer fury. Elected president of the UFA in 1916, he was repeatedly (for fourteen years) acclaimed to the position, although he never collected his salary. Farmers, he believed, possessed a mighty, incipient force. He maintained that the world was divided into nasties and heroes; the nasties were competitive aristocrats who persistently tried to tread on the heroic co-operative democrats. With a combination of messianic zeal and homespun oratory, Wood spread his political philosophy; president of the Alberta Wheat Pool from 1923 to 1937, he had a tremendous effect on Alberta's political shape, and on Alberta's pugilistic positioning. Economic and political issues were tied to faith—one of Wood's first motions as leader was to establish UFA Sunday, the Sunday nearest May 24, to discuss farmers' issues from a religious perspective.

With the UFA's formidable organization behind them, the farmers of Alberta battled economic boom and bust, the optimism surrounding growth and new settlement, the horror of the First World War, drought and depression, and most of all, Alberta's distance from the Centre, where all the important decisions were made. And the force of the UFA went beyond the political. Aside from its religious bent, it sponsored social gatherings like picnics and fairs, advanced adult education and co-operative work, and most particularly, insisted on educating farmers in collective action, and in legal matters. Virtually serving as a UFA/Liberal alliance during Sifton's and Brownlee's terms as premier, the UFA became the most powerful agricultural force in Alberta. Its members' adamant local pride marks Alberta to this day.

But the centres of power were still far away. The First World War—when Canada exported 56 percent of the world's wheat, but prices were set in Winnipeg and Minneapolis in response to a world price determined in Liverpool—and the exodus of farmers from the southern dry belt in 1919–20 ultimately steered the UFA toward a recognition that sideline political action was not enough—they had to run for office. From 1917 farmers in Palliser's Triangle had faced heat, wind, and drought, leading to debt and destitution. Schools were closed, farms were auctioned by judicial sale, and whole communities tumbled into windswept dereliction. The dry belt, which was fit for ranching, was far less predictable as crop land, and farmers there suffered plagues of biblical proportions—grasshoppers, rabbits, sawflies, cutworms, sow thistle, smut, and black rust. Refugees abandoned their land on wagons pulled by horses so thin their ribs were ladders. Auctioneers disposed of pitiful, threadbare belongings. In 1919 and 1920 the UFA sent boxcars of hay and feed oats while the feds turned their backs, saying that whatever was happening was a provincial concern. Experts doled out advice on summerfallowing, but drifts of dust piled against the fences like snow, and in the terrible battle against nature people either committed suicide or simply abandoned everything and moved away.

It is unsurprising that a messianic farmers' organization seemed to offer if not relief at least understanding, some concept of hailstorms and gopher holes. To everyone and no one's astonishment, the UFA obliterated the Liberals to form Alberta's second political dynasty, on July 18, 1921, and subsequently spent four-teen years in power. Henry Wise Wood, who mistrusted politics and didn't want to serve in public office, chose to work behind the scenes. Despite their inexperience and despite urban Albertans' reacting in shock at being governed by a bunch of clodhopper farmers, govern they did, with astonishing skill, until 1935, when they were defeated by the next unpredictable tornado—William Aberhart's Social Credit movement, which was a wilder variation on the original UFA movement and its protest politics.

There were a few success stories. Charles S. Noble, who gave his name to Nobleford, started farming by walking barefoot behind an ox team; he acquired land until he owned fifty-six sections, and ran six hundred horses and sixty-one binders. Then in 1922, defeated by a number of crop failures, he lost everything to the banks. Eight years later he had recovered his wealth and his reputation as the best and biggest grain farmer in the empire. In response to the land's sensitivity, he invented the Noble Drill—a seed-planting machine—and the Noble blade, an oddly shaped cultivator blade that turned the earth in such a way that it left behind enough trash cover (old roots and stalks) to prevent the soil from blowing. Although the biggest depression was yet to come, farmers used their ingenuity to fight Alberta's unforgiving weather and climate.

Settlement in the West was not a romantic story of agricultural worker bees and grateful immigrants subjecting a fertile landscape to their civilizing ploughs. Ottawa wanted a lucrative commercial colony, a shy and willing hinterland, to buy goods and to produce exportable goods; settlement and government-approved land speculation fulfilled those objectives. The CPR whistled across the prairie, the Centre rubbed its hands in glee and greed, and investors in the Western Canada Land Company became millionaires. Except they didn't live in the West, nor did they ever intend to.

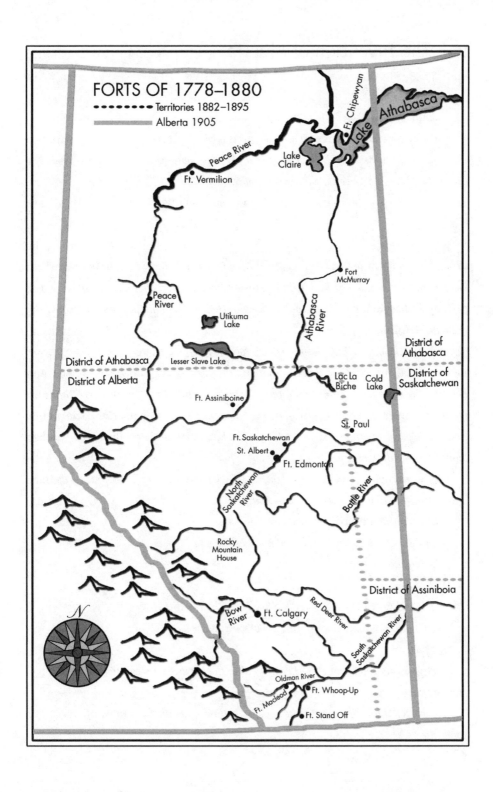

FORTS OF 1778–1880
●●●●●●● Territories 1882–1895
━━━━ Alberta 1905

Ft. Chipewyan

Lake Athabasca

Peace River

Lake Claire

Ft. Vermilion

Fort McMurray

Peace River

Utikuma Lake

Athabasca River

District of Athabasca

District of Athabasca

Lesser Slave Lake

District of Alberta

Lac La Biche

Cold Lake

District of Saskatchewan

Ft. Assiniboine

St. Paul

Ft. Saskatchewan
St. Albert

Ft. Edmonton

North Saskatchewan River

Battle River

Rocky Mountain House

District of Assiniboia

Bow River

Ft. Calgary

Red Deer River

South Saskatchewan River

N

Oldman River

Ft. Whoop-Up

Ft. Macleod

Ft. Stand Off

9 | The Invention of Alberta

Just a little wild rose, with petals soft and pink,
Creeping o'er our prairies and along our rivers brink
Up on the highest mountain peaks it holds its place supreme,
The Wild Rose of Alberta, our Emblem and our Queen
                    —Jeannette Forsyth, "The Emblem of Alberta"

When I left home to go to the University of Alberta, I didn't know that the buildings there were named after men who had helped to invent the province. They were sonorous, dignified names, like Alexander Cameron Rutherford, Henry Marshall Tory, and they sanctified the halls of learning.

Studying late one night, I went to search for a book in the warren-like stacks of the old Rutherford Library, came around a corner and there, in a few chairs tucked into a corner between the stacks, I stumbled on a pair of ghosts. I knew they were ghosts—they were almost transparent, eerily distinct from the solid shelves and volumes surrounding them. Their clothes were nothing like the clothes of the late 1970s and their haircuts and collars looked turn-of-the-century.

They were having a vociferous argument. They seemed not to know that I was there, and I seemed unable to turn and move away.

"Alberta!" said the rosy-cheeked one.

"Buffalo," said the other, paler and not as stout as the first.

"The buffalo are gone."

"Buffalo."

"You lost. It's Alberta."

"Stupid name, Sandy. Doesn't suit the place at all."

"It's pretty."

"Pretty. Is this good enough"—he gestured to the books that staggered to the ceiling—"for you?"

"It's better than nothing. Come on, Fred, having a library named after you is a good thing."

The other looked gloomy. "You got what you wanted, a university. I would have been happy just to have a sensible name for the province."

"Fred," said the large one, "nothing in politics makes sense. Provinces, buildings, get named after the least likely people."

"It should have been Buffalo. One big province called Buffalo." With surprise, I saw that he was smoking, a cigarette held between the fingers of his left hand.

"The Haultain plan."

"Nobody knows who I am, Sandy. But I'd have been happy with Buffalo."

"That's a different place, Fred."

It was the smoke from the cigarette that made me sneeze, not the book dust or a developing cold. In the proverbial resolution that concludes dreams and supernatural meetings, I blinked and they vanished.

They were surely ghosts. But I have never forgotten their argument. What would have happened if the Haultain plan had been adopted, and instead of Alberta and Saskatchewan, the West wrote "Buffalo" as its return address?

• • •

Before the farmers could get elected, Alberta had to become a province.

The idea of a geopolitical region called Alberta came about almost accidentally. At first it was nowhere, just out there, part of Rupert's Land. Then in 1875 Ottawa's North West Territories Act put into place a rudimentary system of representative government enabling collection of taxes, administration of justice, imposition of punishment, regulation of all matters concerning cemeteries, public morals, nuisances, police, roads, highways, bridges, and jails. Any district not exceeding an area of one thousand square miles that contained a population of not less than a thousand inhabitants—excluding, of course, aliens, women, children, or Indians—could form a district and elect a man to the Territorial Council.

In 1881 the area that would be called Alberta elected its first member, Lord Boyle (a Fort Macleod–area rancher who was elected because he was literate) to Regina, the seat of the territorial government, which tried to exercise some say over its future. By that time, J. S. Dennis, deputy minister of the interior—it's not clear if he ever went west, but he must have—made a recommendation that the territory, too big for Ottawa to wrap its imagination around, should be subdivided.

Sure enough, in 1882, "for the convenience of settlers and for postal purposes" (the post office really runs Canada), the North West Territories, that big lump of land, was divided into four provisional districts: Assiniboia, Saskatchewan, Athabasca, and Alberta. The District of Alberta was "about 100,000 miles in extent, to be bounded on the south by the international boundary; on the east by the District of Assiniboia; on the west by the Province of British Columbia; and on the north by the 18th correction line . . . which is near the 55th parallel of latitude."

Alberta was the lucky district that got saddled with the name of one of Queen Victoria's daughters; the rest all had more fitting aboriginal names. Princess Louise, who was no doubt used to vague and far-flung landmarks being christened after her, wrote some years later that, yes, "the beautiful, sunlit and prosperous Province of Alberta was named after me by my husband, the Marquess of Lorne, when Governor-General of Canada. He was asked to name it, [and] he decided to call it after my last name, Alberta, of which he was very fond. Indeed, he mostly called me by it, or abridged it to Alba. I am intensely proud of this most beautiful and wonderful Province being called after me, and that my husband would have thought of it." But Albertans grumbled about the name. One letter to the *Edmonton Bulletin* suggested that Alberta be named Buffalo: "It would be much better to perpetuate the name of the animal which once overran the province and which will soon be extinct." Alberta, said the writer, "may be a very nice name for a baby girl, although that is a matter of opinion, but there can scarcely be two opinions as to its being inappropriate as the name of a great province of a great country."

Getting Ottawa to recognize Alberta's greatness took a lot of work. The Territories wanted responsible government, and in one hell of a hurry. There, in Regina, sat their government, the Territorial Council, a lonely discombobulated body presided over by an Ottawa-appointed lieutenant-governor and without funds to do much of anything. Aside from monies granted from Ottawa, which were paltry, the council could only extract fines from local sources, primarily for gambling and whisky trading. Licensing of ferry operators and billiard tables were other revenue sources, but together didn't amount to much. The Territories needed schools; the Territories needed roads; the Territories needed all manner of attention, and Ottawa was content to let the Territories cool their impetuous heels.

Until 1883, when the six elected representatives on the council began to out-number the Ottawa-appointed four. They started to complain about the lieutenant-governor controlling all the funds. They were, they claimed, not servants of Ottawa but representatives of those people who had elected them. Most vociferous of all was the member from Edmonton, Frank Oliver, editor of the *Edmonton Bulletin*, who, although he was a transplant from Ontario, considered himself a hardcore Westerner. No one is more stridently Albertan than an immigrant from Ontario, and Oliver went so far as to compare the position of people in the West to Russian serfs living in Siberia and suffering under a central despotism.

The 1885 Rebellion only underlined how strongly the West craved autonomy. Then Lieutenant-Governor Edgar Dewdney, the Macdonald puppet who had dismissed the Métis concerns as "petty grievances," was attacked by the Territorial Council, and a group of citizens travelled to Ottawa to demand seats in the House of Commons and increased control over local funds. Most important of all, they demanded that residents of the Territories, not Centrals who'd been awarded patronage positions, fill local positions. Still stinging from the sand flung in its eyes by the Métis uprising, Ottawa reluctantly conceded a few points, including House of Commons representation: four seats—two for Assiniboia, one for Saskatchewan, and one for Alberta. True to its contrary nature, Alberta's first sit-ting member of Parliament, elected in 1887, was D. W. Davis, one of the border-hopping whisky traders from Fort Whoop-Up who had welcomed the Mounties. An adaptable fellow, he became a trader of more acceptable goods and went to work building the fort for the Mounties, then managed I. G. Baker stores in both Calgary and Fort Macleod. His election gave rise to some sarcasm from south of the border. In 1888 an American journalist visited Calgary and then claimed in the *Cedar Rapids Daily Republican* that "the majority of the people are anxious for annexation to the United States. I should judge at least nine-tenths of the votes in Alberta would favour it. . . . Even the Alberta seat in the Dominion parliament is occupied by an American."

Whatever the West's republican desires, Macdonald was determined to control both the territory and territorial revenue, and the fights in the Territorial Council were fast and furious. The maturity and responsibility of the people in the colony was much debated, a duplication of Canada's desire to declare sufficient adulthood from Great Britain to run its own affairs. The irony was lost on Ottawa, which considered the cost of quashing the 1885 Rebellion a loan to the Territories, even though it collected from the Territories taxes on every resource. Even more galling, instead of the subsidy per capita that the "real" provinces were awarded, the Territories were given a vague annual grant, subject to Macdonald's mood, and usually inadequate.

When Boyle, southern Alberta's local representative to the Territorial Legislative Assembly, resigned, an English-born, Ontario-raised, but Alberta-spirited lawyer called Frederick Haultain stepped into the arena of territorial politics. He'd arrived at Fort Macleod in 1884, as green and well-shod as any other Central, but he went to work defending horse thieves and range men, and fell in love with the spectacular scenery and the forthright people. His one bias, which would later haunt him, was his distaste, shaped by his boyhood in Peterborough, Ontario, for Franco-Albertans and the Catholic Church; he would always be a thorough-going Anglican. And he rapidly discovered that in Fort Macleod, political debate was conducted around Taylor's Table, the twelve-person dining-room table in "Kamoose" Taylor's (another brewmaster originally from Fort Benton) Macleod Hotel, the only stopping place in town and the nexus for every traveller and migrant to that part of the country.

When Boyle resigned, the community of Lethbridge assumed that their man, a lawyer called Connybeare, would win the place, but with typical belligerence the Taylor Table, determined not to be outmanoeuvred by Lethbridge, persuaded Haultain, who already had a nose for local politics, to run against him. He defeated Connybeare 201 to 156, and in 1887 he was off to Regina, where he quickly moved into the oratorial gear of governance. He first proposed changes to the cumbersome liquor permit laws, which were supposed to halt illegal whisky traffic but in truth enhanced it. But more important was his call for amendments to the administration of the Territories. And immediately clear was Haultain's belief that national political parties would never serve the Western cause well. Although he was a Conservative, convinced that the good of the Territories had to come before partisan politics, Haultain aligned himself with Oliver from Edmonton, who was a Liberal. This optimism would dog Haultain's footsteps all his life and would eventually lead to his erasure from Alberta's official history.

The process toward self-government for the Territories plodded as slowly as any I. G. Baker bull train. Representatives to the legislature pushed for quasiprovincehood, sending writ after writ to Ottawa, all of which were filed and ignored. Macdonald replaced Lieutenant-Governor Dewdney with Joseph Royal, an urbane Québécois protégé of Bishop Taché's (the powerful Quebec church leader), who was absolutely dedicated to the federal agenda. Despite the formation of a four-person "advisory committee," a version of Western cabinet, the elected representatives had no power to accomplish anything without the permission of this lieutenant-governor, who was firmly in Ottawa's pocket. While it repeatedly sent out endorsements of democracy as a good thing, the Centre was about as likely to give the Territories responsibility for its own administration as it was to move Canada's capital to Battleford. The men in Regina were reduced to debating legislative measures on prairie fires, gopher control, and ferry operations.

Finally Haultain and his colleagues on the advisory commitee were so frustrated that they resigned, leading to a series of votes of non-confidence and resignations, and the lieutenant-governor declining the resignations. The big bone of contention was Ottawa's repeated refusal to let this elected body control the expenditure of what were called "dominion funds." Arguments over the autonomy of the Territories pushed and pulled until Royal dissolved the deadlocked assembly and called an election. When the legislature was recalled, the re-elected dissenters kept making noise and boycotting proceedings until finally Ottawa got tired of all the whining coming from Regina, and in 1890 amended the North West Territories Act, effectively acknowledging responsible government on the prairie. Through it all, Haultain acted as mouthpiece, pest, and suave debater, the real leader of the Territories between 1890 and 1905.

Haultain, beginning to understand the symbolic distance between Ottawa and the West, persuaded the feds to provide some monies toward various pressing territorial needs, including schools, roads, and bridges. That might have been a victory, except for the inflammatory potential of the schools question, particularly with regard to separate schools and the right of French-speaking Roman Catholics to educate their children in French. One-quarter of the territorial population in 1891 was French, and they wanted to ensure their schooling privilege. But Haultain believed in uniform, non-sectarian schools as much as he believed in non-sectarian politics, and he objected to denominational schools, thereby making himself the enemy of every priest and every francophone Catholic in Canada. That position, too, would haunt him. In a precursor to current debate, Haultain thought that religion belonged at home and not in the schools, and that Catholic and Protestant children should be educated together and in English, thereby pitting himself forever against Father Lacombe and Sir Wilfrid Laurier, which would be his undoing. The larger question, although politics obscured it, was that the West needed teachers and schools of whatever denomination; building a one-room schoolhouse and hiring a literate teacher was difficult for settlers, and they didn't give a damn about the teacher's religious denomination.

Frederick Haultain, the father of Alberta, who wanted Alberta and Saskatchewan to be one province called Buffalo

But politics in the West was just as contentious then as now. In an unusual resistance to male herd behaviour, Haultain hated and fought against the party system on the grounds that it restricted the consciences of elected members, and did not permit them to represent their electorate, instead inducing them to follow a party line. Haultain was both idealistic and shockingly unrealistic about the extent to which party politics would govern the whole of Canada, but he persisted in his belief to the end of his life, even though he joined the Conservative Party.

During the 1890s Haultain kept hammering away at autonomy, his correspondence repeating that "we want that substantial control of our own affairs which is enjoyed by all autonomous bodies." Slowly, amendment by amendment, the Territories moved toward provincehood. As early as 1890 southern Alberta's newspapers eagerly imagined a province between British Columbia and Swift Current, with Calgary as its capital. A mass meeting in Calgary in March of 1895, promoted by a former mayor, James Reilly, took up the cry for provincehood. Out of that initiative came an optimistic pamphlet titled "Provincial Government for Alberta," which demanded adulthood. "The pretensions of Ontario and Quebec to know what we want better than we do ourselves, will speedily collapse before a show of unanimity on our part, and the present attitude will speedily change to one of welcome to the last new Province of the Dominion—youngest in point of date, but designed...to become the greatest and most important of them all." The *Edmonton Bulletin* ridiculed that optimism by suggesting that Calgary was displaying its "hog-like propensities," and that it would be better for Alberta to argue for more federal representation than to try to grow up too fast. But however nervous Calgary's ambitions made Edmonton, home rule had been proposed. Clearly territorial independence had shifted to a desire for local or regional government, and Alberta's proactive push for provincial status prompted 1896 debates on the thorny question of whether the Territories should be united or separate provinces.

That was the year the federal Conservatives were soundly routed, and Liberal Wilfrid Laurier, the man who had promised the West responsible government, took over in Ottawa. Politicians from Alberta had begun to align themselves with national power and influence. Frank Oliver went off to Ottawa as Liberal MP for Edmonton; the brash young lawyer R. B. Bennett got himself elected in Calgary and set out to balkanize the territorial assembly in Regina. Patronage, which had always stocked the ranks of Mounties and Indian Affairs men, increased. Clifford Sifton began his groundbreaking immigration campaign, advertising to the world "The Last Best West" and its open arms. Haultain wrote to Sifton, saying, "At the risk of being tedious..., I must ask your earnest consideration once more of the financial and political position of the Territories as it presents itself. Though Parliament has created a Government for the Territories, with responsibilities to the people of the country..., it is continually being forced upon us that the Dominion Government does not consider that fact any warrant for its withdrawal from the paternal attitude adopted in the earlier stages of our history."

It was now some thirty years since Manitoba and British Columbia had been admitted to the Dominion as provinces. What was the holdup for the rest of the West? Arguments for provincehood were supported by population increases, the result of Sifton's aggressive settlement policies. Between 1897 and 1901 homestead entries rose from 2,384 to 8,167, and by 1905 would rise to 30,819. Still, grants from the Centre to the Territories did not increase, and Regina fumbled along, utterly hamstrung. These people needed schools, hospitals, roads, but Ottawa refused to provide funding, even though money from the sale of lands went to

Ottawa. The Territories could never guess what federal grants would amount to, while they were prohibited from borrowing funds and were not allowed to tax the CPR. The small fees and licences they collected were laughable. The structure that would so irritate the West—the Centre's seeming indifference to the actual circumstances of people in these regions—was already in place.

But the pressure for provincehood was fierce, and in May 1900 Haultain made one of his eloquent three-hour speeches, resulting in a unanimous resolution reciting the constitutional progress of the Territories and lamenting the inadequacy of the annual federal grant. In effect, *demanding* autonomy. The resolution was passed by the territorial government on July 20, 1900, and laid before the federal cabinet five days later. Then Ottawa did what it always does: nothing. The government of the Territories waited. Finally, in March 1901 Sifton, as minister of the interior, sent a stilted letter that seemed to signal approval, suggesting a "conference" where federal and territorial representatives could meet to discuss the issue.

The meeting, which took place in October 1901, ranged eloquent Haultain and the territorial treasurer, Arthur Sifton (Clifford's brother) against Laurier, Clifford Sifton, Walter Scott (member for Assiniboia who supported responsible government), and three other feds. The Ottawa boys seemed remarkably cool, raising questions and difficulties but at last asking Haultain to set out his proposal in the form of a draft bill that could be used to frame an act to establish a Western province. Ottawa obviously expected dissension, which would nicely delay the process. But the territory was hot, and this draft bill, outlining provincial control of land and natural resources, provincial right to tax the CPR, and full provincial control of education, landed on Ottawa's desk two months later.

Haultain dreamed of one big Western province named Buffalo, and perhaps Ottawa resisted because even if the federal functionaries had not visited the West, the sheer size of the proposed province gave pause—404,000 square miles would make it bigger than Quebec, as large as continental Europe. While Ottawa hemmed and hawed, the West waited and discussed its future. If the Territories were splintered into four districts, would their potential be diluted? Haultain believed passionately that they should, together, form one province. But Ottawa wasn't having it. Despite arguments about the West as a geographic unit, there was nothing that the Centre feared more.

Alberta in 1900 was a district that reached from the western edge of the Rockies, where the provincial boundary is now, to just east of Lethbridge, then north to Lac La Biche and Athabasca Landing. Medicine Hat lay in the District of Assiniboia, Lloydminster in the District of Saskatchewan, and north of Lac La Biche stretched the larger District of Athabasca, encompassing the whole of the Lesser Slave Lake area, the Peace River, and Fort McMurray, up to Lake Athabasca and Fort Chipewyan. Although many of its cities were already begun, although the trail from Calgary to Edmonton was well-worn, the boundaries of the District of Alberta were permeable. Aside from Haultain's one-big-province dream, there were other proposals. BC suggested moving eastward to annex the area, and Manitoba proposed extending westward, arguing that the Territories had everything to gain by joining Manitoba, which was already a province.

But Haultain had not reckoned with Ottawa politicians, who after another delay sent a chilly rejection in March 1902, stating that "it is the view of the government that it will not be wise at the present time to pass legislation forming the North-west Territories into a Province or Provinces." What made Laurier hesitate? Territories could be treated as colonized, but provinces were political bodies with expectations and rights. When asked, Central excuses ranged from saying that the West didn't have enough people to saying that the West was growing too fast and wouldn't know how to control rapid population growth.

Certain aspects of the proposal had unnerved the Centre completely. Haultain's bill left the issue of separate schools up to the new province. All the schools in the territory were public, but their curricula were under the control of the territorial government. And because Manitoba had waged a battle over their Catholic school system, and lost, Ottawa faced a battle with Quebec. Laurier's willingness to respect distinctive rights marked him as different from other Central politicians, but he was not above connivance, and as prime minister dealt with constant lobbying. The bishops in Quebec spent considerable time and energy persuading Laurier that if he did not establish Catholic schools in the Territories, he could expect opposition in the next federal election. So when Haultain's optimistic bill arrived in Ottawa, Laurier's cabinet, fearful of the political fall-out between Catholic Quebec and Orange Ontario, flatly rejected the proposal. Once again, the Territories had to wait for the Centre to resolve ancient differences.

Haultain refused to stop his crusade. He called a territorial election on the platform of provincehood, and along with a strong contingent of provincial status supporters he was re-elected. Elected too was a lawyer named Alexander Cameron Rutherford, the man who would conveniently become Alberta's first premier. The federal MPs in the Territories now occupied an uneasy position. Although they had earlier supported provincehood, they were now expected to fall in behind Laurier's opposition. Of course, the federal Tories saw an opportunity and came right up the middle, declaring themselves in favour of provincehood, exactly the kind of party politics that Haultain so loathed.

Clifford Sifton now backpedalled and claimed the reason the bill had been rejected was that the Territories couldn't agree on how many provinces there should be. Several provincial boundaries had been proposed. Haultain wanted one big province, his argument that two governments would duplicate work and that greater diversity would create greater economic stability. He did not say aloud that such a large territory would effectively counterbalance the power of Quebec and Ontario. The Two-Province North-South plan, Frank Oliver's favourite, which was ultimately adopted, divided the territory into Alberta and Saskatchewan. Oliver argued that in one big province, the seat of government would be too far from most of the people it was supposed to represent; two provinces would enable administration to keep track of local interests. Calgary, then the largest city in the area, laid claim to becoming the capital of Alberta, but Oliver was secretly lobbying for Edmonton.

Haultain claimed that unanimity was impossible and that the voting majority, who favoured one big province, should be obeyed. Meanwhile, he was being wooed by the Conservatives to declare himself openly as a member of their party. Smelling the direction of partisan politics, Haultain couldn't resist attending the Conservative convention in Moose Jaw, although he still urged the Tories to remain neutral in territorial politics. Nevertheless, his party affiliation was noted and all hell broke loose. Laurier Liberals attacked Haultain, pushing him toward an increasingly anti-government position. Shrewd Laurier knew that if he agreed to this one province, Haultain would likely be elected its premier. Laurier dangled the bribe of a patronage position, a judgeship, but Haultain could smell Ottawa's desire to get him out of territorial politics, and wisely or not, still engrossed in his larger dream, he refused the offer. Nothing could have made the federal Liberals angrier.

Delay and more delay, and pressure from the federal Tories under Robert Borden, who had now conveniently taken up the cause of Western provincehood, mounted. Laurier had to develop a plan and, intelligently enough, began by increasing grants to the West. This quieted the outcry somewhat, but the question still stood. Why was Laurier against autonomy? Finally, of course, people figured it out. Provincehood was being delayed because of the Catholic school issue.

Laurier's second move, in a ploy to make the West feel better, was to increase the number of federal seats in the Territories from four to ten. Then, confident that he could win, he called an election. Despite his non-partisan position, Haultain flung himself into the fight, now campaigning for the Tories. And Laurier, in one last bolt from the blue, suddenly promised that if the Liberals were re-elected, the Territories would be given autonomy within a year. Completely unprepared for his sudden capitulation, all the parties were thrown into confusion. Liberal candidates had to reverse their positions, and the Tories lost the main plank of their platform. Chaos reigned, the Liberals were returned to power, and Haultain's credibility was forever tainted. He had succumbed to partisan politics himself. And once again the West was jerked around by the strings of the Central puppeteers.

Early in December 1904 the *Edmonton Journal* published a fiery article declaring, "Politically speaking, surely we are of age—are old enough to demand that what is ours be given to us to use and to enjoy." On January 4, 1905, Haultain, with George Bulyea, the territorial minister of public works, boarded the train and headed east, ready to begin provincial negotiations. The territorial population then was around 450,000 people, not many, but enough to have aspirations and dreams. These included equal rights with all the other provinces, control of the public domain in the West, control of natural resources, both surface (soil and forest) and subsurface (coal and minerals).

There are no minutes of the various meetings and conferences that took place in Ottawa between January 5 and February 4, 1905, but it is not hard to imagine the round of Ottawa lobbying, rumours, and backroom double-dealings. The West sent various emissaries, delegations from Fort Saskatchewan and Prince Albert and Saskatoon, from Calgary, Edmonton, Lethbridge, and Red Deer, to argue why they should be capital cities. Catholic clerics were on hand to ensure that the separate school question was not forgotten. Haultain presented his 1901 draft bill again, but discussion in whispering Ottawa only seemed to make the process muddier. Every morning Haultain and Bulyea outlined Western provincehood to a poker-faced cabinet, not knowing that every afternoon Laurier held a mirror meeting with his Western caucus, as if seeking counterproposals. In the end, that federal Western caucus and not the territorial representatives determined the future provinces.

Sure enough, Haultain, the man who had fought so long and hard for autonomy and who, as leader of the territorial government, could have expected a bit of consultation, was treated like a mere messenger boy. On February 21, 1905, he was called into Laurier's office and handed drafts of the Alberta Act and the Saskatchewan Act. He had wanted education to be a provincial concern, but to appease Quebec schools were relegated to church control; Crown lands that he believed should be under provincial jurisdiction would be controlled by Ottawa; and the CPR's Western tax exemption continued. Every one of Haultain's logical requirements had been abrogated. Laurier obviously trusted his Western caucus and felt that the members of the territorial government could be thwarted. On March 11, 1905, Haultain wrote a final blistering letter to Laurier, stating his exceptions to the legislation as proposed; in doing so he wrote off his own future in the new provinces.

Laurier introduced Bills 69 and 70 on Alberta and Saskatchewan autonomy on February 21, 1905. The debate that followed was one of the longest to take place in the House of Commons, ten weeks, with twenty-eight days of solid discussion. People were puzzled. Government-supported church-run schools were the antithesis of everything Interior Minister Sifton had stood for. Only later did Laurier's correspondence reveal that to assure his re-election in October, he had drafted this birth-of-two-provinces legislation with several members of his caucus who had decided that despite a general desire for provincial autonomy over education, separate schools in the West would be a given.

All hell broke loose, not because this was a bad education idea, but because the trust between Laurier and Sifton, who was supposedly in Indiana taking mud baths for his health, was broken. Sifton rushed back to Ottawa to discover that Laurier had humiliated him, introducing the Alberta and Saskatchewan bills with a speech that decried secular schools, the model that Sifton had always endorsed. Laurier was torn between a French-Canadian clergy that saw schools as a bulwark against Ontario's militant Protestantism on one side and his adamantly anti-Catholic senior Western minister, determined to promote prairie secularity, on the other side. Sifton began a palace revolution, meeting with

Western representatives, then making it clear to Laurier that he could not support the bill—and handing over his letter of resignation. Laurier agreed to consider amendments to the school clause, but Sifton resigned anyway. The West was taken aback, and Protestant Ontario attacked Laurier. On the eve of the birth of Alberta and Saskatchewan, old Central enmities overshadowed Western issues. Sifton recruited caucus support, and Laurier ultimately gave in to an amendment establishing schools that were run by Catholic boards, but with teachers and curricula certified by the provincial government. This simply retained the way schools were currently governed in the Territories. But in true Central paroxysms, Ontario Protestants raged at the insidious nature of the bill and demanded its withdrawal, while Quebec Catholics raged at what they understood as compromised rights. Nobody was happy. Debates in the House of Commons dragged into the wee hours. Sifton meanwhile recommended the acerbic Frank Oliver, member from Edmonton, as his successor, a move that would significantly influence Alberta's future.

The West watched Ottawa's little firestorm with raised eyebrows. The immigrants arriving to claim their free 160 acres of homestead land (one-third from Britain, one-third from continental Europe, one-third from the US) were a polyglot lot, and although Sifton was adamant about uniform schools because he was afraid that the different interests of Germans, Ukrainians, Finnish, or French would splinter the West, those newcomers were more interested in prosperity than in clinging to their respective cultures. Laurier's famous quote about Canada's mosaic, "I want the marble to remain marble...," romanticized the unique strengths of these new arrivals, while they were concerned with the pragmatic issues of survival.

Ultimately the new provinces were treated to the same solution as Manitoba—an optional half hour of religious instruction at the end of the day by a minister of any denomination, parental approval required. Separate schools fell under state control. French could be the language of instruction in French-speaking communities, a lot like the choices today. Nobody was entirely happy, but it was a workable compromise. As one resident of the territories said in an interview with the *Toronto News*, "The people of the West will never rest until they get Provincial Autonomy on the same terms as the older Provinces. We want control of our own timber, of our own minerals, of our own lands and, especially, of our own schools. And let me tell you the West will not forget."

Laurier, throwing his Quebec and Ontario dogs occasional bones, paid no attention to Western objections. Haultain, although he was the premier of the territorial
government and about to be declared redundant, valiantly struggled on. Although
he didn't even have a forum to express his opinions, he kept articulating the
West's past, present, and future outrage. While the provinces were to be compensated for potential revenue in terms of public land, the pay-out was something of
a red herring. In 1902 the feds had made $1 million in revenue from the West, and
their subsidies hardly compensated for that. The two new provinces were to be
established by unilateral action under the general terms of the British North
America Act. The Dominion believed that the free homesteading policy should
continue and retained control of public lands and resources. Although given compensation in lieu, natural resources were not turned over to Alberta until 1930. The
debate about these details dragged on, past the original inauguration date, which
was postponed from July 1. The Alberta Act received vice-regal assent on July 20,
and the new province celebrated its inauguration on September 1, 1905, with
Saskatchewan doing the same a few days later.

Haultain was a politican cast adrift, and yet his influence in the West was such
that neither the Liberals nor the Tories in either new province dared to nominate a
leadership candidate until they knew his intentions. As a respected politician and
acting premier of the Territories, he was considered an unbeatable foe in any riding, and yet he was homeless, non-partisan, but seduced by the Tories, full of
integrity but lagging in decision.

Meanwhile, there were other discontents. The division between Alberta and
Saskatchewan gave Saskatchewan 251,000 square miles and Alberta 255,000 square
miles. That purely arbitrary fourth meridian ran right through the middle of
Lloydminster, which upset the Barr colony and turned Lloydminster into a Janus-
faced two-province town. The eastern movement of the boundary had put
Medicine Hat in Alberta, and the fact that it was one of the first big CPR towns
made Calgarians uneasy. Through all of Ottawa's paroxysms, Alberta was most
obsessed with the compelling question of where the capital would be. Edmonton
had been named interim capital, but every town—Calgary, Red Deer, Banff,
Lethbridge, and Medicine Hat—claimed to be the best potential capital, and began
exaggerated lobbying, although the final selection would be left to the newly
elected members of the province when that election took place. And now that

Frank Oliver, an unabashed Edmonton booster, had been made minister of the interior, he would exert undue influence in favour of Edmonton.

In July Laurier made a decision, again forever colouring the future of this nascent province. He named George Bulyea the first lieutenant-governor of Alberta, writing, ".... your long and faithful services to the party, entitle you to the best that may be in the gift of the party." Pure and simple reward for good behaviour. But being lieutenant-governor was a ticklish job. Bulyea was required to designate, with Laurier's advice, an acting premier, who would then call an election in Alberta's twenty-five new constituencies, properly selecting MLAs and the new premier. This interim premier would have the wonderful advantage of handing out all the cushy jobs in the not-yet-official government.

Laurier was nervous about the potential controversy around this appointment, nervous about which way Haultain would jump, nervous about Bulyea's friendship with Haultain, and nervous about making sure that this interim premier was a Liberal who would set up a Liberal government in the real election. Ottawa practically swam with intrigue. Finally the Central powers decided to ask the leader of the Liberal Party in Alberta, gossipy, companionable Peter Talbot, to serve as interim premier. But for some reason, Talbot, although he was a staunch Liberal, did not want the job and suggested instead his Strathcona friend, Alexander Rutherford. Although perfectly aware of Rutherford's tendency to favour the north of the province, Talbot assured Laurier that Rutherford would serve as a good Liberal.

Rutherford was an Ottawa Valley man. He had graduated from McGill law school in 1881 and, bored with Ontario practice, took a trip out west, travelling to Calgary on the CPR and then north to Strathcona, that rival town across the North Saskatchewan River from Edmonton. He decided to stay, moved his family to Strathcona, and successfully practised law. He had a finger in every community pie, from education to religion, got involved with local and territorial politics, and bought a lot of real estate around the burgeoning young settlement. Although he was considered an unambitious man, the scope of his activities was so broad that it seems hard to believe he abjured public office. During his term as an elected servant of the public, Rutherford ultimately favoured an independent attitude that resisted the Centre, even though Central politics had anointed him the first premier of the province.

Shockingly Haultain was not even invited to the ceremonies held to inaugurate either of the two provinces he had worked so hard to create. On the heels of that terrible snub, he began the Provincial Rights Party in Saskatchewan, thereby relegating himself to leader of the opposition and remaining politically marginalized. He was eventually recognized for his singular abilities in another sphere entirely, as chief justice of Saskatchewan, and as chancellor of the University of Saskatchewan, an institution that regards him as its founder. The shy, eloquent man who was premier of the North West Territories from 1896 to 1905 died in Montreal in 1942. His ashes, though, lie in the ground beside the gates of the University of Saskatchewan, as firmly rooted in the West as any tough prairie grass.

Alberta was official. Laurier ignored the Territorial Legislative Assembly's support of Haultain, argues historian C. C. Lingard, because of "the fear in the older provinces that one large province would assert a preponderant influence in the dominion of parliament." And so we are a smaller province, Alberta, and an angrier province, too.

• • •

The rivalry between Edmonton and Calgary, which continues to this day, began when the CPR chose to follow the southern line and the first train into Alberta reached Calgary in 1883. The two cities competed acrimoniously to be the capital of the new province, with Red Deer, Vegreville, Wetaskiwin, and Lacombe writing to Ottawa to argue their own advantages. When Edmonton was designated interim capital, the citizens were jubilant—and determined to change its provisional designation to permanent status.

When Conservative lawyer R. B. Bennett returned to Calgary at the end of January in 1905, warning that the stories about Edmonton's becoming the capital were true, Calgary pushed the panic button. They sent a delegation off to Ottawa to plead for, not Calgary, but Banff, assuming that the real capital would then come to Calgary. Edmonton sent its own delegation, headed by Frank Oliver, who was in Laurier's caucus and who argued simply that Edmonton was Liberal, and Laurier was Liberal, while Calgary was Tory. Laurier put on his poker face and told Calgarians that their suit would be given careful consideration, although he had already decided that Edmonton would be the provisional capital.

When the announcement was made, Calgary was furious, Edmonton jubliant and contemptuous. The *Calgary Herald* on February 21, 1905, stated the case bitterly: "The provisional capital of the western provence will be located at Edmonton.... The north country supported the government in the recent election. The southern half of Alberta was equally loyal in favor of the opposition. That the one was thus rewarded and the other punished by the Dominion for the public expression of political preferment cannot be doubted. In fact official circles in Ottawa boasted that 'Tory Calgary' had no right to expect any consideration at the hands of the Liberal government." In response, the *Edmonton Bulletin* gloated on March 2, 1905, "From the attitude previously assumed by the press of that city, it was not to be supposed that the announcement that Edmonton had been selected as the temporary capital of the province of Alberta would be received by the Calgary papers with satisfaction nor with equanimity. Few passions are more desperate or vociferous than baffled greed...." Calgary *Eye Opener* editor Bob Edwards drew blood. "Edmonton now estimates that it has a population of over 4,000. Estimates are easy to make. Calagary with her bona fide population of 11,000 is seriously thinking of estimating her population at 25,000 just to prove that its imagination is not inferior to Edmonton's."

But worse was to come. Laurier delegated the task of drawing up the twenty-five constituencies of the new provincial legislature to "our friend Oliver." He expected Oliver and Peter Talbot (leader of Alberta's Liberal party) to appoint a committee to undertake this task, and in truth a committee was struck, but it never met. Instead, Oliver and Talbot sat down and composed the electoral map of Alberta themselves, drawing the constituencies, as historian J. G. MacGregor says, with "extreme Edmontonian care." Oliver's map was a masterpiece. Calgary was allocated one seat; Edmonton and Strathcona were effectively given six, one in the city and five triangular constituencies surrounding its core. Suspicious Calgarians, anxious that a judicial commission should determine constituency boundaries, presciently pointed out that favouritism would preclude Calgary's supporting anything Liberal for all time, but Edmontonians paid no heed. When Oliver presented his electoral map to the House of Commons, it was seen as an injustice to the whole of southern and central Alberta. Even Liberal Calgarians cried foul. Laurier, finally alarmed, summoned Oliver and Talbot, who convinced him that the distribution was fair, although the two had gerrymandered the boundaries. Despite Laurier's doubts and a population count indicating that the south had 120,834 people to the north's 69,021, Oliver pushed the map through, and not only was the capital settled on Edmonton but the gross inequities of the electoral districts were retained. Apoplectic Calgarians screamed themselves hoarse, even threatening to warn immigrants that wheat wouldn't grow around Edmonton, but it did no good. The bill was passed.

Ottawa was still arguing over the Alberta Act when Edmonton started to make plans for the launch of the province of Alberta. Calgary, to the south, watched skeptically, hoping that the inaugural celebrations were indeed provisional. Determined to outshine Paris, Edmonton declared that electricity would be free for a week and, despite curses flying up from the south, a gaily decorated city welcomed September 1, 1905, without mosquitoes or snow. On Thursday, Governor-General Grey and his party arrived at Strathcona, and on Friday, September 1, the inaugural parade included three bands and all the city's organizations in carriages and on foot. Twelve hundred schoolchildren marched the parade route; another three hundred, too small to walk, rode. Ochsner's beer float brought up the rear, handing out cold beer bottles. Women and men in feathered hats and bowlers made their own laughing parade down McDougall Hill to watch a Mountie cavalry charge on the Exhibition Grounds, and then came the pinnacle moment, the swearing-in of Lieutenant-Governor George Henry Vickers Bulyea. At high noon, Bulyea kissed the Bible and Alberta became a province. The cannons above derelict and crumbling Fort Edmonton went off with varying booms and wallops, and cantankerous Alberta was officially born.

Laurier smiled in a very white collar and a very dark suit; he had visited Edmonton once before in 1894, and looking down at the crowd, he declared, "In the vast sea of upturned faces I see the determination of a young and vigorous people; I see the calm resolution, the courage, the enthusiasm to face all difficulties, to settle all the problems which may confront this new province." James Lougheed and Clifford Sifton and R. B. Bennett were present, although the man who had served as the West's midwife, Haultain, was not. After Bulyea kissed the Bible, Lord Strathcona (Donald Smith) and newly minted Premier Rutherford celebrated with tea and ice water.

If Inauguration Day was heady, the day after it was time to roll up the shirt-sleeves, and Bulyea formally asked Alexander Rutherford to form the provisional government. Rutherford immediately chose a five-man cabinet and called an election for November 9. Because this was a new and untested government, nobody was clear about which side stood for what, except that the Liberals had been shown favouritism by the federal government, and much of the ink that was spilled had to do with federal rather than provincial politics. The Tories claimed that the Liberals were merely instruments of the feds; the Liberals claimed that a vote for the Tories was a vote to move the capital to Calgary. Both promised voters more roads and bridges, setting in stone Alberta's continuing demand for good highways. There were brawls, charges and counter-charges, but the Liberals swept the province, winning twenty-three out of twenty-five seats, with only High River and Rosebud dissenting. Humiliatingly R. B. Bennett, the Conservative CPR lawyer, was defeated in Calgary by a mere twenty-five votes. On November 10, the *Calgary Herald* declared, "By the worst exhibition of Ottawa interference ever displayed in a provincial election, the coercion plot has been forced upon the electors of Alberta." Ottawa had been designated as whipping boy, but that sweeping one-party victory initiated a pattern that persists into contemporary times, so that each Alberta election suggests the swath of a tornado picking up every straw in front of it. The Strathcona gentleman, Rutherford, and his supporters celebrated their victory with a torchlight procession and a bonfire, but under Liberal jubilation lurked Tory discontent; and in fact the number of Tory votes that had been cast exceeded the number of Liberal votes. The constituency boundaries had rigged the election. There would be no doubt that the capital would stay in Edmonton, and although Rutherford agreed to an open vote on the permanent location of the capital, the contest was over.

The first speech of the first session of the first Alberta legislature took place on March 15, 1906, in the Edmonton Thistle Rink, the rink where hockey fans threw coal on the ice to confuse the visiting teams. The new legislature opened with the same energy that had marked the inauguration ceremonies. At the opening dress ball, the incorrigible Bob Edwards of Calgary's *Eye Opener* expressed his delight at the opportunity for "getting on a glorious drunk." Until a proper legislature could be built, McKay Avenue School hosted the sittings. Edmonton now had the home-team advantage. When Calgary MLA William Henry Cushing moved that the capital of the province be transferred from Edmonton to Calgary, the motion was defeated sixteen to eight, with three southern MLAs (Liberals, of course)

The rising legistature with Fort Edmonton huddled in the foreground

unbelievably voting for Edmonton. The battle was over, although it is a well-kept secret that by the provision of the Great Seal, Edmonton is still only a provisional capital. At any moment, any day, a majority vote in the legislature could move the capital.

But back in 1906 the competitive anger between the two cities refused to be banked. Before Calgarians could blink, the premier himself, "Sandy" Rutherford, introduced a bill enabling development of a university. What was the hurry? Unprepared for this swift action, because there were not even sufficient primary schools, the puzzled public watched while the bill establishing a non-denominational and co-educational University of Alberta was passed. Its location was not named, and Calgary assumed that having lost the battle for the capital, they would play host to education. But in 1907 canny Rutherford announced that the university would be located in Strathcona. He had purchased, in his own name, a river lot on the Saskatchewan River's south bank. Uncle Sandy wanted to be a visionary and Alberta gave him that chance, even though Laurier had chosen him as premier because he looked manageable. But Rutherford was not so easily controlled. He passed legislation for the university and then asked Ottawa for the money. When

Ottawa refused, he funded the university through the provincial treasury, infuriating Calgarians once more. But they were learning a hard lesson: loyalties are to "friends" and to "parties" and justice is seldom even-handed. Even Liberals from Calgary were hard-pressed to forgive Rutherford for the university presumption, and that final betrayal cemented the acrimony between the two cities. When the newly designated president of the university, Henry Marshall Tory, toured the province canvassing for both students and funds, Calgarians wouldn't even speak to him.

The legislature building was less contentious. In 1906 the new government struck a deal with the Hudson's Bay Company to buy twenty-one acres on the bank of the North Saskatchewan, where Fort Edmonton still stood. Fur-trading Fort Edmonton, ratty and moth-eaten, would have to go, and in 1915, designated an eyesore, the entire jumble of fort buildings was cleared away. History-minded groups wanted to dismantle the fort, number the logs, and reconstruct it, but although the old timbers were stored by the High Level Bridge for years, nothing came of its reconstruction. Now the lawn-bowling greens sit right on top of the old site of the fort, and government offices ring the grounds.

Excavation for that high-browed Minnesota-lookalike legislature building started in 1907—in typical Alberta haste, the foundations were dug even before a design for the building had been finalized. Changes were made until 1912 when the structure was formally opened, although the politicians had been arguing under the incomplete rafters since 1911. Ironically, except for its granite base, the exterior of the building is fine, yellow-brown sandstone cut from the Glenbow Quarry in southwest Calgary. Calgary's revenge on Edmonton for having stolen the capital continues—the external details are slowly eroding because sandstone is soft and susceptible to environmental damage. As the frame of the building rose, the giant legs for the CPR's High Level Bridge were being raised across the valley just to the west, two mammoth structures playing against Alberta's optimistic sky.

The cornerstone to legislative activity was laid on October 1, 1909, accompanied, of course, by a big parade, including groups under banners like Men of the North, Young Idea, and Votes for Women. Edmonton loved to emphasize its ideals of youth and progress. At the legislature's inception on September 3, 1912, the Duke of Connaught was presented with a gold key, a key that opened nothing, since even the hand-carved oak doors were unfinished. Since then, the building has been perpetually under redesign. But it still hunkers beside the High Level Bridge like an inverted Yorkshire pudding, now dwarfed by the high-rises on Jasper Avenue reflecting the increased power of oil companies and banks. The legislature building has provided employment for everyone from cafeteria workers to gardeners, as well as politicians. It has watched royal visits, parades, concerts, and anniversaries. In the past it was always accessible to Alberta citizens, but after several security breaches, and especially during the recent debate over Bill 11 (the private health care issue), it is no longer a building that any Albertan can freely enter. A site for rallies, a symbolic centre of Alberta's political decisions, it is now a dowager rather than a beacon.

• • •

Now that Alberta was a province, there was bound to be trouble. At first, backed by his impregnable government, Rutherford enjoyed a honeymoon, but he was eventually undone by a combination of the railways and his innocence. The most urgent concerns of the new government were roads, railways, phones, and railways, bridges, and railways. Alberta was much bigger than had been expected because the feds had pushed the boundary of the new province 340 miles north to include most of the District of Athabasca, as well as some sixteen million acres of prime farmland in the Peace River, enough to make even an optimist falter. Edmonton no longer sat on the northern edge of the District of Alberta, but in the middle of the new province. And now the capital was supposed to fix everything, and in one hell of a hurry.

Telephones were the first big problem, and Rutherford vowed to make the telephone a fixture in every farmhouse, even if it meant running Ma Bell (who held the monopoly) out of town. In 1905 there were two long-distance lines—between Calgary and Edmonton and between Lethbridge and Cardston; but there could be a dozen farmers stacked up on one rural party line. By 1908, under pressure, Bell sold out to Alberta Government Telephones, and gangs of men from Ontario or Ohio or Scotland started stringing telephone line, meanwhile checking out the lay of the land in case they wanted to settle in the West for good. The switchboards were often in a corner of a store or post office, but one long, three short, and the people of Alberta were connected, happily talking to their neighbours. When the whole system was completed in 1922, twenty thousand farmers had the telephone and eight thousand miles of long-distance lines spidered over the province. Everybody wanted the phone, all right, but the public utility of Alberta Government Telephones, which ran up a debt of $21 million, would fail in the Depression and would need to be rescued.

Transportation was a thornier problem. Long after the canoe brigades of the fur trade and before the railways, steamboats and scows did most of the work, and when they couldn't handle the rough rivers, wagons hauled goods around the rapids. Navigating the rivers into the north was fraught with difficulty. The land barrier between the North Saskatchewan and the Athabasca River system was one hundred to two hundred miles wide, much of it impassable muskeg. The Athabasca Trail, an old Hudson's Bay Company trail that skirted the North Saskatchewan to Victoria, then at Sturgeon turned north, connected Edmonton with Athabasca Landing. It was fine when the weather was dry, but more often turned into mud, potholes, and nasty fords, destined to result in broken heads and broken axles. The later Edson Trail, which went from Edson to Sturgeon Lake and then on to Grande Prairie, was another corduroy nightmare, but until the railway arrived it was the main road to the Peace country. Once the railways actually got there, those old trails and their stopping houses became obsolete. The Canadian Northern Railway would reach Athabasca Landing in 1912; the Edmonton, Dunvegan & British Columbia (or the Northern Alberta) Railway would reach Peace River Crossing in 1916; and the Alberta & Great Waterways Railway would reach Waterways in 1919. Rutherford believed that railways would meet every one of Alberta's challenges. Determined to open up the northern part of the province, he dreamed of two major railway lines into the Peace and the Athabasca, making him a hero. And so he implemented his infamous railway policy, which decreed that even if the feds would not, his government would guarantee the bonds of any railway that would raise 35 percent of the capital cost of its own construction. That utopian policy, under the slogan "Rutherford, Reliability and Railways," would get Rutherford re-elected with a landslide in 1909. But the Strathcona Gentleman, so eager to serve as banker to the railways, underestimated the crass motives of railway companies and their investors. Railways made money building lines, not maintaining or operating them; that burden fell to the commissioning governments. Rutherford felt confident guaranteeing railway bonds because he believed

The coming of the train brought the coming of the province

that railways would always be profitable, and so the Alberta government eagerly passed bill after bill guaranteeing one steel rail after another. The Grand Trunk Pacific planned to build 491 miles of branch in Alberta, guaranteed at $13,000 a mile; the Alberta North Western planned to build from Edmonton to Athabasca Landing to Lesser Slave Lake to Peace River Crossing; the Canadian Northern planned a line from Edmonton to Athabasca Landing, and most peerless of all, the Alberta & Great Waterways Railway put in its bid for 350 miles of track from Edmonton to Lac La Biche and then Fort McMurray, guaranteed at $20,000 a mile. Railway promoters played poker with politicians, and railway mania escalated.

But railways are harbingers of busts as well as booms, and bust they did, blowing up right in Rutherford's face. At first the rumours were of conflict of interest, the supplier and contractor the same company, meaning that one could inflate the cost to the other. Then began more serious claims, that the Waterways rail was light, laid on an uneven, buckling bed, that poor construction would derail the success of the project. To Rutherford's surprise, he was nastily ambushed by R. B. Bennett, that stalwart Conservative from Calgary, who launched into a scathing denunciation of what he considered graft and incompetence, claiming that various ministers of Rutherford's cabinet were profiting from the deal signed to construct the railway. Bennett argued that the Alberta & Great Waterways contract was the most irresponsible arrangement ever made by any government, and served a motion to cancel the contract on the grounds that the line to Fort McMurray needed to be no longer than 230 miles, not 350; that the line was overcapitalized; that no neutral engineer had inspected the route; and that construction specifications were inadequate. Worse, Calgary's W. H. Cushing resigned his post as minister of public works, saying that the government had acted without his knowledge and consent, and then, heading up a group of insurgent Liberals, accused Rutherford of negligence, claiming, "You have utterly failed to protect the interests of the people."

Through weeks of mudslinging, Rutherford discovered some uncomfortable facts, including that his own attorney general, Charles Wilson Cross, appeared to be on the take in the construction of the Alberta & Great Waterways Railway, that the railways had provided conflicting estimates, and that money had been raked off by someone, possibly quite a few someones, somewhere. Party lines be damned, the entire Alberta legislature was at war. Rutherford did not resign, but weathered the first non-confidence vote (twelve of his own Liberals voted against him), twenty to seventeen. He then named three judges to investigate. But Rutherford's caucus was out of control, and now Ottawa pulled its long-distance strings. Rutherford had screwed up royally, and he needed to go. The federal Liberals, in consultation with Lieutenant-Governor Bulyea, anointed in his place Arthur Sifton, a hard-edged, uncompromising character who could clean up any mess, even one this big.

On the morning of May 26, 1910, after a tense meeting, with Bulyea presiding as the long arm of Ottawa's Liberals, Rutherford resigned, and Sifton took over as premier. Compared to the kindly warmth of Rutherford, Sifton was as cold as ice. And although the independent commission's report ultimately found that the case against the ministers of the government was "not proven," it did conclude that the government's contract with the Alberta & Great Waterways Railway was badly conceived, not thoroughly investigated, and a terrible financial deal for the new province. Alberta had enjoyed the first of many scandals. The bloom was definitely off the rose, both tame and wild.

10 | Crazy Politicians

"Backstrom, what have you got to offer?"

Let me say flatly that when I walked into the doctor's rented hall there in that water stop called Coulee Hill I did not intend to promise anything. But we are so often mistaken; we confuse beginnings, endings. They are so alike so often. Especially when it comes to politics. Politics, or, I might add, love. They had me cornered all right, the bastards. And then the answer came without my thinking—I had been drinking a little; I looked at the speaker and saw he was a farmer and I said: "Mister, how would you like some rain?"

—Robert Kroetsch, *The Words of My Roaring*

(narrated by Johnny Backstrom, a fictional political candidate)

On July 14, 2000, the black cloud on the horizon to the north begins to resemble a theatre curtain. So dark and thick is the air that everything feels muffled. I'm driving through Alberta's tornado zone, and by the ragged clouds, the building anvils, and the almost emerald sky, it looks as if I am getting close to a possible tornado. The clouds race overhead, pulling in different directions, and it feels as if the wind begins to spin. I turn south and drive as fast as I can in the opposite direction. I'm not a storm chaser, but if you live in Alberta you will meet storms, hailstorms, and thunderstorms, and even tornadoes. Towering clouds are a common skyscape.

That day, a sudden tornado struck a campground at Pine Lake, south of Red Deer, resulting in twelve people dead and 131 injured. The campground was ripped to shreds, a twisted mess of metal and wooden matchsticks. Called the deadliest Canadian storm in 2000, it crushed motorhomes, splintered trees, and levelled houses. With utter perversity, the same twister picked up Ashley Thomson, just four months old, sucked her from her car seat, spun her as high as a three-storey building, and then put her back down as gently as a nanny. Called the miracle baby, she suffered only a cut foot. I wonder what she dreams about now—that monster wind or her safe recovery?

Alberta hosts about twenty-eight tornadoes a year, most of them spinning out in the area from Edmonton to Red Deer and east toward Saskatchewan, that "tornado triangle"

Glenbow Archives, Calgary, Canada, NA-1662-?

Woman sitting in her home after a tornado

exacerbated by hot, humid summer air mixed with unstable updrafts and thunderstorms, harbingers of disaster.

The Pine Lake Tornado wasn't quite as destructive as the tornado that hit Edmonton on July 31, 1987. That date would be renamed Black Friday, for the tornado left twenty-seven people dead and more than three hundred injured, resulting in $300 million in damage strewn along a forty-mile path. It shattered the Evergreen Mobile Home Park, tossing seven hundred trailers into heaps. The nearby industrial park was destroyed—a huge oil storage tank was flipped, cars and trucks were thrown around, roofs torn away, and workers hurled into walls. Twelve freight cars flew off the railway tracks. The wind was so loud that it deafened people. Some hailstones that day weighed almost seven pounds. But it wasn't the worst tornado in Canadian history; the credit for that goes to one in Regina in 1912.

In Alberta, big tornadoes hit every couple of years. They're not something we look forward to, but we've learned how to survive them, to comfort the bereaved, to pitch in with the cleanup, to repair the damage and to feed and clothe the victims. And those huge, sweeping storms are more than storms. They pull at our grassroots, suggest a new direction, obliterate our good sense. They leave crystal vases whole and break plastic dishes; they tear the pants off us and leave them swinging on a tree miles away.

Our politicians and our political parties come by their history honestly. Every massive political change in this province emulates the wide sweep of a tornado.

• • •

Albertans have always hated government, its sticky fingers, its interfering ways. They hate politicians almost as much, although they practise a wild combination of adulation and revolt that swings politicians into power and then just as suddenly flings them out of power and onto the streets again.

When it was obvious that Alexander Rutherford had to resign as provincial leader, a number of Liberal candidates were more than eager to sit in his still-warm chair. But no election was held, no caucus vote taken. Lieutenant-Governor George Bulyea (on whose instructions?—probably Laurier's) simply called the house into session, announced Rutherford's resignation, and then announced that Arthur Sifton would be his replacement. This gave the Liberal Party time, with Sifton's caulking, to repair its leaky boat. He dumped every MLA and cabinet minister who had supported the Alberta & Great Waterways deal, and cleaned house. The Royal Commission on that mess was a whitewash job that found no one guilty of outright misconduct.

And the railway still didn't exist—when the Alberta & Great Waterways defaulted on its interest payment, the government met the payment and tried to transfer the more than $7 million in bond money raised to build the railway to the province's coffers. But even the banks resisted, and both the money and the railway were in limbo, making a train to Fort McMurray seem an unlikely dream until J. D. McArthur (already planning the Edmonton, Dunvegan & British Columbia Railway up to Peace River) stepped in with an offer to finish laying steel for the Alberta & Great Waterways. By that time, Sifton, who resembled a bald Sherlock Holmes, had reconciled his party's factions, appointing some of the most vociferous to new cabinet posts. Somehow he held the fractious Alberta Liberals together and got ready to test them against the electorate. Having corralled his disputatious caucus, he confidently called an election.

That April 1913 election, Alberta's third, went down in history as corruption carried to the furthest possible degree. Wild accusations were met with even wilder accusations, Conservatives and Liberals battling one another with every weapon available, while voters were disgusted and disillusioned by turns. Electoral irregularities (on every side) were reported and exaggerated, and the headlines rang with exposures and seizures and falsehoods, retaliations and crooked deals and illegalities. The Tories charged Sifton's Liberals, often correctly, with vote tampering, vote buying, ballot stuffing, bribery, and even physical attacks on scrutineers. They were doubtless taking revenge for Liberal stories that a gang of thugs hired by the Conservatives were sneaking around Alberta intimidating farmers into believing that they were going to be foreclosed on their debts, all so that the farmers would believe that the government was out to repossess their land. No member of this "Rogers Gang" was ever caught or charged, but it made for some great headlines and presaged the marvellous Alberta tendency to believe the wildest of tales. Exaggeration and gullibility are two of our most enduring traits.

But the election of 1913 was filthy. In Peace River, the process had to be delayed until September because some helpful person accidentally or on purpose threw the electoral official's bag (containing the election writ) into Lesser Slave Lake. In Clearwater, which had enumerated only eighty voters, 103 people voted. Ballot boxes and election clerks disappeared. Bribery flourished, and votes were mysteriously assigned to vacant lots. Even in an era when crooked elections were sport, this one took the ribbon, and after it was over, with Sifton winning thirty-eight seats to his Conservative opposition's eighteen, there were still disputes and recountings that needed to be settled.

During the real estate boom of 1910–13, everybody wanted a "government" job, especially Centrals who had come west to make their fortunes the easy way. Real estate brokers, auctioneers, homestead inspectors, all the hangers-on who follow the industry of primary producers flooded into Alberta. By 1912 Edmonton's business directory listed thirty-two real estate brokers, 135 financial agencies, and 336 real estate agents, all going great guns. And as with any time of change, social upheaval grew. Sifton, dour political cynic that he was, had to negotiate the suffrage movement, considerable labour unrest, the temperance movement, and farm revolt.

Prime Minister Robert Laird Borden's relationship with Alberta was flinty-eyed. With the outbreak of the First World War, the Wartime Elections Act disenfranchised all immigrants from the countries governed by the Central Powers (Germany, Italy, and the Austro-Hungarian Empire) who had not been naturalized before, a move that did not make the feds popular with Alberta's many ethnic groups. Borden raised instead of lowered tariffs, and while Eastern manufacturers were benefiting from war production, the farm economy was not. Immigration slowed, the land boom stopped, there was a shortage of labour, and although wheat prices went up, so did the prices of equipment and transportation. The farmers were convinced that the feds worked only for central industrial, financial, and transportation interests, the fifty big shots in the East. At first farmers were exempt from conscription, but then men twenty to twenty-two years old were removed from exemption. The frustrated agricultural West and the Canadian Council of Agriculture produced a Farmers' Platform, which demanded graduated income tax, taxes on corporate profits, and nationalized railways and telegraph companies. Ironically these desires are exactly the opposite of what the Western parties want now.

The United Farmers of Alberta were growing in number and in strength, and after the war ended, the Farmers' Platform declared that if politicians wanted to win the agricultural vote, they had to endorse farmers' demands. Although the UFA was initially against running candidates in elections, the pressure was on. They effectively controlled the provincial government anyway; why not get a few seats?

In the same year that women first exercised their franchise, the tame and uneventful election of 1917, the Non-Partisan League, an agricultural political movement that believed in the nationalization of elevators and flour mills, banking and credit systems, ran four candidates in Alberta's election. Two won, James Weir of Parkland and Louise C. McKinney of Claresholm, the first woman to sit in a provincial legislature in the British Empire. Nursing sister Roberta McAdams, representing the armed services, was also elected, but it took her a while to get back to Alberta from France, so McKinney was sworn in first. In 1917, right after the election, Sifton resigned to go to a presumably happier appointment in Ottawa, where he entered the Unionist—Conservative and Liberal cross—Borden cabinet as minister of customs, a fitting task for a chilly man. Rumours say his resignation was prompted by a woman, or even women. In February 1914, when two hundred women flooded into the legislature building to demand the franchise, Sifton stood outside the chamber doors, listened to their demands, and then asked if they had washed the dishes before coming to petition him.

Sifton was replaced by Liberal Charles Stewart, a singularly uncolourful figure in Alberta politics, except for his coming humiliation at the hands of the UFA. An Ontario-born farmer who had moved to Killam, Alberta, Stewart was an unsurprising choice of walk-in premier. He had been a member of Sifton's cabinet since 1913 and was generally well regarded. Of greater interest was his attorney general, the same C. W. Cross who had been so thoroughly investigated and exonerated for his role in the Alberta & Great Waterways scandal. Cross, a Laurier loyalist, had a tendency to act as if he and not Stewart were the leader; and Stewart headed up a provincial Liberal party that was beginning to show cracks, a result of the arguments in Ottawa between traitor Unionist Liberals and Laurier Liberals. Not nearly as dictatorial as Sifton, Stewart immediately encountered backbench criticism over his failure to press Ottawa for Alberta to gain control over natural resources. And "soldier" MLAs who had returned from the war refused to follow party lines. Alberta's Liberal Party was beginning to implode, the division between Unionist and old-order Liberals and the conscription issue causing serious pressure. When Stewart asked Cross for his resignation, Cross refused, and Stewart was messily forced to rescind Cross's appointment. Partisan politics prevailed again.

When the war ended, the Liberals tried to be as optimistic as everyone else. Stewart was personally popular, but his government far less so. Now that people were grappling with the problems of peace instead of war, they were impatient with the old hard-line parties. A 1920 slump in agricultural prices encouraged general discontent. Railways were still a thorny issue, and added to that were new and thirsty difficulties related to prohibition and irrigation. Under pressure from the farmers, Stewart bestowed provincial guarantees on irrigation bonds, and by the fall of 1921, almost two million acres of land were due to benefit from irrigation. But the long-projected railway lines were still unfinished, and the ones that were finished were in terrible condition. The province kept paying to improve the lines, and the CPR took over running a couple of the worst ones. Meanwhile, the government's debt was mounting.

But that wasn't the worst. Prohibition, in force since July 1, 1916, created more interesting problems than it had solved. The legislation enhanced rather than prevented thirst, and bootlegging became commonplace. Illicit stills were hidden everywhere, and the respectable members of one congregation were treated to a rich, fruity smell, which disclosed that the church janitor was nursing along a raisin whisky still in the hallowed basement. The very judges and lawyers who were expected to pass judgement on liquor act violators were themselves drunk the night before ascending the bench, statistics claimed that as many as 65 percent of the population regularly broke the liquor laws, and Attorney General John Boyle estimated that by 1921, bootlegging was generating an economy of more than $7 million. Doctors and druggists, who had the power to write scrips for "medicinal" beverages, made not a few fortunes. The friction between the wet and the dry side was fierce and furious, and the government, caught in the middle, could only squirm. To make matters worse, the newly formed Alberta Provincial Police couldn't seem to stem the tide of whisky. Soldiers returning from the war discovered that Alberta's complexion had changed considerably.

Poor Stewart. Not a smart lawyer like those who had preceded him, he was a real farmer, and more a supporter of the UFA than the Liberals he was leading. Grumpy veterans and people with declining fortunes were hard to please. In 1919 six thousand Non-Partisan League members and nineteen thousand United Farmers of Alberta members merged, becoming a formidable bloc of influence and encouraging UFA locals to go political. Unitarian preacher William Irvine, the founding father of the radical democratic socialist movement in Alberta and advocate of the Non-Partisan League as a working-class movement, was out on the stump, rabble-rousing at UFA meetings. He charged that while big-shot millionaires had made huge profits from the war, Canadian soldiers had been paid nothing for their deaths and suffering. Elected to a federal seat in 1921, he became a co-founder of the Co-operative Commonwealth Federation, which later shaped the New Democratic Party. But meanwhile, he was fomenting discontent.

Signs of change began in November 1919 when the first UFA candidate ever to contest a seat, Alex Moore, handily won a by-election at Cochrane. The Liberals sniffed the wind but could not believe what Moore's win presaged. Utterly controlled by the farmers, Stewart sat on the fence, amended a bunch of bills, and sure enough, the heat of UFA discontent seemed to cool. Stewart relaxed, had an appendectomy, and decided that he could afford to call an election. Besides, what was there to worry about? The *Edmonton Bulletin* predicted Liberal victories in at least thirty-five seats. But on June 17, 1921, in true Alberta fashion, the electorate swept the Liberals right out the door, and made the UFA victorious in thirty-nine out of sixty-one ridings. An old, established, Centralist party had been defeated by a class-conscious, labour-interested bunch of farmers, without formal leadership and without a rigid platform, who would rule Alberta for the next fourteen years. The tornado of Alberta politics had touched down, and Alberta's second political dynasty had arrived.

• • •

The UFA candidates hadn't promised the moon, and they didn't deliver it either. They were populists, against special class legislation and against privilege but not sure how to act on those beliefs. They wanted not only a better deal for farmers, but a new societal order, with government no longer handing out favours to the rich and the well-educated. What most raised their ire was the protection of Central manufacturing concerns and Central bankers controlling the primary produce of the West, which was wheat and meat. In many ways, the farm movement came out of a powerful moral rectitude, which reacted to an industrial and financial world wielding all the political clout. In truth, every farmer knew and understood the malignant fury of an indifferent nature, and the frustration of unpredictability.

Henry Wise Wood, who'd refused to wear a political mantle, preferring to work behind the scenes, declared that the procedure this neophyte bunch should follow was simple: "Put them in office, leave them alone and let them do it." The leader they chose, Herbert Greenfield, who served from 1921 to 1925, was a simple man and a reluctant premier. Urbanites made caustic comments and welcomed the new legislators by spreading straw on the steps of the legislature; the cities of Alberta were dominated by Ontario people, who felt themselves more sophisticated than this unusual grassroots movement. The farmers' government, however, recruited one very sophisticated member, John Edward Brownlee, alumnus of Victoria College at the University of Toronto. When he finished his studies he travelled west in search of an up-and-coming city where a man could make a future for himself. In 1908 Brownlee articled with Lougheed, Bennett, Allison and McLaws in Calgary, already a firm considered prestigious. Bennett, who was the main lawyer for the

CPR and would soon be prime minister of Canada, took Brownlee under his wing, catechizing him on the details of sources and precedents. Once Brownlee was called to the bar, he joined Muir, Jephson and Adams, the law firm that took care of the UFA's legal work, which put the successful young lawyer directly in Wood's path, and when the United Grain Growers was formed, he served as its general counsel. The advantage of having a Toronto-trained tongue in a city full of hustlers and homesteaders was a given, but Brownlee had a firm interest in farmers, and when Wood asked him to join the new UFA government as its attorney general, Brownlee was delighted to accept. He ran in a by-election in Ponoka and represented that constituency until 1935.

A. C. Rutherford, first premier of Alberta, looking pleased with himself

Glenbow Archives, Calgary, Canada: NA-1514-5

Brownlee was, in effect, the power behind the throne. Greenfield was not ready for the tough questions lobbed at premiers. He enjoyed showing off the legislature building to visitors, but he always hoped that political issues, like bad thunderstorms, would clear off by themselves. As if to underscore his reluctance, Greenfield suffered from unpredictable laryngitis, making him temporarily but frequently speechless. All the more important that his second-in-command be an eloquent and able debater, which Brownlee was. For the four years that Greenfield was premier, Brownlee did the work for him.

The UFA government passed the necessary Drought Area Relief Act, but resisted providing too much help to the stricken farmers of the south, worried that they would come to expect that support and more. And because of the infernal railways, the province was deeply in debt. Brownlee wanted Greenfield to sell off the northern railways, which were bleeding the province dry, but he did not manage to orchestrate that until seven years later. There was nothing for it but to curtail spending, making the farmers less than happy with this new and yet predictably unhelpful government.

Albertans were getting testy. Greenfield seemed inattentive, and had been haunting the watering holes of hotels. By 1924, discontent brewed within the UFA ranks. Greenfield's inability to man the helm was becoming a liability, and it was clear that he might scuttle the next election. Brownlee conducted himself with absolute discretion and told the unhappy rebels that if Greenfield were asked to resign, he would resign as well. Then, after some discussion with Wood, urbane Brownlee did agree to lead the farmers, provided that Greenfield be assured of his loyalty and that Greenfield himself anoint Brownlee his successor. The deal was done, and Greenfield went back to farming, relieved of the weight of office. After Brownlee rewarded him by appointing him Alberta's agent general in London, England, Greenfield regained his voice and enjoyed promoting the beauties and economic promise of Alberta, this time to awestruck British questioners.

Brownlee, though only forty-two when he became premier, was an adept negotiator, with an imposing physical presence—over six feet and more than two hundred pounds, his spectacled stare impressed everyone. While he was attorney general, his most important action had been to pressure Prime Minister Mackenzie King into restoring the Crowsnest Pass freight rate, which had been suspended during the war and which King's Liberals, not overly anxious to please the West, were reluctant to do. Even better, Brownlee managed to secure reductions in westbound freight rates, which brought the price of machinery down. As premier, he lobbied Ottawa for Alberta to get control of her natural resources, and amazingly, he was successful. On December 14, 1929, King signed the agreements for the transfer without a whimper, and although Brownlee could not have seen the future, the signing was the beginning of Alberta's transformation into a powerful economic force.

In the election campaign of 1926 both Liberals and Conservatives took potshots at the UFA, while the UFA simply argued for its return on the strength of its position as a party that did not serve a federal master but was answerable to the people of Alberta. Because Albertans voted by preferential ballot—an unwieldy system used in Alberta between 1926 and 1955—marking their candidates 1, 2, 3, it took forever for votes to be counted, but the UFA was returned with even more seats than before. The final count in 1926 was forty-three UFA, seven Liberal, five Labour, four Conservative, and one Independent. Because rumours were always circulating that Brownlee was about to become head of the Alberta Wheat Pool or that he would leave for some other plum job, he was wooed and worshipped and obeyed.

Brownlee pressed the feds to provide assistance in building roads, now desperately needed. And he introduced the first gasoline tax in the country, first two cents on the gallon, then five cents on the gallon to subsidize the $5 million needed to upgrade roads. The first gasoline tax, and in Alberta! He had his nerve. In addition, all those pie-in-the-sky railways were bankrupt, so control over them fell to the Royal Bank of Canada, who, in true Central fashion, not thinking that Albertans might need a railway or two to move grain and cattle, just wanted to shut them down. Abandoning the lines would alienate northern Alberta and destroy its growth, so Brownlee bought control of the failing railways and worked at persuading both the CNR and the CPR to take them over. After negotiations, the CPR actually purchased, for $25 million, the troublesome Edmonton, Dunvegan & British Columbia, the Central Canada, and the Alberta & Great Waterways railways, relieving Alberta of a heavy weight. Of course, the purchasers were far from philanthropic and would certainly make money on those lines, but Brownlee had done what was considered almost impossible: negotiated return of the province's original investment and balanced the books. He was a hero.

But he was no philanthopist. When Mackenzie King introduced the old-age pensions, Brownlee at first resisted. The terms of the legislation were that any Canadian over seventy who had lived in Canada for more than twenty years was eligible to receive a pension; Ottawa would pay 50 percent, the province of residence 40 percent, and the municipality in question 10 percent. Brownlee objected that Alberta could not afford to support the pension, but a wave of public support made his objections seem ridiculous, and Alberta, shamefully, became the last province to bring in an old-age pension.

In the federal election of 1921 Alberta had sent eleven of their now-renowned farmer activists, dubbed Progressives, to Ottawa, forcing Mackenzie King's minority government to negotiate with them in a Liberal/Progressive coalition. In the messy 1926 political tug-of-war between King and Conservative leader Arthur Meighen, the Progressives helped to defeat two minority governments in the space of a week, which did not help their credibility. They seemed never to know their own minds and that period spelled the end of the farm movement's federal influence.

Few people know it, but the Co-operative Commonwealth Federation (CCF), whose legacy to Canada was medicare and unemployment insurance, was born in Alberta, at a Calgary meeting on August 1, 1932. Now considered a Saskatchewan invention, the CCF offered an alternative to the UFA, and at its first convention in Regina after its founding meeting, its dream of a socialized state was clearly laid out. Historians argue that it could not have thrived in Alberta and so transported itself to Saskatchewan, but in a world looking for populist movements the CCF probably found a home in Saskatchewan because Alberta was already so firmly committed to its own populist party, the UFA, which, in order to retain its power, deliberately opposed CCF principles.

Meanwhile, UFA Premier Brownlee was set to enjoy his successes. But the unpredictable funnel of tornado politics was building again. The stock market crash of 1929, the Depression, unemployment, and labour unrest began to infect even the harmonious farmers. Wheat prices plummeted as fast as people jumped out of windows. Brownlee called in the Mounties to disperse a peaceful hunger march; one thousand men surging toward the legislature made Old Silver Tongue uneasy. And Brownlee's early mentor, R. B. Bennett, had defeated Mackenzie King to become prime minister of Canada in 1930.

Bennett was another carpetbagging Easterner who had arrived in 1897 from far distant New Brunswick to make his fortune in the West. Senator James Lougheed, himself an Ontario transplant, had persuaded Bennett of the enormous potential for making money and for establishing a political career in Calgary, so Bennett packed his books, put on his overcoat, and took the train west. He was as un-Western as any man could be; when he was checking into his room in the Alberta Hotel, one man invited him for a drink. Bennett replied, "I don't drink." Another approached and offered him a cigar. Bennett replied, "I don't smoke." A third man, who had been watching these lobby exchanges, observed wryly, "Boy, oh boy, there's a man who has no future in this man's town."

But Bennett did. His first case was arguing for a man who had been fined for operating a billiard table without a licence. His career, however, would be made in his defence of a crime of passion, the Harris-Gouin case; Bennett successfully got

Harris acquitted of attempted murder for shooting Gouin, the lover of his wife. From then on, Bennett was flying high, running for the Territorial Legislative Assembly, running for Parliament, running his law practice, and investing in real estate. Not averse to employing his inside knowledge of the CPR and where it planned to lay track, he bought farm property and town property, and from his corner table at the Alberta Hotel began to exert a powerful influence on Calgary's corporate affairs. He made money, became an MLA, asked scathing questions about the Alberta & Great Waterways scandal, and made more money. He got elected to Borden's Conservative crew down in Ottawa, but failing to win a cabinet appointment decided he didn't want to serve as a mere backbencher and went back to Calgary, where he bought more real estate and made more money and invested in interesting ventures like the Calgary Brewing Company. This was essential stock-holding for a teetotaller; the way to defeat drinkers was to make money on their dearest desire. A man who bore long grudges, Bennett practised law and making money through various litigious arguments and disagreements, including a fairly acrimonious separation from Lougheed in 1922. And he frequently travelled to England, honing himself as an anglophile and defender of the empire. He kept up his connections with powerful political men in the centre, and oversaw his shares in the E. B. Eddy Company, of which he owned more than half. An issue-driven Conservative, Bennett was preparing himself for the job of prime minister, and sure enough, when Meighen was defeated and the Tories needed Bennett, he was ready to become first the leader of the Opposition and then a millionaire prime minister during a time when most people didn't have a dime.

Rigidly Methodist and a friend of business and manufacturers, Prime Minister Bennett passed a lot of legislation that was no help to the suffering West. He might have lived in Calgary for thirty years and Calgary might have made him his fortune, but he felt no loyalty to his old friends and took a hard line with everything from cutting free railway travel for unemployed men to refusing to put money into relief. The West had nothing but words to use as weapons. Horse-drawn cars (gas was too dear for purchase) were christened Bennett buggies; boiled grain was Bennett coffee; abandoned farms were Bennett barnyards. A man so rich that he had always lived in hotels, and so doubtful about sharing his wealth that he never took a wife, he had very little comprehension of the plight of the ordinary family. Although he declared that the drought in Alberta and Saskatchewan was the greatest national calamity that had ever happened in Canada, he did little to alleviate its effects. He did, however, set up the Canadian Radio Broadcasting Commission, and in 1935 he came up with a whole series of radical reforms that he claimed would regulate the nasty capitalists who had created the Depression. Eyebrows were raised; was this R. B. Bennett talking? But it was too little too late.

He made matters worse when he sent the Regina Mounties in to disperse one of the protest meetings of the "On to Ottawa" train, where they broke a few too many heads. Bennett was setting himself up to take a licking from the Liberals, and in the federal election of 1935, Mackenzie King happily defeated this oddly dapper, oddly lonely man. Although he hung on as Opposition leader until 1938, he had a miserable time of it, and finally, claiming that if Canada "no longer wants me, it will be easier for others if I am no longer there," he moved to England, where he died as Viscount Bennett, as rich and lonely as he had been in Ottawa.

Although he, too, was wooed by Ottawa, J. E. Brownlee opted to stay in Alberta, and after being re-elected in June of 1930 he just tried to steer Alberta through the dirty thirties. He couldn't know that virtually every provincial government would be defeated by the Depression. He couldn't foresee his own defeat, although he should have known better.

On August 3, 1933, the law firm of Maclean, Short & Kane informed Brownlee that they had been instructed to commence action against him for damages for his seduction of Miss Vivian MacMillan, a twenty-two-year-old stenographer from Edson, Alberta. She claimed that the premier had first seduced her in 1930 and had had an ongoing affair with her (despite her reluctance) until the spring of 1933. It was the most enthralling sex scandal ever to hit Alberta, and coming at a time when most people couldn't afford entertainment, it was followed as avidly as a hockey match. Every element of skulduggery and lurid sexual activity was present.

Visiting Edson in 1930, Brownlee had apparently taken an avuncular shine to Vivian MacMillan, the daughter of the town's mayor. He had invited her to come to Edmonton, where he suggested she take a business course, after which he might be able to provide her with a position in government service. Vivian did move to Edmonton; she enrolled in secretarial school and began to visit the Brownlee home quite frequently. The most prurient details of the case came from Vivian's testimony that Brownlee had convinced her to have sex with him on the basis that he had no conjugal relations with his wife, Florence, because she was in danger of dying were she ever to become pregnant again, and he entreated Vivian to have sex with him in order to save Mrs. Brownlee's life. Eventually Vivian succumbed, reluctantly, according to her testimony. She claimed that Brownlee seduced her in his car, at his home, in his office, and on drives in the country; also, that he employed both endearments and threats to keep the relationship going. She was often invited to stay at the Brownlee home, where the unusual bedroom circumstances—Mrs. Brownlee slept with her son Alan, and Brownlee himself slept in a bedroom with his other son—did not inhibit the relationship. When she stayed over, Vivian shared a room with the maid. Brownlee would get up and go to the bathroom, then flush the toilet, and by that prearranged signal Vivian would follow him back to his room, walking in time with his footsteps so that the creaky floor would not betray them. Apparently they would engage in intercourse while Brownlee's son slept in the other twin bed. When Vivian suffered a nervous breakdown in 1932, she went back to Edson for three months, but she chose to return to Edmonton and then resumed her relationship with Brownlee. Only, she claimed, after meeting and falling in love with another man, John Caldwell, to whom she confessed her affair, was she determined to break with Brownlee. Caldwell convinced her that she ought to consult a lawyer, and in July, after Vivian had confessed all to her parents, they hired legal counsel and sued the premier.

Was this suit a thinly veiled means of blackmailing Brownlee? Was this a Liberal plot to discredit him? Brownlee denied the allegations, saying they were "false, frivolous, vexatious and scandalous." He hired his own crack lawyer, and at the much-publicized trial, sat beside his wife, exuding authority. Brownlee's lawyer argued that Vivian's allegations made no sense, while Vivian's lawyer argued that Vivian couldn't possibly have invented such an incredible story. It was her word against his, and the jury, after five hours, came back with a verdict declaring that the premier of Alberta, Methodist and all, had seduced Vivian MacMillan. Despite disagreement from the judge and despite subsequent appeals, Brownlee had to resign. His happy time as premier of Alberta was over.

If Albertans remember Brownlee, it is for the entertainment the trial afforded. If they remember Vivian, they remember she was awarded $5,000 in damages. Some versions of the story claim that the result says a lot about Alberta's strict moral template. Vivian MacMillan went back to Edson, eventually married, divorced and

J. E. Brownlee, a sadder and wiser man

Glenbow Archives, Calgary, Canada: NA-2784-9

married again. And Brownlee, after the spectacular defeat of the UFA government in 1935, returned to his work with the United Grain Growers. There is one last footnote to his name. Not only was he the premier who fought for Alberta to control her own resources, he was the only non-banker on the Royal Commission investigating Canada's economic position in 1933, where he had a long-lasting influence on Canada's monetary future by arguing that the Bank of Canada should be a public institution, arm's length from profit. His good sense with regard to public policy was obviously not something that spilled over into his private life.

• • •

The embarrassed UFA replaced Brownlee with his dour Scottish minister of resources, Richard Gavin Reid, who would govern Alberta for only fourteen months. A new, more charismatic movement was sweeping across the province—Social Credit, based on the theories of Major C. H. Douglas—promising money and jobs, and a whole new system of credit and its application.

Social Credit in Canada started as a voice from the radio, a voice that proclaimed, with rising intensity, that he was a true apostle who had an infallible system by which the world ought to govern itself. Founder of the Calgary Prophetic Bible Institute, a fat, rosy-cheeked man who might have passed for Santa if he'd had more hair and grown a beard, William Aberhart broadcast exaggerated interpretations of the Bible that seemed to invite political application. Only in Alberta, you say? Well, certainly in Alberta, an Alberta patched and thirsty, down at the heels and disillusioned and drought-stricken, eager to hear a good yarn, a means of escape. Robert Kroetsch's 1966 novel, *The Words of My Roaring*, explores the carnivalesque element of Social Credit that was its most appealing feature—it promised hope. It promised a dime for a glass of beer, it promised a green tomorrow, it promised rain. Was it any wonder that the plummy voice of Aberhart pouring out of the radio seemed to provide a cure for the Depression?

That political tornado was Bible Bill Aberhart, furious and fundamentalist, messianically, thunderously, ungrammatically eloquent. And a transplant straight out of the heart of old Ontario. Born on a farm there, he went to teachers' college, got his arts degree by correspondence from Queen's, then began teaching at Central Public School in Brantford, Ontario. Although he'd had only a desultory interest in religion as a boy, in 1906 when he was twenty-eight, he fell under the spell of a Presbyterian minister who roused his interest in the Bible, particularly the hallucinatory Book of Revelations. With exceptional powers of concentration and boundless enthusiasm and self-confidence, Aberhart became an autodidact in Bible studies.

In 1910, offered a considerable raise in salary to teach in Calgary, he packed up his wife and two daughters and came west, becoming principal of Alexandra School, later moving to Crescent Heights, one of Calgary's premier high schools. Aberhart organized and timetabled and chivvied teachers and students into the routines of learning, but his real interest lay in his evangelical work. At first he moved from church to church, Grace Presbyterian to Wesley Methodist and finally to Westbourne Baptist, teaching Sunday school and preaching so compellingly that his Bible classes quickly began to overflow. Eager to bring the wayward to true faith, he converted Westbourne Baptist Church into a booming business, increasing membership and conceiving the Calgary Prophetic Bible Conference, a wild ride on religion that became so popular that meetings had to be moved to the Palace Theatre, a venue that could hold more than two thousand people. The success of the conference generated the Calgary Prophetic Bible Institute, where earnest young men—including in particular one Ernest called Manning—and women could gather to discuss the portentous parts of the Bible, and by the mid-1920s Aberhart had a huge and growing flock. Exceedingly blond, a powerful athlete, and as scholar Harold J. Schultz says, weighing "an eighth of a ton," Aberhart was a celestial bean-counter who loved systems, charts, and diagrams. Numbers supported his authority, as reflected in the titles of his lectures: "The Four Different Attitudes toward Bible Truth," "The Twelve Points of Difference between the Old and New Theology," "The Two Great Characteristics of the Down-Grade." He separated human history into four sections he called "God's Great Divisions": "The Peopling of the Earth," "The Time of the Hebrews," "The Time of the Gentiles," and "Dispensation of Grace," the latter encompassing the present age. In an elaborately conceived system, Aberhart contended that each period of time was interrupted by man's breaking his covenant with God. After the "Rapture," when true believers would vanish into thin air, transported to a better world and leaving the wicked and unredeemed behind to endure the "Tribulation," would come seven years of terror and destruction, after which Jesus would return to earth and a thousand years of peace would precede the final Armageddon. It seems wildly unlikely now, but Aberhart could actually fill the Palace Theatre, as he did on February 1, 1925, with a lecture titled "Seducing Spirit and Itching Ears: The Place of Women in Religion" about how the Bible warns against allowing women to form religious sects. Aberhart chased the elusive enemy he called apostasy, convinced that all modern thought or revisionism was heretical. His fundamentalist tear utterly dismissed the social and communal approach of the United Farmers of Alberta.

And in 1925, building on the spirit of the times, Aberhart began to use the new medium called radio, broadcasting his lectures over CFCN, the West's most powerful station, at his peak logging five and a half hours of air time on Sundays. This gave Aberhart a huge audience. CFCN reached Alberta, Saskatchewan, and BC, and at one point nine thousand children were enrolled in the radio Sunday school. Aberhart roused Westbourne Baptist with his charismatic practices, especially the laying on of hands and rebaptism. He began publishing a magazine, *The Prophetic Vision*, and raised money to build the four-square Calgary Prophetic Bible Institute. First, Aberhart sold "sods," each $100, to purchase the lot, then used the radio to talk up the building campaign and, to boost donations, urged listeners to buy bricks at twenty-five cents. The Bible Institute opened in 1928, smack between a white frame house and a used-car lot, on Eighth Avenue and Fifth Street, a site that would become Eaton's, itself now a memory of failure. And his ideas certainly linger; when Calgary was raising money to build the Olympic Plaza for the 1988 Olympic Games, the city sold bricks for $19.88. Who would have traced this innovative fundraising venture back to Bible Bill Aberhart?

While marking year-end external examinations for the Department of
Education, Aberhart met Charles Scarborough, an Edmonton high school teacher
who was a fresh convert to Major C. H. Douglas's Social Credit movement.
Scarborough worked hard to convert Aberhart to the theories of Social Credit, and
for a while Aberhart resisted. But in the summer of 1932, on the heels of a student's
committing suicide because of financial difficulties and the banks and loan companies foreclosing on farmers, Aberhart read an accessible analysis of Social Credit
theory called *Unemployment or War*, by Maurice Dale Colbourne. Literally
overnight, he became a convert, and began to incorporate these new ideas into his
sermons and lectures. Via Colbourne, Douglas's theories held that private control
of credit creation was responsible for a perpetual insufficiency of mass purchasing
power; he argued that Social Credit would improve everyone's standards of living
by the "velocity theory" of compulsory spending. "Poverty in the midst of plenty"
could be cured by the distribution of "social dividends."

A bundle of contradictions, Social Credit asked only that its followers exercise
faith. Capitalism was its devil, but "free enterprise" its hero. Credit was positive,
but money as a medium was devalued, and hoarding wealth was considered an
offence. Banks were to blame for general poverty because they withdrew money
from the natural flow of business; with only the federal government controlling
banks and currency, the people had no chance to flourish. Under Social Credit,
banking's monopoly would be broken; and given a fair price for their goods and
services, ordinary people would have better purchasing power. Citizens would be
asked to tender their life insurance, real estate, or other collateral to support government bonds, which would then provide every citizen with dividends. Poverty
and want would vanish. Social Credit did not initially reject socialist ideas, and
they were ambivalent about the state's interfering in economics. Certainly they
believed that no person should suffer want, which is the basis of public conscience, but while they argued that the state should not appropriate money from
the rich, they also expressly felt that the state should not permit any company to
make excessive profits through consumer exploitation. Neither duck nor fish, they
muddled between promising overt interference in free enterprise and promising
that the state would not intervene. They railed against the country's economic
controllers, "the fifty big shots" in the East, and swore to break the hold of the old
capitalist system. Most of all, they promised the tattered and thirsty citizens of

Bible Bill Aberhart, at home

Depression-era Alberta $25 a month. That was the real carrot on the stick for every family scraping to live on scarce dimes and nickels.

Slowly the movement proliferated, with Aberhart educating and instructing in the same charismatic way he taught religion, through a series of lessons and classes. Invited by the UFA to address their members, Aberhart began to infiltrate the farmers' movement, his formidable organizational skill multiplying converts who themselves spread out through the province to promote Social Credit. It was a movement on fire, one person converting two people who each persuaded two more. Listeners to Aberhart's Bible broadcasts became targets of energetic field men and women (although Aberhart didn't believe in women leading religious movements, he wasn't averse to using them as support workers), Aberhart missionaries who fanned out from the Bible Institute to cover virtually all of rural and urban Alberta, meeting in living rooms, an environment that made the "study groups" cosy and inclusive.

For all that this was now a considerable political force, Aberhart, years ahead in terms of riding-by-riding organization, had not yet formed a political party. Certainly, Social Credit ideas exerted political pressure, a pressure that was beginning to make the UFA government squirm and to have an effect on UFA membership. Aberhart's interpretations of Douglas's theories were somewhat confused, but in 1934, Aberhart organized a petition to bring Major Douglas himself all the way from England to Edmonton to address the legislature. Douglas first shunned Aberhart and then argued with him, refusing to endorse Aberhart's version of his monetary policies. But the result was that Aberhart seemed more persuasive than Douglas, and Douglas's visit intensified interest in the economic cure that Social Credit promised, even though the UFA government concluded that Social Credit did not offer a real solution to the difficulties the people faced. Aberhart offered hope, and the UFA offered futility. Throughout that summer, Aberhart toured Alberta with his lieutenant, Ernest C. Manning, and people flocked to see the face that belonged to the radio voice. Study groups informally canvassed the population to gauge their response to Social Credit; the numbers demanding political action astonished even absolute supporters, and Aberhart himself stated that the movement had "spread like measles." Pretending to be nothing more than an educator, Aberhart continued his road show, which included a skit with a "patched-up coat of many colours" representing the futile policies of old political parties. (During the 1935 campaign, his dramatic dialogues featured a Central apologist explaining to a man from Mars why Albertans lived in such poverty in the midst of plenty.)

Then, in a striking move, Aberhart broadcast an appeal for "One Hundred Honest Men" to offer themselves to the Social Credit cause. The response was phenomenal, with so many volunteering that Aberhart could select between three and four hundred "honest men" to lay the foundation of what would become a Social Credit landslide. Aberhart was gearing up, but not until March 1935 did it become clear that Social Credit would run a candidate in every riding, and at the pre-election conventions, it was decided that Aberhart himself would choose the candidates who would run. Ironically a man who despised the theories of social gospel had invented a political party entirely in response to the wretched economic conditions of the 1930s.

Much historical discussion has focused on Saskatchewan's endorsement of the left-leaning CCF in contrast to Alberta's embracing a conservative Social Credit movement, but their initial platforms were remarkably similar and appealed to the same population base. The development of both radical movements was very much inflected by historical events, and their success relates to the governments that preceded them. They were, in truth, two sides of the same coin, who initially supported social, economic, and health reforms, and who represented a populist protest against capitalism.

Aberhart himself has been characterized in many ways—as an arrogant demagogue, as a naive and vain schoolteacher flattered by the attention his eloquence evoked, as a crusader against poverty, as a dictator, and as a religious madman. Yet he demonstrated a capacity for organization and planning, if not analysis. Famous for his strategic resignations, which always resulted in a grief-stricken clamour from his disciples, and wound up with his occupying an even stronger position, he was masterful at exploiting challenges. He wrote to his sister, "I am not anxious to go into politics, but the people are urging me to do so." All the newspapers of Alberta were essentially critical of his proposals, but people were desperate to believe any promise. As tireless a campaigner as he was an evangelist, Aberhart stomped the hustings, railing against the UFA (he called the United Farm Women the "Undernourished Fool Women of Alberta," although women voted for him in record numbers). He excoriated his critics as crooks and hypocrites and fornicators. At a picnic rally at the Edmonton Exhibition Grounds on July 6, Aberhart addressed some five thousand supporters, saying that Social Credit, as the dark horse, was the one to watch. (That day is the setting for Bruce Allen Powe's 1983 novel, *The Aberhart Summer.*)

Aberhart himself did not run for a seat, as if he were above the election fray. His candidates were a mix of farmers, merchants, preachers, and schoolteachers, most strikingly the first generation of native Albertans elected to govern their own province. Still, Aberhart was probably as surprised as everyone else when the UFA government, bedevilled by the Brownlee scandal, by Reid's lacklustre leadership, and by internal fragmentation, as well as their own refusal to take Social Credit seriously, went down to resounding defeat on August 22, 1935. Despite their inexperience, their wild promises, and their megalomaniac leader, Social Credit swept the province, winning fifty-six seats, with the Liberals taking five, and the Conservatives two. In a record voter turnout, the beleaguered UFA was eradicated. Jaws dropped all over the world, and headlines read, "Alberta Goes Crazy." In his acceptance speech, Aberhart seemed almost dazed by what he had wrought. The next day, in conversation with reporter Fred Kennedy, Aberhart asked him for advice about political process, making it suddenly obvious that the persuasive preacher was utterly unprepared for what he was now faced with—keeping the promises that he had made to a ragged, struggling province.

Aberhart became premier, and a seat was cleared for him in Okotoks–High River (coincidentally, Joe Clark would come from High River). But where were they going to start? Alberta was broke. There wasn't even enough in the treasury to pay the civil servants, let alone hand out $25 to petitioning citizens. Aberhart had no choice but to take the train east in order to beg and borrow from "the fifty big shots," including former Albertan R. B. Bennett, now the prime minister of Canada (although he was about to be defeated by Mackenzie King). Aberhart came home with a measly $2 million, a stopgap measure and he knew it. Desperate for advice, he appointed a full-blown capitalist, Robert Magor, president of the National Steel Car Corporation, to advise the new government on how to handle its financial imbroglio. Meanwhile, he kept trying to persuade the guru, Major Douglas, to return to Alberta, the site of such a great Social Credit triumph, but Douglas refused. Through letters and cables, Aberhart asked Douglas for guidance, but all Douglas suggested was that Aberhart tax the rich and stay suspicious of bankers, who, in Douglas's scenario, were always Jewish. (The anti-Semitism of Social Credit's original designer was an unhappy aspect of its legacy, and the province's still overt racism can in many ways be credited to the half-life of Douglas's doctrines.) By the time Douglas and Aberhart stopped talking, eighteen months later, the two hated each other.

Despite Douglas's abandonment, Aberhart tried to live up to Social Credit principles. In 1936 the government actually issued a version of credit, or scrip, Prosperity Certificates, which could be exchanged for goods in an elaborate system of stamps and validations. Although by the terms of the BNA Act, only the feds could issue legal tender, the Alberta government did honour some $12,000 worth of this "funny money," while Ottawa did not interfere but sat back to watch the experiment fail by dint of its sheer cumbersomeness. Businesses refused to accept scrip and the scheme was doomed to failure. Only a few were kept as souvenirs.

The year 1936 was a confusing one for Alberta. Aberhart ignored the opposition and waited, as if he did not know how to govern this ungovernable place. In February 1937 Aberhart chose his *Back to the Bible Hour* radio program to announce that, regretfully, he could not immediately introduce Social Credit economic reforms, and in his favourite ploy, asked the people of Alberta if he should resign. His diehard Social Credit caucus was by this time unanimously unhappy with him, and a group of "insurgents" met every night in a room in the basement of the Corona Hotel, plotting to unseat him. These backbenchers fomented revolt and began to holler for Aberhart's head. They made trouble for him even in his own riding. In 1936 his government had passed a Recall Act (sound familiar?), whereby two-thirds of the voters in any riding could recall their representative. A determined group in Aberhart's Okotoks–High River constituency demanded his resignation and circulated a petition to that effect. Aberhart barely escaped recall by passing a motion to repeal his own act. He never mollified the insurgents, although those who supported the original tenets of Social Credit were beginning to understand that he could not implement his election promises. They fought and argued and resigned and stormed in and out of the house, watched by a bewildered electorate, who were still ragged and hungry. Why was nothing improving? In order to distract his internal critics, Aberhart set up the Social Credit Board, whose task was to advise the government on Social Credit polices. But one matter became abundantly clear. Aberhart had learned how to unmask his enemies; a petition calling for his resignation actually originated from his own office because he wanted the names of those conspiring against him in black and white.

Economically things were not going well. The province was still deep in debt and became the only province to renege on paying its bonds, partly because the treasury was bare. When the government sought to meddle with the private sector, business interests fled. The Act to License Trades and Industry effectively proposed the government as the arbiter of trade, making some call it communist and others call it fascist. The Socreds did establish credit corporations, or "treasury branches," which now (a legacy that has actually lasted) function very much like ordinary banks. But they were still trying to find a way to distribute $25 a month. Using a rationale rather like the War Measures Act, they then tried to implement several acts that would preclude constitutional challenges to any legislation in Alberta and would strictly limit the rights of individuals and organizations. Although the bills to take control of the banks were passed in the assembly, the legislation was ultimately disallowed because the feds controlled all currency, credit, and banking. In a confused and disorganized way, Alberta was trying to have a revolution, trying to bring about a peculiar form of governmental control that would overthrow what this particular band of outlaws read as the hegemony of the Centre. But every piece of radical legislation, from the press-restricting Accurate News and Information Act to the Credit of Alberta Regulation Act, was overruled as ultra vires, or unconstitutional, first by the lieutenant-governor, then by the governor general, then by the Supreme Court, then by the Privy Council. Furious at Lieutenant-Governor John Campbell Bowen's refusal to sign the government's bills, MLAs demanded his resignation, but since he was in Ottawa's employ they could not fire him. Instead, because the province paid for his residence and office, he was evicted from Government House, the lieutenant-governor's official residence, a beautiful sandstone mansion overlooking the North Saskatchewan River valley. He moved into a hotel and settled in for a long and rancorous fight.

The most interesting quarrel was probably over the Accurate News and Information Act. Because it had so condemned him, Aberhart hated the press, and this act would be his revenge; newspapers would be required to reveal their sources and to print statements handed out by the government, without emendation. Further, the Social Credit Board could ban any material it chose. This was downright censorship, and the *Edmonton Journal* put on boxing gloves. It appealed the act before the Supreme Court of Canada and the Privy Council of England, and won, and on April 2, 1938, the *Edmonton Journal* was awarded the Pulitzer Prize for its passionate work in defence of freedom of the press. Ultimately Alberta's radical/reactionary new laws were all disallowed, and it soon became evident that even staunch Social Credit party members had difficulty swallowing bills that controlled the press or refused to honour debts. Social Credit wasn't getting anywhere, and Alberta was in a financial mess.

Added to that came the scandal of the Bankers' Toadies case. Two Social Credit diehards, Joseph Unwin, government whip and member for Edson, and George Powell, a member of Douglas's staff who had come to Alberta to provide advice on implementing Social Credit policy, were arrested and tried (despite Aberhart's attorney general trying to declare that the trial could not proceed) for "counselling murder, criminal libel and seditious libel," because of a pamphlet they had written and printed calling for all "Bankers' Toadies" to be "exterminated." Maverick senator and war hero William Griesbach, named as one of the "toadies," had laid the charges against the two and, after a spectacular court case, won. Both men were found guilty and, despite appeals, were imprisoned in Fort Saskatchewan jail, where they cooled their heels for a couple of months, entertained by carloads of Social Credit supporters who motored out to sing to them every night. Although Powell and Unwin were released fairly quickly—Powell returned to England and Unwin to the legislature—that trial demonstrated the palpable impatience of the business establishment with Social Credit shenanigans.

Albertans had elected a government that called itself Social Credit but couldn't implement a Social Credit mandate, that claimed to be left when it was right, and right when it was left. Although later Social Credit governments would denounce public health care, early Social Credit conventions passed resolutions calling on the government to establish state-supported medicine and hospitalization. True to the social gospel tradition introduced by the UFA, Alberta voters were still interested in the spirit of collectivity. There were both fascist and labour patches in the Social Credit coat, uneasy alliances that formed and dissolved. In 1938, for example, although Aberhart censured them, Calgary Social Creditors approved a platform supporting trade unionism. Radical thought in Alberta can turn on a dime, can insist on a merging of left and right that makes the more conventional thinkers of Canada breathless.

Aberhart more and more removed himself from the very policies that had got him elected. Unbelievably, he did not make his maiden speech in the Alberta Legislative Assembly until February 17, 1939 (he was elected in 1935), instead using his radio broadcasts to inform the public of his decisions. In that first speech, he claimed to be concerned with "the work that we have successfully accomplished in Alberta, and to indicate what may yet be expected from our policies." He criticized socialists and conservatives alike, and defended his government's poor results. Populism was a wonderful tornado to ride into office, but a poor whirlwind to retain that office. The electorate was growing critical, doubtful. Party membership dropped, constituency meetings attracted hecklers, and Aberhart's German name raised open suspicion. His only consolation was the official visit of King George VI and Queen Elizabeth, which he enjoyed with tremendous gusto.

The rest of the country, under the shrewd eyes of Prime Minister Mackenzie King, watched the squabbling and the drama and the brawling (fisticuffs threatened in the legislature) and the botched monetary rebellions with combined horror and amusement. The colonials out in Alberta were revealing just how crazy they were, and how very much they needed the steadying hand of paternal Ottawa. Of the twelve specifically Social Credit acts introduced in 1936 and 1937, none came into operation, and all their efforts at economic reform were constititionally disallowed. Once war was declared in 1939, Ottawa's War Measures Act superseded all Alberta's attempts to control business. Over time, the influence of the staunch Douglasites who wanted Aberhart to follow a strict Social Credit economic platform waned, until under Ernest Manning's leadership it faded altogether, with Manning exerting executive power over the "funny money" crowd.

Even that long ago, Alberta refused to co-operate with the Royal Commission on Dominion-Provincial Relations, instead publishing in 1938 *The Case for Alberta*, a set of proposals for economic and constitutional reform. When in 1941 Mackenzie King called a conference to discuss the commission recommendations, Alberta, along with Ontario and British Columbia, sabotaged the meeting.

Despite the general assumption that Aberhart was doomed—he even called himself "the most unpopular man in the province"—in 1940, just a few months after war broke out, Albertans re-elected Bible Bill. Social Credit had fulfilled none of its promises, had raised taxes, had defaulted on bonds, and had alienated every newspaper in the province, but Bible Bill, despite vituperative attacks, came back. The war wiped away the bitter taste of the Depression with a bitter taste of its own. Aberhart's electoral success was bittersweet, too. In powerful contrast to the heady victory of 1935, Social Credit won only thirty-five seats in 1940 and held a slim majority of nine.

One positive measure that the government did implement was the Métis Population Betterment Act, which designated for the Métis people, who had been marginalized and homeless since the Riel Rebellion, nine settlements in northern Alberta. And although he hadn't managed to find a way to install Social Credit economics, Aberhart's education reforms were positive and effective. Before they were in place, rural teachers especially were poorly paid, and rural education did not match the level of education available in urban centres. So Aberhart established school boards with responsibility for bringing relative uniformity to the province's schools. Salaries and conditions improved, and by 1939 the province had been divided into fifty school divisions, all under the direction of divisional boards, much better than the previous ad hoc system. Alberta's learning was at last brought to an acceptable level. The one tension that arose concerned the teaching of evolution within the schools. As the head of a presumably Christian government, Aberhart was lobbied by fundamentalist groups to take an anti-evolutionary stance. Eventually he wrote a tract that he wished inserted into all school textbooks as an antidote to the perfidious theories of evolution, but his minister of education, Dr. G. F. McNally, persuaded him that such an action would be unwise because it would provoke undue controversy.

In 1941 Aberhart was treated to the full extent of the contempt that the province's intellectuals, mostly from the Centre, held for him. It had been the University of Alberta's custom to award every premier an honorary doctor of laws degree. When the president of the university, W. A. R. Kerr, received approval from the university senate's executive, he went ahead and asked Aberhart if he would accept the honour. Aberhart was pleased and confirmed his acceptance, but at the next full meeting of the senate, when Aberhart's name was proposed, a majority of one member voted against the motion, and Aberhart's honorary degree was defeated. The president protested strenuously and asked for a second vote, but got the same results, leaving him in the embarrassing position of having to inform Aberhart of the senate's refusal. Kerr resigned, but Aberhart, although he accepted the decision with grace, was deeply hurt, and the government later stripped the university senate of all its power except that of awarding honorary degrees—it cannot be said that Aberhart had no sense of irony.

The war was very much Mackenzie King's theatre, with Alberta's wide skies providing training for pilots, bombers, and navigators. Aberhart's voice now had competition from the sonorous pronouncements of Churchill and Roosevelt, and while he shepherded a newly prosperous Alberta through the war Aberhart became obsessed with post-war reconstruction, taking up the obvious points of democracy relating to the newly tested allies of the British Empire, fighting together to defeat the evils of fascism. A shortage of manpower, with a particular shortage of farm workers and teachers, made unemployment a vague memory. Aberhart's interest in economics continued, but he had accepted the fact that Social Credit was a fiscal dream that could only be implemented at a federal level or not at all.

At the same time, his characteristic energy waning, Aberhart was suffering from a liver disease that would eventually kill him. He left for Vancouver in the middle of April 1943 for "rest and recuperation," but died on May 23. His wife, Jessie, insisted that he be buried in BC rather than Alberta, where they had lately suffered such unhappiness. And the press, for all that they had waged all-out war on Aberhart, was relatively kind, calling him a champion of the oppressed. Whatever his peculiarities, the writer George Melnyk has correctly summarized his effect: "The name Aberhart is now part of Albertans' genetic code."

• • •

When Aberhart died, Ernest Charles Manning, his figurative son, the young man who had been his right hand, who in 1935, at the age of twenty-seven, as provincial secretary became the youngest cabinet minister in the British Empire, was anointed as Bible Bill's successor. Manning was no dummy, and although he had tried to implement the failed Alberta economy bills, he rapidly began to demonstrate a political savvy that would save Social Credit as a name if not a theory. As soon as Aberhart had taken over the reins of power, Manning set out to educate himself in the problems of practical governance, working so hard at his political education that at the beginning of 1937 he required six months' leave because he had nearly killed himself with overwork and developed tuberculosis. He had just married Muriel Preston, the pianist for the *Back to the Bible Hour* radio program, and she took a crash course in nursing and kept him at home to recover. Probably because of his illness, he was deemed unfit for military service.

That was merely the beginning of a long career that would see Manning steering the province further and further right, navigating resource wealth and prosperous times to set Alberta firmly on its populist but pragmatic feet. Born in 1908 to British immigrant parents struggling to make a living near Rosetown, Saskatchewan, Manning went to a one-room schoolhouse, and grew up like every other prairie farm boy, doing chores. But he was fascinated with the new medium of radio, and by seventeen had somehow managed to save enough money to buy one. When he and his brother raised the antenna from the roof of their house, he picked up CFCN's powerful transmission, and the voice of Bible Bill. Enthralled with Aberhart's vision of change, a year later, at eighteen, he visited Calgary to investigate attending the Prophetic Bible Institute. His two-week stay, during which he met Aberhart, was a happy conjunction for both, and his serious determination convinced Aberhart that this was exactly the kind of young convert who could forward the future of prophecy and persuasion. The next year, Manning moved to Calgary, enrolling in the institute's three-year Bible-study program and becoming, in 1930, its first graduate. He not only studied with Aberhart but lived under his roof and worked as a janitor for the institute, returning to Saskatchewan in the summer to earn enough money doing farm work to continue his clearly happy studies. When Manning graduated, Aberhart was reluctant to see him leave and asked his protégé if he would like to remain in Calgary as the institute's secretary. Manning readily agreed, thereby setting in motion his journey to the longest premiership in Canada, which Manning held for twenty-five years, six months and twelve days, between 1943 and 1968.

Manning did everything in his power to mirror his mentor. He travelled with Aberhart, stood in when Aberhart was unavailable to speak, and learned about Social Credit at his knee—he even mimicked Bible Bill's mannerisms. People said that they could not distinguish between Aberhart's and Manning's voices on the radio. When Social Credit swept to victory in 1935, Manning led the polls in Calgary. A witness to every triumph and confrontation, Manning worked assiduously to acquire the knowledge that Bible studies had not included—parliamentary procedure and political science. When he began his political career, Manning was described by journalist C. W. Peterson as "a conceited, half-baked youngster whose sole business experience has been gained as assistant preacher at the Aberhart Bible College," but in point of fact Manning managed the government on the floor of the house.

As premier, Ernest Manning ruled with an iron fist and enjoyed a political strength that was nothing less than exceptional. He had walked with Social Credit through its failures and as provincial secretary and then as minister of trade he had absorbed experience, becoming in the process an able administrator. Acutely aware of the effects of economic comfort or deprivation, he carefully arranged that when he came up for re-election in 1944, he represented himself as opposing all socialist movements, which by that time were considered dangerous and unstable. The war's economic boom brought monetary relief, and Manning, his religious beliefs at his elbow, common sense apparent in his high forehead, concentrated on serving as a model semi-theocratic leader, all the while proposing plenty of post-war planning and development. People's memories are short. Despite the absolute mess Social Credit had made of Alberta, in 1944 the province elected the party with Manning as its leader in another landslide, a repeat of the tornado that had funnelled Aberhart into office. Perhaps voters were convinced by Manning's nerdy determination or had simply got used to his face hovering below the headlines.

Manning was deeply concerned about what would happen to the economy after the war ended. Alberta, for all her incipient resource wealth, seemed to be headed for quiet stagnation. Her population had dropped, agricultural development was levelling off, and it looked as though she might slip into a slow and sleepy adult-hood. Manning formed a committee to develop an ambitious program of post-war reconstruction, emphasizing Christian values of consensus and co-operation. But he also suggested practical measures, like assistance to young farmers, improvement in teachers' salaries, an extensive building program at the University of Alberta, an industrial development board, and not least, an aggressive policy of natural resource development. A pulp and paper industry was to be pursued, Alberta's road mileage would be doubled, and road and highway quality improved to attract tourists to the magnificent parks. Town planning and the installation of electricity, waterworks, and sewage would be subsidized. In short, Manning's subcommittee on post-war reconstruction imagined a new and improved province. Modern Alberta was about to be invented.

But he still had to deal with his crazy fringe element, the Social Credit Board, who were pathologically suspicious of socialism and any movement like the League of Nations, which they saw as dangerous international conspirators. They were convinced that socialists and global banking interests were secretly working together to control the world monetary supply and to establish a worldwide tax. (One wonders how they would have reacted to the global economy measures that now proliferate.) They became more and more embarrassing to Manning, and their 1947 report, an overtly anti-Semitic document that proposed government ownership of all land and abolition of the secret ballot, pushed him to the limit of his tolerance. Manning publicly denied that Social Credit was anti-Semitic and condemned all anti-Semitic sentiment. Then he dismissed the members of the board and terminated the appointments of all their supporters.

The regional insularity that might have contributed to the eccentric opinions of diehard Social Creditors had taken a beating during the war years. Alberta had begun to identify herself within a larger world. Albertan racism during and just after the war made for some impassioned debate. During the war, obvious discrimi-nation against Germans and Japanese aroused little controversy, and after the war Manning's government demanded that Japanese-Canadians who had been exiled to Alberta from British Columbia be sent back to BC. But public opinion turned, and three years after the end of the war Alberta invited the Japanese-Canadians to stay. (Joy Kogawa's novel *Obasan*, which is set in southern Alberta during the war, addresses the situation of Japanese-Canadians.) Alberta also exercised considerable bias against pacifist sects like Mennonites, Hutterites, and Doukhobors, who were exempt from conscription, especially Hutterites, perceived as increasing their land-holdings at the expense of regular farmers who were off fighting in the war. Hearings after the war reflected a pervasive hostility to Hutterites, leading Manning to implement the Communal Property Act, which stayed in force until 1972 when Peter Lougheed's government repealed the measure. The bizarre para-noias reflected by Social Credit theory were relegated to the sidelines of chimera, where they lurk still, discredited but occasionally aroused to speak through the mouths of characters like James Keegstra, sent to remind Albertans of our history of intolerance.

But Manning's regime was blessed by those primordial coral reefs that bequeathed to the province huge, ripe pools of oil and gas. Eager to find the fuel to keep its four-wheel horses going, a newly mobile Alberta drilled the caprock of the province in an energetic search for oil. When Leduc No. 1 decorously came in as scheduled the day before Valentine's, 1947, Alberta marked itself as an energy power. When Atlantic No. 3 blew in on March 8, 1948, oil and gas spewed every-where, pooling on the ground; six months later the wildcat well was still wild. Alberta had lit a beacon. Subsequent discoveries at Redwater, Pembina Valley, and Swan Hills put Alberta politicians in the unusual position of riding a provincial tornado of new wealth. And to sprinkle gold dust over everything, they quickly realized that natural gas was itself a valuable asset, not just an irritating by-product.

The government began to make money from selling the right to explore on Crown reserves and from royalties on subsurface rights. Hundreds of millions of dollars poured into the treasury and Manning was sailing. Alberta got busy building roads and pipelines and schools, polishing its infrastructure, and enjoying its pros-perity. This was the age of development and investment, takeovers and miracles. Drillers drilled and wells blew in and pipelines were built and Alberta got richer. Large American oil companies like Chevron and Amoco and Texaco came visiting, setting up Canadian subsidiaries and giving Manning advice on how to draw up guidelines for the marketing and production of fossil fuels, thereby colouring Alberta's American accent even more strongly, especially in Calgary. They stayed, bought houses, became active managers in this burgeoning industry. Curiously, or not so curiously, Central Canada was initially uninterested in investing in the potential of Alberta's oil industry—they put their money in mining. Maybe they didn't believe the statistics or thought the boom was just another example of Alberta exaggeration. It was because the Centre shrugged and didn't return Manning's telephone calls that by 1963, 62 percent of Canada's oil and natural gas was controlled by Americans. But the Alberta government possessed the authority to impose procedures for the production and marketing of oil and gas. What a windfall. Albertans were busy and cheerful and prosperous. They re-elected Manning with a majority seven times between 1943 and 1968, happy to forget his eccentric adoptive father, happy to buy houses and cars and to invest in ever-rewarding oil and gas shares. The birth rate went up, immigrants flocked to the province, the population grew, the universities grew, the cities grew. And over this burgeoning empire presided King Manning, a farm boy with a Bible school education.

Manning learned very quickly to appease naysayers and to ally himself with business. His avowed anti-socialist, anti-unionist support of individualism attracted the business crowd like a magnet. The Cold War was heating up, and Manning embodied all the right attitudes, rejecting government ownership and supporting the private sector, even while he maintained that these resources belonged to the people of Alberta. The provincial Energy Resources Conservation Board regulated exploration and development, and that was, as far as he was concerned, sufficient. With its prosperity and its American cousinage, Alberta had little interest in nationalist movements, although one of the most vociferous defenders of cultural and political sovereignty, Mel Hurtig, would come from Alberta. That is the nature of this province; we grow our own dissent.

Manning, eccentrically, continued one old Social Credit tradition. Every Saturday he drove all the way back to Calgary from Edmonton to broadcast, on Sunday, a sermon over Aberhart's old *Back to the Bible Hour*, reaffirming his Christian beliefs and perhaps deliberately underscoring his character as that belonging to a man of integrity—moral, upright, and sober. On Monday morning he was back in Edmonton, ready to rule over his kingdom, truly a one-party state. In 1955 his government was questioned about favouritism with respect to some property transactions that a couple of MLAs had been involved in. This could have resulted in a bloodbath, but Manning handled the allegations and the subsequent inquiry with consummate finesse, and effectively silenced his opposition.

In 1957 and 1958, when the government paid out some $20 million in oil dividends to the citizens of Alberta, Albertans began to lobby for the money to be applied to programs of benefit to the populace. Accordingly, Manning built homes for senior citizens, spent money on street paving and campsites, began to build improved medical facilities, and proposed the building of a provincial archives. Scholarship support for students, home improvement loans, and a huge road improvement program were implemented. If we look now at this overt investment in the province's long-term social and cultural welfare, it is tempting to become nostalgic. Even then, at an extremely conservative time, there was greater concern for public welfare and public good than is articulated now. King Manning was determined to leave a legacy of public works that would reflect well on his stewardship of Alberta's wealth. By then, Alberta's voting system had been changed from preferential to straight ballots, and overall the government began to behave like that of an urbane, although not yet sophisticated, place. Albertans found it easier to drink and smoke, and for all their assiduous censors they could even catch a glimpse of flesh above stockings at the movies.

And at a federal level, the province finally got sick of sending fringe Social Credit MPs to Ottawa. Nobody listened to them, everybody laughed at them, and when John Diefenbaker became leader of the national Conservatives in 1956, Albertans abruptly changed their federal voting patterns and shifted their support to the Tories. Diefenbaker wasn't an Albertan, but he certainly had the makings. Despite the Conservative attraction for big business and the status quo, Diefenbaker, by appointing James Gladstone, a Treaty Indian from Cardston, Alberta, to the Senate, signalled that the First Peoples had a voice in the daily governance of their land. And in 1965, under Manning, Alberta's First Nations people were at last granted the right to vote in Alberta elections. (Status Indians had gained the federal franchise in 1960.)

The sixties saw a rise in nationalism that seemed to bode ill for the protectionist interests of the province. Everything sexy was happening in Montreal, in French, and with a flower in its lapel. Alberta sniffed the blossoming air of tear gas and insurrection and decided that she, too, wanted to go out into the world and meet experience. The baby boomers were in university, and there was suddenly more than one university in Alberta. Their parents had paid off their mortgages. In the last twenty-four years, Alberta's population had doubled to 1.6 million.

King Manning sensed that it was time to retire. He wrote a book, *Political Realignment: A Challenge to Thoughtful Canadians* (published in 1967), which proposed that existing political parties should realign into two camps, the binaries of right and left. It would be a recognition of political realities, he suggested, for Social Credit to unite with the national Progressive Conservative Party and to work for the establishment of a social conservative party. Quite a foreshadowing of current affairs, with the Canadian Alliance Party and the Progressive Conservatives in turmoil over the same idea.

Manning saw through one more election in Canada's Centennial, 1967, winning easily, but when the dust settled he faced across the floor the Lougheed six, a new and tenacious Conservative group armoured with the determination and energy of youth, the sure knowledge that another of Alberta's political storms was building. In December 1968, six months after Pierre Trudeau became Canada's fifteenth prime minister, Manning, at the age of sixty, resigned as premier of Alberta, no longer the Social Credit mecca, but still the wildcat well, the tornado province. It was as if he knew that a completely different animal had now entered the arena of politics—savvy, young, in favour of the sexual revolution, and wonderfully footloose. No two people could have been as different from each other as Pierre Elliott Trudeau and Ernest C. Manning, and their remote crossing of paths predicted the changes about to mark both nation and province. The ultimate in collared respectability and conservatism, Manning was appointed to the Senate in 1970 and for the remainder of his life was a quiet, unassuming presence, even though he sat on the boards of a number of large corporations, becoming one of the very "Fifty Big Shots" who had been the butt of so much of Aberhart's sarcasm. Manning died thirty years later, in 1996, having bequeathed to Alberta a period of seeming stability and to Canadian politics his own chip-off-the-block son, Preston, and a whole new grassroots eccentricity.

Manning's boots were leagues too big for anyone, and although the Social Credit Party elected a leader as similar to Manning as possible, his replacement, Harry Strom, was far out of his depth and far out of sync with the new Alberta. Unassuming and quiet, a rancher from Bow Island who had served as minister of agriculture, Strom had no idea what kind of challenges he was facing, although he was the first premier born in Alberta. His province was no longer the rural, agricultural Model T that it had been before the war. It was now a high-powered Buick with a flashy, high-living urban style. Alberta was no longer religious but secular, no longer shy and self-effacing but brash, well-off, and ready to test her prowess.

Poor Harry Strom was about to be carried away by the new political tornado hovering on the horizon.

• • •

Strom kept his head down and pretended that Lougheed and his young quarterbacks weren't mocking him every minute of every debate in the legislature. They were polite, well-groomed, but in the face of their suave, well-educated urban ease, Strom must have felt heavy, mud-laden. He wasn't a good speaker, he disliked publicity, he lacked political judgement, and he thought his party was invincible. By 1971 those maverick Conservatives had somehow, through defections and by-elections, grown from six to ten, and Strom hadn't even called an election yet. He should have called one the moment he became the Socred leader, but he dallied and waited until July 1971 to dissolve the legislature and call for a vote at the end of August, tornado month.

Lougheed was a new penny with an old name. Bare-headed, in shirt sleeves, he literally ran through the province (his team was famous for jogging), visiting every riding (one day he travelled 1,600 miles)—talking on main street, talking on television, convincing Albertans that he was a live wire, a new Kennedy, not tired old deadwood. Under their one-word election slogan "NOW!" he and his team touched down and then ran off again, youthful and exuberant and full of future. Recognizing that the white males of the Socreds weren't exactly representative of multi-ethnic Alberta, Lougheed tried to collect candidates from a wider range of backgrounds. There still weren't many women, but at least a few Ukrainian names appeared.

Edgar Peter Lougheed is as close as possible to being a blue-blood Albertan, the grandson of Senator James Lougheed, entrepreneurial lawyer and land speculator from Brampton, Ontario, who came to the Territories determined to make his fortune. James Lougheed graduated from Osgoode Hall, then caught up with the CPR railway barons at Medicine Hat, and with a combination of intelligence and talkative flair persuaded the lot of them that he was their man. Decreed a bona fide CPR solicitor, he rented the back of a log cabin in Calgary in 1883 and began to practise. And he bought land. Either he was more prescient than others or he had an inside scoop—the CPR station would be located just one block from his property.

In 1884, Lougheed made another advantageous move, marrying Isabella Hardisty, nothing less than Western aristocracy, the daughter of a Métis woman and an official of the Hudson's Bay Company. Belle was well connected; one of her uncles was Lord Strathcona (yes, the guy pounding in the last spike in the famous picture) and another was Senator Richard Hardisty. While he enjoyed his privileged connections with both the CPR and the Bank of Montreal, James became a confirmed Western booster, arguing for Calgary and the West. He persuaded R. B. Bennett to come west to be his law partner in 1887, and when Senator Hardisty died in 1889, John A. Macdonald named Lougheed as Hardisty's replacement, making him the youngest man in the Senate and a lifelong supporter of the Conservative Party.

Lougheed owned valuable property and oil shares; as one of the original backers of the Dingman Well in Turner Valley, he had a fair chunk of Royalty Oil stock. He built a sandstone mansion, Beaulieu, which has now been restored as a historic site. Knighted in 1916, Lougheed enjoyed a prestige and authority that almost no other Albertan could claim, although gossip around the family was wildly inventive— some stories went that Sir James tried to marry his daughter to the Prince of Wales, who resisted.

When Senator Lougheed died of pneumonia in Ottawa on November 1, 1925, he left behind a lot of property, a fair measure of public work, and five children, only one of whom had gone east to fetch a gilt-edged university degree. That son, Edgar, went to McGill, served in the Royal Canadian Army in the First World War, returned to attend the University of Alberta, and then hied across the country to Dalhousie to study law. A serious bon vivant, he married Edna Bauld, from an almost-wealthy Halifax family, and returned to Calgary in 1924, where Sir James presented them with a bungalow on a street behind Beaulieu. Peter Lougheed was their second son, born in 1928 just before the big crash that would make all high living and optimism redundant. When Sir James died in 1925, Edgar gave up law to try to sort out the affairs of his father's estate, which in the Depression slowly began to atrophy in value. Pressured by the demands of relatives and his own lack of management skill, the fortune dwindled and Edgar Lougheed was reduced to the demeaning position of "estate manager." His mother, Lady Lougheed, died, Beaulieu was seized for non-payment of taxes, and Edgar lost his own home. He took refuge in the one remnant of his bon vivant days still available—alcohol. He would, it's said, walk into the Lougheed Building bright and early, as if on his way to work, walk straight through the building out the back door and into the door of a beer parlour across the alley. His wife had a brief nervous breakdown, and Peter Lougheed's childhood seemed to be very much at the mercy of the "Fifty Big Shots" and their callous disregard for the terrible grift of the West's economic misfortune.

There are apocryphal stories of Peter Lougheed, then ten years old, watching the auction of all the contents of Beaulieu and swearing that he would right his family's fortunes. Growing up in Calgary in the Depression, he heard the voice of Aberhart, and throughout his childhood watched Alberta's political circus. When the Second World War broke out, the Lougheed family moved to what was then the outskirts of the city and settled into reasonable steadiness, only occasionally interrupted by Edgar's drinking bouts. The family might have been on the brink of financial ruin, but they always had a maid. Peter Lougheed himself is unembarrassed by his family's history—he claims he enjoyed an easygoing childhood, lacking restriction and full of the pleasures of growing up next to the Bow River. And when, after the war, real estate values and rentals began to improve, his family's situation improved too.

Lougheed credits his mother with instilling in him the drive to succeed and an appreciation of life's finer things. In school, he was a natural organizer and leader and, surrounded by a gang who admired and emulated him (and who would later join him in politics), Lougheed enjoyed the popularity of a high school athlete. His whole group went up to the University of Alberta together, and it was as a football player for the fledgling Edmonton Eskimos that Lougheed began to garner even more attention. One of those campus men active in extracurricular life, he was sports editor at the *Gateway*, president of a fraternity, and ultimately president of the student council. Lougheed was practising for the push and pull of life as a politician.

Just before setting out for Harvard Business School, he married Jeanne Rogers, and together they met the challenge of the Ivy League, experience that would later give Lougheed tremendous confidence in his dealings with American business executives. Despite job offers in the East, Lougheed returned to Alberta, articling with a Calgary firm and becoming the first third-generation Albertan to be admitted to the bar. Six months later, he accepted a position as legal adviser to Mannix, a huge company with fingers in all kinds of business and building and contracting pies, then he left to open his own law firm in 1962. When he decided to go into politics, he was more than primed. But according to biographer Alan Hustak, Lougheed had never even been inside the legislature, and in March 1965 he sat down in the visitors' gallery to see what he was getting himself into. Manning, on the floor, spotted him and sent a note: "Mr. Lougheed. I hope your visit to the assembly doesn't dim your enthusiasm to enter actively into provincial public life. The first twenty-five years are the worst. It's good to see you here. E. Manning." His visit did not dim Lougheed's enthusiasm. The Progressive Conservatives were leaderless; Lougheed had connections throughout Alberta; and with a burning desire to do battle in the arena of public approval, in 1965 he out-hustled all competitors to win the leadership of that stumbling party. Lougheed was ready to run with more than a football.

He surrounded himself with people committed to his political cause, including Joe Clark, who worked for two years as the party's paid organizer. Through 1966 and 1967, Lougheed drafted party guidelines and covered territory. Little did he suspect that one of his lines, "We believe in a provincial government which gives strong support to the need in Canada for an effective central government," would come back to haunt him. In the election of May 1967, Manning's last, the Progressive Conservatives, under Lougheed's leadership, won six whole seats. Hardly a landslide, but a start.

Lougheed left his old law firm and became leader of the opposition, quickly teaching himself parliamentary procedure, while down in the Centre, Pierre Elliott Trudeau succeeded Lester Pearson as leader of the Liberals. After Manning resigned, no one was more surprised than the Conservatives when one of their own, a Romanian-Canadian with good Ukrainian connections named Bill Yurko, upset the Socred candidate in the by-election for Manning's seat.

When Strom finally called an election, Lougheed's team, which had been planning since 1968, swung into high gear, determined to hit every one of Alberta's sixty-five constituencies. A sense of humour and persistence were huge assets, and Lougheed's campaign was hot and persuasive. On election night in August 1971 the Socreds went down to permanent defeat, bringing in the last whirlwind of politics—Alberta conservatism of its own peculiar brand.

Lougheed hardly seemed to know what to do. He waited at home until Strom conceded defeat, then went to his party headquarters, where he made a subdued speech. Once it was clear that the Conservatives had swept Edmonton, he borrowed a Learjet and flew north, arriving at midnight to the cheers of hundreds of supporters who would barely let him off the plane. After a reception at campaign headquarters there, Lougheed and his wife, Jeanne, returned to the airport and boarded the plane to return to Calgary, but Calgary was weathered in and the runway was so obscured by fog that the plane almost crashed. The pilot had to turn and fly them back to Edmonton, but there were no hotel rooms to be had. So Peter Lougheed, on his first night as premier-elect, not only almost died, but enacted a ritual that still describes the political shape of this province—he flew to Edmonton, flew back to Calgary, then flew back to Edmonton, marking the life of an Alberta politician, and in a strange way echoing Manning's weekly trips to present his *Back to the Bible Hour* broadcast.

The Conservatives had swept the province, winning forty-nine seats over Social Credit's twenty-five. The one true maverick now in opposition was Grant Notley, New Democrat from Spirit River, who, although he never enjoyed political power, until the end of his life enjoyed respect as Alberta's self-appointed ombudsman for social justice. Thirty-nine of the forty-nine Conservatives were new—inexperience on the hoof—and, since there hadn't been a change of government in thirty-six years, no one had any idea of the protocol for picking up the reins of power. Lieutenant-Governor Grant MacEwan, historian and humanist, swore them in, and through chaos and complication, they began to shape a new identity.

Their first act was to pass the Alberta Bill of Rights, a reiteration of individual liberty, freedom of religion, thought, and speech. The rookies worked through the session, learning by their own mistakes, changing almost everything from the rural telephone system on up. To promote solidarity between the western provinces, and to strengthen federal/provincial relations at a time when Ottawa was in the thrall of Trudeau, Lougheed started the Western Economic Opportunities Conference, which became the Western Premiers' Conference, a venue for finding ways to make the Centre listen to the West. Trudeau came to the first one but was unhappy about being outflanked, and at the end of the conference he summarized his irritation by declaring, "I hereby close the first and the last Western Economic Opportunities Conference." As a strategy, the conference worked, but tension was brewing over that elusive and desirable commodity—energy.

Alberta had it and the rest of Canada wanted it. Resources were the lollipop that everyone fought for, and an epic struggle it would be. Lougheed's new brooms thought first that Albertans deserved a bigger cut from the industry—royalties from the oil companies that had been so liberally welcomed to exploit this resource back in the 1940s. Second, they thought that they should be consulted on any international trade agreements having to do with oil and gas. This situation required a tightrope walker to manoeuvre. Lougheed devised a plan whereby oil companies had the option of paying tax on unexploited oil (still in the ground) or of accepting a revised royalty system, which would increase the province's share from 16.66 percent to 21 percent. Oil companies were given incentives to explore for more oil and gas, and they would be allowed to claim this new tax as a deduction—against federal tax returns. This was when the trouble began; but worse was to follow. Lougheed wanted more money for natural gas; and he proposed a two-price system, in which Albertans would pay a lower price than the rest of the country.

Would this go over well with industry? Would this go over well in the Centre? No and no. Neither was happy, but the Centre was especially suspicious. Not only was their gas not cheap, but now their supply was threatened. Central premiers started flying west, a reversal of centuries-long supplicatory trips. The premier of Ontario threatened to sue, on the grounds that Alberta's proposed two-price system impeded free and open interprovincial trade. While Trudeau pretended interested concern for the West, Ottawa added fuel to the fuel by slapping controls on crude oil exports—the Federal Oil Export Tax. Regional bias and unfairness blossomed into bruises. The Crowsnest freight rate raised its head again, and the Centre started up its old whine about the "regions" wanting special consideration, while the "regions" were none too happy about being relegated to their old colonial place.

Finally Trudeau introduced his own two-price system, simply by imposing a tax on Alberta crude. To counteract the loss in revenue, Lougheed again raised royalty rates, and the oil companies fumed. Meanwhile, in the rest of the world, OPEC had decided to cut back oil production and prices were going through the roof. But Ottawa still expected Alberta to provide oil and gas to the Centre at cut-rate prices. In another act of brinksmanship, Lougheed proposed increased royalties again, arguing that Alberta had the right to administer and control her own resources.

With the feds insisting that 50 percent of any increases to the cost of oil would go to the federal treasury to protect Central and Eastern consumers against price hikes, Western consumers were on their own, and regional disparity was right out in the open. Nor did the compromise that was eventually arrived at do Alberta a service. Alberta agreed to subsidize fuel prices in Central Canada by selling crude at $4 a barrel lower than the international price; and Lougheed introduced a whole new complicated royalty schedule.

But Ottawa and Alberta had not agreed on who would ultimately reap those new windfalls, and when the 1974 federal budget came in it became clear that Alberta's oil industry incentives—those deductible royalty costs for development and exploration—had been choked by the feds to one-half of their previous level. Lougheed had one hell of a problem on his hands. Albertans were mad at the feds, mad at what seemed to them an encroachment on a clearly provincial jurisdiction. And they got madder when the federal energy minister unveiled a new plan to cut exports of crude oil, which would cut Alberta's income to nothing by 1982. This was almost a repeat performance of Aberhart's constitutional confrontations. Bumper stickers saying "Let the eastern bastards freeze in the dark" blossomed overnight. This was a struggle about power—and it wasn't pretty.

The big American companies that had been invited up to Fort McMurray to get the oil out of the sands in a consortium called Syncrude got more and more nervous and declared that opening the oil sands would take $1 billion more than they had anticipated. Everybody gulped. The economists flew in and the ministers flew in and Fort McMurray buzzed, but the Syncrude project looked as if it might just end up on the shelf.

Meanwhile, Alberta bought an airline, Pacific Western Airlines, for $80 million without consulting the feds, who were sure to say no, Alberta wasn't allowed to buy an airline, only Ottawa was allowed to own an airline, and Air Canada was an exception to all the rules anyway. But even Conservatives were horrified. Buying an airline made it seem like Alberta wanted to be its own country and was entering into "state capitalism." But despite the Canadian Transport Commission's predictable reaction, the Supreme Court upheld Alberta's right to purchase an airline in the name of the province. (It was resold to the private sector in 1983.)

By the end of November 1974, there was all-out war between Trudeau and Lougheed, with Trudeau, confident of Central backing, stating that Alberta's oil revenues just didn't allow the feds a big enough slice of the pie. To keep the oil industries happy, Lougheed revised his oil royalties again, but that didn't solve discontent. And then Alberta had to swallow her pride and invite the feds and the other provinces in to help them rescue Syncrude. In an incredibly complicated negotiation dividing resource spoils between the oil companies, the provinces, and the feds, Syncrude was saved, although nationalists argued that Canada's resources had just been sold down the river and Lougheed had given foreign companies permission to steal our soup. Political commentators argued that the deal made even Alberta a loser. Some cartoons portrayed Lougheed as pandering to the oil companies; others were nasty enough to provoke lawsuits.

In the budget of February 1975 Lougheed's government announced the invention of the Alberta Heritage Savings Trust Fund, a bag of money that was supposed to ensure the prosperity of Albertans who hadn't even been born yet. Confident that his province was behind him, Lougheed called a snap election, asking Albertans to support him in his ongoing war with the federal government on oil-pricing and energy policies. This time, Albertans were far readier to ride their own tornado power and they swept the Socreds out the door forever, sixty-nine seats to four, garnished by one NDP (Notley) and one Independent. That was the end of Aberhart's fundamentalist vision, in Alberta, at least.

For a while Trudeau and Lougheed pretended to get along, which made Ontario nervous. Quebec, Newfoundland, PEI, and Saskatchewan agreed with Alberta's claim that the price of oil and gas should match international levels, but Ontario in particular, imagining long cold winters, opposed. Meanwhile, Alberta's minister of culture was accused of handing out too much largesse to nonexistent ethno-cultural groups, and more press wars erupted. Lougheed loved television cameras and tried to stand in front of them as much as he could, practising statesmanlike behaviour. Sure enough, the centre starting talking about Lougheed as a replacement for Robert Stanfield, then national Conservative leader. Lougheed sent his scouts to check out the likelihood of prime ministership, but the reports from the Centre weren't positive, so he took to answering the queries of whether he would run for leadership of the Conservatives with the line that Ralph Klein would later happily repeat: "Why should I be prime minister of Canada when I already run Alberta?" Instead, he took a trip to Europe, and by saying the word "oil" over and over, got himself invited to quite a few nice dinner parties.

Back in Canada at the Conservative leadership convention, Lougheed watched while Joe Clark, another Western maverick, but a dark horse, worked the ground and the grassroots to become Stanfield's successor. Lougheed deliberately bypassed endorsing any candidate, but he had also bypassed an opportunity that might have crowned him king of the Conservatives. Whether he would have been able to defeat the charismatic Pierre Elliott Trudeau was another question entirely, and his awareness that Trudeau was unbeatable might have kept him firmly in the Alberta saddle.

Lougheed enjoyed working Washington almost as much as he enjoyed working Europe, and in 1976 he started some intricate negotiations with the Scary States; an early proponent of free trade, he threw down another gauntlet in the energy wars, vowing to recruit American support to back Alberta's demands about tariffs on oil. The Centre got very nervous; at the same time as they were trying to deal with importunate Alberta to the west, they were trying to figure out how to deal with an importunate Québécois, René Lévesque, directly to the east. Constitutional reform looked like a necessity. But Quebec did Alberta a favour. By emphasizing differing regional aspirations and dreams, the two provinces effectively worked together against the Centre's intruding into provincial affairs, ultimately declaring that any amending formula would require the unanimous consent of the provinces.

Ontario cursed Lougheed for being obstinate, and Trudeau castigated Lougheed for trying to gain provincial power at the expense of federal patriation of the Constitution. Alberta, they said, was making a bid to unseat the federal government completely, to devolve virtually all powers to the provinces. This might be called, within another political context, sovereignty association, especially over natural resources. Lougheed claimed throughout that he was only trying to equalize the feds and the provinces, but the Centre didn't exactly see it that way. Alberta's natural suspicion of Ottawa was beginning to resemble paranoia. And it was all about energy, energy, energy. Lougheed visited the Middle East, determined to learn the negotiating strategies of the OPEC nations and bring them back to implement them. Lougheed, as Larry Pratt has so succinctly stated, articulated Alberta's "politics of resentment" while the Centre kept talking about Albertans as "blue-eyed sheiks."

The price of oil was going up, and in 1979 the premier of Ontario escalated Canada's internal energy war by arguing that Ontario had a right to participate in

setting the price of Canadian crude. Alberta had never asked to participate in negotiations about setting the price of Ontario-made automobiles, and they were surprised. By that time Joe Clark was the prime minister and Albertans naturally
expected better of him, but this was the first salvo of the National Energy Program,
which singled out Alberta's resources for treatment different from any other
province's resources. The pressure from the consuming province was on, with Joe
Clark caught in the middle. Every proposal seemed an echo of those old Trudeau
arguments, and Lougheed was getting mad. At one meeting he threw his briefing
book over his shoulder and it hit the wall with a smack. Poor Joe. He was fighting
with his own party and in his own end of the field—and added to that, at a subsequent first ministers' conference, eight of the other nine premiers backed
Lougheed. Despite the security blanket of Petro-Canada, it looked as if energy
shortages were galloping down the backstretch, bringing all kinds of misery to
Central Canada. So John Crosbie's "energy package," with its eighteen-cent-a-
gallon surcharge on gasoline, was a red flag, and all the parties united to vote
down Clark's budget and to tumble his not-even-a-year-old government.

Leaving Trudeau free to come back and take another bite out of upstart Alberta,
which he set out to do with relish and wryness. "Welcome to the eighties," he said.
Albertans groaned. Nothing irritated Trudeau more than provincial power, embodied for him by the Heritage Trust Fund, which, by 1980, bean-counters claimed,
approached $10 billion. Alberta was building itself a nest egg that would make it
immune to the Centre, which did not please the feds. The way to bring Alberta to
heel was to control as much of her resource money as possible. The way to do that
was to come up with elaborate arguments for not paying Alberta the world price
for oil; to shift Canada's focus from oil to natural gas, which was plentiful and
which had a lower price tag; to rationalize control over energy as part of a larger
economic strategy; and to use federal money to explore for this non-renewable
resource. Lougheed fought hard, but he couldn't swim as well as Trudeau, and on
October 28, 1980, the National Energy Program, with its "security, opportunity,
and fairness," was unveiled as part of Trudeau's federal budget.

The feds had their fingers in the barrels, if not the wellhead. Ottawa (read:
Ontario) had won, and now Albertans spent a lot of time in tune with Quebec,
talking about separation. To the rest of Canada the battle was between patriotism
(of the national kind) and special interests, but in Alberta, it felt like a battle over

money and control, and it felt like Alberta had been napalmed. There was nothing for this province to do but turn the oil taps down. We did, in a effort to persuade Ottawa to listen, which Ottawa pretended to do, leading to something called the Oil Agreement, a new "revenue-sharing" plan. Lougheed was tired; he wanted to be an optimist, and he made a few mistakes, including drinking a glass of champagne with his arch-enemy, Pierre Trudeau. Albertans weren't too pleased to see their premier in cahoots with the Centre on the front page of every newspaper; they tended to equate the new Oil Agreement with the not-much-older National Energy Program. But by that time, oil prices were about to take a significant dip and interest rates would climb to something like 21.5 percent, both of which would have other repercussions, namely, a nationwide bust. And Trudeau was losing his glamour; people were angry at him, and he started giving the world the finger. The 1982 election was Lougheed's last, and once again he routed opposition, taking all but four seats. But the damage to Alberta's economy from the fall of oil prices was serious, and Albertans still bitterly complain about the effect of the NEP. That piece of work was phased out following the 1985 Western Accord by Brian Mulroney and Alberta's then minister of energy, John Zaozirny. Albertans breathed a sigh of relief.

Throughout his tenure as premier, Lougheed pursued economic sovereignty within Canada's larger framework. Every ounce of his corporate and oligarchic presence was focused on harnessing the big bucks that ought to be Alberta's. Even the creation of the Heritage Trust Fund in 1975 was a gesture of defiance, a subtle nose-thumbing at the Centre. But challenges to the government's employment of the fund have led to some startling revelations, not all of them happy. And although Lougheed claimed to be accessible to Alberta's grassroots, he practised a governance that was really based on the astonishing force of one man, a man who aroused both respect and fear, and who ran Alberta pretty much with the assistance of his political buddies from back in 1971. His caucus, even when they disagreed, was expected to do his bidding and were often presented with proposals that were really faits accomplis. Lougheed promised that as premier he would run the province like a human rather than a demagogue, but in fact he set in motion the continuing tradition of Alberta premiers who function almost entirely outside the legislature, even to the extent that the current premier, Ralph Klein, openly says that legislative sessions are a waste of time. Lougheed was a private-enterprise man, who nevertheless presided over the bloating of Alberta's civil service, and who really worked hardest for upper-middle-class aspirations of prosperity and pragmatism. In the end it was clear that Lougheed governed by appealing to the province's interest in money rather than any social or cultural agenda. And after all, a restless and dissatisfied populace can always be appeased by a tax cut.

Lougheed's labels—energy and economic opportunity—still stick to Alberta. Attracted by the Heritage Fund and the promise of easy jobs, a raft of newcomers flooded the province, eager for a quick buck and a slice of Alberta pie. Lougheed presided over a newly burnished Alberta pride and a massive boom that increased the province's population; by the time he left, it was reaching nearly 2.3 million.

• • •

In June 1985 when King Lougheed announced his resignation, he had already crowned his successor, Donald Getty, another ex–fooball player who had left the cabinet six years before to pursue his own interests. His race was contested by mavericks Ron Ghitter and Julian Koziak, amid contentions of Lougheed's strong-arming and all kinds of racial and ethnic slurs. For two months, Alberta Tories fought over style and image, and in the end Getty became King Peter's successor, sure to continue what Lougheed had set in place.

Getty, too, was a Central import, born in Quebec, who arrived in Alberta via the University of Western Ontario—in his case, to play football with the Edmonton Eskimos, a team he quarterbacked to two Grey Cup wins. One of the original six who challenged the Socreds back in 1967, he had served as Lougheed's sidekick for twelve years, four as energy minister, the biggest plum in Alberta's cabinet. Then, in the key portfolio of minister of the department of federal and intergovernmental affairs, he had enjoyed the big push of provincial muscle-building that took place in the 1970s. When he left politics in 1979, he ran an oil company, and although Nortek almost foundered in 1982, he managed to pull it through the first part of the bust with a combination of connections and optimism. In the election of 1986 the Conservatives took something of a beating. Not a big beating—they still had sixty-one seats, but they had lost an incredible twenty-two, many of them in the newly aware city of "Redmonton," which had elected an unheard-of slate of sixteen NDP candidates. Even the Liberals had four seats.

Getty's reign was disadvantaged by low, low oil prices, low, low grain prices, and by a Conservative prime minister. Just like all the other Ottawa mandarins, once he was elected Brian Mulroney was less than eager to acknowledge provincial demands, and his government refused to assist in financing an expansion of Syncrude's oil sands project. Alberta was in one of its bust periods, and Getty's lacklustre approach to a place used to Lougheed's well-oiled machinery looked unpromising from every angle, even though he tried to placate small oil producers and promised them that he would try to get a few more concessions out of what had become a tight-fisted Ottawa.

Getty had an endearing habit of chewing on his golf shoes. During the campaign he suggested that things weren't really as bad as they seemed for farmers and small oil producers (to their considerable disgruntlement), that Alberta's oil patch might benefit from the accident at Chernobyl, and that food banks were a great thing. This in a province that had enjoyed unprecedented wealth. Facing one of the worst busts in Alberta's history, Getty responded by appealing to the old chestnuts of Socred family values mingled with free enterprise. And he could be surprising. One of his first public acts as premier was to tour Edmonton's sewers with a city worker, something that Lougheed would never have done. Getty survived by playing quarterback, playing golf pro, playing cowboy. Calm despite Alberta's economy gurgling down the toilet, Getty tried to continue the Lougheed tradition of fighting Ottawa, but the fight didn't go anywhere. His worst trait was that he reacted slowly; it took him almost a year to respond to the oil patch crisis, and then his solutions depended on waiting until the price of oil went back up. Journalist Andrew Nikiforuk contended that Getty "inherited none of Lougheed's luck and too much of his legacy." Government spending, which Albertans had gotten used to, was reduced. In response to slumps in agriculture, oil, and mining, Getty test-drove the roadster called "economic diversification."

In a repeat of the dirty thirties, banks started failing. One of the diversification efforts, Alberta's first home-based bank (if you don't count the treasury branches), Canadian Commercial, collapsed in 1985, quickly followed by the Northland Bank. Both succumbed to the combined drop in real estate and energy markets— ironically, their investments were not sufficiently diversified. Ottawa extended aid to prevent bankruptcy, but they both tumbled to their columned knees. However much the Alberta Opportunity Company (a government incentive fund) approved loans, nothing redemptive happened in areas as widespread as canola oil or motion picture development. And the focus on the petrochemical industry was equally unsuccessful. Nova Corp., the star in Alberta's firmament of oil and gas support services, was battered almost to death. Alberta was a bum's paradise tapped out. The Tory emphasis on private enterprise just wasn't working.

Well, what about the Heritage Savings Trust Fund? Albertans were horrified to discover that the fund was worth far less than they thought, and that it was not growing but shrinking. The 1986 bust killed $10 billion of economic activity in Alberta, and the provincial deficit was rising. The fund, when introduced by Lougheed, was specifically described as a hedge against the unthinkable potential of dwindling oil revenue. Now that time had come. It was also supposed to support diversification. Had it done that? Nobody could tell. People blamed the change in objectives on the 1980 National Energy Policy, which forced the province to use the monies in the fund to keep Albertans happy. Certainly the government had borrowed Heritage money and had used the fund to build hospitals, parks, and other assets, which had not vanished, even though the money was gone. Government agencies like Alberta Government Telephones, Alberta Mortgage and Housing Corp. and Alberta Energy Company had benefited. But not all that windfall money had been invested well, and Albertans were angry. It was going to be up to them to weather the recession by the seat of their collective pants.

Which they did, with the help of food banks and fury, through unemployment and its vicious aftermath of unworthiness, inadequate welfare cheques, and lots of homegrown Alberta rhetoric about self-reliance. Linda Goyette, a writer for the *Edmonton Journal*, says in an article called "Banking on Charity" in the collection *Running on Empty*, "The losers in this recession accused themselves of failure. They, too, were silent believers in the Alberta creed. Pull yourself up by your bootstraps. Don't whine. Be as tough as your grandfather was on that Two Hills dirt farm in 1933." Goyette argues that this attitude partially saved the Conservative government from having to deal with the effects of the recession and pushed Alberta toward its reliance on private welfare—private everything. Churches and community centres and charitable bodies carried the burden of relief while the government conveniently cut social services. Generous with social benefits in high times, Alberta in the eighties was hard on the working poor, and absolutely vicious to unemployed men and women in the prime of their working lives. Almost 100,000

Albertans hitchhiked and drove and rode the dog east or west, just to get away from the province of shattered dreams.

In August 1987, the Principal Group (an Edmonton financial corporate empire) collapsed and hundreds of investors lost money, some of them life savings. Getty's ministers did their variation of a shoulder-shrugging, head-in-the-armpit tuck, although a few of the more obnoxious indicated that they thought the investors were the victims of their own greed. What made their attitude worse was evidence that the government had known about the precarious position of Principal's two arms, First Investors Corporation and Associated Investors of Canada; the Alberta Securities Commission had apparently suggested as early as 1973 and as recently as 1984 that the assets of the company should be investigated. And, adding insult to injury, the same day Principal collapsed, an intrepid press photographer took a wonderful picture of Don Getty testing his golf clubs out on the links when his aide had said he was "working" out of the office. Albertans were livid. They demanded a public investigation. They would have preferred a public execution. The banks in the East, with their Fifty Big Shots, started to look wonderfully stable and reliable. The resultant "investigation" concluded that businessman Donald Cormie had demonstrated some "dishonesty and fraud," and that the government "regulators" had been asleep at the switch, but that didn't return the investors' money. The good times had ended and in the election of 1989, although the Conservatives were returned to power, Getty lost his own Edmonton Whitemud seat. He had to run in a by-election in Stettler to claim a place in the legislature. Now the tally stood at Conservatives fifty-nine, Liberals eight, and New Democrats sixteen. To make matters worse, while Albertans were feeling the squeeze, MLAs got a raise—and slowly it came out that they were enjoying some very healthy living allowances. Something was seriously wrong. The government started talking about how expensive education and health care were. It decided that business would save Alberta, and in a gesture that announced that the boom was definitely over, Getty lowered the royalty rate on oil and gas.

By this time, Getty had in his cabinet a likeable Dumbo-faced maverick called Ralph Klein. In a return to the Social Credit theory of credentials being irrelevant, Klein is a high school dropout with a record of tenacity and hyperbole that warms the cockles of Albertan hearts. The son of a road-builder/wrestler, he was pretty much raised by his grandparents, and is legendary for his working-man appeal and his habit of drinking in the downscale St. Louis Hotel bar. Ralph is a regular guy who never even saw a silver spoon until he became mayor of Calgary, and Albertans love to love him just for that. Whether they love him for everything else is another question.

He started out, despite lacking in education, as first a graduate and then the principal of Calgary Business College. From there he went to work in public relations, and then on to CFCN as a television journalist. His beat was Calgary's city hall, and he had a nose for the interesting stories that seldom come out of municipal politics—Klein interviewed hookers and gas jockeys, Indians and bikers. Married and divorced, he remarried in 1972, and then, in a brilliant chess move, he hired one of his buddies, a television cameraman, to make one good television ad to help him in a bid to run for mayor of Calgary, a city he knew inside and out. On the basis of that short, snappy ad, in 1980 the city elected him with a landslide. And he was a good mayor, conscientious, knowledgeable, and full of civic pride. He loved the job and the job loved him, and even though he said a few precipitate things, like the infamous "creeps and bums" speech, he was in his glory. Even in the midst of recession and cutbacks, the city seemed to glow—and grow.

When Klein went provincial in 1989, he was handily elected, although Calgarians were pictured brushing away tears when he resigned as mayor. Quickly appointed as minister of the environment, Klein had some trouble with pulp and paper mills, but did push through a reasonable environment bill. He was liked, although he practised rude comments and ruder gestures—when an environmentalist gave him the finger, Klein gave it right back. And when Getty stepped down in 1992, eager to spend more time on the golf course and away from crabby voters, Klein took the ball and ran. He was ready to transform the old boys' Progressive Conservatives into a snappy new party. But embedded somewhere in his platform was the subtext "No pain, no gain." He was at first only one of a huge slate of candidates, including Nancy Betkowski, who would later transform herself into Nancy MacBeth and lead the Liberals to defeat against Klein in the 2001 election. In the first round, she was ahead by one vote, but Klein defeated her in the runoff. They have hated each other ever since, and Klein is not averse to taking sly digs at her in public.

Klein has a way of looking straight at people (or straight into the camera) and calling them "folks." Some people trust him for that, and after watching Klein doggedly jog his way through the campaign Alberta elected him in 1993 with a wave of populist and largely rural support. Klein proved he could be just as hard-nosed as the big-business boys, although he went about his slash-and-burn methods differently. While the government pretended to consult with stakeholders at "round tables" and community outreach meetings, they were intent on a new approach that had at its heart one word: cuts, especially to those two previously sacred areas of Alberta wellness, health and education. Klein assigned himself the awful job of getting rid of the deficit, some $30 billion, and balancing the books. Cleverly, he made it seem that the people and not government officials were deciding what should be done with public money; he off-loaded the nasty decisions to them. While Klein pretended to listen, his "fundamental paradigm shift," was really a euphemism for cuts, cuts, and cuts.

By then phrases like "user fees" and "privatization" were beginning to creep into the rustle of the chinook wind. And in 1993, Klein's government announced that it was going to sell its 210 liquor stores, those sacred stills of government control over the consumption and sale of alcohol. In one fell swoop, the Alberta Liquor Control Board cut $67 million in annual operating costs. At the same time, the high end of the board presided over granting licences to a rash of private stores, liquor marts, and wine shops, who began to compete on pricing and opening hours. The only big argument was about whether grocery stores would be allowed to sell liquor (they still have not been granted that privilege). Alberta was living up to its American heritage. Gambling suddenly developed a high profile—video-lottery terminals appeared in almost every bar or lounge throughout Alberta. And newly privatized registry offices were useful sites of information gathering; the government passed an act in 1994 refusing to renew the drivers' licences of any vehicle whose owner was in arrears on child support or spousal support payments.

In typical Alberta political style, the people of the province were behaving like one big herd of lemmings. The round-table meetings, which were supposed to represent populist concerns, were carefully engineered—the invitation lists to these important stew stirrings were pretty much at the whim of government officials. And soon, claiming to represent the voices that spoke at round tables, the government was presenting the people of Alberta with "business plans." Government had become a business. Buddy businesses started lobbying. The business of medicine, the business of private post-secondary education, the business of business. The round tables on health care were a little less sanguine. People were starting to get nervous about what was happening, and there was almost no room or air time for dissent. Cuts to health care were a sensitive matter, and some of the folks who showed up at these meetings had some issues—nasty stories about the way the health care system seemed to be seizing up, how there weren't enough nurses, how people were having to wait atrociously long weeks for crucial tests. But all comments were carefully distilled to help the government arrive at its aim—a slow, steady privatization that pretended to have everyone's welfare at heart. Everyone's welfare translated as no visible provincial tax in Alberta. Some measures had a positive result—government probably did need to be downsized. With some exceptions, Albertans loved it.

And then, there was the Alberta Special Waste Treatment Plant, a joint venture between business and a government eager to implement "diversification." It wasn't exactly a roaring success, and between 1986 and 1994 Alberta poured something like $250 million into its steaming maw. Klein channelled $100 million into expansion of the facility and then defended it by declaring, when interviewed by *The Fifth Estate* in December 1995, "it's actually a tourist attraction." Huh? Klein claimed special consideration for the plant because of its environmental spin; meanwhile, he was selling Alberta everywhere, travelling the world with his Alberta Advantage message.

In the 1997 election Albertans voted King Bluebird in again, with a big majority. Tough, tougher, and toughest. Politeness flew out the window. The cutters started calling themselves "rednecks" with pride. The biggest fight was still coming, and that was the argument over two-tiered health, or Bill 11, the Alberta law presumably regulating private surgical clinics. Petitions and rallies united as people worried about access to public health care eroding and tried to persuade Klein's government that private clinics were wrong. Klein refused to listen, and used what had now become a standard feature of his regime, parliamentary closure (to end legislative debate quickly). The bill was pushed through, although there was practically a riot on the grounds of the legislature. Police were called, truncheons were wielded, and the law was passed, leaving some Albertans complacent about health care and others terribly afraid that general access would be seriously damaged.

But oil prices began to rise again and now, riding another boom, Albertans have begun to insist on better education, better health care, the very infrastructures that were dismantled in the mid-1990s. In the lead-up to Alberta's 2001 election, it was abundantly clear that Klein had not fared well with power deregulation either—he was severely criticized for an electricity deregulation plan that would cost the tax-payers billions of dollars. But the voters were quickly appeased. The government doled out energy rebates in an effort to calm a furious group of users. Klein, des-perate to please everybody, did the politician's shuffle, and in the spring of 2001 Alberta again elected, with a landslide, the same politicians who had cut the province apart. A rosy-cheeked and markedly "happy" premier trundled out to his party's microphone to say to those Albertans who had actually bothered to vote, "Welcome to Ralph's world." And when asked to comment on his surely eventual retirement, Klein remarked, "I'd like to leave the province on auto-pilot—that it's in such good shape, not even the Liberals could mess it up."

As that last election underlines, Alberta is a one-party province. We have never understood the value of a strong opposition, and until we do, this province will remain the crazy political experiment that it has always been. We follow the man who seems to promise us the moon.

• • •

There are, at this moment, three Albertans pacing the federal hustings. Well, two authentic Albertans and one carpetbagger from Ontario who lived in Alberta and served as minister of finance under Klein before resigning from the Conservatives and moving out to Kelowna, British Columbia, to federalize himself.

One of those Albertans is Joe Clark, the man from High River who lasted less than a year as the youngest prime minister of Canada and who has been staging a comeback ever since he lost the Conservative leadership to deep-voiced Brian Mulroney. Clear-eyed, decent Joe Who, the man from Alberta with the best inter-ests of the country at heart.

Clark grew up with politics bubbling in his blood. High River is a pretty, south-ern Alberta town riding the shoulder between the Rockies and the prairie; it has a wonderful vista, which undoubtedly infected Joe's viewpoint. His family ran the local paper, a good place to hone words, but Clark, who fell under the spell of John Diefenbaker early, was determined to go farther than a prairie town famous for its great storyteller, W. O. Mitchell. Once he got a degree from the University of

Alberta, Clark went east to Dalhousie, then to Vancouver's UBC, and then back to university in Edmonton. Clark was seeing the country and taking notes. And priming himself for office, which he ventured into by getting elected to Parliament in 1972. Although he was over thirty, he seemed young, naive, idealistic, and he practised the decency that other politicians talked about.

People and communities are what Clark believes in, and he's not just making it up. When, in 1979, the country was sick of Trudeau arrogance, lo and behold, they voted Clark into the highest office in the land. He was the first prime minister from Alberta, really from Alberta, born and bred, not imported. But when Crosbie brought down the Conservative budget, including that infamous gasoline tax, all the opposing parties got together and voted Clark right out of power again. In the leadership race that Clark insisted on having, Mulroney easily defeated Clark, although he was gentlemanly enough to avail himself of Clark's hard-won experience, and to appoint Clark minister of external affairs. Clark worked hard to help Mulroney, even trying to push through the Charlottetown Accord. But all was in vain, and when the Conservatives under another short-lived prime minister, Kim Campbell, lost to the Chrétien Liberals in 1993, Clark pretended to retire and returned to Alberta for a while.

But this decent man was infected with politics at a time when it seemed only indecent men won elections. Clark brooded and bided his time, and in the federal election of 2000 ran again, in the carefully chosen riding of Calgary Centre, a trendy part of the city where a mixture of high-end urbanites and low-end young party animals live. In one of those astonishing acts of Alberta community resistance, determined not to elect the Alliance candidate, all the Liberals and the NDP and the Conservative voters got together and voted for Clark, thus breaking the Alliance Party's stranglehold on the province. His tongue-in-cheek billboards featured a picture of Clark's saggy countenance proclaiming, "Not just another pretty face." Clark's victory has put him back on the path to recovery. By the time of this book's writing, he was presiding over a sharp increase in voter popularity and getting ready to slaughter his right-wing rival, the Canadian Alliance Party, which was begging him to form a coalition. No matter how the Alliance characters called on Joe to "Unite the Right," Joe just gave his standard Santa chuckle and kept on rising in the polls. On June 2, 2001, the *Globe and Mail* began a lead article on Clark with "For a man who has been ridiculed and written off more than any Canadian politician of his generation, Joe Clark possesses an impressive supply of self-confidence." More like stick-to-itiveness.

Perhaps the happiest indication of Clark's growing popularity was his triumphant performance as marshal of the Gay and Lesbian Pride Day Parade in Calgary on June 10, 2001. There he was in a red BMW convertible, his wife, Maureen McTeer, beside him, smiling and waving to the warm cheers and applause of the whole community, not only the gay and lesbian community. When asked about his motive, he simply said, "I was here because I was invited by a community in my constituency and I am very honoured to do that." Clark's chances of once again becoming prime minister are probably remote, but he could surprise us all. Mostly, he is that quintessential Albertan, a good man. And good men are hard to find.

It is only too obvious that Alberta is the hatching place for strange political birds, including the relatively short-lived Reform Party of Canada, a living emblem of Alberta's recidivist frontier attitude. That party and its long-time leader, Preston Manning, the second Albertan pacing the federal hustings, lumbered to its feet in the tradition of protest, and in the heart of a West still restless and risk-taking, wanting change for its own sake. As a boy and a young adult, Preston inhaled his political experience at the knee of his father, Ernest. Preston ran for election in 1965 and lost; between then and 1986, when he initiated the Reform Party, he honed his beliefs, oxymoronically called Christian politics, which meant that he wasn't likely to be welcomed in any of the existing parties. He had to invent his own—and that's what he did, relying on support from people with sunburnt necks who belonged to charismatic churches. In 1988 Preston ran against Joe Clark in Yellowhead and lost, but Reform was starting to take shape.

The Reform Party felt compelled to revise itself in an effort to appeal to the Centre. Expansion was its mandate, and expand they decided to do, despite their origins as a cry-in-the-wilderness party determined to get the nation's attention. When they went federal in 1993, they won fifty-two seats. Most of them were in the West, granted, but there were the Reformers down in Ottawa, an unruly and ungraceful presence, rabble-rousing and name-calling, the voice of the West in national politics, a raucous parliamentary caucus that wouldn't shut up.

But even that modest success wasn't enough, and determined to woo the right, the Reform Party transformed itself into the United Alternative and then the Canadian Alliance Party, a whole new name with a whole new logo under the old Reform desires. After the birth of that "new" party, which was supposed to attract all splinters of right-wing disgruntlement, they held another leadership race. Preston Manning manfully fought to hang on, but he was double-crossed and then ousted as leader by Stockwell Day—our third Albertan on the hustings. Day looked like a good bet because after his stint in Klein's cabinet as minister of labour, he had been Alberta treasurer, and he took single-handed credit for routing Alberta's huge deficit. But it was a spurious claim—it's easy to be an effective treasurer when oil and gas prices are high, and money is pouring into provincial coffers.

With a grassroots pedigree, the Alliance Party tries to be urban and urbane, but it still works out of sometimes archaic rural values, and while negative to Central protectionist interests, it is as interested in maintaining a good relationship with those interests as any of the Central parties. Witness Day's deliberate wooing of Ontario, the fundraising dinners, the elaborate obeisance to big business. In the federal election of 2000, Alliance fought hard to throw egg at Jean Chrétien, who was only too ready to throw egg at the West, which kept insulting him by pretending that the Liberals were nearing extinction, which they most definitely were not.

While he pretended to be squeaky clean, a man without an agenda who looked buff in a wetsuit, Stockwell Day was upset by the media's focus on his personal religious beliefs. But they did their homework and dug up Day's 1977 visit to a Red Deer College class where he explained that he believed in the fundamentalist theory that asserts that the earth is just six thousand years old and that humans coexisted with dinosaurs. The journalists couldn't resist naming it the "Flintstones' theory of evolution." Day blustered and fumed about unfairness, saying, "This was clearly a case of a negative and unprecedented attack." The best gag, though, was the Doris Day referendum. One of Day's election planks was that if there were sufficient petitioning signatures, a referendum could be held on any matter. The satirical CBC-TV program *This Hour Has 22 Minutes* happily set up a Web site asking voters to call for a referendum for Day to change his name to Doris. The site got millions of votes, which Day tried to joke about, but which clearly made him uncomfortable.

But his footsteps were dogged by far worse, not the least the question of whether Alberta taxpayers should cough up almost $800,000 to aid and abet Day's out-of-court settlement in response to the defamation lawsuit launched by Lorne

Goddard. The Red Deer lawyer had sued Day because, when he was still serving as Alberta's treasurer, Day wrote a letter to the *Red Deer Advocate* criticizing Goddard for defending a man charged with possession of child pornography. Aside from the question of child pornography being reprehensible, Day appears to have decided to ignore or overlook basic legal rights, including a lawyer's responsibility to mount a strong defence even for a crime that might make that same lawyer gag, that every accused person has a right to legal representation, and that the courts are supposed to operate independently of government intervention. In his suit, Goddard claimed that Day's published letter had defamed him and damaged his law practice. Day hired a team of expensive lawyers who performed some interesting services for him, first of all successfully getting the case postponed until after the fall of 2000 federal election. Once the case was settled, out of court, Day's lawyers submitted a whopping bill for their services, which was presented to the provincial Alberta Risk Management Fund, a government fund set up to cover legal bills for MLAs and other government officials involved in litigation concerned with their public duties. The combination of the settlement and the cost of the legal defence made Albertans furious. To make matters worse, at the Alliance Party's annual meeting, Day apologized for the cost, but refused to concede that he had crossed any legitimate line. In the end Albertan taxpayers paid most of the tab, and Day pretended it had never happened.

Since the federal election, Day has managed to hit the news with one faux pas or another almost every week. Little wonder that he is now facing insurrection in the party ranks, a dissatisfied and disgruntled caucus nostalgic for the more measured leadership of Manning, who is probably just biding his time. Nor is it a surprise that a renegade group of Alliance members, which has now brought about a leadership review and an upcoming leadership election, refuses to toe the party line and are calling for a leadership review. Whether the Alliance Party survives will probably end up being Joe Clark's decision.

So, there they are, Alberta's crazy politicians. We seem to specialize in growing them. It's always a sunny day in Alberta politics, and if it rains just a bit more, it might actually be a good year—for yet another wildly eccentric political party. Perhaps the best politician in the province right now is Lieutenant-Governor Lois Hole, a wonderful, down-to-earth woman with the best green thumb in the West and a genuine example of where politics might go in a rainbowed future.

11 | Urban Rivals: Cities of the Plain

Abram dwelled in the land of Canaan, and Lot dwelled
in the cities of the plain, and pitched his tent there...
—Genesis 12:12

I grew up as a rural Albertan. "Town" was the village where I went to school and where my parents collected the mail, bought occasional groceries and gas, and connected with their neighbours. Camrose, once called Sparling, sat smack in the middle of Wild Rose County. A small city, it had a good library, a doctor and dentist, St. Mary's hospital, an auction market, and enough car dealers to supply both used cars and trucks. Edmonton was the big city, destination of infrequent trips to track down special things, a graduation dress or imported Dutch chocolates, a visit to family friends who were immigrants like my parents. I moved there finally to attend university, leaving home to enter an alien and breathtaking world called education.

My shift from rural to urban was bittersweet. I loved the city, but I missed the crisp frost of farm mornings, the yipping call of coyotes, and the shapely ripple of the northern lights I could see at home. When I didn't yet live there, I was awed by the streets, the panorama of things to buy, schedule-bound people, and sociable and cheerful shops. The country still held a brooding darkness, the possibility of drought and failure, and although frogs in a spring slough could be noisy, they did not match the jumbled cacophony of city voices and traffic and the hum of congestion.

When I had lived in a city long enough, I learned to take for granted the rush of traffic, good coffee, and the easy reach of banks and supermarkets. I also take for granted the openness of Alberta's cities, their relative safety, their friendly generosity. That demeanour covers the same sludge and sleaze, the same petty viciousness and secret criminality that any crowd of humans conceals. But Alberta's cities are seductive, slow enough to suggest intimacy and large enough to be anonymous, friendly but briskly determined to get ahead.

I live now on the edge of Calgary, facing west and hoping that the sprawl of roofs won't reach the mountains in my lifetime. Of course, knowing Alberta, I realize there is faint hope of that.

• • •

Until the 1970s Alberta carried its rural heritage within its heart. Only this last generation, grown into the twenty-first century, lacks a connection to parents or grandparents who farmed for a living. Before that time, cities were an alien environment, to be regarded with suspicion and a healthy measure of mistrust, growths that were decadent and flamboyant, hot with people, density, and dust.

The legacy of that rural perspective has coloured the reputation and development of Alberta's cities, so that they are not configured as real cities, not "world-class," never aspiring to the tough, sophisticated swagger that other urban centres effortlessly affect. Montreal and Toronto are the Canadian models, strutting the catwalks of cool urbanity while the rest of us gape admiringly from the cheap seats. Even though Edmonton is technically older than Vancouver, Saskatoon, and Ottawa, a recalcitrant localism has constructed our urban spaces, one that persists despite the growing urgency to be more global, more competitive, grittier, and less bucolic. Our cities are distinct in character, and for all we have tried to camouflage their genetic structure, they still maintain close cousinage to the agricultural and resource-saturated surroundings that spawned them, arising out of a prefixed relationship between transportation (the rivers, the trails, the railways) and resources and staples (fur, land, coal, oil, gas). Our cities may be mavericks, but they are still subordinate to older Central cities.

The two main urban centres of the province were both first located and controlled by large national companies. The Hudson's Bay Company started Edmonton, and the Canadian Pacific Railway started Calgary. But their sites are ancient beyond HBC and CPR. Alberta's First Peoples found and enjoyed their generous locations long before a European fur trader or surveyor set foot there. Edmonton sits high on the banks of the North Saskatchewan River, providing a vista of poplars and water, rich land and swirling skies; Calgary stretches across the shoulder of the foothills, beside the confluence of the Bow and Elbow rivers, with the mountains a panoramic rampart to the west. During the 1970s they boomed magnificently. Then with the 1983 bust, they curled in on themselves and waited for better times, which have come with the current boom, both cities now reaching toward a million inhabitants each.

The relationship between Edmonton and Calgary embodies the Alberta character. They hated one another and they still hate one another, although they pretend to be more mature now than at the turn of the last century. Edmonton was an older city, but the underdog; Calgary, brash young upstart, was unwilling to concede an inch to its more historic cousin, and by 1910 Calgary was ahead in population, 60,502 residents to Edmonton's 57,045. Furthermore, Calgary was on the CPR line to the Pacific, and despite the proliferation of railroads in Alberta, Edmonton had no arm connected to a coast. Calgary had a greater concentration of British and American settlers, while Edmonton was more ethnically diverse. They disparaged one another, made fun of one another, and set the tone for what would be an entire century's tug-of-war. Their ongoing rivalry is still bitter and funny. To this day they are fierce competitors and loving siblings both.

Surrounding them are the smaller but equally identity-conscious cities: Red Deer, the spur in the middle; Lethbridge, hunkered close to the American border; and Medicine Hat, guarding the prairie and the Alberta-Saskatchewan border. Even grittier is the boom town of Fort McMurray, the most economically advantaged city in Alberta. Balancing its heft, Peace River lies in the northwestern reach of the province.

What do Alberta's cities do for a living? In the crisp twilight of winter afternoons, it may seem they exist solely to send steam into the air, strange space-station shapes breathing in the cold. In the long, late light of the summer solstice, they become a dome of sky for the cries of ballplayers, the buzz of mosquitoes, the thwack of golf clubs. They are gentle cities, safe, almost bucolic. Of course, that cloak is as misleading as their newness.

Edmonton

On its dull side, Edmonton's current economic base is oil and gas refining, pipeline transportation, and agricultural, wholesale, transport, and processing industries. Although it claims to be a lunch-box city, its base of government and education give it a stability that resides in those institutions rather than other commodities. And Edmonton's political ideology is less anti-Central than Calgary's. Ethnically diverse, the city has always had far fewer citizens of Anglo background than Calgary. Originally French and Cree, its orientation was not north/south like Calgary's, but because of the fur trade, east/west.

On October 5, 1795, a Hudson's Bay Company party led by William Tomison, searching for a place to build Edmonton House, settled on a spot practically next door to Fort Augustus, the North West Company's already established fur-trading post on the North Saskatchewan River. After changing locations four times (whenever firewood was too much trouble to haul, they moved), the traders finally settled, in 1813, close to where the legislative building now stands. Edmonton was named after some English town or estate as remote from its western location as humanly imaginable. Not many of the early fur-trade posts lasted as cities; most of them slumped back into the ground they rested on.

Edmonton House, which funnelled furs from the Peace, Athabasca, and Mackenzie regions, was the ultimate destination for the noisy Red River carts, carrying goods the one thousand miles from Fort Garry. From 1826 onward, the little palisade, balanced on the cusp between the impenetrable boreal forest to the north and the sweep of the open plains to the south, was the main stopping point on all routes to the North and to the Pacific. Goods came by canoe and York boat to Edmonton House from Hudson Bay, then were packed overland to the Athabasca River. The fort swarmed with noise and work. Blacksmiths hammered horseshoes and metal hinges, carpenters built sheds and troughs and chairs, women dug garden beds for barley and potatoes, all the activities of a metropolis writ small but efficient, a village-sized city.

Dr. James Hector, a member of the Palliser expedition, described Edmonton in 1858:

> [It is] wholly built of wood and...furnished with strong bastions and palisades; the latter, however, being rather rotten to be a very sure defence. It stands on a high steep bank immediately overhanging the river, about 100 feet above the water. Along and below this point are large flats of rich land, only 40 to 50 feet higher than the river, which lie at the base of the higher bank. Both of these were at one time under cultivation to a considerable extent; but now the farm attached to the establishment, though the only one in the Saskatchewan, is of very small size, not exceeding 30 acres. On a hill behind the fort stands a windmill, in which the stones were made by splitting a granite boulder that was found near the spot, and these, as may be supposed, are not very serviceable. However, they manage, when they get a gale of wind, to grind some tolerable flour, quite enough to

prove that, if the business was properly conducted, it might be a valuable source of support. . . . As it is here that the boats for navigating the
Saskatchewan are mostly built, 10 or 12 new ones being turned out
every year, the Company have a larger staff of tradesmen and servants
at this place than at any of the other posts of the district. In all they
have about 50 employees here, and the usual population within the
fort is about 150 souls. These are all fed on buffalo meat, and if there
happens to be a good crop they get a certain small allowance of potatoes. The consumption of meat is enormous, amounting to two buffa-
los a day on the average. It is no easy matter to supply this demand,
especially of late years, and the loss of horses from dragging meat during the severities of the winter, and the number of men employed for
this purpose, alone renders it a very expensive mode of feeding the
establishment, although the first cost of the buffalo, when killed in
the plain, is merely nominal. This year these animals are within a few
days of the fort, and it is accordingly well off; but many years there is
a great scarcity, and even starvation here.

The languages spoken in early Edmonton were French, Cree, Blackfoot, and
Gaelic, very little English. The first missionaries who stopped, in 1838, on their
way to Oregon, were French Catholics, quickly followed by Methodist Robert
Rundle, who recorded how very unimpressed he was by the amount of drinking
and fighting and dancing and, presumably, sex that sustained the little fort
through the long winters. In 1842 an Oblate father named Thibault set up a mission at Lac Ste. Anne; he was replaced in 1852 by Father Albert Lacombe, who
became one of Alberta's most important religious figures. In 1859 Lacombe
recruited three Grey Nuns from Montreal; everyone predicted these delicate convent flowers would wither and die, but they didn't. Lacombe built a mission overlooking the Sturgeon River, about eight miles northwest of Edmonton at St. Albert,
and tried to establish a Métis settlement there in 1861. And he helped Father
Constantine Scollen open Alberta's first school in Fort Edmonton in 1862. By then
his religious efforts were augmented by a Methodist father and son, George and
John McDougall, who established the first Protestant schools in Alberta, one at
Victoria and one at Pakan, seventy miles east of the fort. The McDougalls would

become Alberta fixtures—George McDougall's Methodist church, completed in 1873, is the oldest surviving building in Edmonton. They enhanced their services with the melodic wheezing of the small pedal organ that the preacher managed to cart west.

The rich promise of the lands surrounding this rude tangle of buildings and the glints of yellow in the North Saskatchewan meant that Edmonton would not dwindle into obscurity once the fur trade declined. Miners dug into the riverbanks and panned for gold, and a sprinkling of squatters built shacks; the first settler, Kenneth McDonald, staked his claim in 1871, although the settlement was not properly surveyed until 1882. These newcomers brought the smallpox plague that would so devastate Alberta's First Peoples. At St. Albert two-thirds of the nine hundred people there contracted the disease, and 320 died. No missionary could save them, and at Victoria two of missionary George McDougall's children succumbed to the disease as well. It was enough to make Edmontonians demand a doctor in residence, which they didn't get until Dr. Edward Braithwaite, who had served the Mounties in the Riel Rebellion, set up in private practice after his discharge, performing the first surgeries and becoming in 1896 the town's first coroner, a post he held for fifty-two years.

After the 1870 transfer of land from the Hudson's Bay Company to Canada, Edmonton was confident that civilization—railways, people, and goods—would arrive quickly, but in 1872 the settlement was still ferociously rough-hewn; packs of wild dogs roamed everywhere, and sled dogs, kept outside, howled through the night. In 1875 the Mounties stumbled into town and, once they had rested up and recovered, spent the winter trying to decide where to put their police fort, which they finally located at Fort Saskatchewan—the Royal North West Mounted Police did not take up official residence in Edmonton proper until 1915.

In 1875 Rowand's Big House, the marvel of the West, was torn down, and Chief Factor Richard Hardisty—who married George McDougall's daughter—used the timbers to build his own Big House. One of Hardisty's friends, Donald Ross, opened Edmonton's first hotel in 1876, a hostelry with enough character to make up for its discomfort; the sheets doubled as tablecloths and the billiard room was famous for its gambling. Ross kept his guests warm by burning coal dug from the riverbanks. Later James Goodridge would build the first "brick" hotel, Jasper House, which combined boardinghouse manners with excellent food. By then, Edmonton was the northern terminus for North Saskatchewan River travel, and the *Northcote* became the first steamship to ply the river. The North Saskatchewan is wide and deep, and only frozen for four months of the year. On April 26, 1882, boatbuilder John Walter conducted his trial run for the Edmonton ferry, which carried horses and cows and freight and people across the river for more than thirty years.

The city grew, shacks and clapboard stores inhabited by retired HBC employees, carters and carpenters and blacksmiths both European and Métis, mostly single men in their twenties and thirties, as well as men who stopped off on their way to the gold fields. The settlement quickly connected itself to the world; by 1880 the telegraph reached the town, thanks to Alex Taylor, Edmonton's front man in communications, and on December 6 of the same year the *Bulletin* appeared, printed on a second-hand press and published by the same Frank Oliver who later became a mover and shaker in the political theatre of the province. He also imported the first apple trees to Alberta, wrapping the trunks in barbed wire to protect them from rabbits. Because Oliver had lost the box of type containing the banner, Alex Taylor carved the headline letters out of wood. Pig-headed and politically astute, Oliver was determined that Edmonton would become an important place, and he used his newspaper to disseminate his opinions. His only competition was short-lived. Publisher Bob Edwards spent a brief alcoholic stint across the river in Strathcona, but detoured by drinking, he frequently could not produce his paper, the *Strathcolic*. He hated Edmontonians; their homes, he said, "contain nothing but enlarged pictures of deceased Ontario relatives." In 1900 he went south to start the *Eye Opener*, settling happily in Calgary, which was rougher around the edges and did not enshrine Ontario relatives. He and Oliver never liked each other, perhaps because of Oliver's overweening political ambition. Representing Edmonton from 1883 to 1917, Oliver served first in the territorial government and then, with absolute and studied partisanship, as minister of interior in Wilfrid Laurier's government. He and independent trader John McDougall (not the missionary) bought the first lots along what would later be called Jasper Avenue, thereby ensuring their prosperity. Oliver's newspaper did provide useful information. "Raspberries are ripe. Heavy rain on Sunday last. New potatoes are in general use. Hogs are scarce. Butter plentiful." The paper signalled prosperity, an Edmonton busy planning for the arrival of the CPR.

In 1878 whites and Métis in the area numbered around 450, compared to more than three times as many First Nations people (whose numbers didn't matter to the census bean-counters). Matt McCauley, an early Edmonton booster, started a school, complete with a blackboard but lacking efficient heat. Fingers and toes went numb, and frozen bottles of ink, put on the stove to thaw, exploded into wonderful stains.

In 1880–81 a brief land boom resulted when Edmontonians took to gambling on where the railway would run, and when the CPR announced it would follow the southern route across the prairies and through the Rogers Pass, Edmontonians were furious. Calgary thumbed its adolescent nose, making Edmonton fume even more. Without a railway, its future looked less promising. The citizens took out their frustration on the itinerant squatters who were beginning to erect rough houses on unsurveyed land, land that old-timers felt they had a greater claim to. In 1881 the Edmonton Vigilance Committee was formed to uphold their claims, and in March 1882 a group of otherwise respectable citizens paid a visit to an American squatter named J. L. George, who had begun a shack on land that Chief Factor Hardisty was convinced belonged to him. George met his remonstrating neighbours at his new door with a pistol, and although they handily disarmed him he refused to leave his partially built home. Slowly the forty or so men pushed the building toward the edge of the cliff near the present site of the Macdonald Hotel, until it tottered and tumbled over the bank, with squatter George jumping clear at the last minute. Surveyors were obviously long overdue; the whole town was eager for them to arrive, to divide everything into neat measures, to upgrade the jumbled and unimpressive two-storey wooden facades built for survival, not posterity.

Long before Edmonton and Calgary hated each other quite as much as they do now, Edmontonians hated Strathcona, or South Edmonton, which snottily prided itself on being more British, more Ontario, and less Métis than North Edmonton. When the railway went through Calgary, northerners whined so much that the CPR agreed to run a branch line up to Edmonton, but when that railway refused to cross the river, Edmonton was once again thwarted. Walter's ferry did a booming business. But at least the northern side got electricity. In 1891 Alex Taylor's Edmonton Electric Lighting and Power Company turned on a fuzzy buzz of light, and in 1892 Edmonton was incorporated as a town, which meant it needed a mayor—and Matt McCauley, balding and slightly cross-eyed, became that designated driver.

At their first meeting in 1893, the town council determined to find a good spot for a public market, that measure of life where vendors and customers met to exchange not just cabbages and eggs, but gossip, the connection between townies and farmers. Like good food, keeping the burgeoning town healthy required medical support, and the General Hospital was consecrated on August 15, 1895. Run by the Sisters of Charity of Montreal—the same Grey Nuns everyone predicted would wither—it became the city's centre of healing.

Slowly wagonloads of newcomers appeared, and the Dominion Land Office began to buzz with activity. The feds decided that the land titles office would serve newcomers better if it were on the south side of the river, close to the train station where prospective settlers disembarked. The Dominion land agent had obediently loaded his record books onto a wagon to move to Strathcona when an irate Edmonton crowd stole the wheels right out from under the wagon and set the horses free. They refused to let the land agent cross the river. When Ottawa realized that every piece of paper might end up in the river, the land office stayed where it was. Settlers began to throng the muddy streets, eager to file on free land. Galicians, Ukrainians, and Germans brought pigs and cattle and sheep, animals that had been scarce. The *Edmonton Bulletin* bragged about Edmonton's importance, and at last, in 1897, with contributions from the city fathers and a dare from Ottawa, work on the Low Level Bridge began, holding out a promise that the city would no longer be divided by the North Saskatchewan.

For a brief period in 1897–98, farmers gave way to wild-eyed miners determined to get to the Klondike. Edmonton made a fortune supplying greenhorns with gold rush supplies: shovels and picks, flour and tea, horses and dogs and tents. The gold rush advertised Edmonton as a jumping-off place for riches. It was the first time most Canadians and Americans had even heard of the city. Klondikers needed to take a year or two's worth of supplies, which promised a tidy profit, just as long as Edmonton could keep marketing itself as the Back Door to the Gold Rush. That short year of brawling teamsters and packhorses and hardware gave birth to Edmonton's summer carnival, Klondike Days. Outfitters like John A. McDougall and Richard Secord (their store was McDougall and Secord) did make money. They published a euphemistic pamphlet called "Guide to the Gold Fields: How to Get There, What to Take, Where to Get [It]." Slightly exaggerated, their pamphlet claimed that Edmonton, the largest fur market in

America, had 1,500 people, electric light, a telephone system, a branch of the Imperial Bank of Canada and the Bank Jacques Cartier, Dominion Land and Registry Offices, Customs House and Excise Offices, steam grist- and sawmills, two pork-packing establishments, a butter factory, cold storage, two brickyards, five coal mines, three large hotels, two breweries, several restaurants and boarding-houses, two wholesale grocery houses, three hardware stores, three drygoods and clothing stores, two drugstores, two bakeries, several provision stories, fine schools, Baptist, Methodist, Presbyterian, Episcopalian, and Roman Catholic churches, a large three-storey hospital, a semi-weekly newspaper, a first-class steam fire engine and fire brigade, and of course, McDougall and Secord's outfitting store. But what the pamphlet failed to say was that the overland route was terrible: heavy forest, muskeg, snag-strewn tangles of brush, mountainous terrain, and treacherous rivers, a route that was left littered with broken boxes, rusting hammers, and smashed dreams. Historians estimate that only about seven hundred reached the Klondike via the overland route, compared with the thousands who stampeded through Seattle and the Pacific ports. Only the stupid and the stubborn went through Edmonton, which became a combination of staging post and sorting centre for inevitable failure.

By April 1898 its population was stretched to 2,500, mostly newcomers asking dumb questions. Could one reach the Yukon by bicycle? Were there good boarding-houses along the way? A few Edmontonians joined the craze, but most preferred to make a profit supplying the needs of the gold rushers. And even the most optimistic overlanders suffered discouragement, scurvy, destitution. Some drifted back to Edmonton and begged the city to lend them cab fare home. By March 20, 1899, the *Bulletin* referred to the now-historic rush in the past tense. Edmonton had benefited economically, with up to half a million dollars passing through town. But just as suddenly as it had started, the Klondike boom collapsed.

Edmonton and Strathcona waited for the next boom, between 1901 and 1916, when the twin cities saw a combined population increase from 4,000 to 54,000, a growth spurt in keeping with a frontier town. But to consider itself substantially important, Edmonton still needed a railway. Until it had rails, Edmonton would be nothing more than scattered individual farms, the old HBC fort, and a few build-ings akimbo along Jasper Avenue, muddy, disorganized, and sleepy, a jumble of staked fences and frame houses, scarecrow-armed telegraph and electricity poles, wooden sidewalks, and a wide, dirt-packed main street that was dust at the height of summer and mud during rain or snow.

Finally the first bridge over the North Saskatchewan—the Low Level—opened, and in 1902, at last, at last, the Edmonton, Yukon, and Pacific Railway crossed the bridge. With the railway and more people came breweries and dairies and bakeries, lumberyards and flour mills. As if in preparation for the parties that Edmonton would host, Secord was building the huge-hipped arena of the Thistle Rink, completed in 1902 (and destroyed by fire in 1913; now the location of the Edmonton Gardens). Despite Edmonton's ever-present mud and horse-drawn wagons and packs of roaming dogs, the Edmonton Cigar Factory and the California Restaurant promised that sophistication was just around the corner.

The *Bulletin* got a rival, the *Edmonton Journal*, and Mr. J. H. Morris, an up-to-the-minute man whose wife had a big hat and was known for playing on the first women's hockey team in Edmonton, started driving Edmonton's first automobile up and down Jasper Avenue. Mr. Morris, who sported a large moustache and a cigarette, drove the car for two years before the province required a permit, when he was issued with licence no. 1. Meanwhile, in 1904 Edmonton applied for incorporation as a city and when it was granted threw itself a swank ball in the Thistle Rink. Kenneth W. MacKenzie was acclaimed the first mayor. Edmonton was practising for 1905, hoping that their loyalty to a personage no less important than the federal minister of the interior, Frank Oliver, would earn the city the plum of becoming the capital of the kingdom of Alberta. Calgary, that upstart to the south, might have eleven thousand people compared to Edmonton's eight thousand, but it did not have political influence on its side. Besides, Edmontonians knew they deserved to be the capital, simply because they were better than Calgary. And sure enough, as a reward to Oliver, Laurier annointed Edmonton the provincial capital. Becoming the capital meant that the city had the fun of a massive boom, its population multiplying by ten while men in homburgs and dark overcoats began to populate the sidewalks in front of brick bank buildings. Visiting dignitaries like Lord Strathcona and Governor General Grey brought a statesmanlike gait and cutaway coats to the ceremony; the bands played, the sun shone on a beautiful September day, and Prime Minister Wilfrid Laurier, who was staying in the spanking new Alberta Hotel, which boasted Edmonton's first elevators and a shower bath, enjoined them all to behave like good British subjects. What a hell of a party that was. Edmonton had a hangover for a month.

The town had been declared a city, and the city a capital, but declarations were not enough. The city needed paved streets, sewers, water pipes, schools, police, and proper transportation. It needed streetcars and dial telephones. Even more urgent, the city needed to close the brothels and clean up the streets and replace the old plank sidewalks, which were rotting and dangerous. It needed to hire a fleet of garbage collectors. It needed to arrest the drunks and discourage the pickpockets, and most of all, it needed houses. The housing shortage was so acute that in the fall of 1907 some five thousand people, about a third of the population, were living in tents, without sanitary facilities and without much law and order. Smart tent dwellers tried to get a spot on the riverbank—it was uneven and hard to sleep on a slope, but at least the coal in the banks could be dug out and used for fuel. And sure enough, the less-than-sanitary state of affairs provoked that old accompaniment to human clumping—disease. Edmonton needed dedicated doctors and nurses and a bigger hospital. The doctors assigned to the rudimentary medical facility were never there, the attendants who were there were drunk, and the nurses had to pee in the creek, not a good solution to a tyhoid epidemic.

William Griesbach, a hero just back from the Boer War, tried hard to serve as the new mayor, but the city was growing so fast that taxes couldn't be collected fast enough to pay for improvements, and finally, in July of 1907, the city had run out of money and the Imperial Bank refused to extend any more credit. Still, the whole elaborate charade looked prosperous: McDougall and Secord's had expensive awnings over its windows. Strathcona, which became a city in 1907, was already building a streetcar line. Schools were better organized on the south side, and there weren't quite as many bars and brothels. Griesbach knew how to be a Boer War hero, but running this wildcat place was beyond him, so the Edmonton Board of Trade, knowing that Edmonton would soon seem ridiculous, put their collective heads together and persuaded John A. McDougall, merchant and real estate magnate, to run for mayor. McDougall had made a fortune in the Klondike and a further fortune buying and selling Métis scrip, but he had a powerful sense of civic responsibility, and after he won the 1907 mayoralty race, the first thing he did was go down to Toronto to see the Lorimer Company, who had the contract to build Edmonton's automatic telephone dialling system. McDougall discovered that not only had they not even started on the switchboard but they were still trying to sell shares to raise money to do the work. He made a quick detour to Chicago and negotiated with Strowger Automatic, who agreed to create the switchboard, ship the equipment that month, install the lines by April 1, and even cover legal fees if Lorimer decided to sue. By April 20, 1908, the city of Edmonton had an automatic dialling system. But that was just a start. McDougall set up streetcars and paved a mile of Jasper Avenue. The spectacular High Level, a railway and vehicular bridge that crossed the North Saskatchewan River valley from the upper banks just to the east of the university on the south side, and to the west of the legislative building on the north side, costing a dollar a rivet, hung its latticed cat's cradle above the deep, lush valley.

Rough-and-tumble cities, raw with their own invention, crave elegance. Edmonton moved from a hodgepodge of false-fronted wood-frame buildings to brick and stone with all the flourish of the nouveau brash. At every real estate boom, banks appear, eager to flaunt the trappings of wealth and security. Brick, oak, and even Tyndall stone brought all the way from Manitoba supported their claims to financial solidity. New commercial buildings boasted retail and office space, and apartment buildings finished with mirrored oak buffets rented space. Schools got drinking fountains, but there were parts of the city that were harder to spruce up. The river was a mess, floating with ordure and garbage, although that same river provided both drinking water and ice. The coal-fired electrical plant could not keep up with demand, and there were frequent outages. The city needed sewer lines and water lines and sanitary facilities. The isolation hospital, next to the slaughterhouse at Rat Creek, was nothing more than a leaky tent. Paupers who died were buried at public expense, but not kindly. The ramshackle buildings of Fort Edmonton served as chicken houses and storage sheds, and the whole mess was demolished in 1915 because it spoiled the view.

But history was dispensable. Between livery stables and flophouses, Edmonton flexed its muscles and dreamed of emulating Montreal. Small industries put out tentative shoots: Anderson's brickyards, quite a few coal mines, bakeries, and laundries. There was work enough for everyone, even if the coal mines were dangerous, and six men died in a horrific fire in John Walter's mine on June 8, 1907. Edmontonians thronged to pay their respects, but still felt death was a small price to pay for development. Flour mills and grain elevators raised a fine dust. Printers and taxidermists inked and stuffed. People flocked in, and visitors could put up in new hotels like the King Edward or the Cecil, and visit either saloons or houses of ill repute. The city could hardly keep up with itself.

Thanks to Premier Rutherford and much to Calgary's chagrin, the as-yet-imaginary provincial university was bestowed on Strathcona. Some laughed. This wasn't a college province—if anything, Alberta needed horse doctors and water diviners, not professors, said Frank Oliver. But a University of Alberta was almost dearer to Rutherford's heart than the province itself, and he hired a McGill mathematics man, Henry Marshall Tory, to shape this nascent institution. E. K. Broadus, one of the first professors recruited, recalled his initial meeting with Dr. Tory. "On a day in June 1908, the president of a university not yet in being, in a province which I had never heard of, in a country which I had never visited, came to Harvard and offered me the professorship in English. The offer sounded like midsummer madness." But Broadus took it. That early ivory tower was straight as an arrow, marked by obligatory church attendance, a strict dress code, and a very formal attitude in the classroom. Student behaviour was strenuously policed. Although classes began in September 1908 in the attic of Queen Alexandra School, the first building, Athabasca Hall, wasn't ready for students until 1911, when they moved to a campus as bare and rough as any homestead.

Civilization came calling. The Macdonald Hotel hosted tea dances. Churches pointed spires to heaven. More of Jasper Avenue was paved. More land was annexed. Subdivisions spread, and rackety streetcar lines spidered their way through brush and sinkholes to provide outlying areas with transportation. Graft and bribery played cards behind closed doors, and Edmonton's council meetings had fisticuffs over everything from protection rackets to police control. More telephone cable was strung, more sewers dug, more sidewalks and watermains laid. Strathcona and Edmonton circled the advantages of joining forces, and after elaborate trade-offs and bargains, in February of 1912 the two cities, through the provincial Edmonton-Strathcona Amalgamation Act, united.

But housing was at a premium and the squatters tenting on the river flats could hardly wait to get a wooden shack, any kind of shack. For a short time in the 1912 land boom the price of building lots in Edmonton rose above the value of land in the centre of New York City, the beginning of a provincial tradition, Alberta still home to more real estate agents than good sense. Some 30,000

Americans, eager to invest, invaded Alberta. There were line-ups and fights at the land offices. At the height of the craze, in May 1912, the Hudson's Bay Company decided it was a good time to sell a block of its reserve land at public auction. As part of the deal made with HBC when it sold Rupert's Land to Central Canada, the company had retained title to one thousand acres around each of its forts, and the Hudson's Bay Reserve in Edmonton was a prime piece of real estate for this wound-up time. In an escalation of suspense, the HBC decided that the right to purchase land would be determined by lottery the Monday before the sale. The location of the initial draw was supposed to be kept secret, but lurking scouts and spies noticed a couple of men lugging a Hudson's Bay Company safe into a church hall on Sunday afternoon and within minutes, prospective buyers were lining up, ready to sit it out overnight. That lottery featured all the habits of the land boom itself. First, the people in line sold their spots in the line, their admission to the sale. When the actual lottery numbers (there were 1,500 tickets giving people the right to bid on the available property) were drawn by those in line, people sold those tickets to other gamblers. Then those people resold the rights to the lots they were allowed to buy, and once they had bought a lot, tried to resell the lot at a profit. In the end, more than 1,500 chunks of HBC property were traded for something like $4.3 million. Now that's a land boom, a gambler's paradise. Flipping properties became a habit that Albertans have never given up.

The inevitable crash came. A few months later, the vacant prairie reaches that the city had annexed flourished with dandelions and gopher holes again. Close to 90 percent of those lots remained empty for years, and forty years later some of the Hudson's Bay land was still unoccupied. Ultimately 75,000 lots reverted to the city for non-payment of taxes, making the municipal government the principal owner of land in Edmonton. The city had learned a hard lesson—not to succumb to speculation.

Men with hands in empty pockets began to walk the streets. By 1913 real estate speculators had left town and the population dwindled, boosterism bottomed out. The First World War probably prevented a deep depression, but the Centre benefited from the war boom more than the West. Typically, Centrals claimed that Western cities had no manufacturing base and so war industries should not be located in Alberta. Given the economic roller coaster, why didn't more people leave? Stubbornness, an attachment to place, a determination to succeed, no matter what? All Edmontonians could do was pray for an oil strike—although it didn't get one until Leduc blew in in 1947.

But booms and busts bestow sophistication, and Edmonton began to look toward the outside world. When war broke out in 1914, the *Edmonton Journal* posted a huge bulletin board where people could read the latest about events in Europe. Thousands of men enlisted and Edmonton sent carloads of relief provisions to Belgium. Still, hardly able to meet its payroll, the city faced bankruptcy. Despite its investment in a positive attitude, Edmonton was falling asleep on its feet. Billboards on the street declared that every consumer was either a "booster" or a "knocker." The injunctions had a tone of desperation. "Your own INCOME depends on the success of Edmonton stores and factories. Spend your money where you make it." Another warned, "HE'S A KNOCKER. Don't give business to a merchant who doesn't push goods made-in-Edmonton. He's a Knocker." As if honing its competitive spirit, one read, "Boost for Edmonton. Insist on getting goods made in EDMONTON." And this strange metaphor, "You can't saw wood with a hammer. You knock Edmonton when you send away money that could be SPENT HERE. Don't be a knocker." Despite those efforts, despite the war, the population dropped from 72,000 people in 1914 to fewer than 55,000 in 1918, and the losses were not all soldiers.

Because of the demand for coal and other fuel, the war prevented the bust from being a complete rout, but it was devastating enough, and Edmonton would never forget the humiliation it suffered at the bang of the auctioneer's gavel as lot after lot reverted to the same city that had optimistically developed it. And natural disasters contributed. The heavy rains of 1915 helped the North Saskatchewan to rise forty-eight feet above its normal level and overflow its banks, flooding the entire valley and destroying so many houses that eight hundred families were left homeless. Was this the payoff for hopes and dreams?

Then, with the returning soldiers, came the Spanish flu. The Grey Nuns, who had begun the city's first hospital, the General, were an uncloistered order who believed in community service. They had already encountered their share of political struggles. In 1899 several doctors refused to work at their hospital because they wanted admitting authority transferred from the nuns to an external board. It was clear that there was a mercenary consideration—doctors who worked at the General were expected to provide care to poor patients free of charge on a rotating monthly basis; in that month doctors could expect their income to drop. Despite pressure, the nuns refused to back down, and a group of doctors and members of the Protestant clergy spearheaded the development of the Edmonton Public Hospital, which was not religiously affiliated. In fact, the General accepted patients from every religion, and the new "non-sectarian" hospital was markedly Protestant. Here, then, was Alberta's first fight over health care access, based on a division over money and culture, since two francophone doctors continued to serve the General Hospital. And the argument was also about women; most doctors were used to male municipal boards of directors and did not enjoy having to negotiate with Sisters of Mercy.

But the Spanish flu epidemic of 1918 made the city recognize the need for serious health practices. The Grey Nuns cared for 150 patients at a time in a hospital designed for one hundred, every available space transformed into beds. The only treatment for the flu was good nursing care, hard to find in the stricken city. By the fall, theatres, schools, and dance halls were closed, public meetings were prohibited, and everyone was required to wear cheesecloth face masks outside the home. Businesses shut down, while undertakers did a perversely booming business, although funerals were cancelled because of the fear of infection, and bodies had to be buried at night. By the end of the epidemic, in 1919, more than three thousand Albertans had died, 445 of the recorded deaths in Edmonton.

The peaceful city the returning soldiers had left was changed, now full of automobiles, empty lots, labour unrest. In May of 1919 the Winnipeg strike reverberated west, and a general strike in sympathy spread to electric and even dairy workers throughout the province. The saloons were gone, but Edmontonians went to football games, where the Eskimos began their slow ascent, and to cheer the triumphs of the Commercial Grads Girls basketball team, who won again and again, right up to the Paris Olympics in 1924, the Los Angeles Olympics in 1932, and finally the Berlin Olympics in 1936. In 1920 the Empire Theatre, which would become the Trocadero Ballroom, opened its doors. In 1922 CJCA Radio came on air. Mercifully, in 1923 prohibition was repealed. Civilization had at last returned, with beer parlours attached to hotels, their barn-like caverns echoing with shouts, and Ladies and Escorts isolated next door because women, with bobbed hair and sleek dresses, everyone knew, were a corrupting influence. Finally, in 1924 the

Alberta & Great Waterways Railway reached Fort McMurray, and Edmonton could really claim to be the gateway to the North.

What a rush, what a headlong tumble! Edmonton lusted after railways, but its real future began in 1927 with the opening of Blatchford Field, later to become the much-disputed Edmonton Municipal Airport. Edmontonians were lukewarm about gambling on air travel, and in a 1928 plebiscite rejected expanding the airfield, but an event just a few weeks later showed them the error of their ways. At the remote northern Alberta community of Little Red River, near Fort Vermilion, HBC factor Albert Logan came down with a case of diphtheria. Fearful of an epidemic that could devastate both Little Red River and Fort Vermilion, the doctor in the area sent a message with two Métis men who travelled by horse and wagon to Peace River, the nearest telegraph office. After their eleven-day trip, they were themselves ill and exhausted, but the telegram was received by Alberta's deputy minister of health on December 31, 1928. "Logan, Hudson's Bay man at Red River, fifty miles below Fort Vermilion, bad case laryngeal diphtheria. Voice is gone and throat paralysed. Serum old. Have started immunizing people around but quantity limited.... If possible rush aeroplane. Good landing and no snow.... Send intubation apparatus and several hundred units antitoxin for two hundred. Cannot leave Logan's bedside. Real emergency. Do all possible." Northern flights had stopped for the winter, but flying ace Wilfred "Wop" May and his co-pilot Vic Horner took off in a tiny, open-cockpit Avro Avian to fly more than six hundred miles in forty-below temperatures to deliver the serum. It was foolhardy more than heroic: the plane had wheels and not skis, landing strips along the way were few and far between, and it was so cold that their engine kept cutting out. CJCA broadcast the plane's progress, asking trappers along the way to light fires for beacons. When they landed on the frozen Peace River, they were so cold that they had to be physically lifted out the airplane and Wop May's hands pried from the controls, but the men refuelled, warmed up, and took off again, in temperatures dropping to forty-five below. At Little Red River they landed safely and handed the serum over to the doctor and the relieved community before heading south again. After resting in Peace River for two days, they returned to Edmonton, where their mercy flight had taken on the proportions of radio drama. On the afternoon of Sunday, January 6, 1929, 10,000 people descended on Blatchford Field, where, in the cutting wind, they stood and watched the snowy sky, listening for the drone of an engine. Their wait encompassed the silence of the North and the future of aviation, and although the small engine was hard to hear, at 2:43 p.m. the plane swooped low from the snowy air and landed, and a new kind of hero was born. Wop May couldn't smile, because his mouth was frozen shut—but when he had time to thaw, he did say to the assembled newsmen, "You can tell the world it was a cold trip." That trip began Edmonton's role as home of "seat-of-the-pants" aviation.

Edmonton was on the move again, the messy old city demolishing raffish buildings to make way for more stately contenders. In December 1928, the first dazzling neon sign in Edmonton appeared over Darling's Drug Store, despite blizzards and windstorms doing all kinds of damage. Fires were so common that it was clear the city needed improved firefighting equipment, especially after the 1932 fire in the Corona Hotel, one that sent Alberta's first female cabinet minister, Irene Parlby, out into the street in her nightgown.

By 1929, the Great Depression was seeping over the horizon, bringing with it hunger, unemployment, and theft, bread lines and gunny sack dresses and canned gophers. In despair, many jumped from the High Level Bridge. The population grew again, Centrals and Easterners coming west because they thought it would be easier to get a job. Every year the number of people on relief increased, along with the city's debt.

And then, another war. The Loyal Edmonton Regiment signed up men and prepared to sail off to Europe, and the Salvation Army erected a large canteen on the Prince of Wales military encampment in 1939, but the war seemed unreal—until May 1940 and the invasion of Holland and Belgium. Edmontonians enlisted as soldiers, sailors, and air-force men, and the once-contentious airport became the busiest on the continent, sprouting barracks and hangars and extending runways. At the beginning of the 1940s, Edmonton was the least densely populated city in Canada, but by 1944 the war boom boosted it to the "Crossroads of the West" and air traffic confirmed it as the "Gateway to the North." The Americans invaded, stopping in Edmonton on their way to build the war defence systems of the Alaska Highway and the CANOL Pipeline. There wasn't a bed to be found in the overcrowded city, with both girls and fine china appropriated by the servicemen from the Scary States. The airport zoomed and zoomed; one day in 1943, 860 planes took off and landed. There was gold in Yellowknife and wheat in the surrounding

Men in Edmonton relief kitchen, 1933

farmlands. Sleepy little Edmonton was bustling; and best of all, it had at last sur-passed Calgary in population. The war brought back prosperity, and when it was over no city celebrated more fervently.

Returning soldiers went to university, married, got jobs, and built families, which became part of the baby boom of the fifties and sixties. But the real trans-formation came in February 1947, when Leduc No. 1 blew in. Edmonton discov-ered it was sitting on an oil field, and Alberta was in the money. Three major refineries were built in the city between 1948 and 1951, and would result in the development of a major petrochemical industry. And with the oil came natural gas, both wearing dollar signs. The government counted a surplus, people moved west to work, and the empty lots in the suburbs began to fill up. By 1956 Edmonton was the fastest-growing city in Canada.

But growth was not always happy. Battles erupted between Edmonton and sur-rounding towns, which were gobbled up by the sprawl of the city. St. Albert, Beverly, and Jasper Place were all annexed. Meanwhile, the city elected one of its most colourful mayors, William Hawrelak, the Ukrainian-Canadian who ran the city between 1951 and 1959, twice re-elected by acclamation. He was accused of misconduct over conflict of interest, resigned, then was re-elected in 1964, again disqualified in 1965, but won another election in 1974. Only his death in office in 1975 stopped his return.

Oil and gas are highly capitalized industries, not themselves labour-intensive, but they spawn huge infrastructures of technical, financial, and physical services connected to the business. And with oil money came everything else. Restaurants and hotels, apartment blocks and shopping centres. Virtually overnight, Edmonton graduated to twenty-four-ounce steaks and picnics in well-groomed parks (some nine thousand acres within the city); its university sprawled along the banks of the North Saskatchewan River; it had annexed and filled in all the areas that had been left as gaping stump lots in 1913. In the 1960s what had been urban bungalow residential turned into the era of high-rise heaven, buildings stacked along the picturesque banks of the North Saskatchewan.

A new international airport opened twenty-five miles south of the city, and the entire centre of the city was bulldozed and rebuilt, with a new city hall, a new library, new law courts, a new art gallery. Newness was what counted, urban renewal with a vengeance, complete with freeways and thoroughfares, a zoo, and the Queen Elizabeth Planetarium, the first in Canada, officially opened in 1960. In the 1970s Edmonton enjoyed wild, unfettered growth, prompted by the promise of the Heritage Trust Fund and high-rolling times; by 1976 it was home to 450,000 people. As eager as ever to make tracks, Edmonton officially opened its sparkling Light Rapid Transit system in April 1978. At first the trains didn't go far, only four miles, at a cost of $65 million, but finally, in 1992 the LRT crossed the river to the university, mass transit for students and workers.

When Ottawa's 1980 National Energy Program hit, Edmonton began the downward spiral that would end in the bust of 1982, when oil fell to $29, and Alberta started recognizing that its prosperity depended on the price of a barrel of crude. To add to the bust's bitterness, while Ottawa rescued Central banks, it let a number of Western banks fail. That was hardly offset by the extravagant opening of the extravagant West Edmonton Mall in 1981. Supposedly the largest mall in the world, it covers 119 acres, has eight hundred stores and services, an amusement park, water park, wave pool, skating rink, and hotel. It symbolizes what

Edmonton is most famous for—indoor shopping—appropriate for a city that began as a fur-trading post.

Today, Edmonton works hard to shed what often seems to be its white-elephant complex and, instead, markets itself as the City of Champions—once home to Wayne Gretzky and a number of Oiler and Eskimo championships—and as the Official Host City for the Turn of the Century. It's still a mecca for entrepreneurial Centralists who come west to make their fortunes, like Ontario-born Peter Pocklington, who leveraged his way from car dealerships to real estate, meat packing, and sports. But when he sold hockey star Gretzky to the Los Angeles Kings in 1988, the city turned its back on him, and now Pocklington is persona non grata.

But there is more to Edmonton's unique character. What makes the city Edmonton? Refinery Row, that column of tanks parading the east side of the city? Its ethnic diversity? Its fur-trade ancestry, the old ghosts of the trading post still haunting the valley at night? The beaver that refuse to leave and that chew at the tasty trees along the water just as they did hundreds of years ago? Edmonton points north, bends toward the northern part of this rich province, taking in with a wide sweep of the hand Fort Saskatchewan, St. Albert, Clover Bar. The downtown may languish under the green fluorescence of government offices, strip malls and suburbs may secrete desire, but Edmonton belongs to its river, the North Saskatchewan.

The river is its true character, the 160-foot banks of that magnificent valley the site of human habitation for millennia. Over time, the city has come to embrace the powerful aesthetic of that river and its valley, the sudden leap of the natural world close and intimate, a haven for biking and walking trails. Its green and gold in the fall are so beautiful that the spectator must close her eyes. And so Edmonton looms, above what was once the prime pelt-gathering spot in the world, high-rises and hotels and office complexes, parks and green spaces and art galleries and river raft races and the Fringe Festival and the Folk Festival and the Jazz Festival and the Commonwealth Games. Is this a grand metropolis built between rising and falling oil prices? Or is this just a comfortable city, shrugging along in its old beaver coat, no longer ashamed that it grew out of trade and daring to claim its rough squatters and crooked politicians and schemes and dreams and its awful paranoia and its dislike of its twin 125 miles to the south? This

Edmonton is a home place for citizens, always conscious of being a booster and not a knocker. The latest booster, Mayor Bill Smith, says the same thing every year: "This'll be the greatest year in the history of Edmonton."

And so it will be.

Calgary

Sitting beside the juncture of the Elbow and the Bow rivers—a gentle destination, a confluence, a meeting place—Calgary is a conundrum. There are those who haven't a good word to say about this brash young city, and scoffing at Calgary has long been a national pastime. Cowtown or oil town, too American by half, a town that mixes ranching and business, oil and dark water, full of briefcase-carrying cowboys, computer hackers and pickup trucks. It's a raw city, all elbows and knees, sprawled on the cusp of the prairie and the foothills of the Rockies, gazing toward the mountain scenery to the west and reeling from the inebriating air. Whisky was white Calgary's progenitor, bringing the North West Mounted Police, F Troop arriving in 1875 under the command of Inspector Ephraim Brisebois. They had been commissioned to chase out the American whisky traders, to keep the peace with the Blackfoot Confederacy, and to police a stiff prohibition. Zealous boys, they set out to follow their orders.

The first settlers called the place "the Elbow," but Mounted Police Commissioner James Macleod recommended to his superiors in Ottawa that it be named Fort Calgary—the name of a castle belonging to his mother's relatives back in Scotland. And so, Edmonton and Calgary echo each other's naming, both christened after a place with no connection to the West. To the Blackfoot, Sarcee, and Stoney people, Calgary was simply "Elbow," *Moki'nstsis*. But as Hugh Dempsey says in *Calgary: Spirit of the West*, "the best name for Calgary was devised by the Slavey Indians of northern Alberta. They called it *Klincho-tinay-indihay*, which simply means 'horse town.'"

By the time the police built their little fort, there were already settlers and missionaries in the area. Sam Livingstone, a mountain man who freighted and hunted all over the West, had settled his family on a homestead/private trading post on the Elbow River. Realizing that police presence would encourage settlement, he established the first successful Calgary-area grain, vegetable, and livestock farm, fathered fourteen children with Jane Howse, granddaughter of the man who named Howse Pass, and became a big Calgary booster before he died in 1897. John Glenn had ranched in the undulating coulees of Fish Creek since the fall of 1873. In 1872–73, lay missionary Alexis Cardinal and Father Constantine Scollen set up a log-shack mission some twenty-five miles up the Elbow River. When they heard that the Mounties were coming, Father Scollen got busy building a mission on the Elbow River, an area that is still the heart of Catholic Calgary, now called Mission; when he left, Father Doucet took his place. And John McDougall of that energetic missionary dynasty established a Methodist mission at Morley for the Assiniboine people in 1873.

As for the unemployed whisky traders, the Mounties put them to work, building between September and Christmas of 1875 a vertical log palisade about 150 feet square that enclosed officers' and men's quarters, storerooms, stables, and a guardhouse. Other whisky traders, although their goods had been confiscated, decided to hang around, thus establishing a pattern that Calgary would follow for the next century of playing host to Americans, whisky traders, and oil men ready to change their stripes when the occasion demanded, carpetbaggers eager to deal on anything. Trader Henry Taylor, for instance, hauled a pool table up from Fort Benton, Montana, and built a dance hall around it, selling candy and dry goods on the side—Calgary's first store. And the HBC, now that it looked like a settlement was starting, floated a trading shop down the Bow from the mountains. A few Métis families from Edmonton, ready to undertake freighting between Fort Macleod, Calgary, and Fort Saskatchewan, built cabins along the Elbow and became the rudimentary village's first citizens. The unlikely, unruly, preposterous city of Calgary had begun.

It was quiet for a few winters until 1880, when Sarcee Chief Bull Head, who did not think that Treaty Seven had given his people adequate compensation, rode into town and virtually took the fort hostage. His demands were simple. His people were starving. He wanted provisions for the winter and land for his tribe, or he would burn down the fort. It seemed like a reasonable request, and the Mounties brought up two wagonloads of food from Fort Macleod, then escorted the people south to the Oldman River. Later, Bull Head negotiated for a reserve to the southwest of the city at Fish Creek, now almost within the city. But that early incident marked the way Calgarians handled uprisings of every nature. Wave your guns, but stay calm, listen, and make a deal.

When they learned that this little missionary post and Mountie detachment was going to welcome the CPR, the flimsy Mountie post was immediately enlarged and more permanent buildings erected in preparation for the speculators and construction workers who would flood the town. Sure enough, within a month, a tent city of butchers and bakers and candlestick-makers had spread out on the east side of the Elbow River. When the train pulled in on August 13, 1883, the town was waiting, eager to cheer a new mode of transportation. The day the track was laid across the Elbow, four hundred men received their pay, and despite its being Sunday the next day's celebration included fights, prostitutes, whisky, and no less than $5,000 bet on horse races, one of Calgary's favourite occupations. Nothing has changed.

But where would the official townsite be? The CPR was supposed to survey a site, but they dragged and lagged, and did not choose a location until February 1884. Then they plunked the station not on the east side of the Elbow where most of the tents were pitched and the first tentative buildings leaned, but on the west side, making James Lougheed, who had purchased land there, rich, and locating the heart of the city a mile to the west of the Mountie post. Almost overnight, the entire city of tents and shacks shuffled over to the west side. So now the settlement was tucked into the curve of the Bow River on the north and the railway tracks on the south, a location that would eventually determine the downtown's shape. At first a shantytown, Calgary was always willing to tear up stakes and build anew.

When it was incorporated in 1884, Calgary enjoyed its first mini-boom. Although there were more cattle and horses than people, when the CPR indicated that Calgary would host its regional maintenance depot the town knew it was off to the races. It even had a newspaper, the *Calgary Herald*, founded in 1883 by T. B. Bradon, an early booster who was fond of comparing Calgary to Chicago. He was joined by Major James Walker, another local promoter who, after seven years with the NWMP, became the manager of the Cochrane Ranche. Bow River Mills supplied lumber for city sidewalks and houses, and in 1886 Peter Prince's Eau Claire and Bow River Lumber Company began floating logs down the river from Cochrane to help build the growing town.

During the 1885 Riel Rebellion, Calgary panicked, along with all the other cities in the West. The train brought in troops from the East, and regiments and infantries and mounted corps rode through the streets, which made the town feel very safe, although more guns than ever were brandished. The happy merchants doubled the prices of everything—disaster and impending attack were good for business. But the troops trained and paraded before marching north to defeat Riel, returning some months later a little tattered but ready to celebrate. Again Calgary was happy to oblige, and between licit and illicit whisky suppliers, gave them one hell of a party.

The Mounties might have killed the whisky trade to the Indians, but whisky never became extinct. Bottles snuggled safely in flour barrels, imperative "medicinal" prescriptions were scrawled, and stills hid in the folds of the coulees. The Mounties were supposed to enforce territorial law; and Calgary's chief of police, a hard-knuckled knockabout named John Ingram who had come west to escape various assault charges in Winnipeg, was supposed to enforce local laws. The important struggle was over who, Ottawa or Calgary, got to keep the money for the fines, which were the prevalent punishment and source of revenue. It was one thing to be fined for galloping your horse down Stephen Avenue; it was quite another for the money to go to Ottawa. Then, to complicate matters, Ottawa sent out a hard-line temperance man, Jerry Travis, to fill the role of stipendiary magistrate. The Centre wasn't trying to make a statement, they just needed to reward him with a patronage appointment, and those were usually somewhere out west. The war between the respectable and the reprehensible was on, Travis on the side of the former, and Ingram on the side of the latter. The town of Calgary worked on a fine edge of give-and-take. Prostitutes, gamblers, and bootleggers were occasionally arrested, but fined and released rather than imprisoned; in exchange, the police protected them if someone threatened their business. This was good for business and good for the town's coffers. Travis was appalled, especially when he discovered that the mayor and other town worthies were happily complicit in this "whisky ring." He fired the mayor and didn't hesitate to hand out jail sentences, which caused a serious uprising. At a vociferous meeting, the local reprehensible demanded that Travis be run out of town on a rail. To make matters worse, Travis fired his clerk, Hugh Cayley, for being drunk and unreliable, but Hugh Cayley was also the editor of the *Calgary Herald*, and now the press was on Travis's heels. Chaos ruled, and in the end Ottawa realized that Travis's draconian approach was more of a liability than an asset and simply eliminated his position, giving him a whopping pension and advising him to go into private practice. Instead, he

Calgary begins to look substantial, 1890

bought Calgary real estate and became a rich man. The irony was that both Travis and Murdoch were from New Brunswick, not the West; most of the social and business tycoons who ran the place were Centrals, with the addition of a few Englishmen who called themselves gentlemen.

On November 7, 1886, a huge fire burned half of the developing downtown, which had a few stone and brick buildings, although most were hastily framed wooden shells, perfect for a blaze. And blaze they did. The whole town turned out in their Sunday best and fought the fire as well as possible, even dismantling some buildings and dragging them out of the way of the flames. Eighteen structures, stores and houses and hotels, were utterly destroyed, with considerable financial loss, and Calgary knew it was time to figure out a strategy to deal with fire, the common scourge of prairie towns. The biggest after-effect was that everyone rebuilt, not with wood, but with the honey-coloured stone quarried from the local cliffs, rich, warm sandstone. So many stone buildings went up that Calgary earned the name "Sandstone City."

Between 1892 and 1896, Calgary endured one of those periodic busts that characterize its history, even though with the help of municipal lawyer Arthur Sifton, Calgary became a city, a real city, the first city in the North West Territories, in

1894. The new mayor, Quebec export Wesley Orr, chose "Onward" as Calgary's motto, a motto to which it has clung with all its go-getting heart. Becoming a city gave Calgarians the chance to thumb their noses at Edmonton, which trundled along with fewer than a thousand citizens and no railway, while Calgary had twenty-five hundred people and the heart-stirring whistle of the CPR. The comparison was delicious, made even sweeter when the CPR made Calgary a divisional point in 1898, building a roundhouse and repair shops. It was obvious that Calgary was the hub, the West's connection between nothing and everything. To the arriving settlers, though, many of them migrants from the United States, Calgary looked scurvy and down-at-heel. The piles of horse manure behind the stables stank. The cesspools stank. Flies buzzed and lice jumped from greasy head to head. Cows wandered through the streets. It didn't even have a hospital until an elderly Chinese man, Jimmy Smith, died of tuberculosis, and left $600 to start a public hospital, which the more elevated citizens had not done.

By the turn of the century R. B. Bennett showed up and started lawyering; and outrageous newspaperman Bob Edwards showed up, fresh from Strathcona, and started drinking and reporting, reporting and drinking. Originally from Edinburgh, Scotland, he was, his friends insisted, a man of culture and literary ability despite his drinking, and although he satirized everyone from priest to prostitute, he was shy and reserved. Only a town like Calgary could appreciate him. He lived in the Cameron Block, drank at the Alberta Hotel, competed sartorially with R. B. Bennett, and by 1908 circulation of his newspaper, the *Eye Opener*, topped eighteen thousand. This in a city of ten thousand. But Edwards was read all over the West and as far away as New York. The paper was supposed to appear weekly, but this schedule depended on the extent to which Edwards was under the influence. Certainly he was a first-hand observer of bars and hospitals; his debauches in the former would usually lead to a stay in the latter, five to six days in the Holy Cross, where he would dry out and swear to reform. Not surprisingly he argued for better pay for nurses, but surprisingly (and cantankerously) during the prohibition plebiscite he came out on the side of temperance. The reason? He disagreed with greedy hoteliers charging the same for weak beer as they did for good whisky, making everyone choose whisky, which led to alcoholism and children falling asleep with empty bellies because their daddies had drunk away the milk money. Before the vote, he published his unpopular opinion.

The resulting bootlegging and moonshining made him even more cynical, and by 1918 he had reversed his opinion and began to recommend that prohibition be repealed. He believed that government-owned and -controlled liquor stores were the answer. He also supported medicare, prostitution, and equal rights for women at a time when most places were trying to mimic Edwardian Ottawa. Fearless and independent, Edwards loved Calgary and hated self-righteousness. At the age of fifty-three, he even fell in love and married—Kate Penman, a law clerk half his age. And in the most surprising turnaround of all, he became the very character he had lampooned most, a politician. Although he refused to make even one campaign speech, he was elected to the Alberta legislature as an Independent in 1921. "Isn't it wonderful?" he gloated. "I'm in the legislature and McGillicuddy [a rival newspaperman who had recently died] is in hell." But Edwards was not there long. He himself died on November 14, 1922, of heart problems, complicated by the flu and no doubt a worn-out liver. Poignantly, his wife buried the last issue of the *Eye Opener* and his pocket flask, filled with good scotch, under his gravestone.

But with men like Edwards, Calgary showed its developing character, headstrong and unpredictable, but interesting. At the beginning of the twentieth century, the town wasn't much to look at, a scattering of two- and three-storey buildings with a handful of small frame houses sprouting between the Bow and Elbow rivers. It was bare and windswept, for only a few people had managed to plant trees and shrubs—all imported. In a grasslands desert, trees are strange, almost alien. Settlement developed in clutches, around the CPR buildings, the packing plants, the sawmills, the flour mills, as people tried to live as close as possible to their work. Work was the all-consuming interest of every citizen, even though Calgarians were serious about play. There was an open-air market every Friday, and dancing was popular, especially at special events like the Firemen's Ball. Horse races and foot races were constantly planned, and Calgarians wagered with the same intensity that they do now.

Most lived in frame houses, and for heat used what they could find—wood and coal and occasionally horse dung. They worried about water. Calgary had laid its first watermains in 1899, but the steam-driven pumps of the waterworks were unpredictable, and the city was quick to create the Calgary Gas and Waterworks. The place was growing so fast that the utilities could hardly keep up with the demand. Water wasn't predictable at all, and taps often ran dry, until the Calgary Power Company built a dam and a hydro-electric powerhouse at Horseshoe Falls on the Bow River. It provided much of Alberta's electricity for the rest of the century.

And the city developed different ghettos. Mission or Rouleauville had always been the French neighbourhood. Germantown was on the north side of the Bow, book-ended by the Italian neighbourhood. Pedigrees and sandstone and cattle were none too friendly to ethnic foreigners, and people who weren't part of those early aristocracies had to efface themselves. In this city of opportunity the best opportunities

The irascible Bob Edwards, loudmouth of the West

came to those who were white, British, or from Ontario. Especially those from Ontario, who fancied themselves established Canadians and looked down on the immigrant "scum of Europe." They were no happier about Americans, who built big houses on "American Hill," later renamed Mount Royal. The very change in name reveals something about Calgary's insecurity. "American Hill" smelled too much like new money, while Mount Royal, with its obvious reference to Montreal, suggested a sophistication the city would invent even if it couldn't adopt it.

Still, immigration boomed, and as it did, the big ranching outfits, who had never strung a barbed-wire fence or believed in surveying the land into sections, died. The ranches around Calgary became smaller; nevertheless, the nickname Cowtown persisted right up until 2000. More than any other spectacle, Calgary celebrates its ranching heritage with the Stampede. It still balances the aristocratic urge of show jumping and dressage with the rougher tricks of bronc busting.

Calgary was the biggest booster of provincehood for Alberta, believing itself destined to be the capital. It had the air, the prestige, and the energy; it had the railway, the panache, and the experts. But it hadn't bargained on partisan politics, the fact that Calgary had sent only Conservatives to an Ottawa run by a Liberal prime minister. And when the Rutherford government committed what Calgarians felt was criminal favouritism by bestowing both the provincial legislature and the university on Edmonton, Calgary had another tantrum. Thus developed a raging competition that has never truly abated. Bob Edwards could claim that Calgary was not sore, but the truth was that Calgary smarted with soreness. Only after time and then reluctantly did these cities reconcile themselves to sharing the same bed or even the same ideals. Even when they needed one another, they were wary. During Calgary's 1906–7 coal shortage, Edmonton generously shipped trainloads of local coal south, but not without the *Edmonton Bulletin*'s making snide comments about Calgary's reliance on chinooks to help it through fuel shortages. As small compensation, in 1906 Calgary was assigned the normal school, which trained teachers, in a four-month course, complete with a strap and a lunch pail, in how to handle students in the one-room schoolhouses popping up next to every crossroad of the province.

So Calgary elbowed its way into the twentieth century with an American pedigree and a massive inferiority complex, making it all the more determined to prosper and grow and beat the world at its own game. Veterans of the city's boom-and-bust cycles rushed from one side of the river to the other, giving rise to quite a few real estate swindles. Calgary city council's sudden decision to sell about five hundred city-owned lots led to the Great Land Scandal of 1904. In a quick half-hour March meeting, the council agreed on land valuations and then put the pieces up for sale, without bothering to inform the public. By noon of the next day, the lots were all sold, but the citizenry, figuring out that the land had been purchased by investors who had been tipped off, was irate. After a year of public outcry, the mayor had no choice but to order an investigation, although key people in the scandal—the city clerk and the city solicitor—had already resigned and most of the land had been returned to the city. That scandal was merely practice for the coming Great Land Boom, and it foreshadowed a Calgary hobby called property flipping, more accurately defined as gambling, a fever that would return at intervals through the twentieth century.

During the first decade of the 1900s, about a quarter of Calgary's labour force worked in construction, a percentage that would repeat itself only in the building boom of the 1970s. Although Calgary counted eleven thousand houses by 1911, there was a housing shortage. Still, people and businesses kept pouring into Sunny Alberta, bringing with them bigger dreams and automobiles and streetcars and electricity, and of course, money and the desire to make more money. But money isn't everything, and by 1907 Calgarians could roller-skate at the Sherman Rink, go to a picture at the Orpheum or the Lyric theatres, ride a streetcar, dial a telephone, and worship at their church of choice. They could brag about the amazing Calgary Dominion Exhibition, held in 1908 on the ninety-four-acre fairground the city had purchased from R. B. Bennett and leased to the Agricultural Society. The forerunner of the "Greatest Show on Earth" began with a mile-long historical parade that proceeded chronologically from Indians and settlers to modern merchants and automobiles. The parade was followed by horse racing and rodeo events, brass bands and fireworks, and the priceless thrill of death when a rancher was thrown from his horse and killed in front of the grandstand.

Meanwhile, the university location—Edmonton—still rankled, so in 1912 Calgary decided to start one of its own. Dr. Thomas Blow got the ball rolling, W. G. Tregillus donated 160 acres of land in the west end by the Bow River, and city council donated $150,000. But they had to contend with dog-in-the-manger Edmonton. The legislature simply refused to accord the institution degree-granting powers, defeating the proposal with the excuse that the province could not afford another university, even though the Calgary bunch promised that it would be self-sustaining. For a few years the school struggled on, but by 1914 enrollment was down and the land had to be sold for taxes. In 1915 a federal commission on higher education concluded that there was no need for a second university, and Alberta remained the only degree-granting body until 1966, when activist students argued the University of Calgary into existence. So Calgarians were furious all over again, that fury developing into a political resistance that would as soon vote Liberal as cut off an arm. Arthur Sifton, claimed newsman Bob Edwards, would get no votes in Calgary—he was a Liberal and Calgarians were Conservative to the core. Which, given the plums doled out to the northern city, was shaping up to be a fair prediction. But Dr. Blow didn't quite give up. He simply shifted tactics and instead focused on founding the Provincial Institute of

Technology and Art in 1916, which successfully weathered all of Edmonton's efforts to look down on its worth. Eventually Edmonton would get one, too, called the Northern Alberta Institute of Technology.

Calgary's great land boom kept growing. By 1912 there were sixty-two thousand people, rich and poor, hopeful and beyond hope, a mixture of real estate magnates and expensive lawyers and hard-working labourers. To a poor policeman, trying to control the citizens of this burgeoning city was like trying to herd pigs, and trying to impose manners on those pigs was a hopeless task. The police believed that brothels and bars kept public temper under control. Besides, punishing people was difficult. Fines were easy enough to levy, but there weren't enough jail cells to incarcerate all the lawbreakers. The city supported a brewery and a meat-packing plant and a cooperage—and Whisky Row, the ten hotels lining Ninth Avenue from Third Street East to First Street West, ready to quench a prairie thirst. While Bob Edwards argued that the solution to drunkenness was a good hearty lager at five cents a glass, Calgary polished its reputation as a reliably wet town, with a predictable drunk tank but a forgiving attitude. Silk stockings waved from the bordellos on Sixth Avenue, and anyone with an ear to the wind knew where to find women, whisky, and a place to gamble.

But social evil is part of growth, and the city was preoccupied with its own frenzied development. The CPR carried lumber and cement and nails and hammers into town, sixty teams working twelve-hour days unloaded materials, and right across the CPR tracks was the biggest horse barn west of Toronto for the horses hauling that freight. Every other wagon was carting dirt and bricks and limestone and sandstone to build the booming city, which was going up between the tracks and a mesh of livery stables and blacksmith shops and piles of manure. Horses were king, but by 1911 the streetcar system covered thirty-eight miles and had carried more than six million passengers. Calgary was a city on the go, in love with motion.

After years of argument over a privately built bridge that wobbled across the river at Centre Street, the city finally built the present Centre Street Bridge, its four columns topped by resting lions, crafted by a stonemason named James Thomson in imitation of the lions on Nelson's Column in London, England. The bridge and its felines have recently been refurbished, although the ninety-year-old stone cats were in a sad state and copies had to be recast. But even for a city guarded by a bridge guarded by lions, the bust was coming, and in the fall of 1913 the boom collapsed as energetically as it had started, leaving eerily abandoned streets and the bare skeletons of half-finished buildings, just as another bust would leave cranes stranded in midair in the 1980s.

The winter of 1913–14 was cold and cheerless and shadowed by unemployed men, but Calgary's spirits were lifted by the May 1914 discovery of oil at Turner Valley, when Dingman No. 1 drillers hit oil at 2,700 feet, crude so clear that cars could drive on it. This discovery was almost as crazy as the land boom, and oil became the next lunatic speculation, with people pawning personal effects to raise money to invest, while curb traders, agents, and brokers told tall tales and got into fist fights. Oil-stock promotors echoed all the habits of real estate promoters, but names like Archibald Dingman, together with James Lougheed, A. E. Cross, T. J. S. Skinner, and A. Judson Sayre formed Calgary Petroleum Products Co. Ltd. and the beginning of Alberta's oil patch. Calgary Natural Gas piped gas into the city, and twenty new oil companies invented themselves every week. Alberta's natural resources were then still vested with the federal government, but all that any prospective oil man needed to make a claim was a $5 filing fee, and $80 for the land rental of $.50 per acre per year. Still, the actual findings did not keep up with the bragging; promoters made more money selling stocks in bogus companies than they did from actually selling oil. The biggest profits accrued to printing companies, who ran off beautifully designed share certificates worth nothing. Of the more than five hundred companies that were formed, only nineteen drilled, and only six completed wells. Still, between the fumed oak panels of the newly opened Palliser Hotel, which became a private trading floor, more than $500,000 changed hands every twenty-four hours.

Only the declaration of the First World War slowed the crazy speculation. Then the same men put on their boots and started marching, and the first contingent of soldiers left for England at the end of August 1914. Every day the lists of deaths in the newspapers grew, while women knitted socks and prayed. And that wasn't all Christian and Temperance women did; on July 1, 1916, prohibition hit the well-lubricated city like a shock of cold water. When the men who'd survived returned, drinking returned with a vengeance, along with the Spanish flu and labour unrest. In the spring of 1919 Calgary hosted two major labour meetings: the Western Labour Conference and the BC Federation of Labour conference. Demanding a six-hour day and a five-day week, boilermakers and mine workers, loggers and machinists fought through rowdy meetings where they summarily dismissed their American-based union leaders and set out to form One Big Union, a leftist voice uniting all Canadian workers. When the Winnipeg strike started, Calgary black-smiths, pipefitters, plumbers, and boilermakers walked out in solidarity, although carpenters and electricians kept working. Blaming the unrest on the Bolsheviks, the city encouraged people to hire non-union men, and the federal government fired 185 post office workers. But after two weeks, the striking workers slowly trickled back. The One Big Union seemed to be a qualified failure, but its formation in Calgary suggested the extent to which this now right-of-the-right conservative city once had a labour conscience.

Calgarians have never learned that nature can't be beaten and culture can't be invented. Instead they rely on exaggeration and manic creativity. When times were tight in the early twenties and the city was thinking about cutting wages, city hall got a few threatening letters and a bomb threat. None were treated seriously, but "Chief Buffalo Child Long Lance," whose real name was Sylvester Long, a journalist for the *Calgary Herald*, saw a chance to spark a good story. As the reporter covering city hall, he had an idea of how nervous the city council was. On the very day of the meeting they had convened to discuss the latest threats, Long Lance borrowed a black leather toolbag, a round-faced pres-sure gauge, and a length of fuse, put a handkerchief over his face, and crawled into the mayor's meeting pushing what resembled a bomb ahead of him. Leaving his evocative device and the indelible effect of his bandit face, Long Lance pulled the door closed. Panic erupted. Commissioners ran from the room and jumped out windows, while others sat transfixed in their chairs waiting for the explosion. When they finally realized they had been the butt of a joke—and mainly to provide a reporter with a story—the esteemed city men were furious. The *Herald*, in a departure from its usual bluster, printed an apology and fired Long Lance, who went on to further exploits in Winnipeg and Banff before he was discovered with a bullet through his heart in the mansion of a lady south of the border. His effect, though, lingered. He apparently planned the playful kidnapping of Mayor George Webster at the 1923 Calgary Stampede, when a group of Blackfoot and Sarcee Indians made the mayor cook pancakes and sing cowboy songs on a downtown street to obtain his release, the beginning of

Stampede breakfasts where bank managers and politicians cook flapjacks for ordinary people.

Long before the 1930s, hobo jungles and shantytowns leaned beside the tracks. But despite hard times, between 1921 and 1931, Calgary's population grew to eighty-four thousand people. In February 1929 Eaton's new million-dollar store opened, and the city turned the sod for the Glenmore Reservoir, a massive project that included a dam, an earthen embankment, a water-purification plant, a pumping station, and 270 miles of longed-for watermains, since city taps often ran dry in the summer. At the end of 1930, Calgary was better off than any other Western city; it actually had a balanced budget. But optimism that this was a shortlived depression was soon squelched and Calgary became famous for its soup kitchens and woodpiles. In the spring of 1931 Calgary generously decided that any legitimately needy person could apply for relief, which led to a huge influx of transient men. Desperate to control the numbers, the city stiffened its requirements, which led to unrest and mob violence. In Victoria Park, what was described as the British Empire's biggest soup kitchen fed more than two thousand people a day, using 600 loaves of bread, 170 pounds of butter, 1,100 pounds of beef, a ton of potatoes, 200 pounds of sugar, and 140 gallons of milk. Doctors complained about treating people for free; abandoned wives begged for help; and it was hard to tell whether the relief system was riddled with abuse or utterly overloaded.

The year 1936 was one of bush fires and high winds, but it was also the year the economy turned around, with Turner Valley hitting its biggest crude strike and, in 1937, farmers harvesting a bumper crop. Despite Aberhart's promised reforms, Mayor Andrew Davison, Calgary's kindest and longest-serving mayor, got on the premier's bad side when he refused to accept his prosperity certificates as legitimate currency. But by 1938 prosperity was creeping back, although it would take another war to consolidate its return. When the Second World War broke out, Calgary men, patriotic but even more eager to earn a decent wage, enlisted quickly, and the area became an important centre for airforce training. The Calgary Tanks and the Calgary Highlanders were only two of the many regiments that distinguished themselves in Europe, and the city threw itself into wartime campaigns. Used to doing without, Calgary managed the rationing of gasoline, alcohol, and sugar with good humour, and following its now-determined tradition of community spirit, always exceeded its quotas in the Victory Loan campaigns.

On VE day the entire city thronged the downtown in a celebration that was both a wake for the many men listed as dead or missing and a thanksgiving for those who would return.

Now, like most of the Western World, Calgary entered a slow-rising boom that would last well into the fifties. In 1948 the rookie Calgary Stampeders football team won the Western Conference and the right to challenge the East for the Grey Cup. The game was in Toronto, against the Ottawa Rough Riders, and after the team had left, a group of Calgary boosters decided that they were going east to cheer. They organized a chartered Stampeder Special train that included Sarcee chiefs and chuckwagons and cowboy bands and square dancing, which entertained people at every stop across the country. When they reached Toronto, determined to stop the city in its tracks, they danced with bankers and fed flap-jacks to secretaries, put the mayor on a horse, and seduced the city. Toronto gulped and did stop in its tracks. Centrals had been under the impression that Calgary was a rural city, minding its own business somewhere out west. And to everyone's surprise, the Stampeders won, 12–7. The Calgary fans tore down the goalposts, and if Toronto thought Calgarians were wild before, now they watched dumbfounded. Nobody parties like Calgarians.

In the aftermath of Alberta's late-1940s oil strikes, the city mushroomed, becoming a hotspot for trading, speculators, and bankers. Respectability followed. The normal school became an arm of the University of Alberta's Faculty of Education. The Southern Alberta Jubilee Auditorium raised its rafters to celebrate the province's fiftieth anniversary in 1955. Like Edmonton, Calgary annexed sur-rounding communities. After years of enduring the humiliating experience of being called the University of Alberta at Calgary, students and faculty demon-strated until, in 1966, the provincial government gave in and the University of Calgary gained autonomy, never again having to answer to the parent institution.

Then, in 1967, the city implemented an expensive urban-renewal scheme. Shabby old downtown buildings were dismantled or pulverized, replaced by glass-and-concrete plinths, linked by extensive glass walkways called plus-15s because they ride fifteen feet above the ground, ensuring that no lightly clad oil executive had to walk outside in the winter. Calgary bulldozed its history and invented its future, choosing to transform itself into the most postmodern city in Canada. Intent on private jets, big skies, and soft beds, it did not realize that it was exchanging character for a mess of pottage. Mordecai Richler grumpily commented that the city "looked like it had been uncrated yesterday," a fair assessment. And Walter Chell, the bar manager at the Westin Hotel, invented the Caesar—not the salad, but the drink, a spicy concoction of Clamato juice and lime and pepper swirled with vodka and propping up a celery stick, destined to become the hangover cure for Westerners.

Between 1973 and 1981 Calgary had the boom to end all booms, with real estate shooting through its own roof, and tradesmen and building contractors running to keep up. Branch offices and head offices rolled into town, and prices skyrocketed, at least until the NEP was imposed, but even that didn't put a damper on the city's growth. By 1981 building permits passed $2 billion, and Calgary's growth rate was second only to that of Houston, Texas. The usual array of carpetbagging sophisticates from the Centre arrived, too, happy to collect big salaries and sneer at Cowtown culture while eating in the city's gourmet restaurants, visiting its high-end art galleries, or attending dressage events at Spruce Meadows. Calgary revelled in every sophisticated bend of its elbow, in the authentic Chinese-Calgarian dish called ginger beef, and in its hot new speedway, Deerfoot Trail, named after the Blackfoot runner who was once the fastest man in the West. By 1975, when Deerfoot Trail opened, Calgary had learned the value of its unsung First Nations heroes and was starting to celebrate them.

In the eerie silence following the 1982 bust, regret ruled. People pretended that this was just a hiccup, but bumper stickers saying, "Please God, send me another boom, and I promise I won't piss it all away this time," proliferated. Downsizing and bankruptcies and foreclosures increased exponentially, and Calgarians, riding the bear instead of their usual bull, swore and patched their shacks with cardboard again. How to ride this one out? The city had a Saddledome but no saddle. And then, the usual Calgary solution, well-supported by Mayor Ralph Klein and two energetic boostermen, Bill Pratt and Frank King—throw a really big party, and this time invite the world. The party was the 1988 Winter Olympics. The money came from the province, the feds, and most of all, the citizens themselves, serving the winter games as willing worker bees. Calgary had swallowed its own reputation as volunteer valhalla and it worked. The crazy home of cows and cars managed to pull off the fifteen days of athletic spectacle without breaking the bank. When it was all over, Calgary had made a profit and somehow broken the back of the latest bust. And to ice the party cake, the Calgary Flames, led by Alberta-born Lanny Macdonald, won the 1988–89 Stanley Cup. Slowly, over the next ten years, through Klein cuts and privatizing, the city staggered to its cowboy-booted feet again and imagined the price of oil rising, the politicians falling, and maybe, just maybe, a little more growth and glory.

At the beginning of the nineties, Calgary was one of the best cities in Canada to live in. For a while, it wore a peaceful, almost contemplative air and even began to recover some of its past, opening a reconstructed Fort Calgary, refurbishing the Lougheed house, and remembering the future. It gave the polar bear at the zoo Prozac, put poetry on the buses, and mourned the death of W. O. Mitchell, its great snuff-taker and raconteur. And it mourned its premier historian, Grant MacEwan, the one who had first told Calgary's story. Other mourners watched the destruction of the General Hospital, splintered in a giant explosion that seemed to symbolize Alberta's embattled health care system. But Al Duerr served the decade out as a gentle, responsive mayor, quite unlike the pugilists of the past. The city watched the Boom Town Ghost—one of the buildings left half-unfinished after the 1983 bust—rehabilitated into the Separate School Board's shiny new glass home. It watched million-dollar condominiums mushroom opposite Prince's Island, and microbreweries grow into macrobreweries without spoiling the beer. Now, on the cusp of a million people, Calgary is having another boom, symbolized by sport utility vehicles and road rage and newly hatched vegetarians. The out-of-towners are showing up again, eager for jobs and Golden Fridays (various companies encourage people to work an hour or two longer each day, to earn Fridays off) and high-end dental plans. Because it is the most over-illuminated city in North America, the city moms and dads have now decreed that the streetlights will slowly be replaced with low-wattage bulbs so that the stars are visible again.

And maybe the deer will come out, as they do in the green light of dawn, to nibble suburban grass. Bob Edwards would be proud.

12 | Bread and Circuses, Culture and Bigotry

There is much tea and tennis...'mobiling, dancing, dining and wild riding across
the hills; for when people are healthy and prosperous they are instinctively hos-
pitable, and always in a big-handed, big-hearted way.
— Emily Murphy, *Janey Canuck in the West*

On a sweltering July afternoon, the grandstand at the Calgary Stampede groans under the
weight of thousands of tourists and locals, intent and sweating in their costumes of blue
jeans and cowboy hats. I'm there, bent toward the dust of the infield where a Brahma bull
churns and fishhooks, horns swiping a parabola in the air, the man fastened to his back
like a burr exercising some insane ritual that believes this ton of moving muscle can be
subdued. The clowns dance toward the bull's peripheral vision, their baggy antics frantic
with responsibility. The longest eight seconds in the world, with a man one-tenth the size
of the bull holding only a rope, legs scissoring, head snapping, the animal twisting in a
hallucinatory circle. When the horn blows, both bull and man will try to disentangle
themselves from this brief embrace, the man in his padded vest—that flimsy comfort—
needing to release the rope so that he can fall toward the safe solidity of trundled ground.
And the bull, snorting, red-eyed, having rid himself of another puny frame of blood and
bone, will head for a rest in a winter pasture, to dream of next year's men and circling
horses, next year's unrideable seconds.

Later that evening, in the same grandstand, the klaxon will sound, and the senator of
chuckwagon racing, Joe Carbury, will growl his famous, "And theeey'rrrrre off!"
Thousands of people will rise to their feet in one concerted roar as sixteen horses, four
drivers, and sixteen outriders thread the loop of two barrels and fight for the rail, wagons
and horses and men locked in a dangerous thundering career around the half mile of hell.
The royalty of Alberta chuckwagon families, Glass and Sutherland, Dorchester and
Nevada and Bensmiller, will risk their necks and the necks of four expensive thoroughbred
horses, for money, yes, but mostly for the sheer adrenalin of that heart-stopping race.

The sport was born in that short period of time before barbed wire, when big cattle out-
fits ruled the west. Cowboys hated cooking, and good cooks were highly prized. Getting
food to a nomadic cattle drive was no small feat, and the first chuckwagon was invented

by a Texan who bought an old army wagon and turned it into a travelling pantry and kitchen, complete with stove and water barrel, and covered with a canvas top. Chuckwagons became a necessary fixture of cattle drives, leading the way from camp to camp. And in the Western tradition, competition between outfits led to a little gambling, with one cowboy betting his cook's horses were faster than another's. Those first races, chuckwagons loaded with food and tools and camp supplies, were careering stampedes across the rough, open prairie toward the nearest saloon. Guy Weadick, the American who invented the Calgary Stampede, knew about their legendary thrills and organized the first timed races at Calgary's 1923 Stampede. At those, the drivers were supposed to figure-eight the barrels, race around the track, bring their outfits to a stop, jump off, unhitch their team, and light a cookstove. The first sign of smoke declared a winner.

But speed and cooking don't compete well, and speed has won. Now, collapsible cookstoves are thrown into the back of the wagon by the outriders, and the fastest wagon is the winner, although drivers, outriders, and wagons can lose the race to penalties for anything from wagon interference to knocking down a barrel. This is no rough, amateur race, but a complex mix of horses and harness and weather and temper and track. And it's carefully monitored: the wagons are a standardized weight, the men and horses are tested for drugs, and whips are forbidden.

Still, it's called a killer sport, reckless and inhumane. Yes, horses sometimes die. And men. Human beings haven't changed, and at the Roman circus, death was the biggest attraction. But for all the animal-rights complaints about both rodeo and wagon horses, these animals live well. Bulls and broncs work only a few minutes a year. Chuckwagon horses train for three months, race for three months, and graze the rest of the year. The thoroughbreds are unsuccessful racehorses the drivers buy for this second career. If they weren't pulling a chuckwagon, they'd be waiting in the corral at "the can"—the cannery at Fort Macleod that slaughters and processes fifty thousand horses every year. They're loved and pampered and cared for like children until, hitched together in front of a colourful wagon, a team of four transforms fury into victory.

• • •

In the middle sixties Edmontonian Henry Kreisel, that most Albertan of characters, a Viennese of Jewish heritage who ended up in Canada as a German-speaking enemy alien and ultimately became the vice-president of the University of Alberta, published a brilliant short story called "The Travelling Nude." The story centres on a painter who has a difficult time balancing the demands of daily life and his aspirations as an artist, because no one in Alberta will buy paintings of blue horses or cubist abstractions. He is forced to take a job as an extension lecturer in art, a job that requires him "to travel the length and breadth of the province and give a series of short courses . . . in various small towns," but he is ultimately fired because he decides that his students, who paint nothing but mountains and lakes, need to "be initiated into the secrets of female, figure, sitting, nude." The story beautifully satirizes Alberta culture, an oxymoron that causes derisive chuckles even today. Does Alberta have a culture? Does Alberta's culture go beyond paintings of mountains and novels about the Depression? It does, of course, but in the national register, Alberta's artists, for all their amazing range and sophistication, are treated more like bears raiding a campground than serious practitioners. Outsiders trek here in droves, eager to enjoy the landscape's inspiration, and from Paul Kane to the current inhabitants of Banff's Leighton Colony, visiting Alberta is just fine. But painting and writing and singing in Alberta? Surely Alberta is too unsophisticated to have a cultural identity.

Culture in Alberta has always been confused with sport and spectacle. We don't like our culture lying on a plate, boring and passive. We want it alive, biting back, an articulation of our love for carnival, for excess and excitement. Early entertainment was a mixture of song and dance, booze and gambling, and those escape routes are still an important part of our cultural life, even though we now have our share of symphonies, performers who win accolades on European tours, writers who win Governor General's Awards, painters who exhibit all over the world, and filmmakers who run off to New York.

In early Alberta, children were sent outside to entertain themselves, and childhood was short. John Nyman of High River went to work on the Bar U when he was only eleven. One of his jobs was to crawl into wolf dens to kill wolves. Chores were part of children's lives, feeding and watering horses, milking cows, chopping wood, or hauling water. Because of the work expectations that children faced, high-toned morals were difficult to impose, and the very air contributed to a healthy rebelliousness, which was about having a good time, dancing, drinking, smoking, and joyriding. And for all Alberta's Bible-belt reputation, more people went dancing than went to church.

Deerfoot, the fastest runner in the West

Glenbow Archives, Calgary, Canada: NA-250-3

Historically, the province has been more interested in gambling than gentility, and wagering incited Alberta's first spectator sports. It was John Palliser, in 1859, who proposed that several Blackfoot Indians run a foot race for his entertainment. Deerfoot, the fastest runner on the prairies, proved that the Mounties could be outrun, and in 1886 at a specially arranged race trounced two challengers from Britain and Ottawa. The problem was, his backers had bet against him. His life, too, bet against him. He ended up in and out of jail for various crimes and misdemeanours, and ultimately died of tuberculosis, although he is remembered as one of the swiftest Albertans ever. Canada's first native police officer, Alex Decoteau of Edmonton, was an outstanding runner as well, breaking middle-distance records between 1909 and 1916. He was the one Alberta representative at the Stockholm Olympics in 1912. He joined the Canadian army in the First World War and was killed in action in 1917.

Horse racing is more indigenous to Alberta than any other sport, and Edmonton still holds the world record in per capita betting on the horses. The first races were always won by First Nations ponies, whose sure-footed flight over the prairie or the parkland put the thoroughbred Mountie horses to shame. Horse breeders and race weeks, turf clubs and polo tournaments, gymkhanas and driving clubs flourished, and still do. Alberta has more horses than any other province, and any attempt to limit parimutuel betting would fail. Early British settlers turned up their noses at the rough-and-ready horsemanship of the West, preferring polo. The Sons of England were so good at polo that a High River group won the Canadian championships in 1905 in Toronto, baffling everyone. Even in 2000,

Cowboy biting the dust at the Stampede, 1923

when trainers and grooms, who sleep above the stables at Northlands Park, might have been evicted because there was no contract settlement for harness racers, horse lovers in Edmonton started counting the days of racing they might or might not enjoy. Nothing matters as much as racing days.

The Calgary Stampede mixes man, cow, and horse sport. Begun with the Dominion Exhibition of 1908, which advertised, "Visit Alberta before the Golden Opportunities, Picturesque Riders, and Indians are Gone," it could never have predicted its own longevity. The first successful rodeo, backed by the Big Four— Pat Burns, Alfred E. Cross, George Lane, and Archie McLean, all of whom had made a fortune on cattle—took place in 1912, then reprised in 1923, and finally became an annual extravaganza in 1932. Guy Weadick, the American trick rider who put the event together, wanted a copyright on the celebration, and when the Stampede board refused to do that or to pay him what he thought was enough, he got excessively drunk and at the closing ceremonies in 1932 shouted, "I put on your first Stampede and I've just put on your last." Someone pulled the plug on the microphone, but Weadick was still fired. He sued for wrongful dismissal, which the Stampede Board defended by pleading that Weadick's drinking had interfered with his ability to do his job. But in one of those cultural reversals Alberta is so famous for, the judge said that drinking was part of Weadick's job as Stampede promoter and awarded him six months' salary and legal costs. Weadick wasn't welcomed back until the Stampede's fortieth anniversary, the year before he died in 1953. Buried in the High River cemetery, he still haunts the Calgary Stampede grounds, and of a chill November evening his ghost rides through the Round-up Centre.

Albertans have a soft spot for reformed criminals and Wild West characters. When Buffalo Bill Cody visited Edmonton with the Sells-Floto Circus in July 1914, he was treated like a king, although he didn't do much more than smooth his goatee and award prizes for an essay contest on "Who is Buffalo Bill?" sponsored by the *Edmonton Journal*. Edmonton hoped he'd become a local booster, and he teased the city fathers, saying, "I will have to move to Alberta myself, for there are now more buffalo here than in any other part of the world."

Edmonton's Exhibition, a mixture of agricultural fair and circus, was first held in November of 1879. In 1918, as a publicity stunt for the Ex, American aviatrix Katherine Stinson made the first airmail delivery in Western Canada, flying up from Calgary with the mail. Over time, the Exhibition kept changing, until in 1962, searching for a catchy theme, it was renamed Klondike Days, in honour of the gold seekers who used the Overland route. The Exhibition, while a chance to watch horse races and play the midway, has never enjoyed quite the thematic focus or intense participation of southern rodeos, and by the 1990s the Klondike theme was faltering.

Edmontonians relish a circus more than most, but the most unusual three-ring was the Sells-Floto Circus in 1926, when a dog's barking frightened fourteen elephants into breaking their chains and stampeding through the streets. They trumpeted down Jasper Avenue, trampling fences and gardens and veering through alleys. They smashed trees and sidewalks, terrifying citizens and charging the keepers who pursued them. They were finally retrieved when the circus trainers used a tamer older elephant as a lure.

Imported exotic animals, risk-taking acrobats, and the less savoury displays of side-shows pushed highbrow culture aside. Albertans loved the excesses of circuses, hot-air balloons, flying machine demonstrations, aeronauts making parachute jumps, high-wire performers, and necromancers. Vaudeville attractions included performing dogs, trick bicyclists, and battle-axe jugglers. One travelling midway passing through Calgary in 1922 presented a young mule deer—for some reason they couldn't take the deer with them—to the Calgary Street Railway. What they thought the street railway would do with it is hard to imagine, but the deer occupied a green spot in Bowness Park and was later moved to St. George's Island, the first animal in the Calgary Zoo.

Early sport followed the seasons. Hunting preceded winter, and the first snowfall reduced everyone to drinking or pool until curling came along. One day in 1890, a bunch of bored Mounties resorted to golf, starting a craze that opens a new course every year. Bars served as informal betting houses, and wagers could be placed on the outcome of virtually any game. Lacrosse attracted large and unruly crowds, eager for bloody fights and blows to the head. At one Strathcona match, the spectactors beat someone (probably a referee) senseless. Baseball, by comparison, was a mild sport, although there were a few instances of umpire buying. Still, the Western Canadian Baseball League fans would sometimes beat players up, and the brawling league was finally suspended in 1914. Again and again, small towns, bigger towns, and Edmonton and Calgary worked out their local pride through competition. Early competition between the Calgary Tigers and the Edmonton Eskimos was so fierce that in 1913 they had to play at Red Deer, because neither would even set foot on the other's home ground.

More than any other sport, hockey matches led to spectacular rivalries. Begun in the 1890s, hockey took off in Alberta like a rocket. As early as 1908 the Edmonton Hockey Club played for the Stanley Cup, but did not win. In May of 1948 the Edmonton Flyers won the Allan Cup, the prize for senior amateur hockey, by defeating the Ottawa Senators. More than sixty thousand people, almost half the city, greeted the Flyers with a victory parade for Edmonton's first major team trophy. In March of 1950 the Edmonton Waterloo Mercurys won the world amateur hockey title, and in February of 1952 the same team won hockey's gold medal at the Olympics in Oslo, Norway. In May of 1963 the Edmonton Oil Kings (now Edmonton Oilers) won their first Memorial Cup.

In 1980, after a brief fling with the now defunct World Hockey Association, Calgary bought the Atlanta Flames, gaining an NHL franchise, and the tension between Calgary and Edmonton got higher and higher. The first owners were a conglomerate of businessmen less interested in the team as a financial deal than as a symbol of civic pride. They stayed in the background, leaving franchise policies to the president of the team. But the Calgary Corral was too small an arena, and while the Saddledome was being built—it was completed in 1983—Edmonton trounced Calgary year after year until finally in 1986 Calgary was able to beat Edmonton. They won the Stanley Cup in 1989.

In recent years neither the Flames nor the Oilers have been doing much winning. The Oilers lose; the Flames lose; the Oilers lose. There are still battles of Alberta, but they are less passionate than in the 1980s. By 2000 the Flames were playing so badly that the fans referred to them as the Lames. Still, a recidivist pride keeps people going to the games, although not nearly as many as in the winning days, when Calgary's downtown was awash in red jerseys and the stands in the Saddledome were a sea of red. Fan disillusionment in both cities has taken its toll. When the players seem only interested in money, when the owners see a city as only a means to make money, and when the game itself has become a commercial zone, everybody loses. It might take another Gretzky to make people believe again.

Skiing and ski jumping are sports naturally supported by Alberta's landscape and climate, and the mountain slopes have encouraged skiers for decades. The first skis touched Banff snow in 1894, when a Norwegian sent a pair of the boards to a friend. In 1910 Conrad Kain brought some skis from Austria, built a small jump on Tunnel Mountain, and the sport was off, but alpine skiing didn't really get going until the 1930s when Banff hosted the Dominion Ski Championships. The Crazy Canucks of the 1970s, fearless daredevils, really made Alberta snow famous. And skiing showcases Alberta's wilderness playgrounds, Banff and Jasper. Albertans can gloat that these two national parks are bigger than some Canadian provinces, and bigger than most European countries.

Indians had always lived in the exquisitely beautiful Bow Valley, but the ferocity of the Blackfoot for a long time kept traders and travellers away from southern Alberta's mountains. Only in the 1870s did the first surveyors reach the Rockies, and it took the railway to open the area to white travellers. The CPR arrived at Banff in the winter of 1883, the same winter that William Van Horne visited and proposed building a resort there. The First Peoples knew about the mysterious healing waters that steamed out of a crevasse at Sulphur Mountain, but three

Skiing in Alberta

railway workers saw the spring as a chance to make money; they staked a claim and sold baths to railway workers and miners (who probably needed them). As soon as the railway was built, tourists began to take the CPR's open observation cars through the Rockies. By 1900 Rocky Mountains National Park, established in 1887, entertained eight thousand visitors, most of them wealthy tourists from outside the West. Meanwhile, interest in the medicinal properties of the springs grew, until Dr. R. G. Brett, medical supervisor for the CPR, promised the cure of clear mountain air at the Brett Sanitarium. When the Banff Springs Hotel opened in 1888, it boasted 250 rooms, the largest hotel in the world. But the foolish architect had designed it so that the kitchens overlooked the river valley, while the guest rooms faced the forest. With typical decisiveness, Van Horne turned it around so that guests would get the benefit of scenery. The Banff Springs became a premier destination, turning away so many guests that it had to expand, and seeing the potential, the CPR built a log chalet farther west at Lake Louise in 1890. Banff was a CPR town, with CPR hotels, CPR restaurants, and CPR outfitters for the recreational climbers eager to test the slopes. But when one amateur mountaineer fell to his death, the CPR wisely imported professional Swiss guides to lead intrepid ascents.

Jasper, named after an early North West Company clerk, Jasper Hawes, grew more slowly than Banff because it was so difficult to reach. Only in the 1920s, much later than Banff, did the northern park become a tourist destination, but even then the road wasn't great, and Jasper became readily accessible only in the 1940s. One way to be overwhelmed by scenery is to drive the most incredible highway in the world, the Banff-Jasper highway, which was built as a labour project during the 1930s, nature curing unemployment.

Alberta's less famous mountain beauty spot, Waterton Lakes National Park, was named by Palliser expedition member Thomas Blakiston after an English ornithologist, Charles Waterton, who never saw it. Waterton's original hunter and guide, Kootenai Brown, lived there from 1879 till the end of his life; it would have been more fitting to let the park keep his name. And in the northeast of the province, Elk Island National Park lives in solitary grace as a conservation area for moose, deer, buffalo, and elk. These parks are Alberta's playgrounds, but they are Canadian territory, and inevitably there has been conflict between Parks Canada and park users. The biggest challenge for conservationists is to reduce the impact of visitors, even while more and more of them arrive in search of a natural world fast vanishing. Although it might seem that these parks make every Albertan a nature lover, most visitors never get out of their vehicles. Automobiling was an early sport in Alberta, relished for speed. Albertans are restless, and driving is a singularly competitive activity that has grown worse with the advent of "suburban assault vehicles" on both rural and urban roads.

Only driving has replaced pugilistic Alberta's interest in boxing. In the late eighteenth and early nineteenth centuries, intense and unprovoked matches took place in smoke-filled basements or old barns, abandoned buildings or tents outside city limits. Illegal fights were frequent, and if the police raided them the spectators just jumped out of the windows and ran away. So popular was the sport that prizefighters would show up in Calgary and spread the word that they wanted a challenger, leading to unpredictable matches—the police and fire chief would not only look the other way but serve as referees. Calgary's reputation as the capital of fist fighting was almost interrupted in 1909 when the city council voted to ban all boxing and sparring events where admission was charged, although free events were fine. But that didn't stop Tommy Burns, a prizefighter, from moving to Calgary as a promoter in 1910. He built a stadium just outside the city limits to avoid breaking the law and orchestrated some amazing fights, including a famous Victoria Day match between Arthur Pelkey and Luther McCarty. The first round had barely begun when McCarty collapsed on the floor and subsequently died of a blood clot. Pelkey was charged with manslaughter, although the jury found that he was not responsible. Four days after the fight, professional boxing was banned, and Burns became a fire-breathing evangelist, putting a damper on pugilistic fun for some years to come.

Walter Twinn, chief of the Sawridge Creek band, was another boxer who made the gyms of Edmonton thud. Although he suffered the hard knocks of residential school and grew up poor, Twinn met luck when his reserve struck oil in the 1960s. As chief, he was willing to use the white man's tools to get a leg up for his band, which some saw as cultural betrayal. But as a boxer and a boxing promoter who tried to use the sport to give tough aboriginal kids an outlet for their aggression, he was admired and recognized. Boxing matches still find a big audience; the province likes blood, and out in the country, if you know where to find them, illegal bare-knuckled matches still go on.

Wrestling too is an Alberta preoccupation, arguably best burnished by Stu Hart's infamous Stampede Wrestling. Known as the King of Harts, Stu Hart initiated the pyrotechnics of pro wrestling, now carried to extremes in the World Wrestling Federation. Premier Ralph Klein's father, Phil, wrestled as "the Phantom" and "the Mask." It all began when Stu Hart, a scrawny teenager in Edmonton in 1930, was taken under the wing of British Empire champion Jack Taylor, who taught him the fundamentals of "submission," or amateur, wrestling. Hart's first major match came in 1937, when he won the Canadian Nationals. He won again in 1938, but in 1939 was run over by a fire engine and broke his back. Doctors said he would never fight again, but like most pugilists he was stubborn, and he set out to prove them wrong. He was soon back in the ring, even considered a possible gold medallist in the 1940 Olympics, which were cancelled by the Second World War. Needing to make a living, Hart moved to Calgary and decided to go professional. By 1946 he was a rising star, and in late 1948 decided to start his own ring in Calgary. Over the next four decades he produced some of wrestling's most celebrated performers, including his legendary sons. Saturday-afternoon Stampede Wrestling, hosted by personality Ed Whalen, who is credited with such vernacular expressions as "ring-a-ding-dong-dandy" and "malfunction at the junction," was pure Alberta. Hart trained all manner of wrestlers in the basement—the Dungeon—of his west Calgary home. The Hart sons remember the groans and screams that filtered from that basement, and their father's unremitting ability to hold the strongest man down. In 1980, though, disillusioned by the sport's craziness, Stu shut down Stampede Wrestling, and the Hart boys ultimately signed with the World Wrestling Federation. Together, they formed the Hart Foundation, which included Bret "the Hitman" Hart, Owen Hart, Jim "the Anvil" Neidhart, and Davey Boy Smith, all ruled by patriarch Stu. Bret "the Hitman" Hart left the WWF when his character was transformed from a hero into a villain, and he has since moved to World Championship Wrestling. But when Owen Hart was killed in a freak stunt at a WWF competition in 1999 and his wife sued the WWF for damages, the family was angry and divided. Wrestling is not a "safe" sport, and this family doesn't take sides against it. For all the tawdry operatics of television wrestling, Stu Hart is a modest, self-effacing man who has never forgotten his Alberta roots—he and his family still live in Calgary. Although frail and wheelchair-bound now, Hart represents the wonderful extravagance that has come to symbolize professional wrestling.

It might seem as if all this gambling and nose busting leaves no room for music or literature, but Alberta takes high culture as seriously as low. The Edmonton Opera company, born of the Edmonton Operatic and Dramatic Society, formed in November 1903, despite the difficulties of importing costumes and finding good tenors and baritones. The Calgary Opera House and Hull's Opera House early on staged *The Geisha*, *Ten Nights in a Bar Room*, and *Uncle Tom's Cabin*, as well as Shakespeare and novelty acts (contortionists and sword swallowers that William would have approved of). At first Edmonton had no theatre company and no real stage; instead, everything from legislative sessions to hockey games took place in the Thistle Rink. But that changed with Alexander Cameron, a cultural maverick who hosted performances at theatres he built, the Empire and the Edmonton Opera House, the Kevin and the Lyric. Visiting vaudeville acts showcased ventriloquists and trained dogs, singers, and jugglers. But the war and moving pictures shut down vaudeville, although vaudeville's cousin, the travelling Chautauqua shows, lasted a bit longer. They toured Alberta offering everything from uplifting lectures to songs. Until 1935, when they folded their tents, Chautauqua's entire Canadian operation was organized out of Calgary.

Live entertainment's demise was hastened by movies. By 1910 there were a good number of theatres in Alberta, their names as poetic as the dreams they hawked—Bijou, Garland, Dreamland, Orpheum, Princess. Movies cost only five to fifteen cents, but upright citizens were nervous about their depiction of crime and murder, and in 1915 moralistic Alberta appointed its own censor, R. B. Chadwick. He took his job seriously and banned moving pictures of the World Championship boxing match, which did not please boxing-crazy Albertans. Howard Douglas, who replaced Chadwick, was content to let the exhibitors snip out potentially offensive sections, and he stored all the cut-out bits in Alberta's Celluloid Morgue, which by 1921 contained ten thousand feet of excised film. Forbidden were portrayals of vampires, drunkenness, drug addiction, robbery, immodest dancing, counterfeiting, white slavery, gruesome bloodshed or corpses, and ridicule of races or classes, but Alberta's censorship was supposedly one of the most liberal in Canada. Movies were not to exhibit women in nightdresses and lingerie, and were definitely admonished to avoid sensual kissing and lovemaking. Nellie McClung urged that women should be allowed to sit on the censorship board—to protect children, of course.

By the 1930s, when money grew scarcer, only eighty-five theatres remained open in Alberta. Instead, listening to radio replaced outings. And Alberta's bad roads and worse weather made the wireless an instant hit, especially since signals were easily picked up by remote farm, as well as town, receivers. At High River W. W. Grant set up what would eventually become Alberta's most powerful broadcasting frequency, CFCN, which he called "the Voice of the Prairies." Radio combined entertainment, news, and education, and Bible Bill Aberhart used the medium to convince Alberta voters that his Socred Party represented all three. Soon other religious groups saw the advantage of the airwaves. When CJCA broadcast the boxing match between Jack Dempsey and Gene Tunney in 1927, the Jehovah's Witness church group who shared the frequency simply started broadcasting over the match, and listeners were furious. Radio wars were conducted between church broadcasts, one openly attacking another. When the Jehovah's Witness station charged the Catholic church with persecution, the federal broadcasting regulators had had enough, and stopped licensing church-owned broadcasting stations, a ban that would last until 1996.

CKUA broadcast extension courses from the University of Alberta and ultimately became the Edmonton outlet for the CBC. It taught on-air foreign languages and courses in zoology, and for refreshment it transmitted recitals. There were even rules for how to listen to the radio—if the national anthem was played, everyone was supposed to stand up. Live music and drama reached into living rooms both rich and poor. Radio was a boon for writers, the democratic theatre of the 1930s and 1940s. Alberta playwrights Elsie Park Gowan and Gwen Pharis Ringwood wrote more than two hundred radio dramas. And radio introduced stars who became more than local. When Wilf Carter first moved to Calgary in 1923, he sang and yodelled in bunkhouses and at dances until in 1930, he conducted his first radio broadcast on CFCN. He wasn't the only singer made famous by radio—Edmontonian Robert Goulet got his start there, and jazz legend Big Miller played for CKUA.

Serious music was another matter entirely and Calgary's Symphony, the first ever organized in a city of fewer than 200,000, was founded in 1913 through public fundraising. Edmonton at first focused on choral music, but in November 1920 the Edmonton Symphony raised the baton to its first concert. Because of the Depression, it was disbanded in 1932, but then reformed in 1952. In 1946 the Alberta government established the Alberta Music Board to promote local musical talent. The Jubilee Auditoriums, built in honour of Alberta's fiftieth birthday, gave each city a well-appointed concert hall. Today classical new music ranges from aurages to neo-consonance, with composers like Violet Archer, Quenten Doolittle, Malcolm Forsyth, Robert Rosen, Andrew Creaghan, Gordon Nicholson, Jacobus Kloppers, J. P. Christopher Jackson, Allan Gordon Bell, and Rolf Boon all coming out of Alberta.

Other music drifts through streets and concert halls, across the green grass of outdoor festivals. Country singers George Fox and Ian Tyson, queen of heartache Jann Arden, Huevos Rancheros, Cindy Church, k. d. lang, and Tom Jackson all hail from Alberta. And despite their international stardom, many still call Alberta home—k. d. lang visits her mother in Corsort, Ian Tyson gets an honorary degree from the University of Calgary, and Jann Arden can stroll into her favourite diner and have a piece of pie.

We're a literate bunch too. We borrow more books per capita from our libraries than any other province. And as for our writers, Alberta writing is a hotbed of activity that has been growing for more than a hundred years. In the late 1800s

Ralph Connor (Charles William Gordon), author of countless morally uplifting novels, lived in Banff for three years, and because Alberta had such an effect on him, set most of his novels here. The province also inspired a number of Pauline Johnson's poems. Arthur Stringer (*Prairie Stories*), Nellie McClung (*Purple Springs*), and Robert Stead (*The Cow Puncher*) wrote books that reveal the mixed agrarian and reformist world of Alberta in the early decades of the twentieth century. Earle Birney, who was born in Calgary in 1904, lived in Banff until 1922. His first poems evoke the Rockies that he knew so well, most famously the poem "David," about two friends who are mountain climbers.

But these writers were only the beginning, preludes to Henry Kreisel and Ross Annett and W. O. Mitchell, whose incredible depictions of prairie life still resonate. Mitchell especially mined the emotion of prairie experience as no other writer has. At the same time, Sheila Watson was writing her modern benchmark, *The Double Hook* (1959) and Rudy Wiebe and George Ryga were exploring their social and cultural displacements, Wiebe in novels and short stories and Ryga in drama. Expatriate Robert Kroetsch was beginning his hyperbolic depictions of Alberta as a tall tale. Kroetsch recalls that when his novel, *The Studhorse Man* (1960), was about to come out, he had lunch in New York with his editor and agent. Chatting over strawberries and salmon, the agent suddenly asked, "Now, Robert. Tell me. This Alberta that you write about. Is it a real place or did you make it up?"

It would have to be invented, over and over again. Thomas King, who taught native studies at the University of Lethbridge for ten years, uses Alberta as the mythical setting for not only his novels, but for his wonderful radio series, *The Dead Dog Café*. Greg Hollingshead, whose amazing short stories trace a revival of the form, will serve as the next writing director of the Banff Centre for the Arts. Playwrights Sharon Pollock and John Murrell, Brad Fraser and Eugene Stickland stage groundbreaking plays in the footlights of the foothills.

Poets have planted gardens all over the province. Wilfred Watson, Charles Noble, Stephen Scobie, Douglas Barbour, Jon Whyte, Dorothy Livesay, Claire Harris, Bert Almon, Christopher Wiseman, and Leona Gom are only a handful of many who crank out unforgettable lines.

Meanwhile, other scribes wrote history and biography, politics and identity. Myrna Kostash echoes her Ukrainian heritage in *All of Baba's Children* (1977), and Douglas Cardinal speaks the unspeakable in *The Unjust Society* (1969) about

Canada's treatment of First Nations people, while Maria Campbell's *Halfbreed* (1973) dissects the life of a Métis woman. Such fine historians as J. G. MacGregor, Grant MacEwan, and Hugh Dempsey have now been joined by cultural commentators like Fred Stenson, Sid Marty, and George Melnyk, whose two-volume *Literary History of Alberta* is a major overview of Alberta writers and writing. And newer writers have begun to call to readers from the shelves of bookstores and libraries. David Albahari, Peter Oliva, Rosemary Nixon, Yasmin Ladha, Ken McGoogan, Suzette Mayr, Roberta Rees, Nicole Markotic, Thomas Wharton, Todd Babiuk, Pamela Banting, Candas Jane Dorsey, and Anita Badami bring to Alberta literature fresh eyes and images. These writers happily upset any notion of Alberta writing as conservative or culturally central. And these are only well-known names; hundreds of others contribute to the word-portrait of this impossible place. Fred Stenson's *The Trade* (2000), a brilliant historical revision of how this province was shaped by the fur trade, and Thomas Wharton's *Salamander* (2001), which imagines the world through the strange mystery of type, are two recent books that symbolize the power and sophistication of Alberta writing now.

There are and have been as many artists as there are writers, and to list them all would require another book. Suffice to say that a museum of art, which grew into the Edmonton Art Gallery, was begun as early as 1923, and the Banff Centre, as well as province-wide art groups and schools—most notably the Alberta College of Art and Design—have helped to establish a thriving visual arts community that paints far more than mountains and lakes.

Alberta has served as a film location since 1910's *An Unselfish Love*, but better known are *The Calgary Stampede* (1925), *His Destiny* (1928), *Little Big Man* (1969), *Days of Heaven* (1976), and *Superman* (1977). Indigenous films, like Anne Wheeler's *Loyalties* (1985) and *Bye Bye Blues* (1988), demonstrate an excellence that doesn't need to look to the Centre for either approval or money. And more than one Alberta local has a story about running into Brad Pitt at a club or sitting next to Clint Eastwood at a sushi bar.

But our own culture is quite another matter, and abashed and self-conscious, we're uneasy about how good it actually is. We need more practice bragging about our artists. The names mentioned here are merely a fraction of the talent that makes art and culture so alive in this province. Albertans have such a wealth of things to see and do that choosing an entertainment can be wrenching. Now mini-festivals of Beethoven rub shoulders with the physical theatre of High-Performance Rodeo, and Handel's *Messiah* precedes Alberta Theatre Projects PlayRites Festival. Edmonton and Calgary have more theatres per capita than any other cities in the country, and stage local plays, Canadian plays, and international plays. The faux-Edinburgh Edmonton Fringe Festival, North America's first and biggest, features mummers and jugglers, serious Shakespeare, and Cirque everything. It follows Edmonton's International Jazz Festival and the Folk Music Festival and the Film Festival and the Heritage Festival, where true Alberta culture is cooked up out of a mélange of ethnicities. Just down the road, there's country music at the Big Valley Jamboree, and a few months later, in Calgary, the world's best young pianists compete at the Esther Honens International Piano Competition. That's after the summer's festivals. Meanwhile, the dance companies, Dancewest, Decidedly Jazz Danceworks, Springboard Dance, and Alberta Ballet, both traditional and outrageous, perform; while in Banff, every variety of cultural expression competes with the silent mountains. There's too much to do and too little time to do it, from the Pyrogy Festival in Glendon to the Banff Mountain Book and Film Festival, to the Alberta Provincial Plowing Competition in Wanham to the Alix Wagon Wheel Museum to the Fête franco-albertaine in Edmonton to the Great Canadian Barn Dance at Hill Spring.

• • •

If Canada is none too eager to believe that Alberta has a culture, the entire country has no compunction about awarding this province first prize for bigotry. Redneck Alberta, intolerant and racist, conservative and neo-Christian, suspicious of anything new, home of white supremacists, gun lovers, and not a few book-banning school boards. True or false? Like any other place in Canada, both true *and* false. The most inarguable truth is that Albertans have never been quiet about their prejudices. As with any world in flux, Alberta staggered from one surprising change to the next, with people continually having to adjust their actions and their ways of measuring others. And while there are no excuses for people's worst behaviours, this place first struggled with and then faced sweeping changes, coming head to head with its own confusions, and in a brusque, completely unabashed way has come to embrace people that at one time scared the hell out of us.

European occupation of what were boundless Indian territories was the first act of dispossession, but the irrefutable racism that First Nations people continue to experience is still an issue neither abstract nor dismissable. The tug-of-war between newcomers and indigenous people has never been resolved. Uneasily, the shift from a reciprocal relationship to a dependent one cast the aboriginal peoples onto the mercy of white man's justice and white man's government. While Albertans have never thought it right to mistreat their original occupants, they have taken for granted their exploitation. Alberta's First Peoples have their own opinions about fat cats and administrators, the hurt and suffering of the residential-school system. Some are called status aboriginal and some are called non-status aboriginal, although the difference is often arbitrary. Ralph Klein recently appointed Métis Pearl Calahasen as minister of aboriginal affairs and northern development, but government has a vested interest in smoothing the path between business and anyone who might get in the way of business. And the facts hover. Unemployment for natives runs around 70 percent. Even though only 6 percent of the province's population is native, 40 percent of inmates in Alberta's jails are native. The suicide rate for natives is twenty times the national average. But statistics obscure the human face of people whose only desire, in this affluent, speed-obsessed present, is to be granted space and respect, and who in a very few decades have made enormous leaps, from a nomadic freedom to agrarian confinement to industrial sophistication.

After First Nations women were cast aside by the European newcomers in favour of white wives, the early social trust of the West was broken, resulting in wary suspicion, the unease of people who no longer share common desires. Difference became a marker rather than commonplace and accepted. In the early West, race and colour were far less fraught than they would become by the end of the 1800s. In 1822 Pierre Bungo, the first black man to spend time working at Edmonton House, aroused the curiosity of the Indians, who called him an odd white man. Sixty years later, speedy Alberta justice ensured that a black man in Bassano was arrested, tried, sentenced, and in jail by the evening of the same day. A white culprit would hardly have been treated to similar efficiency.

And Alberta's reaction to Ukrainians was distinctly unfriendly when the new settlers arrived. In 1905, when the southern part of the province realized that the election had not put them in a favourable position for influencing Ottawa, the

Calgary Herald complained, "A hoard of Polacks and Galicians and innumerable pug uglies has inflicted the province with a form of government that is contrary to British traditions of law and fair play." The terms "Bohunk" (meaning Bohemian and Ukrainian) or "Hunky" (Hungarian) were often inaccurately applied to Ukrainians. Alberta hadn't had much practice at geography and there was general confusion over where people came from and what their social or political origins implied. Central Europeans, who comprised the big wave of immigration in the early 1900s, were called "Sifton's dirty Slavs." In the corrupt 1913 Alberta election, Andrew Shandro, running as an independent Liberal in the riding of Whitford, become the first person of Ukrainian background to win a seat in the legislature. But his election was challenged, an inquiry determined that he had bribed the voters, and he was ousted. Other elections were not challenged, although bribery and corruption were rampant. Would an Anglo representative have been pursued so thoroughly?

Other notions persisted, too. Italians, Greeks, and Jews were thought unsuitable as farmers. Mormons were excoriated for practising polygamy, and concerted attempts were made to restrict their right to buy land. Yet less than forty years before the Mormons arrived in Alberta, polygamy had flourished among both white and First Nations men. Now polygamy was treated as shameful, repulsive, and Mormons were harassed until they renounced the practice. People were afraid of "foreigners," but everyone was a foreigner, including the people who used that word most. These racial and ethnic restrictions were supported by various theories on race, nationality, and religion, such as J. C. Woodsworth's *Strangers Within Our Gates*, which catalogued immigrants according to their desirability and argued that only the most intelligent and "progressive" should be allowed to enter Canada. Dismissals of various European immigrants as quarrelsome, animal, sluggish, or unfit to be trusted coloured both official policy and unofficial behaviour. Concern about how to make these settlers "assimilate" preoccupied various government departments and bodies, as did questions of eugenics. And in 1923 Alberta passed an act that allowed the sexual sterilization of "mental defectives" to prevent them from multiplying.

Blacks and Asians aroused incredible xenophobia. Despite discouragement and harassment, there were, by 1911, some one thousand black settlers in the province, farming quietly, usually in communities of their own like Amber Valley or Keystone. Edmonton had few black residents, but the city was not welcoming; the board of trade tried to impose a $1,000 head tax on all non-white immigrants, but without authority to do so had to settle for a committee to look into the matter instead. A petition to exclude non-white immigrants was circulated, and garnered more than three thousand names. Red Deer joined the racist reaction, stating that "blacks were an undesirable class of settler." Calgary imitated Edmonton; blacks were commonly refused service and barred from public places. Lethbridge behaved slightly better, the *Herald* observing that if a man had the ability to turn bald prairie into a fruitful farm, the colour of his skin did not matter. It seemed as if the more established cities, already settling into social concrete, were the most likely to practise discrimination.

Albertans were most vociferous about the Chinese, who had built the CPR, burying a fellow worker's body beside every mile of track. When the government of Canada refused to pay their passage home, they had no choice but to stay and survive as well as they could. Coal miners hated them because they thought the Chinese would provide cheap labour and rob them of their jobs. Relegated to domestic work, work that the "real men" of the prairies had no interest in doing, they set up laundries and restaurants in every prairie town. But their position was tenuous. The *Banff Crag and Canyon* reported that "Chinamen" and white men mix no better "than glue and perfume." The *Lethbridge Herald* argued that Alberta should deny people of Japanese and Chinese descent the vote, as well as any right to compete with white labour. During the Depression, Chinese were given only $1.12 a week for relief, compared with non-Chinese, who received $2.50 a week— and three unemployed Chinese men literally starved to death in the winter of 1936. Shunned by whites, these lonely men grouped in "Chinatowns" and then had to face misperceptions about their ghettoized life. When Calgary Chinese pooled their money to buy property in the area around Centre Street in Calgary, white businesses protested furiously.

When, in 1892, a laundryman was diagnosed with smallpox, Calgarians panicked. Wanting to eradicate not the smallpox but the Chinese, whom they saw as unclean, three hundred drunken whites attacked Chinatown and tried to burn it down. In this "smallpox riot," the laundry where the man worked was burned down, and all the Chinese in the city were placed under quarantine—virtually imprisoned. Worried that all the other laundries would be ordered closed, Chung

Gee and Chung Yan, his brother, left Calgary for Edmonton and almost vanished from sight—until the *Edmonton Bulletin* reported that Chung Yan was responsible for starting a fire by leaving hot ashes near a stable. The Chinese were blamed for every social evil, with horrific results. In 1907 a Lethbridge mob attacked a Chinese restaurant because a Chinese man had allegedly killed a white person with a hammer. The rumour was false, but the riot was real enough and the mob smashed all the Chinese restaurants on main street and threw stones at the people. In November of 1910 Lethbridge Chinese laundries and restaurants were banned from operating in the city's north ward, supposedly to protect the area from smells and noises associated with the two. The Lethbridge Steam Laundry, however, which was run by whites, was exempted from the ban. If local rowdies wanted to hurt someone, they inevitably picked on the weakest link, so there were frequent cases of gangs or groups of rough men robbing Chinese restaurants or assaulting their proprietors. Penalties for that behaviour meant nothing, although sometimes glimmers of compassion showed through. In 1905, in a case in Edmonton, one Chinese filed an action against another, charging him with stealing $295. Recognition that these men shared a different language was a small gesture of acceptance, and the swearing-in was in Chinese. But there were frequent editorials in all of Alberta's newspapers calling on the Alberta government to disenfranchise the Japanese and the Chinese.

Chinatowns, communities discrete from the Caucasian world around them, became a part of the burgeoning West. There are few first-hand accounts of the way that early Chinese-Albertans lived—they were too busy trying to survive. A 1908 article in the *Edmonton Bulletin* described Chinese businesses as mysteriously exotic. "In the Chinese stores queer wares are on sale; the long strange pipes of the Celestials, strange looking masses of Chinese foods, lacquer work, ivory carvings, silk clothing and other curious and unknown articles. Down in the basement of the building every foot is utilized and the entire under part of the building is connected from end to end with mysterious doors and passages." The Chinese got the blame for two particular offences: opium use and gambling. They were thought to be the main providers of laudanum, a heady infusion of opium in alcohol. Police conducted frequent raids on the backs of laundries in search of evidence and to assuage the socially constructed repulsion for drugs and gambling. But to a lonely person, opium offers a respite, and if a person has money but is not permitted to

Glenbow Archives, Calgary, Canada: NA-2186-33

Hop Wo Laundry being moved, 1920s

buy much and is certainly not encouraged to spend time in the stores and restaurants only a few blocks away, why not gamble? White Albertans did not recognize the cycle of bigotry that they perpetuated. And because such bigotry thrives on clichés, every cliché possible was ascribed to the Chinese, from white slavery to smuggling and conspiracy. Still, until the mid-twentieith century the better-off competed to hire Chinese cooks and houseboys, wanting their abilities in service but unwilling to accord them their rights. The outcome, naturally enough, was the development of Chinese clans, who worked together to protect their families' rights. As time passed, Chinatowns became first ghettos for the poor and the not-yet-assimilated, then trendy urban places to visit.

Racial considerations were not erased from Canada's Immigration Act until 1967, and by then Chinese immigrants were hip, well-off, fluent in English, and motivated by very different desires than the nineteenth-century Chinese who had built the railway. In the early 1970s Edmonton's Old Chinatown was threatened with extinction, but a Save Chinatown committee in 1973 persuaded the city that the streets should not be widened and the area "cleaned up." But by 1981, eager to appropriate prime real estate, Edmonton had razed and relocated its Old Chinatown. Now the federal government's Canada Place sits on top of the ghosts of those struggling, lonely old men. The re-placed Chinatown, called Chinatown South, tries to replicate the spirit of the Old Chinatown that still exists in Calgary. Designed and architectured, it reflects the way that Albertans continue to tear down the old and then try to reconstruct history through renewal. New Chinatown, or Chinatown North, combines Chinese businesses with more recent Vietnamese businesses. These recent and "real" Chinatowns, with their bustle and strip-mall energy, are now everywhere, a powerful presence in a new and more diverse, if uneasily tolerant, Alberta.

Ironically, racism against Asians was mitigated only when, during the First World War, Albertans could blame the Germans for every ill. In June of 1915 miners in Drumheller stopped working because their employers would not fire some one hundred men of Austrian and German descent. In Calgary eight months later, mobs attacked restaurants and other establishments in Germantown. The Dominion Wartime Election Act of 1917 disenfranchised German- and Austrian-born Canadians; by that time, Alberta served as the federal government's arm by hosting a number of camps for enemy aliens. For some reason, the National Parks, Canada's playgrounds, seemed a perfect place to keep prisoners, and Banff and Jasper both had internment camps. The men imprisoned there inched roads through some of the most difficult passes of the mountains and did various other beautification jobs in the park.

While Alberta's crazy politics are often read as conservative, they are also the result of different groups' being marginalized and mistreated. Populist, ultra-right groups were the inevitable result. Through the 1930s and 1940s foreigners were painted as "reds," and immigrants, not entirely happy with bosses who conformed to the old British order, were labeled "radical." Political parties that diverged from established Liberal and Conservative positions appeared to offer an alternative to Anglo-Protestant superiority. Add to the mix the Douglasite conspiracy theories of Jewish world domination, and populist Alberta was a powder keg. Ernest Manning purged his party's anti-Semitic fringe after the Second World War, but anti-Semitism has never entirely vanished.

When the federal government ordered that all of British Columbia's Japanese people be evacuated from the coast, Albertans gained a new enemy alien. The Japanese people brought in to work in the sugar beet fields in southern Alberta faced protest and nasty invective. If the Japanese were a danger to BC, then surely they were a danger to Alberta. Lethbridge and Calgary banned them from entering the cities, even to go to school or to work. The Japanese were not allowed to own property, not allowed to travel more than twelve miles without a permit. Many were interned in camps. When the war ended, Alberta demanded that the Japanese be moved out of the province, but the active work of churches and humanitarian associations finally prevailed, so that in 1948 the Japanese were given official permission to stay in Alberta, even though this had not been a happy place for them. Joy Kogawa's novel *Obasan* brilliantly evokes the terrible displacement of the Japanese and their attempts to make Alberta a version of home.

At the beginning of the Second World War, conscientious objectors from pacifist Hutterite, Mennonite, Jehovah's Witness, and Doukhobor sects worked in alternative service camps, again in Jasper and Banff, beautifying the beautiful. The locals were not grateful, but heckled the men for being cowards and complained bitterly when they were allowed to swim in the Cave and Basin or the Upper Hot Springs pool. The camps were not brutal and the men were fed reasonably well, but the pervasive attitude toward conscientious objectors was disparaging, and no one was kind to the men, even though they worked hard.

Other detention camps in Kananaskis, Medicine Hat, Lethbridge, and Wainwright held German POWs who were in the Afrika Corps and who had been captured by the British. Britain sent thousands of these men to Canada, who dispersed them across the country, and Alberta's four camps held almost twenty-five thousand men. Some people bitterly referred to these camps as babysitting facilities for Nazis, and although at first the men were not required to work, volunteer prisoners were later set to cutting firewood. Quite a number tried to escape, a few successfully, but most were shipped back to Germany after the war, where many of their memories of being imprisoned in Alberta were fond ones.

The post-war period brought almost 200,000 new settlers to Alberta—political refugees, disaffected citizens of countries who had suffered the brunt of the war, and economic migrants. Many of these "ethnics" faced a new discrimination— primitive living conditions, downward mobility, and a soft bias driven by economics and class more than bigotry. When the Chinese Exclusion Act was repealed in 1947, Chinese-Albertans could finally bring their families to join them. And Albertans daily began to encounter South Asian, Vietnamese, and African faces. Not that the province's uneasiness with difference was forgotten, but the new prosperity gave rise to a demand for multiple skills and pleasures that only diversity could supply.

Although now far less xenophobic than in the mid-1900s, Albertans still seize occasions to display their intolerance. In 1982, for example, Sikh taxi drivers faced local discrimination with the Yellow Cab Company. But to its credit, Alberta knows its history, and has never been able to pretend that its ignorance or nativism or racism or discrimination does not exist. Unstable, eccentric, susceptible to unpredictable fluctuations in opinion and moment, Alberta rides a bucking bronco, sometimes called pluralism, sometimes called grassroots, sometimes called populism, and sometimes called downright mean and ornery.

Good old Alberta: bread and circuses.

13 | Ladies, Women, and Broads

Circle the wagons, girls, here the bastards come.
—Robert Kroetsch

This was the way to be a woman in the West.

Figure out how to harness the horse by using the illustrations of harness in the Timothy Eaton catalogue. Read the catalogue and dream about what you do not have. When the new one arrives, cut up the old one for pictures, paper dolls. Flour sacks make durable sheets and pillowcases, tea towels and underwear. The trick is to soak them, then bleach them, then boil them to erase their shameful letters. No one will ever know you're not wearing silk.

Set the bread to rise overnight, punch it down, let it rise again, roll it, punch it, and form it into loaves, then set the loaves to rise again. Make sure the fire is stoked and the oven ready. Nothing is better than a fresh-cut crust spread with homemade butter and Rogers Golden Syrup. Chop wood to keep the stove burning. Carry water from the well and heat on the stove until it boils. Follow the instructions for Whiter Washing with Less Work. "Sprinkle granulated soap into the tub or washer. Add lukewarm or hot water and stir. A few seconds will give a clear, rich, soapy solution. Use enough soap to produce creamy, lasting suds even after the clothes are in. Let the suds be your guide. Soak white clothes an hour or two or overnight in lukewarm suds. Sprinkle dry granulated soap on badly soiled spots, roll garments and push well under water. Water should cover clothes. Rinse thoroughly, one hot water rinse, and one cold water rinse. Colorfast clothes should soak not more than fifteen or twenty minutes." Do the washing in the galvanized tub, rubbing the clothes over the corrugated board, eyes stinging from the yellow carbolic. Hang wet clothes outside until frozen. Iron everything, the iron heated on the same wood stove.

Milk the cow early and strain the milk through cheesecloth, saving some whole milk to churn into butter with the wooden dasher. Remember that the reputation of a housewife depends on the quality of her butter. In the summer, pick berries in the hot coulees, thick with mosquitoes and thunder. Gooseberries, saskatoons, chokecherries, the lucky find of a wild strawberry patch, the careful cherishing of raspberry canes. Sterilize the jars for canning, boil the fruit, and bottle it.

Stuff mattresses with straw, stitch feather and woollen quilts. Pray for chinooks. Pray for a post office, a party line, a midwife, a neighbour with a sense of humour. Pray that soon you'll leave this sod shack and live in a two-storey frame house, with three bedrooms upstairs, front and back parlour, a dining room, a pantry, and a kitchen—and a cellar to keep carrots and potatoes firm enough to eat in February. Pray that your grandmother will send you a barrel of apples from Ontario.

Comfort yourself with facts. Mrs. Alice Parker baked Winston Churchill's wedding cake. Miss Grace Burroughs will conduct the Edmonton Journal *Cooking and Homemakers School, at the Empire Theatre, on February 22, 23, and 24. Annie McKernan walked four miles from her home in Strathcona to attend the first wood-frame school, every day. Mrs. John McDougall was only the fourth white woman to live outside the Fort. She was noted for her teeth, her piano, her pipe organ, and her hospitality. Mrs. Murdoch McLeod was afraid of grasshoppers. Her husband was a prisoner of Riel; she made dresses for social events. Mrs. Matt McCauley came from a family of claim jumpers, also very musical. Mrs. Frank Oliver won prizes for baking bread. She became the most popular hostess in Ottawa. Mrs. James Lauder did not suspect that she would live with baking pans but no furniture. Mrs. Alf Hutchings of the Battle River learned to swim. And Mrs. Thomas Henderson, who survived the gold fever, rode miles with a young baby and a sack of oatmeal. She lost her matches and survived on raw oatmeal.*

And hundreds of now-nameless First Nations women watched over hundreds of births, comforting lonely newcomers. Their daughters endured the rigid rules of residential school, the braids they were forced to wear pulling their scalps tight, the checked dresses hemming them in more surely than the manners and prayers they had been taught.

Pray for forgiveness.

Circle the wagons, girls, here the bastards come.

• • •

Men, men, men, men, men. The plot of Alberta's story bristles with men, a deuce of men, a porcupine of men, as if the West belonged solely to them. In order to see the women of Alberta, it is necessary to peer around the men, who strut and pose, who block the light. All these boy stories of police and politicians, missionaries and miners, leave aside the presence of women.

For a long time, there were more women than men in the West—First Nations women outnumbered First Nations men. And however much anthropological interpretations consign Indian women to the drudgery of carrying and cooking, pounding berries and skinning animals, they were indispensable. No person essential to a culture is powerless, especially one who labours long and hard. Before the advent of the white man, who imposed his version and valuation of them, Indian women exerted their own particular torque on their specific lives. Women were valuable, and commanded a bride price. Skinning, tanning, sewing, cooking, and gathering food were substantial contributions to the daily survival of Alberta's tribes. Babies took their mothers' names; and women together cared for and raised children, teaching them by example and by story. Polygamy was fluid and pragmatic, but a Plains Indian woman could divorce her husband by throwing his clothing, weapons, and medicine bundle out of her teepee, especially if he beat her or failed to provide meat and food. Mobility, that Alberta hallmark, was enabled by women, who might not have ridden the horses or paddled the canoes, but who literally moved, from day to day, their entire household. While we have subtle glimpses of women's lives as told in oral histories and through early white contact, their stories remain mysterious, covert, important for their withholding, and should not be guessed at or ignored.

There is one absolute fact. Without First Nations women, everyone would have starved to death, the Indian men themselves and especially the newly arrived white men. And starving was only the half of it. Although stories present the fur traders as maverick adventurers, their trade would have been limited and unsuccessful without the alliances they made with First Nations women, who served as guides and translators, connections and cooks. Sylvia Van Kirk's groundbreaking *Many Tender Ties* examines this important aspect of the fur trade; and her brilliant study warns against quick and easy assumptions assigning either victimhood or luxurious elevation to women who formed alliances with traders and were the mothers of Métis children. The lives of women are never so simple.

Whatever the rules of the company, and the two trading companies were very different, it was almost inevitable that a white trader would seek the comfort and assistance of a woman, either Indian or Métis. Daniel Harmon, a North West Company trader from Vermont, states in his journal of October 10, 1805: "This Day a Canadian's Daughter (a Girl of about fourteen years of age) was offered me, and after mature consideration concerning the step I ought to take I finally

Blackfoot women, late 1800s

Glenbow Archives, Calgary, Canada: NA-3981-5

concluded it would be best to accept of her, as it is customary for all the Gentlemen who come in this Country to remain any length of time to have a fair Partner, with whom they can pass away their time at least more sociably if not more agreeably than to live a lonely, solitary life, as they must do if single. In case we can live in harmony together, my intentions now are to keep her as long as I remain in this uncivilized part of the world, but when I return to my native land shall endeavour to place her into the hands of some good honest Man, with whom she can pass the remainder of her Days in this Country much more agreeably, than it would be possible for her to do, were she to be taken down into the civilized world, where she would be a stranger to the People, their manners, customs & Language." He had it all worked out, and to his own advantage, but Lisette Duval, the young Métis woman in question, exerted an unexpected effect on her husband. Their life together was "cemented by a long and mutual performance of kind offices." When it was time for him to return to the "civilized" world, he could not countenance leaving without her.

Quite simply, establishing good relations with the indigenous and Métis people required that traders cultivate the goodwill of the women, by giving them presents and often by establishing liaisons with them. Many women were excellent trappers and brought their own furs to trade. They were pragmatists, enterprising and politically astute. There was nothing submissive about these women; they were capable of jealousy and seduction, influence and resistance as well as love, and they were all as individual as their circumstances and their characters. Still, given their position as women of the land, their partners, whether white or First Nations, constrained their world. But that is the story of women almost everywhere.

In the 1800s the West was home to many aboriginal and Métis women, but few white women. Since men had decided that white women were nuisances, prone to fainting and hysteria, they were kept out of the West, even if they wanted to come. Breaking through this embargo was difficult. The story of Isobel Gunn, who disguised herself as a boy to work for the Bay at Moose Factory is well told in Audrey Thomas's novel, *Isobel Gunn*. In 1807 French-Canadian Marie-Anne Gaboury became the first white woman to reach Fort Edmonton, travelling with her husband, a French voyageur and free fur trader, Jean Baptiste Lajimonière. Despite frights and adventures from bolting horses to her baby son's almost being kidnapped, she enjoyed the challenge and came to love northwest life. Her matriarchal power is enshrined in her being the maternal grandmother of Louis Riel through her daughter Julie. And she gave birth to the first white child born in what would become Alberta—Josette.

Eventually the custom of making alliances with Indian and Métis women shifted, in accordance with the model set by the officers of the fur trade, to white women. Once George Simpson married his prim-faced cousin, the entire social fabric of the trade changed. Men became as subject to social arbitration and fashion in the wilderness as in big cities, and their complicity with the racism that began to pervade the West is arguably the greatest insult that the First People endured. As soon as only white women were acceptable as wives, the initial intimacy between First Nations women and white men was forever marred. A potentially utopian world that had enjoyed a brief flourishing was stymied.

In all the official histories, white woman are the brave ones, pioneers, pilgrims, saints, and moral arbiters. Despite their lauding of "tender plants," late-nineteenth-century missionaries and military men felt that a certain kind of woman was needed in the West, tough, cheerful, and dauntless. At the same time they were to keep their clothing spotless, their hair up, and their morals unblemished. Nuns supported their missionary priests and wives their husbands by providing nursing and cooking. Elizabeth McDougall, who came west in 1872, was one of the missionary adjuncts who so impressed everyone by tagging along with her proselytizing husband to establish a mission at Morley. But more than anything, being a woman in Alberta meant a radical shift from propriety to pragmatism.

Women who chose to make their life in the West had to be adaptable. Confronting a completely different world, they learned by the blisters on their hands a new lexicon of femininity. There were few servants in the West, the ones that were available not very tractable, unwilling to serve as maids or washerwomen; a woman with a desire for even middle-class comfort had to rethink her expectations. This new world demanded washtubs and bread-making, the quotidian necessities of a household. And whether they recognized it or not, white women in the West fashioned their lives after their aboriginal sisters, making their own clothes, washing, ironing, mending, chopping wood, making butter, milking, and if no school was close, teaching their children. Those who were homesick wrote letters and kept diaries, and some gave up and fled back to the Centre or across the ocean. Those who couldn't flee had no choice but to adjust. Their first shelters were often tents. Their first houses, which they swept and shivered in, were shacks built of logs or sod, with dirt floors, usually a square area divided into a simple living room and kitchen with beds along the walls. These cabins were so small that chores like churning butter and washing clothes had to be done outside. The sod huts were cosy in winter but come spring when the snow melted would leak and shower dirt. Houses with a crude basement to store canned goods and vegetables seemed more permanent; although best of all was a separate ice-house to keep cream and butter. On Saturday nights every member of the family took turns hunkering down in a tin bathtub full of water heated on a stove. The longed-for "good" house had a wood frame, with rooms for specific purposes and often a second storey and a shingled roof. Until 1890 houses were practical and plain; only after 1890 did they begin to signal social prestige, their design and decoration becoming more elaborate.

Some women fell in love with the land. In 1884, Mary Ella Inderwick, the wife of a range lease holder, wrote in a letter, "This is the only life! I have any number of troubles—in fact too many to mention—but I forget them all in this joyous air, with the grand protecting mountains always standing round the western horizon. . . . It is the spirit of the West that charms one, and I cannot convey it to you, try as I may. It is a shy wild spirit and will not leave its native mountains and rolling prairies, and though I try to get it into my letters I fail, but I must warn you that if it once charms you it becomes an obsession, and one grows very lonely away from it. No Westerner who has felt its fascination ever is really content again in the conventional East."

Adventurous women were able to pursue their interests with far less interference than they encountered in the Centre. As early as 1889 the Rockies were greeted by hardy types who had no intention of letting a skirt get in the way of a steep slope. Mary Schäffer was a Quaker widow from Philadelphia who collected and sketched botanical specimens. Together with her friend, Mary "Mollie" Adams, she undertook two mountain expeditions, in 1904 and 1905, that have become markers in mountain exploration, and in 1908, she made an expedition to Maligne, or Chaba, Lake. She had no illusions about "discovering" the lake; she knew very well that she was merely tracing the footsteps of countless Stoney Indians and trappers. Her

Women's activities varied

miles of trail riding led to the publication of *Old Indian Trails of the Canadian Rockies*, an illustrated volume recounting her various journeys. More and more attached to the West, Schäffer began living in Banff all year round, and she eventually married her guide, Billy Warren, who was some years her junior. It appears to have been more than a marriage of convenience, although Warren used Schäffer's connections to develop his contacts—she was good friends with R. B. Bennett—and to invest in some key properties in Banff. Her photographs vividly reflect the park before Banff was infected with tourists; she grew so attached to the area that the Stoneys called her *Yahe-Weha*, Mountain Woman. Her friend Mary Vaux had come to the Lake Louise area as part of a scientific team measuring the movement of glaciers; she was sensible enough to suggest that women in the mountains wear knickerbockers, stout boots, and flannel shirts, an idea that would never have been accepted in the Centre. And Catherine and Mary Barclay, avid hikers who taught in Calgary schools for more than thirty years, founded the Canadian Youth Hostels. The very first youth hostel in North America was a $19 tent they pegged into the ground near Bragg Creek in 1933.

Fashion in early Alberta had to be adaptable. Women might have wept as they fitted their daughters with rough copper-toed boots, but at least the toes wouldn't wear out. Ready-made clothes were not available and most women sewed their own, although there were dressmakers in Macleod and Calgary and Edmonton. Women relied on ingenuity to make themselves and their homes attractive. The most common denominator was work, work, work, but for all that they had to be willing to pitch in to help with everything, early Alberta was wide open for unmarried women. With three men for every woman, and an even greater ratio in the country, the province was a happy hunting ground for women intent on marriage. Advertisements for mail-order wives and genteel companions appeared. Men wanted a "girl" who was kind to dogs and a good cook more than they cared about housekeeping, but what they needed was someone to look after chickens and pigs and to do the milking. "Alberta needs women more than men or money," the *Lethbridge Herald* declared, and ads were placed in Central newspapers. One read: "Urgent: thousands of nice girls are wanted in the Canadian West. Over 20,000 men are sighing for what they cannot get—WIVES! Shame! Don't hesitate—COME AT ONCE. If you cannot come, send your sisters. So great is the demand that anything in skirts stands a chance. No reasonable offer refused. They are all shy but willing. All Prizes. No Blanks. Hustle up now Girls and don't miss this chance. Some of you will never get another."

Such advertising seems comic now, not to mention blatantly chauvinistic. There is little indication of how well the propaganda worked, but plenty of evidence that women who came west with parents or other family were better off for that support. In truth, "nice" girls wouldn't have been permitted by their families to come. But it's not hard to image that cunning, desperate, imaginative, and adventuresome girls came, the kind of women the West wanted, frontier women likely to do well in a raw, rough, unfinished country. Stacked against them were isolation, loneliness, homesickness, the risk of dying in childbirth, and constant work. Most had to learn to cook on a wood stove, render lard, churn butter, raise chickens, gather eggs, salt pork, garden, butcher, bottle vegetables, brand cattle, milk cows, and make soap for laundry. There is no estimate of how many times a woman, overwhelmed by mosquitoes and dirt, sat down and wept. Invariably, women needed to be able to ride horses, drive buggies, raise children, and make fine cakes out of a few raisins and a handful of flour. They had to be nurses and teachers and morticians and hired hands and mothers and sweethearts, all at the same time.

Class divisions between women consolidated more as the population grew. The elite, the well-educated, usually came from the Centre or from Britain. Their lives assisted by servants—usually immigrant women, since First Nations women were wonderfully resistant to the niceties of service—they enjoyed the leisure to focus on their appearance, attend dances and teas, hold at-home afternoons and garden parties, and emulate as much as possible the world they had left. To their credit, all this leisure time led them to join or start hospital aid groups, women's Canadian Clubs, and the Woman's Christian Temperance Union.

Middle-class women, who usually had a modicum of education, centred their work on their homes. They were the wives of shopkeepers and businessmen, and if single might work as stenographers, maids, teachers, nurses, or clerks. Non-Anglo immigrants, German, Italian, Ukrainian, Scandinavian, or even Asian, could chip their way into the middle class, quite a contrast to their lives in the socially inflexible Centre. And to complicate matters, a number of independent women, mostly Yankees, made no bones about coming to Alberta's boomtowns to improve their financial lot. They wanted to own businesses, not marry them. Attitudes were influenced by background. The British were more class-conscious and stiffer than other women. The Americans completely ignored the social rulebook. Canadians threaded their way somewhere between. Most "respectable" Canadian wives still imported their social attitudes from Ontario, but that could lead to confusion, since rules in Alberta were far more pliable.

Women of the lower classes had to work outside their homes to feed their families. Language-challenged recent immigrants were, of course, treated as if they were beyond social reckoning, and those women, who lived in tents and shacks, did housework or cleaning or sewing to make ends meet. Sometimes, though, the down-at-heel women were unfortunately married to blue-blooded but unredeemable remittance men.

In a completely separate class were the "soiled doves," the prostitutes. The trade of prostitution flourished for its ageless reason: as a means of survival for girls without resources or women without marketable skills. The number of unattached working men with money to burn, cowboys who spent long months without even seeing a woman, and the West's mixture of labourers and layabouts was fertile ground for mercenary sex. Given the numerical imbalance between men and women, prostitution boomed as much as land speculation, and many a frugal madam was able to retire and re-establish herself in a different city as a well-heeled matron or widow. Shunned by respectable women, *filles de joie* were physically as well as socially segregated, living outside town boundaries or lumped together into unsavoury areas. More questionable than their sexual favours was their intimacy with alcohol, what historian James Gray calls the "booze-brothel syndrome" in *Red Lights on the Prairies*. Saloons and houses of ill repute were cousins, with madams providing illicit whisky to whet or quench the appetite. Their shared job was to keep the temper of the times.

From policemen to politicians, including a few lieutenant-governors, it seemed that every man except those with an overpoweringly Ontario sense of social reform frequented bars, billiard rooms, and brothels more or less regularly, and without stigma or apology. Hard-handed men were hungry for touch, eager for a little soft light and the lace trim on a petticoat, and the women who supplied their needs helped to open the West in ways almost as important as the wives who milked cows and harnessed horses. Well-known Calgary prostitute Pearl Miller ran such a clean, pleasant house that men felt that they were sitting in a respectable parlour and imagined that they were courting rather than paying for sex. And the occupants of brothels understood soap and water; brothels and Chinese laundries both used about six barrels of water a week. Respectable women either ignored these houses or, in some cases, became vigilantes and set them on fire. On the whole, though, such houses and residents were treated with tolerance. Jails with room for women were scarce, so if a scarlet lady was charged with breaking the law, usually disorderly conduct, she was fined, a handy way of taxing the oldest profession and adding income to the town's coffers. In 1921 the general law on prostitution broke down into three sections: keeping a disorderly house; being an inmate of a disorderly house; and being a frequenter of a disorderly house. Which of the three was fined most was questionable. The madam paid protection money, but if one of the inmates was charged the madam would try to send a new girl who would get off because she had no previous record.

When Mounties themselves were regular customers, it was futile to pretend that the law fought prostitution. Some said that in Edmonton there were at least a hundred brothels, but one experienced madam put the estimate at between four and five hundred. Cities welcomed gambling and prostitution just as long as the side effects of excess were controlled. Streetwalkers, however, were a different story. They were visible, for one. For another, they were cheap and, because their turnover was high, more prone to disease. They were almost inevitably the ones to be harassed and preached at by moral reformers.

Calgary's "Whisky Row" competed with Edmonton for variety and accessibility, although Police Chief Tom English piously declared that if there were houses of prostitution, he didn't know where they were. Everyone else did. There was even a campaign to replace the lace curtains in the windows of brothels with blinds— apparently too many people were enjoying a free show. Calgary's prostitutes were proud women whose shopping expeditions required high-fashion silk and satin. Her business booming, one lady-of-the-evening, Diamond Dolly, would sweep into a jewellery store to invest in more jewellery, sometimes every week. And the brothels had no compunction about hiring Chinese servants and associating with new immigrants; they were excellent employers who paid a decent wage. The brothels were also more racially diverse than the rest of the town, with black and Japanese as well as white prostitutes.

The houses in Drumheller and Lethbridge catered to a labour-specific clientele and even served double duty as schoolrooms and social centres. There weren't many other places for miners and cowhands to learn the niceties of using knives and forks, how to sign their names, or dancing the two-step. In Drumheller, the best brothels sat where the penitentiary now looms, fancy places that brought in extra girls on miners' paydays, when there would literally be line-ups outside the doors. One house even doubled as a version of convention centre for visiting dignitaries, serving meals and providing classy entertainment for coal-company executives and union bosses; another had the atmosphere of a clubhouse, where miners could go to enjoy a beer and a game of cards. In Lethbridge, Cowboy Jack, a madam whose masculine name belied her femininity, kept the visiting cowboys in hand by pitching them into a horse trough if they misbehaved. Servicing miners meant two really busy days and then twelve slow days; cowboys were a quieter, steadier proposition, who wanted to relax and talk for a while. Every place had its own sexual culture, and the women sought to provide what would satisfy the specific needs of their visitors. Some women even married their customers, although marrying likely meant giving up living in relative comfort for a small and dirty shack. Although they wouldn't have to deal with countless men, they'd be toiling at different unsavoury tasks, and the question of whether or not to marry needed much consideration.

Properly married women didn't relish buying hats or gloves in the same shops as the working girls, but public outrage aside, it was difficult to force policemen to crack down on prostitution when the law was more interested in collecting protection money than closing brothels. Lethbridge tolerated brothels until as late as the middle of the Second World War. Finally, even in towns as wild as those in the Crowsnest Pass, the houses of the more elegant prostitutes vanished, decorum overtaking the West. Of course, prostitution is still present, merely less visible.

The question of prostitution and its tolerance in early Alberta was really an argument about the standards of the Centre being imposed on the differently measured West. The imported concept of "social evil" didn't play as well in Alberta as in the East; and making it stick was much harder. But outraged meetings in high-raftered churches demanded inquiries, and welfare pioneers eagerly denounced the profession and its side effects. In the end prostitution changed with the onset of prohibition, when men were more intent on getting their hands on beer than on breasts, and the business became the street-savage and pimp-driven activity it is today. Perhaps the most interesting reversal was that of Pearl Miller, the Calgary madam who, after making a bundle, bought a house in Calgary's Mount Royal, got religion, and spent the rest of her life trying to reform other working girls, even haranguing them through the bars when they were jailed. How successful she was is not clear, but her fame lasted at least as long as the Second World War. One Calgary regiment was camped next to an American outfit who had put up a booster sign reading, "Remember Pearl Harbor!" In return the Calgary regiment put up its own sign, reading, "To hell with Pearl Harbor, Remember Pearl Miller."

Given that there weren't many professions open to women, prostitution, for all its drawbacks, could be safer and more comfortable than marriage. And choices for women were limited. Women could be book-keepers and seamstresses, telegraph and telephone operators. Slowly, waitressing and sales positions appeared, although the assumption was that women did not need to be paid as much as men. There was a sharp differential between male and female schoolteachers, and despite protest, that did not change until the 1940s. Women who came west to teach often ended up in isolated communities trying to instill some basic knowledge of reading and writing and arithmetic into students ranging in age from five to sixteen, and ranging in ability from frank illiteracy to quick intelligence. Some schools were well equipped, while others were log shacks with barely a bench for the students and no books to speak of. Generally a group of settlers would form a school district by hammering together a building and hiring a teacher by mail. Some teachers from Britain and Central Canada were college students teaching during the summer to earn money. But others were simply young women taking up one of the few professions available to them.

The teacher would suffer her first shock when she arrived at a branch-line station no bigger than a minute and found she was expected to board with a trustee, which could be more or less comfortable, but meant that privacy was limited and her every move scrutinized. She had to get along with the adults who hired and evaluated her, and she had to be entertainer, disciplinarian, and instructor to her pupils. In the country, attendance could be sporadic, depending on the weather and seasonal work; rural children, their parents' labour force, attended school less than half the time. School districts might form, and trustees might set and collect school taxes, but that didn't make the job of a teacher easy, between chopping wood and checking for head lice and hauling drinking water from distant creeks. Outhouses were a nightmare, the subject of endless scatological pranks. Fractious students challenged a teacher's authority, and older students could physically overcome a teacher. The strap seemed a nasty necessity. Just getting to school through blizzards and hailstorms was a challenge, and then the school would be redolent with the smell of wet mittens and rubber boots. By 1905, Alberta had some 560 schools, staffed by 1,200 teachers trying to enlighten more than 34,000 pupils; and two-thirds of those teachers were women. Their pay at first was miserable. Some in the early 1900s made only $1.25 a month, and although they were supposed to be provided with room and board, the accommodation was often minimal, and their salaries often late. In the 1920s salaries rose to around $40 a month, but were always dependent on times being good. The portrait of the king might smile down on these women, but life as a teacher wasn't much fun. Nor were their students always happy to be enlightened. Many were recent immigrants whose command of English was rudimentary. The required *Alexandra Readers*, produced in Ontario, set out to inculcate proper British-colonial notions, which seemed remote and inappropriate to the West. But spelling and geography bees were fun, and the checker matches, story-telling, baseball games, and Christmas concerts made up for the discomforts of learning. In fact, the schools of Alberta became the first places celebrating secular community activity. Hardest of all was keeping teachers. The men usually left to get a higher level of education—in law or business—while the women, of course, left to get married. (There is no record of how many, if any, switched from teaching to prostitution.)

Nursing was another important profession, but the work was so demanding that not many chose it. Diseases of the day were either fatal or communicable, whether smallpox, typhus, diphtheria, or tuberculosis. Doctors were absolute kings and nurses expected to serve not only as helpmates but as emptiers of bedpans, washers of filthy linens. Private nurses who hired themselves out to care for the sick at home commanded a little more money than hospital nurses, who kept long, exhausting hours. Women who married doctors found themselves pressed into service whether or not they had any training. Until Alberta's first school of nursing opened in 1905, the population depended on nurses who'd come from the Centre. Usually, though, wives and mothers had to cope with cut-off fingers, frostbite, burns, diarrhea, and toothaches. The nurses who worked in proper hospitals with proper equipment were fortunate but few. And they, too, gave up their profession when they married.

But the West was a place where women could kick over the traces. One spectacular example, Caroline Fulham, ran a small but smelly pig ranch smack in downtown Calgary in the late 1800s. The possessor of a knife-edged Irish tongue, she rode a bedraggled democrat with a barrel in the back up and down the city streets collecting slops. She had appropriated rights to all the kitchen waste discarded by hotels and restaurants, and her pigs ate like kings. The butt of much local teasing, she liked a few drams and often tangled with police, who could count on needing at least three men to subdue her when they arrested her for her usual infractions—disorderly conduct, drunkenness, or fighting. Her appearances in court were Shakespearean in pitch, and because Calgary's best lawyer, Paddy Nolan, chose to defend her (he had no hope of getting a fee, but he was fascinated with her extravagant tales and he knew the effect of a good performance), the entertainment value for spectators was exceptional. Afraid of no one, the Queen of Garbage Row readily abused police, lawyers, judges, and the city council. Once she accused an officer of tearing a hank of hair out of her head; the hair, which she brought as evidence, proved to be from a horse's tail. While branded a notorious nuisance, she became the city's own version of holy fool, and though illiterate, she had a wit far beyond those who ridiculed her. One day a civic-minded doctor noticed that she was limping and asked what the matter was. She told him that her ankle had been bothering her, and he suggested that she step into the nearest drugstore so that he could have a look. When she peeled down her stocking, he was shocked into exclaiming, "I'll bet a dollar there's not another leg in Calgary as dirty as that." Fulham immediately held out her hand and said, "Put up your money, doctor. I'll show you another." Before the doctor could hesitate, she had exposed her other leg and taken his dollar. When she sold her property and moved to Vancouver, the respectable heaved a sigh of relief, but those with a sense of humour knew the city's loss.

By then, women were edging into the sacred world of men. Alberta's first woman doctor, Dr. Etta Denovan, worked with her husband out of Red Deer until 1903. In 1912, Bessie Nicholls became the first woman in Alberta to be elected to public office, as a school trustee in Edmonton. While she was still campaigning, the city discovered that she was ineligible because she was a woman, but rather than losing such a good candidate, immediately pushed through an amendment to the city charter, enabling her to run. At least they had the intelligence to recognize useful talent. And in October of the same year, Annie Jackson, a square-jawed young toughie with curly hair and a no-nonsense look, became Edmonton's first female police officer. Prior to that, she'd been with the Children's Shelter, and she offered a woman's perspective on law enforcement until 1918 when she resigned her position to marry. Between 1918 and 1923, Annie Gale served as Calgary's first female alderperson and actively campaigned for health clinics for women and children. In 1924 she was elected to the public school board, and there she insisted that the province should pay for eye, nose, and throat operations, since they were essential to a student's being able to perform. By contrast, Esther Marjorie Hill, Canada's first female architect, grew up in Edmonton. She enrolled in architecture at the University of Alberta in 1916, but transferred to the University of Toronto two years later. She moved back to Edmonton in 1921, but was denied registration by the Alberta Association of Architects and had to teach at a country school until an architectural firm hired her as a draftsman. Even then, Hill could not make a living and had to move to Victoria.

Alberta women didn't know how to keep their mouths shut, nor did they want to. Katherine Hughes, a well-known journalist and troublemaker, came to Edmonton in 1906 and worked at the *Edmonton Bulletin*. A Catholic apologist, she wrote a biography of Father Lacombe, which was published in 1911 as *Father Lacombe, the Black-Robe Voyageur*. Avidly opposed to Emily Murphy and Nellie McClung, she took charge of the *Bulletin's* society page, but she also covered the legislature. Most important, in 1908 she was appointed the first provincial archivist, and she left a legacy of records and oral reports from old-timers, who by then were starting to vanish.

Alberta men have never been too comfortable with the formidable and ferocious women of this province, and they are still nervous when asked to explain the feminism and fury of Western women. Deborah Grey might seem the Alliance's version of a motorcycle mama, but she carries on a long tradition of activist women. Mostly men just duck their heads and say nothing, or mutter something disparaging. But the attitudes and behaviour of frontier men probably did a lot to instigate feminism. Men weren't very good at cleaning up the world's dirt, and the West was a grubby place. And while Alberta men, historically and currently, were eager to assign a "higher morality" to women than women wanted, they were also quick to give women the burden of blame. A good number of Alberta's laws, including present laws regarding whether a rape victim's past can be brought to bear on the trial of her accused, have not served women well. To survive in Alberta, women have had to fight, and fight hard.

So it should not be surprising that the country's early feminists came from Alberta. As the province grew, women's choices seemed to shrink. During the First World War, women had pitched in—cutting and sewing at the Great Western Garment factory in Edmonton, rolling cigars at Imperial Tobacco, burning their fingers on the hot pressing rollers at Superior Laundry. Many of them elected to stay at work after the war, a trend of economic independence if not equality. The jobs available to women included a fair degree of drudgery (prostitution aside), and women knew that the better things in life usually accompanied a man and marriage, but that solution was not always available.

And double standards persisted. A man could divorce his wife for adultery, but a woman needed additional reasons; Ottawa only made grounds for divorce equal in 1925. An unwed mother had full responsibility for her child; but a married woman had no legal authority over her children—fathers could choose their schooling and religion.

No one paid attention to the situation of women more than Emily Ferguson Murphy. Murphy was the author of the Janey Canuck books, begun because while Murphy was sailing to England in her youth, she happened to hear a British woman on board disparaging Canadians, or "Canucks," as terribly unpolished and, worst of all, rather too much

Emily Murphy, first woman magistrate in the British Empire, passed over for the Senate

like Americans. Murphy was inspired by the incident to use Janey Canuck as her nom de plume, and by the time she'd moved to Edmonton had published *Impressions of Janey Canuck* and *Janey Canuck in the West*. Her travelogue style and her Canadian perspective were infectious; and her writing reflected her concern with poverty, dysfunctional families, and working conditions, even though she herself came from a fairly comfortable background. After performing exemplary service as a preacher's wife in various Ontario parishes, she moved, with her Anglican husband, Arthur Murphy, to Edmonton. For all Murphy's initial resistance to the frontier town, just become the capital of Alberta, she came to love its rough edges, its lack of social pedigree. And in Edmonton Murphy found plenty of worthy causes to suit her missionary zeal, the most pressing the lot of women with no laws to protect their interests. Murphy had never before encountered the hard facts of women's legal position, and now it so consumed her that she undertook extensive research on exactly what rights women had. She discovered that wife beating, bigamy, polygamy, elopement, rape, drunkenness, and prostitution were rampant. She discovered that women might clean and cook, churn and launder, garden and grub, fetch water and split wood, sew and slaughter, but they had no protection or power over the disposition of family property. A woman faced destitution if her husband gambled away their land; a man could leave land and possessions to male relatives without consulting his wife, who was at the mercy of his kindness. There had been a dower protection act, but the Real Property Act of 1886 effaced dower rights as getting in the way of land registration in the North West Territories. And unless a woman was legally the head of the household, she could not file a homestead claim.

Murphy lobbied like hell for the Married Women's Protective Act, which legally assured a wife one-third of her husband's estate, and which was passed by the Alberta legislature in 1911. She pushed for the Married Women's Home Protection Act in 1915, which meant that a woman could file a caveat to prevent the sale of her home without her permission. And she supported the Dower Act of 1917, which gave a woman the right to stay on her homestead as long as she lived. Murphy moved easily into the role of community protector, serving as convenor of the Committee on Laws for the Better Protection of Women and Children, and working for the Edmonton Local Council of Women, a group that saw women in all manner of sleazy and criminal situations. Members of these groups were tough do-gooders who made it their business to attend court cases and to intervene if they saw fit. One day several shady ladies charged with vagrancy and prostitution were to appear in front of a judge who, while not outright ordering the members of the committee to leave, embarrassed them into withdrawing by asserting that they would be forced to listen to "evidence that no decent women would care to hear." Decency was often used as a weapon to censor women's access to information—and Murphy had had enough. Surely the accused were entitled to have their case heard by women. The group began to lobby for a woman on the bench. Surprisingly Alberta Attorney General Charles Wilson Cross agreed and in 1916 appointed Emily Murphy a commissioner under the Child Protection Act, as well as a police magistrate, meaning that she automatically judged juvenile court. The *Edmonton Bulletin*'s summary of her new post declared proudly, "Edmonton has its first woman police magistrate and Alberta has taken another step in the path of social reform, leading every other province in the Dominion." Even more striking, she was the first woman in the British Empire to be given such a post. Despite having no formal legal training, Murphy set out to learn. And learn she did, very quickly, that she would be persistently challenged, not on her judgement or knowledge, but because of her gender. One lawyer immediately argued that Murphy could not serve as a magistrate because she was not a person under the BNA Act, which defined "person" as "male persons." The fat was in the fire, and there was fire in the fight.

Women by this time could take up homesteads. And women had contributed physically to the province's growth. An all-woman crew had built the grade, near Viking, for the Grand Trunk Pacific railway. During the war they repaired bridges and worked in factories, collected bottles and cans for the war fund, served as nurses. And Alberta wasn't indifferent; it was the first province to set a minimum wage for women—$9 a week in 1917, which was raised to $14 a week in 1923. Then, in April of 1916, the suffrage bill passed, and women could vote in provincial elections. To celebrate, Murphy, McClung, and Judge Alice Jamieson had their picture taken together, looking as pleased as punch. When women first voted on June 17, 1917, their action declared a radical change in attitude. Only Lucien "Little Napoleon" Boudreau, the MLA for St. Albert, had opposed women's suffrage when it was proposed in the legislature, and not because of his French-Canadian background but because, he said, "British women did not vote."

Women were capable of everything, which of course included crimes and misdemeanours. The women who appeared in front of Judge Emily Murphy, persons or not, ranged from respectable and indignant women who had somehow failed to pay driving tickets or dog taxes and were annoyed at being forced to adhere to any law, to disadvantaged or criminal women involved in cases of child neglect, prostitution, family violence, or alcohol abuse. Murphy unflinchingly watched "white slave traffic," vagrancy, domestic abuse, illegitimacy, and the struggles of young women who fell in love with bounders and cads. She offered practical solutions for everything, including making the automobile a public place so that it could not be designated as a house of prostitution. Combining perspicacity and tough love, she corresponded with women in jail, urging them to reform. She instituted changes to the jail, which was in the basement of the Edmonton Court House, insisting that there should be more beds and that prisoners should be allowed to look out the window. Women had always had to use a lavatory pail in the corridor in plain view of the male prisoners; Murphy forced the prison to put a closed pail in the women's cell. Blunt and abrasive, she was not afraid to speak her mind on any subject, from venereal disease to the physical exploitation of girls.

Murphy cleaned up any number of messes with a mixture of moralistic fury and generous pragmatism. She was very much a woman of her time and place; her interpretation of women's circumstances, while reformist, reflected her position as a respectable woman who employed servants. While ready to help the unfortunate and the degraded, she was equally ready to apply a rigid moral measure, which gave rise to one of Murphy's controversial outbursts, a book on drug abuse entitled *The Black Candle*. Because she had seen so many girls and women whose lives were destroyed by cocaine and opium, Murphy felt perfectly qualified to comment on the use of drugs. Of course, the WCTU was in accord about mind-altering substances—alcohol was the villain in home destruction, but alcohol was used by white Europeans, men who were supposed to have moral fibre under their rough exteriors. Drugs like opium and cocaine occupied a more exotic realm, and Murphy accused "outsiders" of causing drug addiction, laying most of the blame for the presence of opium on Chinese-Canadians. Her xenophobia was overt—she mentioned other ethnic groups, but in her crusade generally fingered the Chinese as responsible. *The Black Candle* demonstrates Murphy's centrist Anglo-Saxon position; by birth and design, Murphy considered herself superior to any persons morally or ethnically different, and thus felt she had a perfect right to accuse them of immorality. Of course, Murphy reflected the sentiment of the times, one that feared racial diversity. And she was correct that illicit drug use needed to be curtailed; she thought, for example, that seized drugs should be destroyed because they often disappeared. But her insistence that the ideal immigrant should be assimilated into the mores and standards of Anglo-Saxon Christianity was doubtful and disturbing. Influenced by the beliefs of J. S. Woodsworth, she believed that immigrants of "inferior stock" needed to be denied entry to Canada. But even worse, on the basis that eugenics proved that mental and physical deficiencies were inherited, Murphy argued for sterilization as a means to control the "degradation" of good Canadian stock. Because so many of the cases that Murphy saw in her courtroom suffered from mental illness, her solution to misery and crime seemed logical to her. Sterilize the miserable and insane and mentally handicapped and they would not reproduce. Voila! No more mentally handicapped.

This position of "maternal feminism," arising out of the moral righteousness of women who believed in their own high-minded goals as wives, mothers, and caregivers, was a dangerous but populist feeling. The United Farm Women of Alberta were solidly in favour, and argued to the United Farmers of Alberta that "the adult mental defective of both sexes be kept under custodial care during the entire period of reproduction." So in 1928 the UFA government passed the Act Respecting Sexual Sterilization, one of the most horrific legacies of the twenties, not repealed until 1972. During those forty-four years, 2,822 Alberta women and men were sterilized, most without their agreement. Those victims are now seeking recourse. While some of them have received financial compensation, the terrifying power of such a measure, and the even more terrifying beliefs behind it show the extent to which Albertans, for the sake of "improvement," often do not think through a sticky moral dilemma. Betty Lambert's brilliant play *Jenny's Story* (1981) was one of the first literary works to examine the scars left by this attempt at social engineering.

Murphy secretly wanted an appointment to the Senate, but the federal government held fast to its archaic contention that women were not persons. Federal MPs seemed remarkably reluctant to explore ways in which the Constitution could be amended, and no matter how many letters of protest reached the Hill, the boys in Ottawa didn't think the position of women as reflected by a presence in the Senate deserved attention. The fight seemed to fizzle, until Murphy discovered that if five persons, acting as a unit, could petition the Supreme Court to interpret a part of the BNA Act, the issue would have to be heard by the court. So Murphy wrote to the four women she trusted most—Nellie McClung, the famous writer and prohibitionist from Calgary; Louise McKinney, the MLA for Claresholm and a key organizer of Woman's Christian Temperance Union chapters; Henrietta Muir Edwards from Fort Macleod, an expert on legal matters pertinent to women and children; and Irene Parlby, the MLA for Alix and the second woman cabinet minister in the British Empire—asking for their support, "in order that the women of this Dominion, comprising approximately one half of the electorate, may enjoy their full political rights on the same terms as these are, or may be, enjoyed by men."

Murphy was the point person, leading "the Famous Five." Her letter to them may seem somewhat dictatorial, but such an attitude appears to have been an accepted part of her personality, and at the end of August 1927 the five met for tea. The petition they signed that afternoon asked two questions. First, does the governor general or the Parliament of Canada have the power to appoint a woman to the Senate? Second, is it constitutionally possible for the Parliament of Canada under the BNA Act to make provision for the appointment of a woman to the Senate? Straightforward questions, asking for a clear yes or no. But the answer wasn't simple. That petition drifted all over Ottawa, from department to department, before Minister of Justice Earnest Lapointe decided that it should be referred to the Supreme Court of Canada. Somehow it had been revised without the petitioners' agreement, to read: "Does the word 'persons' in Section 24 of the BNA Act include female persons?" After working so hard to frame their questions without using the word "persons," the women had been railroaded. Murphy was furious, and in a letter to McClung vented at politicians and, most interestingly, the smugness of Central women. She wrote, "I hear, though, that it has been a terrible shock to the Eastern women that five coal heavers and plough pushers from Alberta (Can anything good come out of Nazareth?) went over their heads to the Supreme Court without even saying, 'Please ma'am, can we do it?' We know how to stir up interest in the East—just start it going ourselves." Murphy had become an Albertan. Although she and her friends were born in the Centre, they were now from Alberta, that hotbed of trouble out west.

The Supreme Court of Canada held a pompous hearing and sure enough, ruled that women were not eligible for appointment to the Senate because "they are not 'qualified persons.'" Thanks to the BNA Act and British common law, women were still defined as "equal with regard to pains and penalties, but not with regard to privileges." Despite women's being qualified, despite the precedent of women's having the vote, the Supreme Court simply clung to the pronoun of the law—"he." Innovative gestures were unlikely to come from the Centre, and that this particular appeal had come from the wicked West only made the political Centre more uneasy. So what else were these maverick women to do but go over the heads of the lengthy law-bound Supreme Court and the nervous Parliament and appeal to the Privy Council in England?

When the appeal was heard by the Privy Council in July 1929, none of the Canadian mavericks was present. There were a few British suffragists, but it was strictly a male affair, conducted with pomp and circumstance and a good deal of heavy dignity. Months later, almost anticlimactically, on October 18, 1929, Lord Chancellor Sankey read aloud a ponderous report that wove in and out of the person-and-pronoun labyrinth, finally concluding that "women are eligible to be summoned to and become members of the Senate of Canada." He concluded that the burden of argument rested on those who would deny that the word "persons" includes women. The headlines of the newspapers said it all. "Five Alberta Women Win in Senate Claim" and "Senate List Expands for Government Choice" and "New Legislation is Needed in Ottawa for the Appointment of Women." This became known as the Persons Case.

Not all of Murphy's wishes came true, though. She still had her heart set on being named to the Senate. When the Centrals in Ottawa appointed their first woman to the Senate, they appointed not Murphy but Ontario's Cairine Wilson, soft-spoken and ladylike and pliable. The slap was vicious. When Wilson, dainty and feminine, her gown trailing behind her, quite unlike the chesty Western harridans who had brought this state of affairs about, was escorted into the Senate on the arm of a male Senator, the male body of the Senate refused to stand or to applaud her. But that was scant comfort for Emily Murphy, who saw her ideals reduced to travesty. And to add insult to injury, there was talk of keeping female appointments to the Senate to a quota.

Murphy fought on, but began to lose heart, and in 1931 she retired as a magistrate. Two years later at the age of only sixty-five, she died in her sleep, after asking, just before she went to bed, the score of the latest Edmonton Grads' (the women's basketball team) game. The tributes to her were kinder in death than in life, often the case with people who threaten the status quo. She was famously difficult, and famously long-winded. Women complained that she wouldn't stop talking and that she wanted everyone to work for her—but the truth was, she fought a lot of her battles alone, and she took her gloves off to fight them. In an interesting footnote, no Alberta woman was appointed to the Senate until 1979 when Joe Clark appointed Martha Bielish from Warspite. Ottawa knew enough to be afraid, very afraid, of Alberta women.

Ironically, all of the Famous Five were Eastern imports. Henrietta Muir Edwards came from a fairly privileged Montreal family, but that did not prevent her from setting up the Working Girls' Association, a house where single women could get rooms, training, and legal advice. Edwards's evangelical impulses were not dampened by her marriage to Oliver Edwards, who moved to Indian Head as official doctor for the Indian reservations in 1883. During a brief sojourn back in Ottawa, Muir Edwards worked with the governor general's wife, Lady Aberdeen, to establish the Victorian Order of Nurses, the YWCA, and the National Council of Women, an umbrella organization for the Woman's Christian Temperance Union, the Women's Canadian Club, and the Women's Press Club. Muir Edwards served as the National Council of Women's Convener of Laws, which meant that she spent hours researching legal matters important to women. That was hard work and following Oliver was work too, especially when his next move was to the Blood Reserve in southern Alberta. By then, Edwards was rather stout. She had concluded that corsets, which squeezed and contorted the body, could not possibly be good for women, and so she stopped wearing them, and argued the same boycott to others. Of all the Famous Five, Henrietta Muir Edwards was the least fashionable, the poorest, and the most homespun, belying her well-heeled background. In 1899 she prepared a major summary of all the laws relating to women and children, a chore that signalled her long relationship with property law, pragmatically important to women. She died in 1931, two years after the Persons Case had been resolved, at the ripe old age of eighty-two.

Nellie McClung was born in Ontario, although her family moved to Manitoba when she was only six. She turned into a firebrand, public mischief-maker, and fierce advocate of prohibition—not temperance but prohibition. A powerful feminist, she contended that men wanted to keep women out of politics only because they didn't want women enjoying their cosy, well-paid political positions. "The great army of women workers are ill-paid, badly housed, and their work is not honoured or respected," she stated. Funny, headstrong, and fuelled by fantasies of a life beyond the mundane, McClung wrote moralistic fiction, spoke up in public over any matter pertinent to women, and was ready to battle every dragon. She could take on the worst heckler, her wit her greatest ally, and she was never afraid to fight dirty. She wrote, in her lifetime, some fifteen novels, various short stories, and two autobiographical works. *In Times Like These*, a political tongue-lashing of government and men, was published in 1914.

Her first cause was to unveil the terrible situation of the women who worked in the Winnipeg factories. Then she turned her formidable attentions to women's suffrage, helping to form the Women's Political Equality League and travelling around Manitoba promoting suffrage for women there. McClung believed, naively, that once women had the vote, they would first vote to eradicate liquor, then vote for better health services and dower laws. McClung could not believe that women would enjoy a drink, neglect their children, or elect corrupt politicians. The vote, she knew, would cure every social ill. Getting the vote became a powerful Grail, one that women rallied around. When the Manitoba premier, Redmond Roblin, mocked them, insisting that voting women would destroy the sanctity of the home, the Political Equality League decided to perform a mock parliament, which ridiculed men's duplicity in politics. With McClung playing the role of Roblin, the play was a great success—and in 1916 Manitoba became the first Canadian province to grant women the franchise.

By then, McClung had moved west and turned her attention to Alberta premiers and their failings. Women had been agitating for the Alberta vote since 1910, and various organizations worked for the franchise in tandem with education and prohibition. The concerns of women of that time were aimed at areas that affected them directly: temperance, child welfare, and education. Domestic life was of primary importance to these early fighters, and it served them with metaphors, too—Nellie McClung was likely to say that women were needed to do a mighty piece of housekeeping in politics. McClung arrived in 1914 bearing the banner of having castigated Manitoba's premier, and she was immediately made vice-president of the Equal Franchise League. With two hundred determined women who swept into the foyer of the legislature in February 1915, she made an eloquent address and presented poker-faced Premier A. L. Sifton with a petition of twelve thousand names requesting suffrage. Sifton gave a noncommittal answer and later muttered to the press that "Mrs. McClung and Mrs. Murphy are very determined women." And they were. Again they visited Sifton and got another noncommittal answer. Then, suddenly, he acquiesced—nobody knows why. Perhaps he was persuaded by his almost-invisible wife. In February Sifton introduced bills to enact prohibition and to confer the franchise, and on April 19, 1916, Alberta became the third province, after Manitoba and Saskatchewan, to give women suffrage.

What is it about the West? Determined women? A powerful receptiveness to social change? Only in the West would women's suffrage get such quick response—Ontario didn't grant women suffrage until 1917, and Quebec not until

1940. Why? These backward new-minted provinces were acting like forward thinkers. The federal vote was not granted to women until 1918, not exercised until the election of 1921, and no women from Alberta ran federally until 1935.

But even more surprising, considering that everyone tended to blame prohibition on women, the men of Alberta, in a referendum held before the franchise was extended to women, voted to prohibit liquor. Now this was harder to figure out. Were they stricken with conscience? Did they think that this law would prevent women from getting the vote, maybe shut them up? Were they trying to head the WCTU, those Women who Continually Torment Us, off at the pass, give them a sop? It is hard to know what brought about that strange result, but Alberta went dry, convincing McClung and her colleagues that they could turn wine into water. McClung won a seat in the Alberta legislature in 1921, a member of the Liberal opposition, representing an Edmonton riding. But even then, she refused to adhere to party lines. When it came to matters related to women and children, she voted with her conscience, not her party, sometimes with and sometimes against the UFA government. When, in 1924, another referendum repealed prohibition, McClung was crushed. Prohibition had been voted in by men, but had been voted out by women. Bitterly McClung was learning that women were turncoats, too, and not nearly as interested in social progress and moral uplift as she had assumed. Albertans like to drink.

McClung, who had moved to Calgary by then, was discovering that her moralistic zeal and her stand on prohibition weren't helping her political image—in the 1926 election she lost her seat by sixty votes. The success of the Persons Case must have been a small consolation, but McClung's other causes, too, had mixed results. She was both terribly behind and far ahead of her time. She wanted women to be able to serve as fully ordained ministers, a reform that churches simply would not hear of. She had a fraught relationship with war and pacifism and the draft. When the Alberta government decided that women should not be allowed to enter bars, Nellie came up with another of her famous observations: "With the Senate doors open now, there are only two great institutions that will not accept women on equal terms—the church and the beer parlours." Later, as the first woman on the CBC board of governors, she fought hard for women's programming and women employees, a novel idea that the centralist CBC resisted as strongly as men had resisted the vote and the Persons Case. Overall, Nellie's Alberta years stirred the powerful stew of government change and reform. But she was never appointed to the Senate either. No Western rabble-rousers allowed there.

Louise McKinney, then Louise Crummy, also came from Ontario. She had joined the WCTU while she was still in school and embraced every one of its tenets about alcohol debauching men, debasing women, and destroying children. She wanted to be a doctor, but became a teacher instead, and while teaching school in North Dakota met James McKinney, who was as determined to rid the world of alcohol as she was. Moving north to Alberta, the McKinneys settled in Claresholm, and Louise became a firebrand for the establishment of WCTU chapters, helping to found forty-three of them in Alberta and Saskatchewan. Using the example of abused and neglected women, she worked hard for the white ribboners and even harder for the purification of politics. Confident that suffrage would put an end to the existence of liquor, the WCTU member stamped around Alberta and, miracle of miracles, managed to persuade men to vote for prohibition in the referendum of 1915. Power was a heady mix, and McKinney ran for the Alberta legislature in 1917, winning and becoming the first woman to sit in a provincial legislature in the British Empire. Actually, two women sat in that forward-thinking legislature; Roberta McAdams was elected as part of the Alberta Military Representation Act. Her election handbills asked that soldiers and nurses give one vote to a man and "the other to the sister," promising that she would work for the interests of returning soldiers after the war. But since it took a while for McAdams to get herself back to Alberta from her nursing work overseas, McKinney sat first.

What a time and what a place! Two women in the legislature, and not meek, quiet little yes-sayers. The incredible contradiction of these women was that they espoused a powerful connection with God and religion, and yet lived amazingly emancipated lives. McKinney believed in equal pay for equal work, so while she opposed the use of liquor and tobacco, she supported women's getting a reasonable recompense for the sweat of their brows. The repeal of prohibition was awful for McKinney, too; especially because it was women who had voted to Bring Back the Bottle. McKinney shifted her energy to working for the convergence of the Methodist, Congregationalist, and Presbyterian churches, becoming the only Western woman to sign the Basis of Union that created the United Church. When she died, her grave was covered with the white ribbons of purity and faith that the WCTU cherished so much.

Irene Parlby (née Marryat) was the only one of the Famous Five not born in Ontario, but she could one-up Centrals in breeding and class in every way; she was raised in England and India, and only happened to come to Canada to visit friends who were living in Alix, close to Lacombe, in 1896. There, she met and fell in love with Walter Parlby and decided to stay. Delighted by Western adventure—falling into mudholes and fording rivers—she was thrilled with the beautiful landscape. Both Parlbys were immensely privileged. He had attended Oxford, and she had enjoyed governesses and Swiss finishing schools, but they adapted to life in central Alberta with tremendous zest, endlessly fascinated by the unfolding of a new country. Parlby was active in the development of the Women's Auxiliary of the United Famers of Alberta, and when the UFA became a political party she ran for election in the riding of Lacombe. Astonishingly, the UFA won a landslide, she was made minister without portfolio, the second woman in the British Empire to hold a cabinet post (the other was in BC). Her lack of portfolio might have seemed pointless, but Parlby made it count, sifting through the intricate processes of government as patiently as a nun. Sitting among the men of that government, she could be eloquently persuasive, especially on bills to do with public health. The acts that she sponsored included the Children of Unmarried Parents Act (a woman could sue for child support), the Child Welfare Act, the Official Guardian Act, the Alimony Orders Enforcement Act, the Domestic Relations Act, and the Maintenance Order Act. Parlby was a quiet but effective counterbalance to Murphy and McClung, who were impatient for change; she knew that change didn't happen overnight, and yet she was happy to sign Emily Murphy's petition, thus becoming the fifth of the famous quints. Parlby served three terms with the UFA government, until 1935, when the UFA were completely routed. She did, however, at the request of Prime Minister R. B. Bennett, go to Geneva as one of three Canadian representatives to the League of Nations. Then, having seen her share of politics and political life, Parlby contentedly lived out a long life in Alix.

How could these five women, the signatories of the Persons Case petition, come out of regressive, redneck, provincial, regionally afflicted Alberta? Would they have been able to do what they did had they stayed in the Centre? Would this work even have occurred to them, or would they have been consigned to gloomy Edwardian drawing rooms, gloves and hats eternally necessary, and corsets tight to the point of discomfort? It is as if by transporting themselves to Alberta, they were transported to a land of amazing emancipation, where the very air egged them on, sent them out to fight. Their thirteen-year struggle to change the law did not result in any personal reward. Murphy certainly never received the recognition that she deserved, and only Nellie McClung went to Ottawa to view the plaque, mounted in a hallway near the Senate, with their five names. None of them was appointed to the Senate, doubtless because they made staid Centrals nervous. One old senator is reported to have said, "Oh, we never could have had Mrs. Murphy in the Senate! She would have caused too much trouble!" Exactly. And shame on Ottawa. These women took on the fight for personhood in name and in law and became the most unlikely gang ever to ride out of the West. They are immortalized now, in a larger-than-life bronze group statue that was unveiled in 1999 beside Calgary's Olympic Plaza. There's an empty chair in their circle, a chair that invites any passerby to sit. So many women and men have accepted their invitation that the chair's surface has already begun to wear away. A copy of the same statue was subsequently moved to Parliament Hill in Ottawa, after another great fight, because only Fathers of Confederation, reigning monarchs, and dead prime ministers are allowed to have statues in Ottawa. Getting Ottawa to approve the monument took the efforts of another hard-fighting Alberta woman, Calgarian Frances Wright. Now the Famous Five lift their bronze teacups to success, to the West's having once again overturned the Centre. Centrals who view them there have a vague idea that these must be Ottawa women. In fact they were dyed-in-the-wool Albertans, every one of them, earning themselves a place on Parliament Hill.

The flapper age of the twenties, which featured less-restrictive clothing, short skirts, and more fun, matched the new emancipation. Alberta women were as interested in fashion as anyone else. When the flapper craze arrived, they raised their hemlines, bared their shoulders and flattened their breasts, happy that a new dress, which used to take twenty-five yards of cloth, now took only four. And they bobbed their hair—losing all that weight made them light-headed. At Holy Cross Hospital in 1926, two student nurses who cut their hair were fired, but when all of them did the same, the administration had to give in. Women then were called Mildred and Luella, and even if they were still pushed toward being teachers and nurses, at least in towns and cities, they now had vacuum cleaners and electric stoves. Still, only 3 percent of married women worked outside the home. As for sex and childbirth, they were as cloaked in silence as they were at the turn of the century.

Alberta's best-known women after the Famous Five were the Edmonton Commercial Graduates' Basketball Club, heroines who passed and shot their way from behind their typewriters to the basketball courts of the world. Between 1915 and 1940, the Edmonton Grads won all but twenty of the 522 games they played. Coached by a steady and self-effacing Percy Page, the McDougall Commercial High School principal who would become Alberta's eighth lieutenant governor (1959–66), they dazzled the world, winning local, national, and international championships as handily as they typed. (Their first captain, Winnifred Martin, had the fastest fingers in Canada; she won a 1924 typing championship with 118 accurate words in one minute.) The Grads were strictly amateurs. Page had introduced basketball as part of the school's physical education component; since it was a relatively new game, he had to buy a book to read up on its rules, and given that the school had no gym and the students played on a hard outdoor court, their initial success—they won the provincial championship—was astonishing. At the end of the school year, they didn't want to quit.

Most of the players worked as stenographers or clerks, and by Page's rules had to be unmarried, abstemious, and of sterling character. But with his wife along as a chaperone, Page's girls saw the world. They competed in four Olympics, winning every one of twenty-seven exhibition games, and James Naismith, the Canadian man who invented basketball, called them the greatest team that ever stepped out on a floor. Even more telling, they stared down archaic superstitions about women and sport, and how their natures couldn't tolerate hard physical competition. They were told that they would never have children or that they would die before they were forty, but the Grads ignored all dire predictions and concentrated on their exceptional teamwork. Thirty-eight women played for the Grads over the years, and their almost predictable victories gave Edmonton countless opportunities for celebratory parades. In 1938 captain Noel MacDonald was named Canada's Female Athlete of the Year, and it was only after the outbreak of the Second World War that the team disbanded, leaving behind a legend that is still incomparable, and changing the face of women's sport forever. Allan Stein directed a National Film Board documentary, *Shooting Stars*, on the Grads, in 1988.

The Second World War changed women's circumstances completely. Women joined the forces, although most of them performed tasks—clerks, drivers, and cooks—that would free the men for battle. Best of all was the range of jobs that opened up at home—women could at last get into more than nursing and teaching, and they worked in meat packing, aircraft repair, manufacturing, and heavy industry, and as elevator operators and textile workers, taxi drivers and bricklayers. A telephone operator could earn $36.50 a month. The Great Western Garment Company in Edmonton had always employed women, GWG's overalls famous for their stop-loss pockets and their strength. Lillian Morris, who was president of Local 120 of United Garment Workers of America, wore men's overalls during a trip with GWG management to Drumheller to appeal to miners to wear only GWGs and thus support local industry. When GWG got the contract for military clothing, it became the largest employer of women in the province, and 425 of them worked around the clock, seamstresses as well as machinists and knife pushers. It was a heady, busy time, and when it was over, although women were encouraged to return home, they were not quite so happy to comply. Edmonton women had danced and flirted with all the Americans working on the CANOL Road project, they'd learned the pleasure of money in their pockets, and they had proven that they could do anything men could do. They had also learned that driving a car could be a lot more fun than baking cookies.

After the war a new influx of refugee and immigrant women flooded in to work as servants, waitresses, nurses, and housekeepers. The Anglo configuration of Alberta was changing colour and tone. More and more women went to university. Rural women were becoming aware of the complexities of farming as a business; farm women had always had to carry wood and clean stoves, milk and garden and sew and launder in an unending round of chores. Farmhouses were relatively rudimentary, and women's labour left little room for sentimentality or hobbies. But after the war, women's work took on a greater value.

The voices of Nellie McClung and Emily Murphy seemed distant, faraway. Even with the sexual revolution and political change in North America in the late 1960s, Alberta women lived within a subtle conservatism that still echoes in the treatment of women today. Disgracefully, Alberta was the home province of the notorious Irene Murdoch case of the late 1960s. An Alberta farm wife who had worked for twenty-five years alongside her husband, Murdoch sued for a share in the family's ranch when the two divorced in 1968. Women across the country were shocked at the Supreme Court's upholding the lower court's judgement: they decreed that she had no right to half the property since she had done no more than what was normally expected of a farm wife. All her years of work did not entitle her to any part of the farm, and she was awarded only a lump-sum maintenance payment. The concrete injustice of this decision finally seemed to wake women up, and Alberta's Matrimonial Property Act, ensuring equal division of assets, was finally passed in 1978.

It's still a fight. Women don't drive chuckwagons, and in Edmonton, as recently as 1988, Shirley Benson became the first female firefighter. Christine Silverberg's service as Calgary's chief of police met a lot of resistance, but she proved she was up to the challenge. Nancy MacBeth, Elaine McCoy, and Pam Barrett have met with uneven success in politics, although currently seventeen of the eighty-three MLAs are women. Women run oil companies and write books, women design software and run record companies. Instead of signing up with an agency, Edmonton's "escorts" can now work independently and operate offices in their homes. But the hum of Alberta's boomeranging conservatism still pervades the province, and women here know that they better keep checking over their shoulders, twirling their lassos, and never take anything for granted. That witty and drunken old reprobate, Bob Edwards, a man who loved women, said, "It is our firm conviction that blending of women's ideas with those of reasonably thoughtful men will some day bring about an era of common sense."

We're still waiting.

14 | Buffalo and Beaver, Bluster and Blood

History is a plot. Just when the muddled writer thinks she has finally looked at some event from every angle, another detail appears, a line in a newspaper, or a photo of a person, and all logic spills on the floor. There are facts and there are facts, too many facts, sometimes too few facts. The facts themselves can be as confusing as the truth, and of course there is no truth. But tantalizing fragments of story, all of them deserving their own books, keep ambushing the story of Alberta. Here are some of them (arranged alphabetically).

• • •

Beaver, Buffalo, Bears

The beaver made it, but the buffalo (bison) didn't. The terrible transformation of the emporium of the West reduced their numbers from sixty million to a few dozen, and to heaps of scattered bones. Now, Wood Buffalo National Park, created to protect the wood bison, has about thirty-five hundred animals; Elk Island National Park is home to some five hundred plains bison. Buffalo have no natural enemies other than humans.

Bears, black bears and grizzlies, fight to hold their own. Both prefer berries and plants to meat, but will eat small animals and fish. To fatten up for their long winter's sleep, they gorge themselves; biologists claim that grizzlies can devour 200,000 buffalo berries a day. Not as gregarious as black bears, grizzlies have retreated far back into the parks. They do all they can to avoid humans, and if there is a confrontation the bear is likely to win. People are given suffi-cient warning. The signs read: "You are in bear country." They mean the bears have the right of way.

Beaver brought the white man west. Hunted nearly to extinction in the years of the fur trade, these large, sleek, lustrous, aquatic rodents are now on the increase. They are one of the only mammals besides man to build their own houses. In 1791 in Athabasca country, Peter Fidler ran into the biggest beaver house he had ever seen: "The Indians with me said that it also far surpassed in size any that they had seen. I had on this account the curiosity to measure it & found it to be 44 yard in circumference & 18 feet high, situated in the middle of a small Swamp, but appeared to us to have had no water in it these few years back. The house was old & no Beaver in it. It was not a collection of Houses joined together as the Beaver some times make as the families of the Beaver grow up, but one single intire house & had been made in one season. On account of its prodigious size I should imagine it to have been the collective labour of nearly 20 Beaver." Still sitting on the back of Canada's nickel, beaver are now on the increase, living in cities and happily gnawing down suburban trees.

Alberta is also home to the cougar, *felis concolor*. In January 2000 Frances Frost, a dancer and artist, was attacked and killed while cross-country skiing just outside Canmore. The attack marked the growing friction between humans and animals; if cougars have insufficient wildlife to hunt successfully, they will try for other prey, even human. Because of the declining numbers of deer, elk, and bighorn sheep, the eight hundred or so cougars living in the foothills are hungry. After Frost's death, the park issued a chilling set of directives, instructing residents and visitors not to leave small children unattended and to keep pets on a leash. But most interesting was the reaction of Frances Frost's family. They mourned her death, but felt that she had died doing something she loved, and that the animal was no vicious killer, merely following its nature. Her memorials did not call for park closings or government intervention, but talked about her love of life and her pleasure in the mountain area where she lived.

Coal and the Crowsnest

Coal underlies huge areas of Alberta. The Indians called it "burning rocks," and white newcomers, who first noticed it in seams along the banks of the North Saskatchewan River in Edmonton in the 1860s, quickly learned to mine it. Low in ash, Edmonton's coal fired easily but burned too fast; its low sulphur content made it satisfactory for domestic use, but unsuitable to burn in train locomotives. Coal was cheap and efficient, and a ton could produce 50 percent more heat than a cord of wood, a bonus for settlers who needed heating fuel. When John Walter brought a stove capable of burning coal to Edmonton in 1874, its use spread.

Edmonton's old-timers all owned coal mines. Donald Ross, who dug an air shaft to the surface so he could mine year round, found his hospitality "overtaxed by miners" and so began charging them fifty cents for meals. John Walter's mine near the south end of the High Level Bridge killed six miners in a fire in 1907, but it did not cease production. By 1908 thirty local mines tendered coal to schools, the fire hall, and the hospital. The Edmonton Penitentiary Mine was worked by inmates, digging heat for the prison itself. By 1917 the Clover Bar mine had 250 employees, ten staff officers, and a winter payroll of $20,000 a month. The Humberstone mine at Clover Bar produced eight hundred tons of coal a day and employed two hundred men. The Black Diamond mine lasted forty-nine years and produced three million tons—22 percent of all the coal mined in Edmonton. To the local economy, coal was worth a million dollars every three weeks.

But Edmonton coal could not compete with the burnability of Crowsnest coal, and by the 1930s the city mines had shut down, partly because mining led to cave-ins and sinking of surface land, land the city wanted people to build houses on. Eventually Edmonton purchased all the coal rights on river lots and prohibited mining under the roads because of serious damage to public utilities.

The coal in the south had a longer life. In 1870 Nicolas Sheran, a young Irishman driving a whisky trader's wagon between Fort Benton, Montana, and Fort Whoop-Up (now Lethbridge), recognized a coal seam in the banks around Whoop-Up and made return trips to Montana with loads of coal. Coal in the Red Deer River valley led to the mines in Drumheller. Belgian missionary Father Pierre-Jean De Smet noticed coal in the Crowsnest Pass in 1845, and when the railway put a line through to Nelson, BC, on Kootenay Lake in 1898, they found the coal in the pass ideal for stoking the boilers of CPR engines. Processed into coke, it fuelled the huge smelter at Trail, BC. To finance the line, the CPR accepted an $11,000-per-mile grant from the federal government and in return agreed to haul prairie grain at a cheaper rate to ports on Lake Superior and the Pacific Ocean. The Crowsnest Pass Agreement and the Crow Rate were born, with Western farmers' winning a fixed freight rate they have fought to retain ever since.

Towns blossomed along the Crowsnest Pass. The first mine opened at Blairmore in 1898, and within fourteen months ten other mining towns had named themselves. Wages of $3 a day attracted workers from all over the world, and coal became the crucible for unions; organizers from the United Mine Workers of America signed up miners by translating their creed into Italian, Ukrainian, and Hungarian. The pass boomed and grew, temporarily forced to pause only when, at 4:10 a.m. on Wednesday, April 29, 1903, a 100-million-ton slab of Turtle Mountain's rock crashed down onto the east end of the town of Frank. Located in the valley of the Oldman River, Frank was a model mining town of six hundred crouched under the shadow of the mountain in a spot where the Kootenay Indians had always refused to camp because they knew the mountain was restless. The mine was 165 yards deep, its seams at an easy eighty-five-degree angle that required little blasting, as if the mountain were complicit with its own mining. Still, it had given some warning. In the months before the slide, timbers checked thoroughly at night were found splintered in the morning. Rooms of removed coal would silently and mysteriously seal up. On the night of April 29 there was a sharp drop in temperature, noted by the crew of the 4 a.m. freight train, which pulled up to the mine entrance, and after the crew talked with some night-shift workers headed back to town. The mine bridge was in sight when the engineer heard a deafening rumble. Instinctively he thrust the throttle forward and the train lurched across the bridge with the brakemen clinging to the sides. Behind them, bridge, tracks, and earth convulsed. When they pulled to a halt and rubbed their eyes, they realized that they had to warn the *Spokane Flyer,* a passenger train due into Frank any moment. A brakeman grabbed a lantern and headed across the rubble toward the main tracks, reaching the eastern stretch just in time to wave the lantern at the train and stop it. House-sized boulders filled the valley and climbed halfway up the slope of the opposite mountain. Cottages, the livery stable, and a construction camp were destroyed. The centre of town was spared, but the force of the blast was so great that people were thrown from their beds. Nobody quite knew what had happened. An earthquake? Volcanic activity? Flooding? The cable to Prime Minister Laurier read: "Terrible catastrophe here. Eruption Turtle Mountain devastated miles of territory. One hundred killed. Must have Government aid. . . ."

The number of dead and many of their names are still unknown. William Pearce, federal inspector of mines, arrived the next day. He suspected that the near-vertical mining might have caused the slide, and his report, not made public until 1979, suggested that the company had left insufficient substance between the mine walls, an unsafe practice that might have contributed to the slide. He would prove right. Later it became clear that sedimentary rock destabilization, exacerbated by the warm days and cold nights before the slide, resulting in moisture and freezing, probably caused the slump. In the weeks after, journalists and politicians made the required pilgrimage to the Crowsnest Pass to witness the results of the greatest slide in recorded history. Because the track was impassable, the train stopped at the slide base and passengers had to haul their luggage across the rubble to a train on the other side. Nervous townspeople were moved immediately, and the whole town was shifted to the north, but before the decade was over Frank had become a ghost town. The mine owner died in 1908, some say of "nervous fear," and in 1917 the mine ceased operation. The Indians still call Turtle Mountain the mountain that walks.

That was only the Crowsnest's first disaster. On December 9, 1910, an explosion rippled through Bellevue mine. Forty-two men were working underground and thirty-one of them were killed, not by the explosion but by "afterdamp," that deadly mix of carbon dioxide and carbon monoxide. Rescuers brought the bodies to the surface and put them in the bathhouse, where women tried to identify what was left of their husbands. One thousand miners, full of grief and anger, marched behind their coffins; deaths always created demands for improved safety. An inquest in 1911 found that negligence was the cause of the explosion, but West Canadian Collieries was not penalized. The company's insurers refused to pay benefits, and UMWA lawyers had to fight for damages.

But the worst was yet to come. On June 19, 1914, a series of explosions rocked the Hillcrest mine. Of the 235 men working underground, 189 were killed, the worst mining disaster in Canadian history. The coal dust had loosened with gunpowder blasting, and one spark hitting this dust ignited it. The explosion set off a chain reaction. Toxic gas and carbon monoxide delayed rescue operations while, on the surface, miners' families, the Mounties, and the entire town gathered to wait. After twenty minutes, eighteen men staggered out, and the rescuers pushed through, finding men crushed to death beneath timbers or blown to pieces from the explosions. Others succumbed to the afterdamp or drowned when they tried to use pools of water to strain the poisonous gas. Again the dead were carried to the surface and again the horrific task of identifying bodies and their parts began. The limbs of strong young men lay scattered on the washhouse floor while reassembled bodies lay in rough coffins in the Miners' Hall. Charles Elick, a miner who had dug himself out of Turtle Mountain after the Frank slide, was killed at Hillcrest; his wife gave birth to their youngest child the day after the disaster. On June 21, while the graves were still being dug, the funerals began, the dead grouped—Roman Catholic, Anglican, Presbyterian, Odd Fellows, Masons, Orangemen—and laid to rest in long, shallow trenches. The disaster left 130 widows and four hundred fatherless children; Hillcrest Collieries paid each family

$1,800. At the inevitable inquiry, the fire boss suggested that sparks from a rockfall could have ignited the gas. His analysis was disputed, but years later his theory proved right. Hillcrest mine continued to operate until 1949.

Between 1900 and 1945, more than a thousand miners died in accidents and explosions, most in that fourteen-mile strip between Blairmore, Alberta, and the British Columbia border. Benevolent societies were set up to provide insurance against illness; the union established a fund to help injured miners and widows, and built a hospital in Coleman in 1906. But much of what happened was part of an ancient class struggle, acted out between English bosses and "radical immigrant communities," who only wanted to work and live. In Lethbridge, another coal-mining town, mine owner Alexander Galt was coldly indifferent to miners and their lives. He deliberately hired an ethnic mix of workers hoping their clash of languages and cultures would make them resist unionization. He had broken strikes at Galt mine in 1894, 1897, and 1899, but in 1906 the UMWA organized a strike to end all strikes. In the first sixty days there were two riots, thirteen explosions, and one charge of arson. Galt called on the Mounties to control the strikers, but police interference only made tensions run higher, and the strike wore on through a long summer. In a positive east/west move, William Lyon Mackenzie King (not yet the prime minister) came out to mediate, and successfully resolved the strike. And the union was satisfied; while it had given up a few demands, it had also successfully established a presence in Alberta. When the 1907 Provincial Coal Commission toured the province, its members recommended changes that included setting up of a workers' compensation fund, better mine inspection, and restrictions on child labour (boys working in the mines were sometimes as young as twelve).

There were other strikes and other attempts to unionize. No wonder. Working conditions for miners and railway workers could be outrageous. Crowded into unheated tents and bunkhouses, often cold and hungry, the men were ripe for disease. Everything they received, from the rough blankets they slept under to the mouldy food they ate, was deducted from their pay. Men who fell ill were charged for room, board, and medical care. Men who were injured were fired. As late as 1935, coal town Drumheller was described by Mary Rundle, secretary to the Royal Commission to investigate the coal industry, as a "dreary little mining town set in a strange pocket of weird hills—the valley of the Red Deer River. The formations are most peculiar, not to say sinister." Hundreds of small shacks huddled together in large "camps," mostly grouped around the principal mines. There was no water supply except from a communal tap in the middle of the camp, and no sanitation. It resembled a valley of desolation.

When natural gas flared in 1923, the coal market began to decline, and only recently, with coal a cheaper fuel than gas, is there potential for its recovery. Alberta is still home to coal mines, the not-yet-open Cheviot, close to Hinton and next to Jasper National Park, whose start-up has been postponed by limited coal markets and subject to environmental strictures. The Luscar mine still employs up to 450 people, but it is running out of coal and will close in 2002. The days of collieries, of coke ovens and underground ponies, are over.

Camrose

A pretty city set in the fertile Battle River valley, on the wagon trail between Wetaskiwin and Saskatoon. First called Sparling and begun in 1905, it is the heart of Scandinavian settlement; the farmland is enormously rich and the surrounding parkland peppered with settlements like New Norway, Edberg, Bergen, New Sweden, and Malmo. The Battle River watershed is one of the most beautiful areas in Alberta, especially around Dried Meat Lake, Meeting Creek, and Buffalo Lake. Camrose is home to Sunny Boy Cereal and Augustana University College; Chester Ronning, diplomat and educator, expert on China, lived there.

Drumheller and Dinosaurs

A town that time forgot, first a ranching outpost, then a coal-mining town, home to great whorehouses and magnificent labour unrest—until the discovery of the eerie skeletons of the dinosaurs. For years a pan-baked town huddled between the hoodoos and decorated with shambling plastic dinosaur replicas, it assumed a mantle of dignity and sophistication when it became home to the Royal Tyrrell Museum of Palaeontology. It's also home to the Drumheller Penitentiary, a sprawling medium-security federal facility. The rock formation that cradles the skeletons of the beasts who once roamed Alberta is situated in Drumheller. Charles Sternberg, the great dinosaur hunter, described the area with poetic intensity: "The valley of the Red Deer at Drumheller is a great chasm four hundred feet deep, cut by the river into the heart of the prairie. Across from plain to plain it is nearly two

Paleontologist George Sternberg, son of Charles, taking a break on a hoodoo

miles. Tributary creeks and coulees have cut narrow trenches back into the plain, while in the main valley, especially near the brink of the prairie, are long ridges, tablelands, buttes and knolls, pinnacles and towers . . . transformed by nature's sculpting into fantastic bad-land scenery."

Of course, the better dinosaur park, Dinosaur Provincial Park, is much farther east, closer to the city of Brooks, which feels that Drumheller's fossil museum has robbed it of dinosaur destiny. On a pan of dry bentonite in the park, pilgrims can listen to a paleontologist decoding a message from two hundred million years ago, the washboard of dinosaur bones stretched out as if sleeping, waiting for someone to stub a toe on an exposed rib. Dinosaur scientists study and sort and test dinosaurian ecology, the creatures' habits, their brains, their social groupings. Were they communal animals? What cries did they make and how did they mate? Did they herd or migrate, graze or devour? Visitors kneel in homage to the mysteries of this area now called Badlands, the licorice-striped layers of sand and mudstone a vast prehistoric burial ground. The grave-robber dinosaur hunters roamed here for one hundred years collecting the collateral of fossils, dragging the giant skeletons off to London, Buenos Aires, New York, and Ottawa. Only after years of waving them goodbye did Albertans realize that we were losing our ancestors.

Edson

The town, initially called Heatherwood, at the beginning of the Edson Trail, 250 miles of "mud, muskeg, and mosquitoes" on the way to Grande Prairie. The Peace

River country was rich, open land, and settlers heading there needed a short, efficient route. The Edson Trail was shorter than the original overland route via Athabasca Landing, but it was not efficient. The stopping houses along the way were as rough as the trail itself, and so the Edson Trail served as a baptism of fire for settlers making their way to the land of the Peace. When the Edmonton, Dunvegan & British Columbia Railway pushed through to Mirror Landing, in 1916, it was abandoned.

Fort Macleod, Fort McMurray, Fort Saskatchewan

Towns started by Mounties, therefore the appellation "fort," but each one distinctive. After stumbling around the prairies developing sore feet, the Mounties first slapped together a palisade on an island in the Oldman River and called it Fort Macleod, after Colonel James Macleod. For years the main base for the Mounties, it is not much bigger now than it was in the early 1900s. A peaceful town, it serves, together with Pincher Creek, the ranching area of southern Alberta.

Fort McMurray, on the other hand, is the fastest-growing city in Alberta, developments in the oil sands booming with each passing year. It began as a fur-trading outpost, when floating the rivers into the north was almost impossible. The land barrier between the North Saskatchewan and the Athabasca varies from one to two hundred miles, and much of it was impassable muskeg, until the Athabasca Trail was replaced in 1919 by the Alberta & Great Waterways Railway, Premier Rutherford's downfall.

Now Fort McMurray dances with activity, planes coming and going, hotels full and bars rowdy. The city was recently shocked to discover that it had two hundred homeless people and about eight hundred on the brink of homelessness, simply because builders cannot erect dwellings quickly enough. The city is growing by 20 percent a year. Stranded in a beautiful location, at the confluence of the Clearwater and Athabasca rivers, the city revolves around the oil industry, with Syncrude, Suncor, and Northstar plants located some twenty-five miles away. The sands are as sticky as molasses, their bitumen, or hydrocarbon, content high enough to warrant the considerable investment that has gone into developing new extracting processes and building pipelines. Oil sands reserves stagger the imagination; best guesses claim up to 2.1 trillion barrels of reserve oil, more than in the entire Middle East. The sites themselves are overwhelming. Huge draglines scoop the sand out of pits and onto a pile; then a bucketwheel reclaimer moves the oil sand to conveyor belts, which carries it to the plant for extraction and upgrading. Each dragline is as tall as a 25-storey building. Eventually the conveyor belt systems will be completely replaced by more economic heavy-hauler trucks to transport the sands. The most recent heavy hauler developed weighs 360 tons. Each costs almost $3 million, and each of its four tires costs $40,000 to $45,000. Women are apparently the better drivers—they don't wear out the gearbox quite as quickly as men. In the plant, bitumen is now extracted by a hot water method, then upgraded to synthetic crude oil, so called because it is altered from its naturally occurring state. Because it contains few impurities, Syncrude's patented end product is known as Syncrude Sweet Crude. As long as North Americans use oil products, Fort McMurray will enjoy a prosperous future.

Fort Saskatchewan was where the northern Mounties built their post; it seems they were nervous about staying in Edmonton. As a result, Fort Saskatchewan has become a disciplinary centre with a provincial correctional facility, just enough of an elbow away from Edmonton to have an attitude.

Gophers

Quick, twitchy little ground-dwelling rodents, actually Richardson's ground squirrels, common to fields and pastures, a hallmark of the prairies. Hated by farmers—cows step in their holes and break legs—who try to eradicate them with poison or other means. For years gophers had a price on their heads; small boys got a penny-a-tail bounty for catching them. The whimsical world-famous Go-fur Museum in Torrington, Alberta, has carried gopher mania to extremes, stuffing the little critters and dressing them up, then placing them in anthropomorphic tableaus. Visitors can buy their very own stuffed gopher under glass for the mantelpiece. Torrington even has a gopher song:

> Listen to the whistle, oh hear the gopher call,
> As they roam from early springtime to the late part of fall.
> They dig their holes with pleasure,
> Five for everyone,
> Front door, back door, side door,
> And two dug just for fun!

Grande Prairie

The agrarian city of Alberta's north, which sits at the heart of a tantalizing open area—La Grande Prairie—that invited cultivation. The original destination of the Edmonton & Dunvegan Railway, it struggled with access for years. Now a centre for the surrounding agricultural region, it also supports a substantial oil and gas industry, along with logging.

Eric Harvie

Eccentric and generous lawyer and collector whose oil holdings, right next to Leduc, made him fabulously rich. Instead of spending his wealth all on himself, he established the Glenbow Foundation, then went out into the world and collected everything from sleighs to swords to Queen Victoria's underwear. Harvie rented warehouses in Calgary to hold the material he gathered, which is so eclectic that it can still startle museum staff. Those items formed the basis for the Glenbow Museum and Archives, one of the most outstanding collections of Western Canadian history, including paintings, books, photographs, and other artefacts. A cornucopia of the marvellous, the Glenbow holds First Nations materials, minerals, and medieval armour, and includes stuff as eccentric as shrunken heads and the first Model T every built. An unprepossessing man, Harvie drove an old Studebaker and kept his philanthropy under wraps. Although he died in 1975, the Devonian Group of Charitable Foundations still gives away money in memory of a man who left the province of Alberta a legacy beyond measure.

Icefields Parkway

The highway to Jasper from Banff, without question the most heavenly road in the world, mountains blue and purple to either side, every bend a breathtaking vista. It leads gawking motorhome drivers right past the spectacular Columbia Icefields, where tourists can fall into hidden crevasses and meet slow deaths from hypothermia. The Columbia covers almost ninety-seven square miles, bringing together three fields of ice—the Columbia, the Saskatchewan, and the Athabasca glaciers. At the toe the glacier seems benign, water pouring from its melt. The tongues of ice from the high country seem motionless, but ice and snow live and converse in avalanches and falls, while glaciers calve bergs of old, old water, suspended in blue. Tourists drive by, hardly daring to leave the road, but those brave enough to climb find paradisical alpine meadows. At the legendary Amethyst Lakes, hikers have been known to faint at the exquisite beauty that meets their eyes.

Kananaksis

The shyest mountainous area of the province, designated a recreation area rather than a park, but actually just as beautiful as Banff and Jasper. It was developed to serve as the downhill skiing site for the 1988 Olympics. The slope that was chosen is almost always bared by the chinooks, so Nakiska resort claims the most outrageously expensive state-of-the-art snow-making equipment in the country. Only in Alberta.

Lac Ste. Anne

Pilgrimage site forty miles west of Edmonton where every July more than sixty thousand people seek spiritual and physical healing. Immersion in the lake is supposed to cure every possible illness and grief. First Peoples have travelled to Lac Ste. Anne for centuries; they are now joined by other Albertans prepared to believe in miracles.

Lethbridge

Later known as the city that coal built, originally the site of Fort Whoop-Up, riding between the coulees cut by the Oldman River. The river at that juncture used to be known as the Belly, but squeamish ladies simply could not bring themselves to utter the word "belly," and after years of argument the Geographic Board suggested that the river be called the Oldman all the way to its meeting with the Bow. For hundreds of years its broad valley was a Blackfoot campground, and ghostly aboriginal battles still haunt its terrain. The viaduct bridge was the highest of its type in the world when it was built in 1909, crossing 307 feet above the Oldman River.

Although the Mounties shut down Fort Whoop-Up faster than you can say "bootleg whisky," a few years after coal was discovered in the area, Coal Banks, its original name, was changed to honour mine president William Lethbridge. As a coal-mining town, it enjoyed its share of labour unrest and union building, despite the best efforts of one of its founding fathers, Alexander Galt, son of Sir Alexander Galt, one of the Fathers of Confederation. Galt used his family and government connections to get a grant of more than one million acres of land and mining rights, virtually all of southern Alberta's coalfields, in return for a promise to build a railway, which he never did. But what else was new?

Right up to the 1940s, the city was renowned for its prostitutes and gambling houses. In the referendum on prohibition, Lethbridge voted overwhelmingly to stay wet, but was overruled by the province.

The land around the city benefited from various irrigation projects, making it prime farming country. And in 1971 the University of Lethbridge, architecturally one of the most striking universities in the world, opened. Quite a contrast to the the town's reprobate past.

Maverick

Traditionally, a range calf without a brand and consequently without an owner. If cowboys couldn't poach them, they'd butcher them—fresh meat for the chuckwagon. Also a term applicable to Albertans, especially appropriate for a collective resistance to being caught, owned, herded, taxed, or identified.

Medicine Hat

A city named for an aboriginal legend about a Cree medicine man who lost his headdress in a battle with the Blackfoot. Originally Medicine Man's Hat, it was changed to Medicine Hat to sound more British. Located in the old District of Assiniboia, it looks south to the Cypress Hills, where turn-of-the-century caches of hidden whisky still mellow and age. The CPR helped to make Medicine Hat boom; in 1883, when the railway was under construction, a tent city of fifteen hundred men squatted beside the tracks. Home to ranchers and natural gas, Medicine Hat sits on a field of methane, which CPR crews found accidentally while drilling for water. Citizens could drill a gas well in the back yard for their own domestic supply; gas was so abundant that the town's lights were never turned off.

Because Medicine Hat was home to the West's most northerly weather station, minus-minus temperatures seemed to originate there. Maybe it was the cold that made the cowboys in this area so active. They started the sport of riding broncs, competing to break their necks.

Oil and Gas

Alberta's lifeblood. Oil and gas commodities have governed the boom and bust cycles of the province. Alberta sits on 60 percent of Canada's oil, 85 percent of its natural gas, and all of its oil sands reserves. Some estimate gas reserves at two hundred trillion cubic feet. Although dire warnings suggest that we are depleting this resource too quickly, Albertans believe, against logic, that it is inexhaustible, that they will always find more.

Fossil fuel reserves under Turner Valley, southwest of Calgary, amount to around a billion barrels of oil and three trillion cubic feet of gas. Gas ambushed Alberta in 1883 in Medicine Hat, when a railwayman struck a match over a water well and was blown not quite sky-high, but some distance. More surprised than hurt, he set out to exploit this explosive substance, and Medicine Hat started using gaslight long before it was fashionable.

The search for petroleum incited the worst kind of investor fever, oil promoters competing with real estate agents as obnoxious speculators. Promoters whipped up lunatic behaviour; everybody wanted to buy stock, and people pawned baby carriages and clocks to get enough money to invest in oil-in-the-ground stock certificates. The famed Archibald Dingman, James Lougheed, A. E. Cross, T. J. S. Skinner, and A. Judson Sayre together formed Calgary Petroleum Products Co. Ltd., which became something of a paying proposition. Oil from the Dingman well was so pure that cars could be powered from it. These men were mostly Centrals who'd come west to make their fortunes—and they did. A sixth investor, William Stewart Herron, was squeezed out, got mad, and started a whole series of other companies, including Okalta, which dominated the oil patch until the 1940s. Oil gave Alberta a complex vocabulary: wildcatters, roughnecks, riggers, tool-pushers, seismic crews, survey crews, land men, and all manner of other accoutrements and workers. Finding oil was dangerous work for a driller, who pounded a hole into the ground, lowered a casing pipe into the hole, and prayed he wouldn't get blown up. Other dangers included fires, toppling derricks, and blowouts. Riggers slept in shacks, ate out of cans, drank, and gambled; oil gave rise to a new breed of Albertan, the rough-and-ready rig worker who disregarded danger.

Alberta celebrated when we got control of our natural resources on December 14, 1929, the UFA government's greatest triumph. While Turner Valley was a big strike,

Imperial Oil's Leduc No. 1 in 1947 was the Valentine's Day gift of the century, and Alberta has never looked back, even though we've had some mean and nasty fights about oil and its disposition. Just say the acronym NEP in downtown Calgary and watch the fists ball. Ottawa's manoeuvre in "equalizing our energy endowment" effectively redistributed Alberta's wealth to the rest of Canada, and we've never been quite so sanguine about "national fairness" since. And when in 1986 the big bust came and oil dropped to $14 a barrel, we were on our own.

Leduc No. 1, 1947—Alberta's wealth

Glenbow Archives, Calgary, Canada: NA-555-5

Although Alberta is often flattened by wind, we're determinedly resistant to wind power. The turbines at Pincher Creek provide enough of this alternative energy to run fifteen thousand homes. Still, Alberta drags its feet on establishing a fund to finance alternative energy sources. Even though wind power will reduce carbon dioxide emissions, the government doesn't want to annoy the province's blue-eyed sheiks.

Peace River Region

A northern area where the Peace and Smoky rivers conjoin, originally known as "the Crossing," then named after the peace treaty the Cree and the Beaver people made together (around 1780) at Peace Point—sixty miles upstream from Peace River's junction with the Slave. Fur traders arrived in the late eighteenth century, along with map-maker Alexander Mackenzie, who recorded the reason for the name. Treaty Eight, which applied to all the northern aboriginal people, was negotiated in that region in 1899.

This demanding place had both boosters and detractors, and many a Peace country settler moved south after a few years of struggle. Railway magnates gambled, but it was a hard region to get to, and those who set out had to be very determined. The Dominion government, needing to acknowledge the Métis people, issued land scrip to them in the Peace River District, each scrip entitling the holder to a quarter section of land. But Edmonton boosters saw an opportunity, and land speculators cheated the Métis, exchanging a few dollars or a bottle of whisky for their entitlement. John A. McDougall, in partnership with Richard Secord, respected Edmonton businessmen both, traded in scrip and made a fortune. Selling scrip was not strictly illegal, but it was recognizably exploitative. When Secord was charged with making profits from selling scrip, he was well protected—none of the major papers in Edmonton would report on the case. And after he was charged, the federal government changed the law so that no charges could be laid if the alleged scrip offence had occurred more than three years earlier, which in Secord's case it had. Senator James Lougheed (who had sold scrip for profit himself) piloted the amended legislation through.

When the provincial boundaries were outlined, the District of Alberta became a province much bigger than anticipated—the border moved 890 miles north to the sixtieth parallel to include most of the Athabasca and Peace River districts, and added to Alberta sixteen million acres of prime grain land. That border manoeuvre made Edmonton very happy; no longer was the city on the northern fringe of its district but in the middle of a much larger province.

The Peace has always been a place eager for its own tall tale, its own extravagance, eager to pronounce that its cabbages are as big as children and its hailstones even bigger. When a special Senate committee concluded in 1907 that grain crops could be easily grown in the Peace River, they were too late. Settlers had already started heading there; they'd figured out all by themselves that though huge tracts of good agricultural land had already been settled on the prairie, much more was sitting in the north, just waiting for the bite of a plough. The Peace became "the Dreamland of Canada," the last destination for promoters to promote. Newcomers from many different ethnic backgrounds flocked to the millions of acres of arable land, especially after the railway finally made it through in 1915. Getting a railway into the area was a feat; by 1910 fifteen railways had been given charters to reach Peace River and had failed.

But that didn't stop the boosters. Peace River Jim, James Cornwall, was an early promoter who came to Alberta from Ontario, traded furs, worked as a river pilot on

Peace River maverick Twelve Foot Davis, blind and paralysed, on his way to Edmonton to trade his furs, 1899

the Athabasca, and ignited all kinds of promotional flares, mostly from his safe vantage point in Edmonton. On the other hand, his friend, Twelve Foot Davis, who was hardly a hair over five feet but could pack two hundred pounds, became synonymous with the region's fabled generosity and neighbourliness. A Yankee who drifted farther and farther west, he gained his name from staking a twelve-foot gap between two claims during BC's Barkerville gold rush. Henry Fuller Davis took his gold and converted it into goods for trade, then set up a small post near Fort Dunvegan, gaining fame for his hospitality and his extraordinary pumpkin pies. At the end of his life, blind and lame, he still made his yearly trip to Edmonton. On his deathbed, a nun asked if he was afraid of dying, and he answered that he had no reason to be afraid, for he had never killed, never stolen, never harmed a soul, and that he had always kept an open door. Although he was buried at Lesser Slave Lake, his friends moved his body to the hill above the

Crossing. Fittingly his grave marker reads: "Pathfinder Pioneer Miner and Trader. He was every man's friend and never locked his cabin door."

For a few years the Peace River region was so certain of its economic future that a wavering secessionist movement sprang up. In 1927 Charles Frederick, editor of the *Peace River Record*, argued that a new province should be created, one that merged northern Alberta and British Columbia, giving them the best of both norths and a seaport. Northern Albertans were as fed up with the provincial government as the province was sometimes fed up with Ottawa. The Peace knew that the South and the Centre wanted the North as a colony to exploit and develop. When the province of Peace River became more than a joke, Premier John Brownlee realized he had better take northern Alberta's discontents seriously and went on a tour to reassure the area of his government's support. People showed up to complain about everything from roads to bridges to railways to creameries—or lack thereof. Connecting northern Alberta with the centre of the province was urgent.

In the Great Depression, hundreds of refugees fled prairie drought and destruction by migrating to the Peace Country. There, they were able to start over and make their way. Leona Gom's collection of poems, *Land of the Peace*, celebrates that pioneering spirit.

Rats

Nasty rodents that Alberta has none of, the only province in Canada that can claim to be rat free. The Rockies formed a barrier to rats from BC, but the Saskatchewan border required no passport. When rats began to appear in the southeastern part of the province, the Alberta Department of Agriculture instituted a relentless rodent patrol that killed every rat daring to stick its nose an inch inside the province. The twenty-mile protective zone along the Saskatchewan border is still active, and every year municipalities and the provincial government spend a quarter of a million dollars killing the nasty nibblers. Now, if only they'd spend that much eradicating the human variety...

Red Deer

The city that pivots around Highway 2 between Edmonton and Calgary, right at the halfway point. Sitting on the banks of the Red Deer River, the town began as a stopping house on the Calgary-Edmonton trail. Its advantages were broadcast by an early booster, a Methodist minister from London, Ontario, named Leonard Gaetz (the main street is named after him) and quickly attracted settlers to this heart of the parkland. In 1913 it became the sixth city in Alberta, after Calgary, Edmonton, Medicine Hat, Lethbridge, and Wetaskiwin, but is now larger than all except Edmonton and Calgary.

Early on the town started a ladies' college for business students and even enjoyed its own railway—the Alberta Central. Trains stopped for twelve minutes, plenty of time for refreshments at the Olympia Café right across the street from the station. Aside from the usual booms and busts, and the disasters caused when the river overflowed its banks, Red Deer quietly grew and grew, the rich soil first attracting homesteaders, and the later gas and oil refineries at Joffre keeping the area prosperous. Red Deer refuses to be a bedroom for either Edmonton or Calgary, but its clocking in at the one-and-a-half-hour mark on the three-hour drive between the two cities ensures its historical role as a stopping place. Gasoline Alley, the string of gas stations and fast food outlets beside the highway, serves more cups of coffee than any other spot in Alberta.

St. Albert, St. Paul des Métis, Lac La Biche

Towns that serve as reminders of Alberta's venerable francophone history. Father Lacombe's mission at St. Albert (named after his patron saint, not him) was the first Roman Catholic bishopric in Alberta. St. Paul did not flourish as well, and the settlement that was to have been a model Métis community gradually shifted to a French-Canadian settlement, which still survives. Despite the best efforts of boosters like Father Lacombe, all kinds of people from Ontario eagerly came west, but people from Quebec did not, and attempts to colonize the West with francophone settlers was contested by the sweeping numbers of anglophones. Besides, the church wanted francophones to spread through Quebec, not vamoose to the faraway West. Still, the names of Bonnyville, Plamondon, and Bon Accord echo Alberta's original immigrants. *C'est dommage*. We could have been a truly bilingual province.

Taxes and Tariffs

One of Alberta's much-touted advantages is the absence of any visible provincial sales tax, a symbolic nose-thumb at the rest of Canada. Red-blooded

Albertans would be horrified by the facts, but the truth is, Alberta has a great history of taxation.

Alberta's taxes are crazy. At one time, even horses and buggies and whips were taxed. When the talkies came in, Alberta introduced a one-cent-tax-per-movie admission, which probably went toward the storage costs for the celluloid morgue where all the censored bits curl around one another. Most ironic of all, tax-hating Alberta, the land of petroleum products, was the first to levy a tax on gasoline, implemented in 1922 under the UFA and Brownlee, of two cents on every gallon. The rest of the country quickly followed suit.

In 2000, tax-paranoid Albertans devised a single-rate tax plan, which Premier Klein claimed would enhance the Alberta Advantage, until the government did some math and realized that the plan would have to be revised so that Albertans didn't end up paying more than they were under the old system, which was tied to federal rates.

Visitors

Even in December, it's hard to find an Alberta-born Albertan in a roomful of people. We're a province of visitors who decided to stay, put down tentative roots, and surprise ourselves twenty years later when we notice that we've never left. And now it's too late. We don't want to leave.

And Alberta has had its share of illustrious visitors who came, who saw, who conquered, or at least imagined they did. One of the earliest was the governor general, the Marquess of Lorne, who crossed the prairies in 1881. He was young and energetic, and fired with Victorian imagination, he took the CPR to the end of steel at Portage la Prairie, and set off by wagon to see the great Northwest. Queen Vicky's daughter, Princess Louise Caroline Alberta, didn't come along, but he wanted to name something on his trip for her, and when he got back to Ottawa he insisted that the North West Territories, of which there were three (Assiniboia, Saskatchewan, and Athabasca), should add a fourth, called Alberta, thus foisting this unlikely name on us forever.

Royalty enjoys the West. Edward, the not-yet-abdicated Prince of Wales, came in September of 1919 after a whirlwind tour of the rest of Canada. Wilfrid "Wop" May, the First World War flying ace and later bush pilot, accompanied the train into Edmonton by flying acrobatic loops above, making everyone, including the train conductor, nervous. At a baseball game, Edward threw the inaugural pitch, then lounged on the grass near the first-base line and cheered the home team. Everyone had to watch their etiquette, but he loved the West's lack of pomp and circumstance. At a grand ball in the legislature, he danced with far too many young women, declaring to all of them, "I love the prairies." He went on to the same round of balls and receptions in Calgary, then to High River, where he rode a bronc and joined a cattle roundup. He meant what he said; he loved the prairies so much that he bought the Bedingfeld Ranch, and returned in 1923, 1924, 1927, 1941, and 1950, saying that he had "caught the western spirit." He outshone his brother, King George VI, who came west on a state visit in 1939 and conducted himself with considerably less abandon.

Many visitors to Alberta are intent on reformation or conversion. One of the earliest was Pierre-Jean De Smet, whose goal was to convert the "American Indian." "How consoling to pour the regenerating waters of baptism on the furrowed and scarified brows of these desert warriors,—to behold these children of the plains and forests emerging from that profound ignorance and superstition in which they have been for so many ages deeply and darkly enveloped." His awful platitudes make one wish that he had been eaten by a bear. Instead, he was treated to exquisite *"cuisine à la sauvage,"* which he didn't deserve. "The first dish [an Indian] presented me contained two paws of a bear. In Africa, this ragout might have given some alarm; in effect, it bears a striking resemblance to the feet of a certain race. A roast porcupine next made its appearance, accompanied by a moose's muzzle; the latter I found delicious. Finally, the great kettle containing a sort of hotch-potch, or salmagundi, was placed in the midst of the guests, and each one helped himself according to his taste." He almost lost his cassock and, one hopes, his virginity, but his account is one of the more amusing of the early missionary visitors. He was by no means the last. Alberta seemed a magnet for preachers and evangelists, including Aimee Semple McPherson, who preached in Lethbridge in 1920, and the Maharishi Mahesh Yogi, who visited Edmonton in 1966. Transcendental meditation continues to be a presence; TM even ran candidates in federal and provincial elections in the nineties, campaigning on a platform of meditation resolving all social ills.

Politicians visit often, although they don't stay. The renowned Agnes Macphail, later to become Canada's first federal woman MP, spent 1913 in Alberta, teaching at Oyen for the change of air and to heal an "inward goitre." She became interested in the UFA movement, then almost died in a blizzard in October, which drove her back to the nicer climate of Ontario. Some speculate that she came west to further her long flirtation with R. B. Bennett—but that came later. The renowned suffragette Emily Pankhurst visited Edmonton in 1916, the very day of Emily Murphy's appointment as a magistrate.

Other visitors came to entertain Alberta. Will Rogers, Buster Keaton, Stan Laurel, and Sophie Tucker performed at the Pantages Theatre in Edmonton. Dame Nellie Melba sang at Sherman's Roller Rink in Calgary, and L. B. Morgan, the wonderful jazz pianist, appeared at Calgary's Cabaret Garden in 1917. The higher-brow Sarah Bernhardt played Edmonton's Empire Theatre in *La Dame aux Camélias* in January 1913, without once complaining about the cold, and she returned in 1918. We've hosted hordes of Americans, waves of Americans, from ranchers to fly-by-nights, and when the American army boys were busy building the Canol Road and the Alaska Highway, we saw Bob Hope, who stopped on his way to entertain the troops in Alaska, and Joe Lewis, the world heavyweight boxing champion who played baseball during a promotional tour in 1943. Fiorello LaGuardia, New York's mayor and a member of the Canadian-American Joint Board of Defense, was even spotted biting into a hamburger in an obscure Jasper Avenue café.

The poets passed through, too. Rupert Brooke declared injudiciously that "Edmonton is a quiet little town," but he figured things out fast. "It is imperative to praise Edmonton in Edmonton, but it is sudden death to praise it in Calgary. The partisans of each city proclaim its superiority to all the others in swiftness of growth, future population, size of buildings, price of land—by all recognized standards of excellence." Pauline Johnson was less judgemental, and when her train was stopped by flooding she enjoyed picking berries with the Blackfoot. Rudyard Kipling was a meddlesome visitor, who felt that he had sufficient experience to warn Canadians before the election of 1911 that they would compromise their national integrity (if not their souls) if they embraced reciprocity with the United States. Popular figures like Arthur Conan Doyle toured Western Canada, and Graham Greene and, more recently, Louis de Bernières have immortalized Alberta in their writing.

The Group of Seven spent a lot of time in Alberta scouting landscape, and western artists like Frederic Remington and Charles Russell visited, too. Russell sent this warm thank-you note to his friend Guy Weadick:

Great Falls, Montana

Friend Guy:

I received your postal and letter an was glad to here from you: You
were so bussy when I left I did not get to thank you for the good time
we had at the Stampede. I came west 31 years ago, at that time baring
the Indians an a fiew scattered whites the country belonged to God
but now the real estate man an nester have got moste of it grass side
down an most of the cows that are left feed on shuger beet pulp but
thank God I was here first an in my time Iv seen som roping and riding but never before have I seen so much of it bunched as I did at
Calgary. Ive seen som good wild west showes but I couldent call what
you pulled off a show. It was the real thing an a whole lot of it . . .

With best wishes from your friend
C.M. Russell

Well, he could paint, but he couldn't spell.

We've welcomed priests and acrobats, sword-swallowers and snake-oil salesmen
and contemporary movie stars like Cuba Gooding Jr. (filming a football movie)
and Dennis Hopper, who was arraigned in a Calgary court for possession of twelve
grams of marijuana. After an abject apology in September 2000, he was acquitted
and sent home. They come and go, the visitors, talking about how we aren't quite
what they expected, that they never thought there'd be so many sidewalk cafés, or
that the air would be so tantalizingly pure. And they always seem to come back.

West Edmonton Mall

The world's largest mall rolls out the shopping and the fun to almost sixty thousand visitors a year, but the numbers seem to be slipping a little, and the bankruptcy trustee has had to step in a few times. Edmontonians have mixed feelings
about the mall—some love it, and some claim it's killed the downtown—but the
Ghermezian brothers' dream of a wild bazaar is an actuality, with more than eight
hundred shops, an ice rink, amusement parks, a casino, aquariums, movie theatres, aviaries, and a wave pool, all under one gigantic roof.

Western Alienation

Just to be repetitious, alienation is a habit we've developed into an art, a sport, a way of making Ottawa nervous. We invent political parties, the Western Canada Concept Party, the Alberta Independence Party, the United Farmers of Alberta, Social Credit, the Reform Party (of Canada), the United Alternative, the Alliance Party (of Canada), and at least a dozen more, just to keep the feds off balance, keep them guessing. Alberta looks fat and rich. So why are we unhappy? We're not, really, but Jean Chrétien spends more time in Florida than in Western Canada. And Alberta remains a mystery to Centrals, who criticize and generalize and don't understand our old discontents. The only way to learn is to come out to Alberta, stay quiet, hang around, listen. Pay attention. The real Alberta Advantage is that we know more about the rest of Canada than they know about us. And as for what the Centre thinks it knows about Alberta...well, beware the smoke and mirrors.

The emblem of our province is the prickly wild rose, a hardy fenceline thorn, pretty and tough—just like Alberta.

Growing up in Alberta—the pleasures of Western alienation

Selected Bibliography

Alberta in Stories, Poems, and Drama

Adam, Ian. *Songs from the Star Motel*. Red Deer: Red Deer College Press, 1987.

Almon, Bert. *Deep North*. Saskatoon: Thistledown, 1980. *Mind the Gap*. Victoria: Ekstasis Editions, 1996.

Annett, Ronald Ross. *Especially Babe*. Edmonton: Treefrog Press, 1978.

Balan, Jars. *Salt and Braided Bread*. Toronto: Oxford University Press, 1984.

Ballem, John. *Oilpatch Empire*. Toronto: McClelland and Stewart, 1985. *The Barons*. 1991.

Banting, Pamela, ed. *Fresh Tracks: Writing the Western Landscape*. Victoria: Polestar, 1989.

Barbour, Douglas. *Visible Visions*. Edmonton: NeWest Press, 1984.

Bell, Wade. *The North Saskatchewan River Book*. Toronto: Coach House Press, 1981.

Bugnet, Georges. *Nipsya*. St. Boniface: Éditions des Plaines, 1990, first published in 1924.

Birney, Earle. "David," in *The Collected Poems of Earle Birney*. Toronto: McClelland and Stewart, 1975.

Campbell, Maria. *Halfbreed*. Toronto: McClelland and Stewart, 1973.

Clark, Joan. *From a High, Thin Wire*. Edmonton: NeWest Press, 1982.

Connor, Ralph. *The Sky Pilot: A Tale of the Foothills*. Toronto: Westminster, 1899.

Daniel, Lorne. *Towards a New Compass*. Saskatoon: Thistledown Press, 1978.

Dumont, Marilyn. *A Really Good Brown Girl*. London: Brick Books, 1996.

Edwards, Caterina. *A Whiter Shade of Pale/Becoming Emma*. Edmonton: NeWest Press, 1992.

Foggo, Cheryl. *Pourin' Down Rain*. Calgary: Detselig, 1990.

Fraser, Brad. *Poor Super Man*. Edmonton: NeWest Press, 1995.

Frey, Cecilia. *The Love Song of Romeo Paquette*. Saskatoon: Thistledown Press, 1990.

Gom, Leona. *Land of the Peace*. Saskatoon: Thistledown, 1980.

Goto, Hiromi. *Chorus of Mushrooms*. Edmonton: NeWest Press, 1994.

Govier, Katharine. *Between Men*. Markham, Ont.: Viking, 1987.

Halverson, Marilyn. *Cowboys Don't Cry*. Toronto: Clark Irwin, 1984.

Harris, Claire. *The Conception of Winter*. Toronto: Williams-Wallace, 1989.

Howard, Barbara. *Whipstock*. Edmonton: NeWest Press, 2001.

Howes, Mary. *Lying in Bed*. Edmonton: Longspoon Press, 1980.

Huston, Nancy. *Plainsong*. Toronto: HarperPerennial, 1993.

King, Thomas. *Green Grass, Running Water*. Toronto: HarperCollins, 1993. *Medicine River*. Toronto: Viking, 1989.

Kinsella, W. P. *Dance Me Outside*. Ottawa: Oberon Press, 1977.

Kogawa, Joy. *Obasan*. Toronto: Lester & Orpen Dennys, 1981.

Kostash, Myrna. *All of Baba's Children*. Edmonton: Hurtig, 1977.

Kreisel, Henry. *The Almost Meeting and Other Stories*. Edmonton: NeWest Press, 1981.

Kroetsch, Robert. *Alberta*. Edmonton: NeWest Press, 1993. *Alibi*. Toronto: Stoddart, 1983. *Badlands*. Toronto: General, 1982. *A Likely Story*. Red Deer: Red Deer College Press, 1995. *The Studhorse Man*. Toronto: General, 1982. *What the Crow Said*. Edmonton: University of Alberta Press, 2000. *The Words of My Roaring*. Edmonton: University of Alberta Press, 2000.

Lambert, Betty. *Jenny's Story*. Toronto: Playwrights Canada, 1981.

McGoogan, Ken. *Visions of Kerouac*. Nova Scotia: Pottersfield Press, 1993.

Markotic, Nicole. *Minotaurs and Other Alphabets*. Toronto: Wolsak & Wynn, 1998.

Martini, Clem. *A Three Martini Lunch*. Calgary: Red Deer Press, 2000.

Marty, Sid. *Men for the Mountains*. Toronto: McClelland & Stewart, 1978. *Nobody Danced with Miss Rodeo*. Toronto: McClelland & Stewart, 1981. *Leaning on the Wind: Under the Spell of the Great Chinook*. Toronto: HarperCollins, 1995. *Switchbacks: True Stories from the Canadian Rockies*. Toronto: McClelland & Stewart, 1999.

Mayr, Suzette. *The Widows*. Edmonton: NeWest Press, 1998.

Melnyk, George. *Ribstones*. Victoria: Ekstasis Editions, 1996.

Mitchell, W. O. *For Art's Sake*. Toronto: McClelland & Stewart, 1992. *The Black Bonspiel of Wullie MacCrimmon*. Calgary: Frontiers Unlimited, 1965. *How I Spent My Summer Holidays*. Toronto: Macmillan, 1981. *Jake and the Kid*. Toronto: Macmillan, 1961. *Roses Are Difficult Here*. Toronto: McClelland & Stewart, 1990. *Since Daisy Creek*. Toronto: Macmillan, 1984. *Who Has Seen the Wind*. Toronto: Macmillan, 1984.

Moher, Frank. *Prairie Report*. Winnipeg: Blizzard Publishing, 1988.

Murphy, Sarah. *Comic Book Heroine and Other Stories*. Edmonton: NeWest Press, 1990.

Murrell, John. *Waiting for the Parade*. Vancouver: Talon Books, 1980. *Farther West and the New World*. Toronto: Coach House, 1985.

Nixon, Rosemary. *The Cock's Egg*. Edmonton: NeWest Press, 1994.

O'Hagan, Howard. *Tay John*. Toronto: McClelland & Stewart, 1989.

Oliva, Peter. *Drowning in Darkness*. Dunvegan: Cormorant, 1993.

Patton, Brian. *Tales from the Canadian Rockies*. Edmonton: Hurtig, 1984.

Pollock, Sharon. *Walsh*. Vancouver: Talonbooks, 1973. *Doc*. Toronto: Playwrights Canada, 1984.

Powe, Bruce. *The Aberhart Summer*. Edmonton: NeWest Press, 2000.

Rebar, Kelly. *Bordertown Café*. Winnipeg: Blizzard Publishing, 1989.

Rees, Roberta. *Beneath the Faceless Mountain*. Red Deer: Red Deer College Press, 1994.

Reid, Monty. *The Alternate Guide*. Red Deer: Red Deer College Press, 1985. *Dog Sleeps*. Edmonton: NeWest Press, 1993.

Riis, Sharon. *The True Story of Ida Johnson*. Toronto: Women's Press, 1976.

Russell, Andy. *The High West*. Toronto: Macmillan, 1974. *The Rockies*. Edmonton: Hurtig, 1975.

Ryga, George. *Ballad of a Stone Picker*. Toronto: Macmillan, 1966. *The Hungry Hills*. Toronto: Longman, 1963.

Scott, Barbara. *The Quick*. Dunvegan: Cormorant, 1999.

Sproxton, Birk. *The Hockey Fan Came Riding*. Red Deer: Red Deer College Press, 1990.

Stenson, Fred. *Lonesome Hero*. Toronto: Macmillan, 1974. *Last One Home*. Edmonton: NeWest Press, 1988. *Teeth*. Regina: Coteau Books, 1994. *The Trade*. Vancouver: Douglas & McIntyre, 2000.

Stephansson, Stephan G. *Selected Prose and Poetry*. K. Gunnars, trans. Red Deer: Red Deer College Press, 1988.

Summers, Myrna. *North of the Battle*. Vancouver: Douglas & McIntyre, 1988.

van Herk, Aritha. *Judith*. Toronto: McClelland and Stewart, 1978. *No Fixed Address*. Toronto: McClelland and Stewart, 1986. *Places Far from Ellesmere*. Red Deer: Red Deer College Press, 1990. *Restlessness*. Red Deer: Red Deer College Press, 1998.

Wagamese, Richard. *Keeper 'n Me*. Toronto: Doubleday, 1994.

Wah, Fred. *Faking It*. Edmonton: NeWest Press, 2000.

Wharton, Thomas. *Icefields*. Edmonton: NeWest Press, 1995.

Whyte, Jon. *Mind Over Mountains*. Harry Vandervlist, ed. Calgary: Red Deer Press, 2000.

Wiebe, Rudy. *Alberta: A Celebration*. Edmonton: Hurtig, 1979. *The Angel of the Tar Sands and Other Stories*. Toronto: McClelland and Stewart, 1982. *Far as the Eye Can See*. Edmonton: NeWest Press, 1977. *My Lovely Enemy*. Toronto: McClelland and Stewart, 1983.

Wood, Kerry. *Cowboy Yarns for Young Folk*. Toronto: Copp Clark, 1951. *The Map Maker*. Toronto: Macmillan, 1955. *Queen's Cowboy*. Toronto: Macmillan, 1960. *Wild Winter*. Toronto: Macmillan, 1962. *Willowdale*. Toronto: McClelland & Stewart, 1956.

Wreggitt, Andrew. *Making Movies*. Saskatoon: Thistledown Press, 1989.

Useful, Informative, or Downright Essential Books about Alberta

Alberta Report Newsmagazine, out of Edmonton, and *Alberta Views*, out of Calgary (two magazines that devote themselves to matters relevant to the province).

Archaeology Guide and Tour of Greater Edmonton Area. Edmonton: Provincial Museum of Alberta, no date.

Calgary Centennial Souvenir Book. Calgary: Provost Promotions & Publications Ltd., 1974.

Canada's Oil Sands and Heavy Oil. Calgary: Petroleum Communication Foundation, no date.

Edmonton: The Way It Was. Edmonton: Fort Edmonton Historical Foundation, no date.

Baker, William M., ed. *Pioneer Policing in Southern Alberta: Deane of the Mounties, 1888–1914*. Calgary: Historical Society of Alberta, 1993.

Baldwin, Beulah. *The Long Trail*. Edmonton: NeWest Press, 1992.

Barry, Patricia Steepee. *Mystical Themes in Milk River Rock Art*. Edmonton: University of Alberta Press, 1991.

Belanger, Art J. *A Half Mile of Hell: The Story of Chuckwagon Racing*. Calgary: Frontier Publishing, 1970.

Bercuson, David, ed. *Alberta's Coal Industry, 1919*. Calgary: Alberta Historical Society, 1978.

Bolton, Ken, et al. *The Albertans*. Edmonton: Lone Pine Press, 1981.

Breen, David H. *The Canadian West and the Ranching Frontier, 1874–1924*. Toronto: University of Toronto Press, 1983. Ed. *William Stewart Herron: Father of the Petroleum Industry in Alberta*. Calgary: Historical Society of Alberta, 1984.

Brennan, Brian. *Building a Province: 60 Alberta Lives*. Calgary: Fifth House, 2000.

Broadfoot, Barry. *Next Year Country: Voices of Prairie People*. Toronto: McClelland & Stewart, 1988.

Butler, William Francis. *The Great Lone Land*. Edmonton: Hurtig, 1968. *The Wild North Land*. Edmonton: Hurtig, 1968.

Byfield, Ted, ed. *Alberta in the Twentieth Century*, volumes 1–8. Edmonton: United Western Communications, 1991–2000.

Byrne, T. C. *Alberta's Revolutionary Leaders*. Calgary: Detselig, 1991.

Carter, David J. *POW: Behind Canadian Barbed Wire*. Elkwater: Eagle Butte Press, 1998.

Carter, Sarah. *Capturing Women: The Manipulation of Cultural Imagery in Canada's Prairie West*. Montreal and Kingston: McGill-Queen's University Press, 1997. *Lost Harvests*. Montreal: McGill-Queen's University Press, 1990.

Cashman, Tony. *The Best Edmonton Stories*. Edmonton: Hurtig, 1976. *The Edmonton Story*. Edmonton: Institute of Applied Art, 1956. *A Picture History of Alberta*. Edmonton: Hurtig, 1979.

Chambers, Captain Ernest J. *The Royal North-West Mounted Police: A Corps History*. Toronto: Coles, 1973.

Charyk, John. *Pulse of the Community*. Saskatoon: Western Producer Book Service, 1974. *Those Bittersweet Schooldays*. Saskatoon: Western Producer Prairie Books, 1977.

Christensen, Jo-Anne, and Dennis Shappka. *An Edmonton Album: Glimpses of the Way We Were*. Toronto: Hounslow Press, 1999.

Cole, Catherine C. "The Great Western Garment Company, 1911–1939: 'Who Threw the Overalls in Mrs. Murphy's Chowder?'" Edmonton: Alberta Museums Assocation, 1989.

Cormack, R. G. H. *Wild Flowers of Alberta*. Edmonton: Hurtig, 1977.

Coues, Elliott. *The Manuscript Journals of Alexander Henry and of David Thompson*. Minneapolis, Minnesota: Ross & Haines, 1965.

Cruise, David, and Alison Griffiths. *The Great Adventure: How the Mounties Conquered the West*. Toronto: Penguin, 1996.

Dabbs, Frank. *Preston Manning: The Roots of Reform*. Vancouver: Greystone Books, 1997.

Dawson, J. Brian. *Crowsnest: An Illustrated History and Guide to the Crowsnest Pass*. Canmore: Altitude, 1995.

Dempsey, Hugh. *The Amazing Death of Calf Shirt, and Other Blackfoot Stories*. Saskatoon: Fifth House, 1994. Ed. *The Best from Alberta History*. Saskatoon: Western Producer Prairie Books, 1981. *Big Bear: The End of Freedom*. Vancouver: Douglas and McIntyre, 1984. *Calgary: Spirit of the West*. Saskatoon: Fifth House and Glenbow, 1994. *Crowfoot: Chief of the Blackfeet*. Edmonton: Hurtig, 1976. *The Gentle Persuader: A*

Biography of James Gladstone, Indian Senator. Saskatoon: Western Producer Prairie Books, 1986. *Indian Tribes of Alberta*. Calgary: Glenbow-Alberta Institute, 1986. *The Rundle Journals, 1840–1848*. Calgary: Historical Society of Alberta and Glenbow-Alberta Institute, 1977. *Tom Three Persons: Legend of an Indian Cowboy*. Saskatoon: Purich Publishing, 1997. *The Wit and Wisdom of Bob Edwards*. Edmonton: Hurtig, 1976.

Denny, Sir Cecil E. *March of the Mounties*. Surrey, BC: Heritage House, 1994.

Doig, Ian. *Quotations of Chairman Ralph*. Vancouver: Stellar Press, 2000.

Durieux, Marcel. *Ordinary Heroes: The Journal of a French Pioneer in Alberta*. Edmonton: University of Alberta Press, 1980.

Eaton, Diane, and Sheila Urbanek. *Paul Kane's Great Nor'West*. Vancouver: UBC Press, 1995.

Elliott, David, ed. *Aberhart: Outpourings and Replies*. Calgary: Historical Society of Alberta, 1991.

Elliott, David, and Iris Miller. *Bible Bill: A Biography of William Aberhart*. Edmonton: Reidmore, 1987.

Elofson, Warren M. *Cowboys, Gentlemen, and Cattle Thieves: Ranching on the Western Frontier*. Montreal and Kingston: McGill-Queen's University Press, 2000.

Erasmus, Peter. *Buffalo Days and Nights*. Calgary: Glenbow-Alberta Institute, 1976.

Fardy, B. D. *Jerry Potts: Paladin of the Plains*. Langley: Mr. Paperback, 1984.

Fooks, Georgia Green. *Fort Whoop-Up: Alberta's First and Most Notorious Whisky Fort*. Lethbridge: Whoop-Up Country Chapter, Historical Society of Alberta, Occasional Paper No. 11, 1983.

Foran, Max. *Calgary: An Illustrated History*. Ottawa: National Museums of Canada, 1978.

Foran, Max, and Sheilagh Jameson, ed. *Citymakers: Calgarians After the Frontier*. Calgary: Historical Society of Alberta, 1987.

Foran, Max, and Heather MacEwan Foran. *Calgary: Canada's Frontier Metropolis*. Calgary Chamber of Commerce, Windsor Publications, 1982.

Foster, Peter F. *Self-Serve: How Petro-Canada Pumped Canadians Dry*. Toronto: Macfarlane Walter & Ross, 1992.

Francis, R. Douglas. *Images of the West: Responses to the Canadian Prairies*. Saskatoon: Western Producer Prairie Books, 1989. And Howard Palmer, ed. *The Prairie West: Historical Readings*. Edmonton: Pica Pica Press, 1992.

Fryer, Harold. *Alberta: The Pioneer Years*. Langley: Stagecoach Publishing, 1977. *Ghost Towns of Alberta*. Langley: Stagecoach Publishing, 1976.

Gadd, Ben. *Handbook of the Canadian Rockies*. Jasper: Corax Press, 1995.

Glover, Richard. *David Thompson's Narrative, 1784–1812*. Toronto: Champlain Society, 1962.

Godfrey, John, ed. *Edmonton Beneath Our Feet*. Edmonton: Edmonton Geological Society, 1993.

Gould, Ed. *All Hell for a Basement: Medicine Hat, 1883–1983*. City of Medicine Hat, 1981.

Grant, George. *Ocean to Ocean: Sandford Fleming's Expedition Through Canada in 1872*. Toronto: Prospero Books, 2000.

Gray, James H., *Booze*. Toronto: Macmillan, 1972. *A Brand of Its Own*. Saskatoon: Western Producer Prairie Books, 1985. *R. B. Bennett: The Calgary Years*. Toronto: University of Toronto Press, 1991. *Red Lights on the Prairies*. Calgary: Fifth House, 1995.

Harmon, Daniel Williams. *A Journal of Voyages and Travels in the Interior of North America*. Toronto: Courier Press, 1911.

Harper, J. Russell. *Paul Kane's Frontier*. Austin: University of Texas Press, 1971.

Hart, E. J., ed. *A Hunter of Peace: Mary T. S. Schäffer's Old Indian Trails of the Canadian Rockies*. Banff: Whyte Museum of the Canadian Rockies, 1980. *Trains, Peaks and Tourists*. Banff: EJH Literary Enterprises, 2000.

Hauschildt, Elda. *The Kay Sanderson Collection: 200 Remarkable Alberta Women*. Calgary: Famous Five Foundation, 1999.

Hearne, Samuel. *A Journey from Prince of Wales's Fort in Hudson's Bay to the Northern Ocean*. Toronto: Champlain Society, 1911.

Herzog, Lawrence. *Built on Coal: A History of Beverly, Edmonton's Working Class Town*. Edmonton: Beverly Community Development Society, 2000.

Hesketh, Bob, and Frances Swyripa, eds. *Edmonton: The Life of a City*. Edmonton: NeWest, 1995.

Hill, Douglas. *The Opening of the Canadian West: Where Strong Men Gathered*. New York: John Day Company, 1967.

Hooks, Gwen. *The Keystone Legacy: Recollections of a Black Settler*. Edmonton: Brightest Pebble Publishing, 1997.

Hopwood, Victor G. *David Thompson: Travels in Western North America, 1974–1812*. Toronto: Macmillan, 1971.

Hoy, Claire. *Stockwell Day: His Life and Politics*. Toronto: Stoddart, 2000.

Hughes, Katherine. *Father Lacombe: The Black-Robe Voyageur*. New York: Moffat, Yard and Co., 1911.

Hustak, Alan. *Peter Lougheed*. Toronto: McClelland and Stewart, 1979.

Jackson Jr., L. E., and M. C. Wilson, ed. *Geology of the Calgary Area*. Calgary: Canadian Society of Petroleum Geologists, 1987.

James, Jean. *Orville: An Inside Look at Rodeo and Chuckwagon Racing*. Hanna: Gorman and Gorman, 1992.

Johnston, Alex, and Andy den Otter. *Lethbridge: A Centennial History*. Lethbridge Historical Society and the City of Lethbridge, 1991.

Jones, David C. *Empire of Dust*. Edmonton: University of Alberta Press, 1987. *Feasting on Misfortune: Journeys of the Human Spirit in Alberta's Past*. Edmonton: University of Alberta Press, 1998.

Kavanagh, James. *Nature Alberta: An Illustrated Guide to Common Plants and Animals*. Edmonton: Lone Pine Publishing, 1991.

Kelly, L. V. *The Range Men*. Toronto: William Briggs, 1913.

Kershaw, Linda. *Edible and Medicinal Plants of the Rockies*. Edmonton: Lone Pine Publishing, 2000.

Leeson, Howard. *Grant Notley: The Social Conscience of Alberta*. Edmonton: University of Alberta Press, 1992.

Lingard, C. C. *Territorial Government in Canada*. Toronto: University of Toronto Press, 1946.

Lisac, Mark. *The Klein Revolution*. Edmonton: NeWest Press, 1995.

McClung, Nellie L. *Clearing in the West: My Own Story*. Toronto: T. Allen, 1976.

McCullough, Edward J., and Michael Maccagno. *Lac La Biche and the Early Fur Traders*. Lac La Biche: Canadian Circumpolar Institute, 1991.

MacDonald, Graham A. *Where the Mountains Meet the Prairies*. Calgary: University of Calgary Press, 2000.

McDougall, John. *Forest, Lake and Prairie: Twenty Years of Frontier Life in Western Canada, 1842–62*. Toronto: Ryerson Press, no date. *Pathfinding on Plain and Prairie*. Toronto: William Briggs, 1898.

McDougall, J. Lorne. *Canadian Pacific: A Brief History*. Montreal: McGill University Press, 1968.

MacEwan, Grant. *Blazing the Old Cattle Trail*. Calgary: Fifth House, 2000. *Calgary Cavalcade: From Fort to Fortune*. Saskatoon: Western Producer Book Service, 1975. *Eye-Opener Bob: The Story of Bob Edwards*. Edmonton: Institute of Applied Art, 1957. *Fifty Mighty Men*. Saskatoon: Western Producer Prairie Books, 1982. *Frederick Haultain: Frontier Statesman of the Canadian Northwest*. Saskatoon: Western Producer Prairie Books, 1985. *John Ware's Cow Country*. Saskatoon: Western Producer Prairie Books, 1976. *Mighty Women*. Vancouver: Greystone Books, 1995. *Pat Burns: Cattle King*. Saskatoon: Western Producer Prairie Books, 1979.

MacGregor, J. G. *The Battle River Valley*. Saskatoon: Western Producer Prairie Books, 1976. *Behold the Shining Mountains*. Edmonton: Applied Arts Products, 1954. *Edmonton*. Edmonton: Hurtig, 1967. *Father Lacombe*. Edmonton: Hurtig, 1975. *A History of Alberta*. Edmonton: Hurtig, 1972. *The Land of Twelve-Foot Davis*. Edmonton: Allied Art Products, 1952. *North-West of 16*. Toronto: McClelland and Stewart, 1958. *Peter Fidler: Canada's Forgotten Explorer, 1769–1822*. Calgary: Fifth House, 1998.

Mackenzie, Alexander. *Voyages from Montreal on the River St. Lawrence through the Continent of North America to the Frozen and Pacific Oceans in the Years 1789 and 1793*. Edmonton: Hurtig, 1971.

Mackey, Lloyd. *Like Father, Like Son: Ernest Manning & Preston Manning*. Toronto: ECW Press, 1997.

Maclean, John. *McDougall of Alberta*. Toronto: Ryerson Press, 1927.

McLennan, William M. *Sport in Early Calgary*. Calgary: Fort Brisebois Publishing, 1983.

McLachlan, Elizabeth. *With Unshakeable Persistence: Rural Teachers of the Depression Era*. Edmonton: NeWest Press, 1999.

Mair, Alex. *Gateway City: Stories from Edmonton's Past*. Calgary: Fifth House, 2000.

Mair, Charles. *Through the Mackenzie Basin*. Edmonton: University of Alberta Press and the Edmonton and District Historical Society, 1999.

Malcolm, M. J. *The Pursuit of Ernest Cashel*. Saskatoon: Western Producer Prairie Books, 1984.

Martin, James. *Calgary: Secrets of the City*. Vancouver: Arsenal Pulp Press, 1999.

May, David. *The Battle of 66 Street: Pocklington vs UFCW Local 280P*. Edmonton: Duval House Publishing, 1996.

Melnyk, George. *Beyond Alienation: Political Essays on the West*. Calgary: Detselig Enterprises, 1993. *The Literary History of Alberta*, vols. 1, 2. Edmonton: University of Alberta Press, 1998, 1999.

Mikkelsen, Glen. *Never Holler Whoa! The Cowboys of Chuckwagon Racing*. Toronto: Balmur Book Publishing, 2000.

Miller, Nancy. *The Famous Five: Emily Murphy and the Case of the Missing Persons*. Cochrane: Western Heritage Centre, 1999. *Once Upon a Wedding*. Calgary: Bayeaux Arts Inc., 2000.

Milton, Viscount, and W. B. Cheadle. *The North-West Passage by Land*. Toronto: Coles, 1970.

Morris, Alexander. *The Treaties of Canada with the Indians*. Toronto: Prospero Books, 2000.

Morton, W. L. *Social Credit in Alberta*. Toronto: University of Toronto Press, 1959.

Murphy, Emily. *Janey Canuck in the West*. Toronto: McClelland and Stewart, 1975.

Myers, Patricia A. *Sky Riders: An Illustrated History of Aviation in Alberta*. Saskatoon: Fifth House, 1995.

Newman, Peter. *Company of Adventurers*. Markham, Ont.: Penguin Books, 1985.

Nikiforuk, Andrew, Sheila Pratt, and Don Wanagas, eds. *Running on Empty: Alberta After the Boom*. Edmonton: NeWest Press, 1987.

O'Donnell, Cynthia. *Bitumount: A History of the Pioneers of the Oil Sands Industry*. Edmonton: Alberta Culture and Multiculturalism, no date.

Owram, Douglas R., ed. *The Formation of Alberta: A Documentary History*. Edmonton: Historical Society of Alberta, 1979.

Palmer, Howard, and Tamara. *Alberta: A New History*. Edmonton: Hurtig Publishers, 1990. *Peoples of Alberta: Portraits of Cultural Diversity*. Saskatoon: Western Producer Prairie Books, 1985. Eds. *The Settlement of the West*. Calgary: Comprint Publishing, 1977.

Parker, James. *Emporium of the North: Fort Chipewyan and the Fur Trade to 1835*. Regina: Canadian Plains Research Centre, 1987.

Pattie, Don, and Chris Fisher. *Mammals of Alberta*. Edmonton: Lone Pine Publishing, 1999.

Peach, Jack. *Days Gone By*. Saskatoon: Fifth House, 1993. *Thanks for the Memories*. Saskatoon: Fifth House, 1994.

Potyondi, Barry. *In Palliser's Triangle: Living in the Grasslands: 1850–1930*. Saskatoon: Purich Publishing, 1995.

Poulsen, David. *Wild Ride! Three Journeys Down the Rodeo Road*. Toronto: Balmur Book Publishing, 2000.

Pratt, Larry. *The Tar Sands: Syncrude and the Politics of Oil*. Edmonton: Hurtig, 1976.

Pratt, Larry, and Garth Stevenson, eds. *Western Separatism: The Myths, Realities and Dangers*. Edmonton: Hurtig, 1981.

Rasporich, Anthony, and Henry Klassen, eds. *Frontier Calgary: Town, City, and Region, 1875–1914*. Calgary: University of Calgary, 1975.

Rasporich, A. W., and E. A. Corbet, eds. *Winter Sports in the West*. Calgary: Historical Society of Alberta, 1990.

Regehr, T. D. *The Canadian Northern Railway*. Toronto: Macmillan, 1976.

Reid, Sheila. *Wings of a Hero: Ace Wop May*. St. Catharines, Ont.: Vanwell Publishing, 1997.

Reineberg Holt, Faye. *Sharing the Good Times: A History of Prairie Women's Joys and Pleasures*. Calgary: Detselig, 2000.

Roberts, Sarah Ellen. *Of Us and the Oxen*. Saskatoon: Modern Press, 1968.

Rodney, William. *Kootenai Brown: Canada's Unknown Frontiersman*. Surrey: Heritage House, 1996.

Royal Tyrrell Museum of Palaeontology. *The Land Before Us: The Making of Ancient Alberta*. Red Deer: Red Deer College Press, 1994.

Russell, Dale. *A Vanished World: The Dinosaurs of Western Canada*. Ottawa: National Museum of Natural Sciences, 1977.

Silverman, Eliane Leslau. *The Last Best West: Women on the Alberta Frontier: 1880–1930*. Calgary: Fifth House, 1998.

Silversides, Brock V. *Shooting Cowboys: Photographing Canadian Cowboy Culture, 1875–1965*. Calgary: Fifth House, 1997.

Smith, Barbara. *Ghost Stories of Alberta*. Toronto: Hounslow Press, 1993. *More Ghost Stories of Alberta*. Edmonton: Lone Pine, 1996.

Smith, Don, et al. *Centennial City: Calgary, 1894–1994*. Calgary: University of Calgary, 1994.

Southesk, Earl of. *Saskatchewan and the Rocky Mountains*. Edmonton: Hurtig, 1969.

Spalding, David. *Into the Dinosaurs' Graveyard*. Toronto: Doubleday, 1999.

Steele, Sam. *Forty Years in Canada*. Toronto: Prospero Books, 2000.

Stenson, Fred. *The Story of Calgary*. Saskatoon: Fifth House, 1994.

Sternberg, Charles Hazelius. *Hunting Dinosaurs in the Bad Lands of the Red Deer River, Alberta Canada*. Edmonton: NeWest Press, 1985.

Stocken, H. W. Gibbon. *Among the Blackfoot and the Sarcee*. Calgary: Glenbow Museum, 1976.

Thomas, Lewis G. *The Liberal Party in Alberta: A History of Politics in the Province in Alberta, 1905–1921*. Toronto: University of Toronto Press, 1959. *Ranchers' Legacy*. Edmonton: University of Alberta Press, 1986.

Thomas, Lewis H. *The Struggle for Responsible Government in the North-West Territories, 1870–97*. Toronto: University of Toronto Press, 1956.

Thompson, David. *David Thompson's Narrative*. Toronto: Champlain Society, 1916.

Tingley, Ken, ed. *For King and Country: Alberta in the Second World War*. Edmonton: Provincial Museum of Alberta and Reidmore Books, 1995. Ed. *The Best of the Strathcona Plaindealer*. Edmonton: Pioneer Press, 1999.

Van Kirk, Sylvia. *Many Tender Ties: Women in Fur-Trade Society, 1670–1870*. Winnipeg: Watson & Dwyer Publishing, 1999.

Waiser, Bill. *Park Prisoners: The Untold Story of Western Canada's National Parks, 1915–1946*. Saskatoon: Fifth House, 1995.

Wallace, J. N. *The Wintering Partners on Peace River*. Ottawa: Thorburn and Abbott, 1929.

Ward, Tom. *Cowtown: An Album of Early Calgary*. Calgary: City of Calgary Electric System/McClelland and Stewart West, 1975.

Warre, Captain H. *Sketches in North America and the Oregon Territory, 1844–45*. London: Dickinson, 1983.

Watkins, Ernest. *The Golden Province: A Political History of Alberta*. Calgary: Sandstone Publishing, 1986.

Weir, Joan. *Back Door to the Klondike*. Erin, Ont.: Boston Mills, 1988.

Wetherall, Donald G., and Irene R. A. Kmet. *Alberta's North: A History, 1890–1950*. Edmonton: University of Alberta Press and the Canadian Circumpolar Institute Press, 2000. *Town Life: Main Street and the Evolution of Small Town Alberta, 1880–1947*. Edmonton: University of Alberta Press, 1995. *Useful Pleasures: The Shaping of Leisure in Alberta, 1896-1945*. Regina: Alberta Culture and Multiculturalism/Canadian Plains Research Centre, 1990.

Whyte, Jon, and Carole Harmon. *Lake Louise: A Diamond in the Wilderness*. Banff: Altitude Publishing, 1982.

Wiebe, Rudy, and Bob Beal. *War in the West: Voices of the 1885 Rebellion*. Toronto: McClelland and Stewart, 1985.

David G. Wood. *The Lougheed Legacy*. Toronto: Key Porter Books, 1985.

Zuehlke, Mark. *The Alberta Fact Book*. Vancouver: Whitecap Books, 1997.

Index